THE SECOND CENTURY
OF PSYCHOANALYSIS

With Best
Wishes,
Michael A. Diamond

With Best
Wishes, Chris Christian

CIPS Series on The Boundaries of Psychoanalysis
Series Editor: Meg Beaudoin, PhD, FIPA

CIPS

CONFEDERATION OF INDEPENDENT
PSYCHOANALYTIC SOCIETIES
www.cipsusa.org

The Confederation of Independent Psychoanalytic Societies (CIPS) is the national professional association for the independent component societies of the International Psychoanalytical Association (IPA) in the USA. CIPS also hosts the Direct Member Society for psychoanalysts belonging to other IPA societies. Our members represent a wide spectrum of psycho-analytic perspectives as well as a diversity of academic backgrounds. The CIPS Book Series, The Boundaries of Psychoanalysis, represents the intellectual activity of our community. The volumes explore the internal and external boundaries of psychoanalysis, examining the interrelationships between various psychoanalytic theoretical and clinical perspectives as well as between psychoanalysis and other disciplines.

Published and distributed by Karnac Books

When Theories Touch: A Historical and Theoretical Integration of Psychoanalytic Thought by Steven J. Ellman

A New Freudian Synthesis: Clinical Process in the Next Generation edited by Andrew B. Druck, Carolyn Ellman, Norbert Freedman and Aaron Thaler

Another Kind of Evidence: Studies on Internalization, Annihilation Anxiety, and Progressive Symbolization in the Psychoanalytic Process by Norbert Freedman, Marvin Hurvich, and Rhonda Ward with Jesse D. Geller and Joan Hoffenberg

THE SECOND CENTURY OF PSYCHOANALYSIS

Evolving Perspectives
on Therapeutic Action

Edited by
Michael J. Diamond
and Christopher Christian

KARNAC

First published in 2011 by
Karnac Books Ltd
118 Finchley Road
London NW3 5HT

British Library Cataloguing in Publication Data

A C.I.P. for this book is available from the British Library

ISBN-13: 978-1-85575-800-1

Typeset by Vikatan Publishing Solutions (P) Ltd., Chennai, India

www.karnacbooks.com

*To the courageous, passionate founders and foremost,
first-generation creators of the Los Angeles Institute and
Society for Psychoanalytic Studies (LAISPS)—Charles Ansell,
Hedda Bolgar, David Brunswick, Barbara Carr, Cliff Caruth,
Elaine Caruth, Rudolf Eckstein, Milton (Mike) Horowitz,
Hans Illing, Miriam Landau, Ernest Lawrence, Lars Lofgren,
Ethel Ann Michael, Norman Oberman, Martin Reiser,
Jean Roshal, Jean Sanville, Joel Shor, Marshall Wheeler, Joan
Willens, and Itamar Yahalom—many of whom in 1970, helped to
establish the first fully interdisciplinary psychoanalytic training
program in Los Angeles as an Institute dedicated to psychoanalytic
independence by means of an open-minded, discerning attitude
toward the rich diversity of psychoanalytic theory and practice*

CONTENTS

vii

ACKNOWLEDGEMENTS

A book always reflects a mixture of voices and influences. First and foremost, we owe a debt of gratitude to LAISPS for its commitment to promoting intellectual growth and professional collaborations among psychoanalysts in an institute that boasts a rich heritage of open-minded thinkers, grounded in serious scholarship. We much appreciate the input and collegiality of LAISPS's members and candidates far too numerous to list. In addition, the editors wish to acknowledge the work of William Jock for his careful editing of the manuscript; and Morris Eagle, Tom Helscher, Peggy Porter, Alan Spivak, Peter Wolson, Leon Hoffman, and Jonathan House for their friendship and helpful reviews and comments on several of the chapters. We are most grateful to Meg Beaudoin, the CIPS series editor and liaison with Karnac, for her help throughout the process. On a personal note, Chris wishes to express his gratitude for the emotional and intellectual support of his family, Trudy and June; and Michael, to his wife, Linda and adult children, Maya and Alex, for their constant support and understanding, and to Miles (Davis Diamond), for his unyielding and playful companionship throughout the writing process.

SERIES EDITOR'S PREFACE

In this exceptional volume, leading thinkers of the CIPS community continue a collective effort to wrestle with the critical and vexing question at the heart of this book series and at the root of so many of our controversial discussions, "What are the boundaries of psychoanalysis?" This is a question of many parts, for psychoanalysis is more than a body of theories or a clinical practice. It is also a profession bound to the imperatives of a profession: developing and codifying theory, refining technique, training new candidates, and establishing a respected presence in society at large. The question of boundaries arises with regard to each aspect of our common endeavour: with regard to our theories, our clinical procedures, our research methods, what we teach, and the face we present to the world. Naturally, the establishment of boundaries entails both an empirical, scientific dimension as well as social processes within the professional community.

With this volume, the CIPS community turns to the question of curative factors. As Diamond and Christian observe in their introduction, the history of psychoanalysis begins with the introduction of a cogent and compelling paradigm, comprehensive in its scope, inspiring in its promise and, as Eagle emphasizes, linking the nascent profession of psychoanalysis to the cultural values of the Enlightenment. In the beginning, psychopathology was seen to be a product of repressed desires and fears, psychic conflicts that were unruly, unmanageable, and persistent because they were unconscious. Psychoanalysis emerged as a method of making the unconscious conscious and thus restoring the unity of the mind and its capacity for self-regulation. In his explanation to the Rat Man, Freud noted that the ancient artifacts in his office had survived for millennia because, while buried underground, they were protected from the corrosive impacts of this life. With their return to the world above, they are once again subject to its elements and fated to destruction. The tragedy of archaeology, however, would be the triumph of psychoanalysis, for troublesome childhood desires and fears that move so freely in the dark would not survive the bright light of adult mental life.

The Freudian paradigm was elegant and awesome. Treasured for its truth and promoted as the core of a new profession, the paradigm was the object of intense devotion and emotional investment. But life is inevitably messier than the theories propounded to explain it, and expanding clinical experience would soon challenge the premises of both theory and technique. In the clinical situation, psychoanalysts had to address the twin facts that interpretation did not always illuminate and illumination did not always heal. Thus, even as a new understanding of the ego and its defences was taking shape, even as new approaches to the problems of resistance and the cultivation of self-awareness were being introduced, the primary curative role of insight came into doubt. The psychoanalytic relationship, long recognized as an ancillary factor in promoting the patient's collaboration, came to be considered a curative factor in its own right by some analysts. If the relationship was found to be curative in itself, of what value is insight? And if insight is secondary or inessential, what does this portend for the fate of psychoanalysis and its practitioners?

The ensuing debates have typically taken the shape of a binary, either/or choice, often producing more heat than light but enabling proponents of one view or the other to establish themselves as leaders of social groups or movements within psychoanalysis. As Rangell observes in Chapter Two, such social phenomena are commonplace in psychoanalysis, and can promote the persistence of competing ideologies whose "unique" visions adherents seek to protect even as the professional community as a whole, and each new analyst as an individual, struggles to integrate competing ideas into a higher synthesis.

Happily, the reader will find that the essays in this volume transcend the binary thinking of the past. Taken together, the volume is a colloquy, a virtual conference that leaves the reader in a somewhat altered universe of thought, one that gently—ever so gently, really—has moved from the question of "Is interpretation or relationship the true curative factor in psychoanalysis?" to the far more productive question of "How do each of the curative factors interact to promote cure?" On leaving the volume, it is self-evident that insight and relationship are inseparable, mutually facilitating forces, each potentiating the other, each moving the mind towards awareness of its own mental operations and towards the recognition of the other as separate, distinct from rigid and preformed representations, and alive with new potential.

As a past president of CIPS, I am delighted and deeply proud to offer this short preface. As a profession, we need to nurture new ideas and value the ensuing pluralism, but we must also support a vigorous and continuing dialogue to ensure that our pluralism is productive, that it gives rise to creativity and innovation, but also to a wholesome integration of ideas and efforts. Some social forces may conduce to separatism and a regressive pluralism in which single ideas are put forward and championed as complete theories (*pars pro toto*), a phenomenon observed by Rangell many years ago, and cited throughout this volume. We must ensure that other social forces move us towards integration and unity. This wonderful volume is, in part, the product of a rich dialogue that has been occurring within the CIPS community, both within and across societies, and I am confident that it will move us towards ever more productive dialogue, discovery, and novel integrations.

Fredric T. Perlman, PhD, FIPA
Past President, CIPS

ABOUT THE EDITORS AND CONTRIBUTORS

Hedda Bolgar, PhD, training and supervising analyst, faculty and founding member, Los Angeles Institute and Society for Psychoanalytic Studies; founder and faculty member, Wright Institute, Los Angeles. Dr Bolgar has been teaching and practising psychoanalysis for more than 70 years. She is recognized as one of our profession's most accomplished and creative members, having trained numerous psychoanalysts. Her current interests focus on aging, feminism, political activism, and psychoanalytic training and practice while continuing to see patients today, at the age of 101.

Christopher Christian, PhD, this volume's co-editor, is member, Los Angeles Institute and Society for Psychoanalytic Studies; graduate of the Institute for Psychoanalytic Training and Research (IPTAR), New York; assistant professor of psychology, New School for Social Research; and director of the New School/Beth Israel Center for Clinical Training and Research at the Beth Israel Medical Center in New York City. He has a private practice in Manhattan.

Michael J. Diamond, PhD, this volume's co-editor, is training and supervising analyst and faculty member, Los Angeles Institute and Society for Psychoanalytic Studies; faculty member, Wright

Institute, Los Angeles; and associate clinical professor of psychiatry, University of California, Los Angeles. His major publications are on psychoanalytic technique, psychoanalytic gender theory, treatment of early trauma and dissociation, and fathering and masculinity, including his recent book, *My Father Before Me: How Fathers and Sons Influence Each Other Throughout Their Lives* (2007).

Morris N. Eagle, PhD, faculty member, Los Angeles Institute and Society for Psychoanalytic Studies; distinguished scholar in residence, California Lutheran University; and professor emeritus, Adelphi University. He is past president, Division of Psychoanalysis (Div. 39) of the American Psychological Association. He is the author of over 100 journal articles and numerous books, including *Recent Developments in Psychoanalysis* (1984) and *From Classical to Contemporary Psychoanalysis: A Critique and Integration* (2011); and recipient, 2009 Sigourney Award in recognition of distinguished contribution to the field of psychoanalysis.

Thomas P. Helscher, PhD, president, Los Angeles Institute and Society for Psychoanalytic Studies, and also a training and supervising analyst and faculty member; faculty member, Wright Institute, Los Angeles; and member of University of California Interdisciplinary Psychoanalytic Consortium.

Nancy Caro Hollander, PhD, faculty member, Los Angeles Institute and Society for Psychoanalytic Studies, and professor emeritus, California State University. She is the author of the recently published book, *Uprooted Minds: Surviving the Politics of Terror in the Americas* (2010), in which she explores the psychological meanings of the critical social, economic, and political crises facing the US; and co-editor, *Psychoanalysis, Class, and Politics: Encounters in the Clinical Setting* (2006), as well as author of numerous articles on psychoanalysis.

Beth I. Kalish, PhD, training and supervising analyst, faculty member, and past president, Los Angeles Institute and Society for Psychoanalytic Studies; served on the board of the Confederation of Independent Psychoanalytic Societies (CIPS) and the House of Delegates of the International Psychoanalytical Association. She is published widely with a special interest in the assessment of movement behaviour and non-verbal communication in children and adults in treatment.

Peggy Porter, PhD, training and supervising analyst and secretary, Los Angeles Institute and Society for Psychoanalytic Studies; and member of the board of directors of the Confederation of Independent Psychoanalytic Societies (CIPS). She has a private practice in Los Angeles.

Stephen Portuges, PhD, faculty member, Los Angeles Institute and Society for Psychoanalytic Studies; Director, Psychoanalytic Psychotherapy Program, New Center for Psychoanalysis; clinical supervisor, Community Counseling and Parent Child Study Center, California Lutheran University. He has published numerous articles in professional journals, and is the executive editor, *International Journal of Applied Psychoanalytic Studies*. He has a private practice in Los Angeles.

Leo Rangell, MD, faculty member, Los Angeles Institute and Society for Psychoanalytic Studies; honorary president of the International Psychoanalytical Association (since 1995); past president (twice), American and International Psychoanalytical Associations; clinical professor of psychiatry at the University of California, Los Angeles and San Francisco. He is the author of close to 500 publications in psychoanalysis and related mental sciences, including his highly acclaimed text, *The Road to Unity in Psychoanalytic Theory* (2007).

Linda Sobelman, PhD, training and supervising analyst and faculty member, Los Angeles Institute and Society for Psychoanalytic Studies (LAISPS), and currently director of training; faculty member, Wright Institute, Los Angeles; former associate editor, *International Journal of Psychoanalysis*. She is the recipient of the Jean Sanville Award for creative writing in psychoanalysis from LAISPS for her chapter in this volume.

Alan P. Spivak, PhD, training and supervising analyst and faculty member, Los Angeles Institute and Society for Psychoanalytic Studies; and faculty member, Wright Institute, Los Angeles. He is a former president of the Los Angeles Society for Psychoanalytic Psychology. He presents psychoanalytic papers and lectures nationally and internationally.

Peter Wolson, PhD, training and supervising analyst and faculty member, Los Angeles Institute and Society for Psychoanalytic

Studies, and past president and director of training; resident faculty member, Wright Institute, Los Angeles; and founder, Confederation of Independent Psychoanalytic Societies (CIPS). His publications address topics such as adaptive grandiosity in artistic creativity and fatherhood, the existential dimension of psychoanalysis, as well as a number of psychoanalytically informed op-ed pieces on politics and culture.

Evolving perspectives
on therapeutic action:
where are we after a century?

Michael J. Diamond and Christopher Christian

As psychoanalysis enters into its second century, we seem, as always, to be in the midst of important debates, possibly even paradigmatic alterations, occurring in psychoanalytic theory, epistemology, and technique. Until recently, nearly all theories of therapeutic action have tended to rely on linear, causative models that Abend (1990) refers to as "manufacture models" that emphasize the interconnection between the analyst's actions and the patient's responses in which time and temporality are primary. In contrast, some current thinkers have drawn upon classical, postmodern and European-based ideas that not surprisingly stem from Freud's (1913) timeless notion of therapeutic action. From the beginning, Freud considered therapeutic action to be an unpredictable and independent process that results from the conditions in which analysis takes place, largely in accordance with the nature of the analyst's activity. Comparing therapeutic action to male sexual potency, Freud (ibid.) stated:

> The analyst is certainly able to do a great deal, but he cannot determine beforehand exactly what result he will effect. He sets in motion a process ... once begun, it goes its own way [p. 340].

To the very end of his career in "Analysis Terminable and Interminable" (1937), Freud implicitly held to this exemplar in declaring:

> Instead of an enquiry into how a cure by analysis comes about ... the question should be asked of what are the obstacles that stand in the way of such a cure [p. 221].

The analytic process encompasses a naturalness and unpredictability that coincides with life itself (see Ferraro & Garella, 2009), which in practice (rather than theory) does not favour well-defined objectives. In contemporary writings, moreover, this classical and non-temporal model tends to be represented in spatial and non-linear terms (Ferro, 2008; Galatzer-Levy, 2009; Bolognini, 2011) wherein experienced, psychological time is distinguished from linear, chronological time as in a helical model (Grinberg, 1990; Schlessinger, 2005). As models develop and attempt to fill gaps in our comprehension of the human psyche and strive to resolve the *pars pro toto* fallacy that historically vexes theoretical progress (Rangell, 2007), more complex, multifactor models of therapeutic action are gaining attention.

The debate continues, nonetheless, as to the exact nature of the therapeutic action of psychoanalysis. We see this amply demonstrated, for example, in the recent monograph on the topic published in the *Psychoanalytic Quarterly* (Volume 76, Supplement, 2007), as well as in the commentaries on Abend's (2009.) latest article entitled, "Freud, transference and therapeutic action". Although Abend argues that Freud was convinced from 1910 onward that the analysis by means of interpretation of the transference was the sole factor involved in the therapeutic action of psychoanalytic treatment, analysts today, including contemporary Freudians like Abend (ibid.), though regarding interpretation as essential for "proper analytic technique", do not believe it is the "only agent of therapeutic impact" (p. 871). As Canestri (2009) states, "The definition of what therapeutic action means to a psychoanalyst will be closely connected and will depend on the overall theory preferred by that analyst" (p. 904).

Greenberg (2009), in arguing "that there is no single road to therapeutic effectiveness" (p. 933), reads Freud's formulation somewhat differently and like Loewald (1960) believes that analysts offer at least two major mutative possibilities *"in one and the same act,* seamlessly" (Greenberg, 2009, p. 933, original italics). First, the analyst provides *insight* by making the unconscious conscious and, second, simultaneously serves a developmentally crucial *relational* function. Gabbard and Westen (2003) found support for such clinical hypotheses in recent neurophysiological work suggesting the alteration of the analysand's "unconscious associational network" as a result of free association and interpretation, a new experience with the analyst, and the internalization of the analyst's attitudes and functions (p. 827).

Some consider these claims "neuroreductive" and overly optimistic (Lopez, 2004). Yet, most analysts today would agree with Greenberg (2009) as well as Gabbard and Westen (2003) in arguing for an inclusive understanding of therapeutic action, wherein *more than* the various events going on at every moment affect therapeutic action in intricately related ways. As Jiménez (2009) notes, "[S]ingle mechanism theories of therapeutic action, no matter how complex, are unlikely to prove useful" (p. 244).

There remains considerable uncertainty and controversy concerning the nature of therapeutic action and the technical procedures best suited to achieve favourable results (e.g., Abend, 2007; Canestri, 2007; Friedman, 2007; Greenberg, 2007; Michels, 2007). But this is not necessarily inauspicious. Greenberg (2007), for instance, believes that,

> ... conversations about therapeutic action remind us of the endless intricacy of the psychoanalytic process; they enliven our work and spark our attentiveness to events that would otherwise escape notice [p. 1687].

Certainly, the nature of analytic change is unique to each patient and it is self-evident that change is an *idiographic* issue. The *idiographic* nature of clinical psychoanalysis, contrary to the *nomothetic,* is about the particular rather than the general, the idiosyncratic rather than the universal, and the unique rather than the common. This is not to say that our interest in change as it relates to the unique aspects of each individual, precludes systematic research. However, as these changes pertain to clinical work, we believe that the significance of the analyst's experience of the individual patient requires taking in and becoming impressed by something presented by the patient that is particular to each clinical encounter. Thus, as Gabbard (2009) states, psychoanalysis becomes "a noncoercive collaboration involving a process of two people thinking what either alone cannot think" (p. 581).

As will be made clearer in this and other chapters from this volume (see particularly, Christian and Diamond, Rangell, and Eagle in Chapters One to Three respectively), the diverse historical aims in psychoanalysis are reflected in the various schools favouring outcomes congruent with that school's theory of mind, development, technique, and epistemology. Nonetheless, all schools fundamentally converge in stressing the significance of change that pertains to a patient's mental experience (along with bodily manifestations), which may also be reflected in change regarding significant others and the external world.

Hence, the two primary aims of therapeutic action entail: (1) a *new relationship to one's internal world or mind*, which might be described as intrapsychic structural change, altered internal object relations, destabilization of forces in conflict, achieved depressive position functioning, self-object development, strengthened affect regulation, and/or improved reflective functioning; and (2) a *new relationship to one's external world*, significant others, and the larger, collective world, each of which involves altered attachment patterns and an increased recognition of the subjectivity of others (Benjamin, 1990) and a "theory of mind" (Fonagy & Target, 1996). Thus, when mutative change occurs, patients are better able to *work* and *love*, as Freud (1937) advocated, and more often than not, *play* and *create* as described by Winnicott (1971b) as well as the American ego psychologists (e.g., Hartmann, 1939b; Hartmann, Kris & Loewenstein, 1946; Rapaport, 1967). Despite the potential that psychoanalysis has for effecting such profound changes, Theodore Reik reminds us (1948):

> The "curing" of a neurosis by no means resembles the picture many psychoanalysts paint. The neurotic symptoms do not evaporate into thin air without a trace, but they pale into insignificance. Scars remain after psychoanalysis just as after a successful operation, and they ache when stormy weather approaches [p. 91].

Smith (2007) points out that therapeutic action is often discussed at different levels of abstractions, creating a veritable "confusion of tongues" that make comparisons between different schools difficult. Moreover, he notes that the distinctions have become blurred between a theory of therapeutic action and a theory of technique as if "the activities of the analyst define therapeutic action" (p. 1737). In considering the many interesting articles published in the 2007 supplemental issue of the *Psychoanalytic Quarterly* entitled, "Comparing Theories of Therapeutic Action", we see the various levels of abstraction and confusion between what the analyst does and what happens for the analysand, as well as the idiosyncratic use of terms, such as insight and containment. Consequently, words are often used "to build fences between [analytic] groups" (Smith, 2007, p. 1754) rather than bridges to communicate. In discussing the ironies of analytic "cure", Dimen (2010) paraphrases her relationally oriented colleague, Adrienne Harris (2005) in quipping, "[W]e speak postmodern but inhabit enlightenment" (p. 260).

In this volume, the traditionally Freudian-trained, yet independent-minded authors strive to be cognizant of the limitations and ironies inherent in the concept of "cure" as well as the overly deterministic nature of many accounts of therapeutic action. At the same time, most of the chapters' authors welcome the consensus within the psychoanalytic literature that the mutative process involves both the *internalization of the relationship with the analyst* (i.e., relational/attachment factors) and the *achievement of insight through interpretation,* (i.e., insight/understanding factors; see Loewald, 1960; Friedman, 1978; Cooper, 1992; Baker, 1993; Pulver, 1992; Gabbard, 1995). Each author presents his or her unique perspective on therapeutic action but all would seem to agree that it no longer makes sense to represent the analytic process in a split or bifurcated manner; in other words, the analyst must be both a *transference object*, subject to *interpretive* work, and a *new object*, subject to *internalization*. As Greenberg (1986) articulated, "If the analyst cannot be experienced as a new object, analysis never gets under way; if he cannot be experienced as an old one, it never ends" (p. 98).

However, the issue of *newness* is not without its own inherent controversies. Many, who stress interpretation as the main mechanism of change (cf. Spivak in this volume, Chapter Six), believe that for a long time into an analysis, no matter what the analyst does, he or she is not seen as a new object but rather as a fantasy object (positive or negative). Paradoxically, what accounts for the "newness" to which Greenberg refers, is that the analyst interprets the fantasy, so as to allow a more reality-based assessment of the analyst and others. From this standpoint, he is only *new* in two ways. For one, he is the only person in the patient's life who makes manifest the role of fantasy through interpretations, and secondly, he can be related to, eventually, as an external object because of the interpretations.

Our authors generally concur that transference interpretations are indeed mutative; however, they also seem to agree that it is problematic for an analyst to focus exclusively on transference interpretations as the *only* mutative agent. Most, though not all, would agree with Baker (1993) that in each analysis, it appears that a new phase of growth and development is ushered in by the patient's discovery of the analyst as a new object, which among other therapeutic functions, paves the way for a more complete termination. Consequently, arising from Strachey's (1934) seminal work, the "objective" interpretation of transference distortions is considered an essential step in the process whereby the analyst emerges as a new object. This is what Baker (1993) regards as "the corrective *analytic* experience" as contrasted with the mostly discredited "corrective emotional experience" of Alexander (1950) to the extent that the latter term became inextricably linked with the manipulation of the transference.

Within this frame of thinking, as implied in several chapters (See Eagle, Chapter Three; Wolson, Porter, Diamond, and Helscher, Chapters Eight to Eleven respectively), particularly in cases of structural deficit or developmental arrest, non-verbalized features, such as the analyst's survival, the metabolization and containment of the patient's unprocessed, chaotic material, and the atmosphere of safety and tolerance provided by the analyst's attitude, frame, and mind use, are themselves implicit transference interpretations, or simply therapeutic experiences that can be mutative. Hence, Eagle (Chapter Three) discusses the changes in a patient's psychic structure resulting through these more gradual, non-verbal processes, which he terms, "new corrective relational experiences", whereas Diamond (Chapter Ten) considers intrapsychic change that results from the analyst's ability to make use of the interpsychic experiences occurring in the analytic dyad.

For this volume, the two editors have sought to draw together a number of accomplished psychoanalytic clinician-scholars who are based in Los Angeles and are members of the Los Angeles Institute and Society for Psychoanalytic Studies (LAISPS) to reflect upon their ideas about what makes psychoanalysis work and to contribute an original chapter on the subject. If psychoanalysis is to continue to evolve and blossom in its second century, it becomes crucial to develop heuristically-fertile and clinically-sound ideas and hypotheses on therapeutic action if for no other reason than as a means for researching the nature and effectiveness of psychoanalysis. Along these lines, the recent president of the American Psychological Association, Alan Kazdin (2008, 2010), implored practitioners and researchers alike to take concrete steps to study the "mechanisms of change" in order to make research relevant to practice and thereby optimize the processes critical to change. Equally important is the need for analysts to speak more clearly to one another about what we actually do and how we understand its impact on our patients. Conversations about therapeutic action enliven our work and expand our clinical repertoire.

Building bridges between diverse schools is but one of the many advantages accruing from the study of therapeutic action in psychoanalysis and, as we hope our readers will discover, each chapter author (or authors) values open-minded, independent thinking that is grounded in a Freudian perspective and balances tradition with innovation, reflecting LAISPS' ethos. Each also demonstrates considerable depth and breadth of psychoanalytic understanding in their examination of the vicissitudes of analytic treatment.

Throughout this volume we seek to understand from a range of theoretical perspectives the mechanisms of therapeutic action by which psychoanalysis achieves its therapeutic aims. Is it through the insight gained by interpretation that the functioning of the ego expands? Or, the identification of the analysand with the analyst's attitude that modifies the harshness of the superego or helps develop the ego's synthetic functioning? Or, leaving aside structural theory and possibly even metapsychology, could it come through the development of a new, unique, and even a "real" relationship with the analyst, whose holding and containing functions, maternal provision, and analytic love provide the conditions for growth of internal object representations and/or relations that were stunted in their development? Similarly, might the relationship with the analyst facilitate intrapsychic structural development per se by dint of internalization processes? Might the analytic process itself result in the mutative internalization of the patient-analyst relationship? Or, is there perhaps an interconnection between understanding and attachment throughout a transformative analytic process? For that matter, is there one psychoanalysis or many?

Brief overview of the chapters

The present volume is organized into five main sections. In the first section, *Contextualizing Therapeutic Action*, therapeutic action is examined in its widespread historical and philosophical context. Following this introduction to the volume, we (Chris Christian and Michael Diamond) present a brief history of therapeutic action in psychoanalysis, emphasizing the shifting theoretical trends that have led to today's more inclusive understanding (Chapter One). Next, Leo Rangell in Chapter Two makes use of key developments in the second half of the 20th century along with pivotal personal experiences during his long and illustrious psychoanalytic career to demonstrate his own uniquely inclusive, integrative, and yet classically Freudian understanding of psychoanalytic action as it reflects on the psychoanalytic theory of mind and clinical praxis (i.e., what he terms being a "Developed Freudian"). He notes that his own more diffuse viewpoint of psychoanalytic action moved from a Utopian view that privileges insight to include working through in order to yield reparative action that entails more than *interpretation* alone and thus, makes use of many additional technical procedures, particularly *suggestion* ("… and even *urging*") as part of analytic work.

In Chapter Three, Morris Eagle makes the claim that psychoanalysis is inextricably tied to the *enlightenment vision* of self-knowledge and the abiding belief that it will set one free. He then goes on to show and critique how contemporary psychoanalysis as well as broader cultural-philosophical trends, both theoretically and clinically, fail to undermine the link between the enlightenment vision and the traditional psychoanalytic emphasis on knowing oneself.

The second section, *Conflict, Fantasy, and Insight in Therapeutic Action*, consists of four chapters. In Chapter Four, Stephen Portuges and Nancy Hollander discuss how psychotherapeutic change is promoted when the psychoanalytic dyad identifies, demonstrates, and analyzes resistance and counter-resistance to the psychoanalytic method. In expanding on Paul Gray's technique of *close process attention*, Portuges and Hollander consider the interpersonal relational dimension previously overlooked in this methodology as well as the impact of neglecting social reality in accounting for therapeutic action. In Chapter Five, Chris Christian reviews modern conflict theory as an evolution of ego psychology that is centered mainly on the work of Charles Brenner. Christian shows how interpretation of conflict and compromise formation is the primary means by which psychoanalysis effects meaningful change in terms of the quality of the ensuing compromise formations. Alan Spivak, in Chapter Six, examines the affectively rich and vital nature of the interpretive act in its parallel to a mother's meeting her baby's "first gesture" with recognition. In this respect, while acknowledging the influence of many factors in the analytic process, Spivak contends that the most vital force in analytic action is ultimately being recognized and understood by an "other". It is this that enables the analysand to bear previously warded-off aspects of his own mind and experience, which relieves his beleaguered ego, while increasing the elasticity of his personality. The last chapter in this section, Chapter Seven by Linda Sobelman, focuses on the patient's conscious and unconscious "curative fantasy" wherein the analyst, as an idealized parent, compensates for deficiencies in the *actual* parents (real or imagined). She contends that these fantasies represent pain and deprivation in the patient's early relationships with his or her parents, and express their sense of what was missing in those relationships and thus what they believe they still require for healing those early wounds. Sobelman argues that mutative change rests less on the analyst's decision as to whether or not to accommodate the patient's transference wish than to *the ability to establish a collaborative spirit of joint inquiry* into the multiple determinants and consequences of the patient's fantasy.

The third section, *Relational Experience and Mutative Dynamics*, consists of two chapters. In Chapter Eight, Peter Wolson offers a pluralistic perspective on the importance of "analytic love" in creating the conditions for therapeutic change. Wolson argues that psychoanalytic love, whether object libidinal or narcissistic, is at the core of psychoanalysis and supports his thesis by examining its operation in varying psychoanalytic schools' theories of mutative techniques.

Peggy Porter, in Chapter Nine, argues that the analyst's use of her own emotional, visceral, proprioceptive and mental responses in the context of the patients' splitting operations is crucial in facilitating analytic change. According to Porter, countertransference enactment and projective identification share a common ground in this integrative work.

The penultimate section, *Mental Experience and Therapeutic Action: Unconscious Communication, Internalization, and Non-verbal Processes*, is comprised of three chapters. Michael Diamond, in Chapter Ten, proposes that the constant factor in the complex process of therapeutic action is invariably fashioned from the analyst's mental activities during the work. In emphasizing the analyst's "mind use", Diamond argues that analytic change rests on the analyst's ability to create and utilize an inner space in relationship to the patient's unconscious functioning. Diamond examines how the analyst's mind use, particularly with regard to the unconscious, interpsychic communication, helps patients to integrate *insight* through interpretation and the mutative facets of their *relationship* with the analyst. Thomas Helscher, in Chapter Eleven, explores how analysts uncover and help certain types of patients dismantle the complex set of identifications with powerful, "bad" internal "objects" that stunt the patient from developing more mature and gratifying object relations. Using Freud's theories of narcissism and the object relations theories of Klein, Bion, and Fairbairn, Helscher argues that the core of therapeutic action entails working through identifications in ways that gradually enable them to become symbolizable. For Helscher, analysis entails understanding specific identifications and their functions in order to help the patient risk the release of these internal objects. In Chapter Twelve, Beth Kalish considers the significance of non-verbal expression and unique movements (motility) in the analytic process. Kalish argues that such "movement thinking" is a meaningful tool for furthering therapeutic action.

The concluding section, *Reflections: Psychoanalytic Dogma and Flexibility*, consists only of Hedda Bolgar's chapter (Chapter Thirteen) where she, herself in her second century as a 101-year-old psychoanalyst, discusses the connections between various developments in psychoanalytic theory and technique, and their relevance to the analyst's clinical interventions as well as her/his subjectivity. Dr Bolgar, the first non-medical analyst trained at the Chicago Psychoanalytic

Institute, discusses her first-hand experience with Alexander's technique and what she believes is a fundamental misunderstanding of Alexander's viewpoint that led to such caution and rigidity on the part of mid-20th century analysts. In a revealing interview, Bolgar discusses the changes in her own ways of thinking and working over time and its impact on her views of therapeutic action.

Throughout the volume, the authors emphasize diverse ways by which the therapeutic aims of analysis are achieved. In their distinct opinions, the authors capture the essence of the Los Angeles Institute and Society for Psychoanalytic Studies (LAISPS), which when founded in 1970, strived to position itself as an institute dedicated to psychoanalytic independence. The founders stressed a need to understand in depth the history of psychoanalysis in order to promote its growth, which inevitably includes the influence of contemporary models and orientations. In becoming a full component society of the International Psychoanalytical Association in 1995, and as this volume's chapter authors make clear in their independent-minded, inclusive, and scholarly manner, LAISPS continues its rich tradition of building upon and adding to (rather than replacing) the fundamental, everlasting, and amply demonstrated tenets of psychoanalytic knowledge, theory, and technique.

SECTION I

CONTEXTUALIZING THERAPEUTIC ACTION

CHAPTER ONE

A brief history of therapeutic action: convergence, divergence, and integrative bridges

Christopher Christian and Michael J. Diamond

reud's thinking about how analysis cures and the aims of therapeutic action underwent significant revisions throughout his life. The very notion of "cure" as an aim of psychoanalysis has been evolving, resting mainly on a medical model's conception of an end-state, conveyed as both a noun and verb, which analysts have defined in various ways in accordance with the prevailing state of analytic knowledge and clinical theory. An analyst's conception of therapeutic action depends on his or her understanding of the psychic apparatus or mind and the view of what is mutative in the clinical process. How these issues are approached may be conscious, yet a considerable portion often remains implicit as well as unconscious.

In tracing the history of therapeutic action and its connection to analytic cure, it is useful to consider three different, though interrelated viewpoints: first, the nature of the psychopathology or syndrome that psychoanalysis sought to address at its inception and how particular pathologies and clinical populations challenged established notions of therapeutic action, leading to the emergence of alternative perspectives over time; second, the theory of the syndrome's pathogenesis, perhaps initially in terms of symptomatic

3

expression and subsequently as character; and finally, the various theories of mind or metapsychology.

In the late 1800s, hysteria occupied centre stage among psychiatric syndromes and hypnosis had become re-legitimized by the medical community as a field of inquiry (Makari, 1998). The birth of psychoanalysis is often traced to this specific illness, hysteria, studied through the use of this particular technique, hypnosis, as championed by French neurologist, Martin Charcot (Jones, 1972; Ellenberger, 1970; Sulloway, 1979; Makari, 2008). Unconscious thoughts, Charcot demonstrated, could influence behaviour. This seminal discovery would become the foundation of psychoanalysis and all psychoanalytic psychotherapies. In his famous medical demonstrations at La Salpêtrière, Charcot showed how patients suffering from hysteria were responding to some suggestion (or autosuggestion), the origins of which were often unclear. Although Charcot believed that therapeutic suggestion could counter autosuggestions and alleviate symptoms, he nonetheless held fast to the belief that this was not a cure and that hysteria was a degenerative disease, which no talking remedy could ever cure (Makari, 2008)—an idea that Freud, his reverence for Charcot notwithstanding, would, in time, upend.

Prior to meeting Charcot, Freud had learned from a senior colleague of a 21-year-old patient who exhibited classic symptoms of hysteria. Bertha Pappenheim would become known in psychoanalytic history by her pseudonym, Anna O. (Breuer & Freud, 1893). From this patient, Breuer learned that "if she was allowed to narrate her inner fantasies, her symptoms would abate" (Makari, 2008, p. 40). That is, she would produce the necessary recollections that would inevitably lead to a memory of an incident that had been repressed and was the key determinant of the symptom. Anna O. christened the process "chimney sweeping" (Freud, 1910a, p. 13).

Freud's clinical practice

Initially, drawing on his experience with Charcot at *La Salpêtrière*, Freud experimented with the use of suggestion in his own clinical practice—a process that entailed authoritatively counter-suggesting away the pathogenic idea that was thought to be at the heart of the patient's symptom. Yet, suggestion proved to have limited long-standing success once the patient was no longer under the influence of the authority of the analyst (see Spivak, this volume, Chapter Six for a discussion of Freud's ambivalent relation to suggestion). From simple suggestion, Freud moved to Breuer's method of catharsis by which the strangulated affects tied to the traumatic experiences that were being recollected needed to be released. In 1893, Breuer and Freud wrote:

> [E]ach individual hysterical symptom immediately and perma-
> nently disappeared when we had succeeded in bringing clearly
> to light the memory of the event by which it was provoked and
> in arousing its accompanying affect, and when the patient had
> described that event in the greatest possible detail and had put
> the affect into words. Recollection without affect almost invari-
> ably produces no result [p. 6].

Hypnosis, suggestion, catharsis, and abreaction would eventually give way to other techniques, including free association and dream analysis, as Freud aimed at achieving a new method by which to reach the recesses of the mind, access its sequestered contents, and bring these in line with the patient's present reality.

By 1893, Breuer and Freud believed that they had taken an important step towards uncovering "the psychical mechanism of hysteri-
cal phenomena" but, nonetheless, still lacked an understanding of "the internal causes of hysteria" (p. 17). In his search for causes of hysteria, Freud noted that in the process of recollection, his patients often came upon memories that Freud interpreted as representing traumatic childhood molestation. This led Freud to postulate what became his infamous *seduction hypothesis*, whereby he contended that *actual* seduction was a *necessary* cause in the development of hysteria. Freud (1896):

> I therefore put forward the thesis that at the bottom of every
> case of hysteria there are one or more occurrences of prema-
> ture sexual experience, occurrences which belong to the earliest
> years of childhood ... [p. 203].

However, by autumn of 1897, Freud announced to Fliess that he was abandoning his seduction theory, and instead claimed that seduction fits into a "general category of causes" (Makari, 1998, p. 862)—a

sufficient but not a necessary cause of hysteria as well as other forms of psychopathology. More significantly, Freud began to develop a libido theory of psychoneuroses, postulating that neuroses are primarily caused by inner conflicts over objectionable sexual thoughts, wishes, and impulses (i.e., drive derivatives).

Dreams

Freud became interested in dreams, much as with hypnosis, for what they might reveal about how the mind works and for the clues they might provide as to the contents of the unconscious. Driven by his own need to address unconscious conflicts triggered by his father's death, Freud began his legendary self-analysis in 1897 (Kris, 1950), whereby he recorded and freely associated to his own dreams, while sharing his personal discoveries with his close colleague, Wilhelm Fliess. In the process he uncovered a primal wish that he deemed universal, which he described in an 1897 letter to Fliess (Masson, 1985): "I have found in my case too being in love with my mother and jealous of my father" (p. 272). From this monumental discovery of the universality of infantile sexuality and Oedipal conflicts, Freud (1900) became convinced that dreams were "the royal road to the unconscious" (p. 608).

In the winter of 1900, Freud met a patient, Dora, whom he believed was capable of illustrating the central "importance of dreams" (Freud, 1905a, p. 4) in the analytic method. He would describe his recently completed monograph on the case of Dora to Fliess "as a fragment of an analysis of a case of hysteria in which the explanations are grouped around two dreams; so it is really a continuation of the dream book" (Freud, 1901, p. 433).

Although Freud would ultimately regard Dora's case as a failed treatment, in time, psychoanalytic history would point to her treatment as a watershed moment in which the importance of transference was fully recognized. Freud's willingness to show his clinical work along with his own misjudgments allowed him to see and report on what he recognized as an inattention to the transference. Thus, Freud (1905a) wrote:

> But when the first dream came, in which she gave herself the
> warning that she had better leave my treatment just as she had

formerly left Herr K.'s house, I ought to have listened to the warning myself. "Now," I ought to have said to her, "it is from Herr K. that you have made a transference on to me." ... And when this transference had been cleared up, the analysis would have obtained access to new memories, dealing, probably, with actual events. But I was deaf to this first note of warning, thinking I had ample time before me, since no further stages of transference developed and the material for the analysis had not yet run dry [pp. 118–119, fn.].

Thus, we see the beginnings of the notion that the analysand's experience of the analyst and the analytic process (i.e., transference) is not inconsequential. Indeed, by way of seeking its intrapsychic meaning, analysis of the transference relationship would become the vehicle through which important discoveries were made, and change effected.

Developing psychoanalysis: the structural perspective or "where id was, there shall ego be"

In its beginning, psychoanalysis was interested in the repressed contents of *the* Unconscious, and how this repressed material led to symptoms (i.e., neurotic compromise formations); later, with the development of the tripartite structural model (Freud, 1923a), partly stemming from Freud's recognition that certain activities of the ego operate outside conscious awareness, and that self-punitive behaviours and suicide could not be accounted for by the type of pleasure-seeking ego that Freud had postulated in 1917, psychoanalysis became interested in the interactions among all three mental structures: id, ego, and superego. Attention shifted from id-analysis to the ego and its mechanisms of defence. Anna Freud would write her influential monograph *The Ego and the Mechanisms of Defense* in 1936, and American ego psychology would emerge with an emphasis on defence analysis (see for example, Fenichel, 1941b, 1954; Hartmann, Kris & Loewenstein, 1946). Internalization, the development of a superego, and the expansion of the role of the ego, especially as it pertained to the ego's role in defensive operations, generated numerous and intense arguments about how structures of the mind develop, work, and influence the therapeutic process.

Theorizing therapeutic action: Marienbad and Edinburgh

By the 1930s, a wide-ranging debate was well underway concerning the primary mutative factors in psychoanalysis. The notable Marienbad symposium in 1936 on "The Theory of Therapeutic Results" was convened at the 14th Congress of the International Psychoanalytical Association to air differences, which had as their point of departure Freud's (1923a) last model of the mind. Given a general acceptance among the participants of the tripartite structural model, the disagreements had more to do with the means by which therapeutic change was produced.

Strachey argued that structural change was initiated by introjection of the analyst's superego, which temporarily modulated the harshness of the analysand's more archaic, punitive superego and increased his or her capacity to tolerate drive expression sufficiently well until the mutative interpretations could consolidate the gain. Strachey articulated this view in his 1934 paper, "The nature of the therapeutic action of psychoanalysis", which primed the debate that ensued at the conference. Strachey (1934) believed that interpretation would have its largest impact when directed to the point of most urgency in the transference and concluded: "The principal effective alteration consists in a profound qualitative modification of the patient's super-ego, from which the other alterations follow in the main automatically" (p. 159). Moreover, he added,

> This modification of the patient's super-ego is brought about in a series of innumerable small steps by the agency of mutative interpretations, which are effected by the analyst in virtue of his position as object of the patient's id-impulses and as auxiliary super-ego [p. 159].

In short, as objectionable drive-derivatives emerge in the treatment, and as the analyst remains calm, non-judgmental, and understanding in response to the analysand's impulses, the latter slowly adopts a similar attitude towards his own impulses, becoming less self-punitive. This process entails both identification with, and an internalization of, the analyst's own mental attitude, much as Diamond (this volume, Chapter Ten) expands upon in terms of the analyst's use of his/her "analytic mind" to facilitate deeper understanding of the unconscious interaction as well as the patient's unconscious mind.

It is this change in the analysand's self-punitive trends that represents the important agent of cure according to Strachey. As Arlow (1993b) later points out, this focus on the mechanism of *introjection* represented Strachey's Kleinian orientation, which Arlow characterized as follows:

> Listening to the transference interpretations, the analysand comes to appreciate the difference between the introjected, destructive mother imago contained in his or her superego, in contrast to the reasonable, rational image of the analyst. In piece-meal fashion over the course of the analysis, the bad, internal superego introject is extruded and the good, reasonable psychoanalytic introject becomes ensconced in the superego [p. 195].

Of course, the natural question arises as to why the child's superego is imbued with such intense aggression. Osman & Tabachnick (1988) explain this in terms of the introjection of projected impulses. Thus, in their words:

> ... the oral aggressive impulses of the child toward its earliest objects results, through the perpetual process of introjection and projection, in the development of a subjectively fantastic view of them as being highly dangerous, destructive, and puni- tive. Thus the child, having felt aggressive toward the object, is likely to perceive the introjected object (in the manner of the superego) as more punitive toward his ego than the external object really is [p. 199].

According to Strachey (1934, 1969), and others, including Money-Kyrle (1958) and Rosenfeld (1971, 1983), the focus of the transfer-ence interpretation, then, is on the patient's primitive projections. It requires that the analyst be able to experience and recognize the pro-jections and, in turn, through the analysis of his countertransference, be able to remain in touch with these feelings in order to interpret them correctly (much as Spivak, Porter, Diamond, and Helscher, likewise emphasize in this volume, Chapters Six, Nine, Ten, and Eleven respectively). The analyst who cannot recognize, contain, and then explain to the patient the nature of these projections will provide inexact interpretations, which cause the patient anxiety that often results in acting out. Such acting out ensues when the analyst's failed containment and inadequate explanation lead the patient to believe that the analyst misunderstands out of a need to avoid or reject the patient's "dangerous" impulses.

As an important aside, in regard to the issue of the inexact interpretation, it is worth mentioning that Glover (1931) believed that the inexact interpretation had the effect of in fact reducing anxiety and providing symptom relief because the patient can seize on such an interpretation which, by virtue of being less near the true source of anxiety, is feared less, and more readily accepted. In his words (ibid.),

> It is probable that there is a type of inexact interpretation which, depending on optimum degree of psychic remoteness from the true sources of anxiety, may bring about improvement in the symptomatic sense at the cost of refractoriness to deeper analysis [p. 399].

Returning to Marienbad, Sterba (1934) put forward a contrasting view at the symposium that emphasized the patient's introjection of the analyst's *observing ego*, in contrast to the superego, as proposed by Strachey (1934). It was this that provided an alliance that enabled mutative interpretations. This ego psychological perspective was in line with both Anna Freud (1936) and Nunberg (1937), who believed that the focus of therapeutic action must be on the ego and thus, "[T]he task of therapy consists of resolving the conflict between the psychic institutions, thereby reducing psychic tensions" (Nunberg, 1937, p. 157). The effect would be an expansion of the observing and synthesizing functions of the ego in imitation of the analyst's role. Insight into intrapsychic conflict and defence were the essence of the psychoanalytic process as opposed to the modification of the patient's internal object relations via a new relationship with the analyst. Portuges and Hollander (Chapter Four), Christian (Chapter Five), and Spivak (Chapter Six) extend these ideas concerning conflict and defence in this volume.

As Friedman (1978) points out, what was most conspicuous across both major viewpoints dominating the discussion at the celebrated Marienbad conference was the emphasis on *internalization*, specifically by means of introjection. In Friedman's (1978) description:

Two introjective mechanisms had become important by the time of Marienbad. Both derived from Freud's suggestion that the patient is persuaded to adopt the analyst's attitude. One application was Sterba's formulation that the patient *imitates* the analyst's disinterested way of observing and alters his own ego to match. The other was Strachey's (1934) idea that the patient *incorporates* the analyst's greater tolerance, thus altering his own superego [p. 530, italics added].

The principal aim of interpretation for the ego psychologist was an increased tolerance of drives—"a 'taming' of the instincts" (Freud, 1937, p. 225)—which are synthesized, neutralized, or sublimated by the ego, allowing for more gratification and less inhibition on the part of the patient. For the Kleinian-oriented object relationists, treatment entailed a modification of an overly critical and punitive superego. The patient relinquishes his own superego, and replaces it with a more benign superego in identification with the analyst's more mature, tolerant, and understanding attitude. Moreover, in recalling both classical theory and foreseeing later developments, Bibring (1937) anticipated Kohut's (1971) work on "transmuting internalization" by drawing attention to the affective component in introjection that ensues from gradual frustrations within close dyadic relationships. Helscher, in this volume (Chapter Eleven), explores the importance of *disidentification* from, and releasing of, internal objects that stunt patients from developing more mature and gratifying object relations.

Twenty-five years after the Marienbad symposium, another conference of historical significance on "The Curative Factors in Psychoanalysis" took place in 1961, this time in Edinburgh. Here, the view represented by Gitelson (1962) that *attachment to the analyst* is a necessary pre-condition before interpretation can be effective, became the focus of debate. Gitelson contended that such attachment could also be "an integrating and restructuring experience in and of itself" (Blatt & Behrends, 1987, p. 280).

In a paper published the year following the conference, Gitelson elaborated on the ideas he introduced in Edinburgh. He (1962) stated that the first phase of an analysis is marked by a mobilization of the patient's infantile and primitive feelings of love and hate towards the analyst, the handling of which will determine the following phases of treatment. Gitelson equated the analyst's position in this beginning stage to that of the mother *vis á vis* her child and, in analogizing to *maternal care*, he quotes Winnicott (1960) wherein, "the qualities and changes in the mother ... meet the specific and developing needs of the infant" (p. 589). Likewise, and congruent with Loewald's (1960) important idea, the analyst meets the patient's need for a "fostering figure" to resume the ego's arrested development and progress onto a secondary level of development with more individualized, autonomous, mature forms of relatedness. Of this first stage of treatment, Gitelson (1962) writes that it is a human relationship that "fosters a freer use of primitive mechanisms of projection and introjection in the patient and analyst" and that introduces a "factor of reassurance through rapport which may be decisive" (p. 198). Foreshadowing Kohut's views (1971), Gitelson explains,

> ... the analyst's empathic imbrication with his patient's emotions provides a sustaining grid of "understanding" (or "resonance") which leads toward co-operation and identification, to the partial relinquishment of the anaclitic attitude, and in the end to a collaboration which Sterba has called "therapeutic alliance" [p. 199].

Other analysts held a different position when it came to this idea of establishing a positive transference as a pre-condition for interpretive work. In fact, Wilhelm Reich (1926, 1933), as well as many subsequent Kleinians, classical, and ego psychologists believe that interpretation of anxiety or latent negative transference is an essential and far more reliable vehicle for establishing trust and rapport in the early phase of treatment because it serves, in fact, to diminish the patient's anxieties regarding more destructive, primitive aggression directed at the analyst (see Bird, 1972).

In the wake of Alexander's (1950; Alexander & French, 1946) controversial ideas by which he advocated manipulating the transference to achieve a "corrective emotional experience", many psychoanalysts, including Gitelson, felt it necessary to reassert the primacy of interpretation and insight as the defining feature of psychoanalysis in contrast to other forms of psychotherapy.

In response to Alexander's plea for "flexibility", Eissler (1953) delineated what was acceptable, standard psychoanalytic procedure drawing the line between psychoanalysis and psychotherapy and introducing a special term for any deviation in technique—namely, what he called "parameters," which he defined as follows: "I define the parameter of a technique as the deviation, both quantitative and qualitative, from the basic model technique, that is to say, from a technique which requires interpretation as the exclusive tool" (p. 110).

A year later, Rangell (1954c), likewise felt it necessary to outline how psychotherapy and psychoanalysis differed. The psychoanalytic establishment, as if under siege by these *new therapies*, in many ways became more rigid. Rangell writes, "The various maneuvers engaged in by the therapist in Alexander's system, and in general with the 'corrective emotional experience,' are at times, to be sure, dynamically indicated, but when they are, they distinctly constitute dynamic psychotherapy in contrast to psychoanalysis" (p. 743).

Returning to Edinburgh, it is significant that Gitelson's viewpoint was met with such intense opposition that he was moved to reassure the audience that he was not gratifying the patient's libidinal needs for attachment and, moreover, that he relied on classical techniques of interpretation as the method of cure (see Friedman, 1978). As Abend (2007) has noted, this period was clearly "the high water mark of theoretical orthodoxy" (p. 1425), and thus, in order to mollify the displeasure of most participants at the conference who "did not want to hear about any curative factor except understanding as conveyed by interpretation" (Friedman, 1978, p. 535), Gitelson (1962) took pains to clarify that,

> I certainly am not supporting the view that the essential nature of the analytic procedure is found in its provision of a "corrective emotional experience" aided by magical suggestion and representational gratification. My intention is to extend the classical view that only the ego can be influenced therapeutically, and that to this end accurate *interpretation is the prime curative factor* [p. 203, italics added].

Lest the reader get the wrong impression that he (Gitelson, 1962) was advocating what he called the "impulsion towards the kind of overt conduct that has been called 'interpersonal', 'supportive', and 'human'" (p. 196), and in contrast to "those who have overtly 'humanized' the analytic situation because of their misunderstanding of 'analytic passivity' and their consequent reaction against it" (p. 198, fn.), Gitelson devoted the first third of this paper to the task of making unequivocal his conviction that the "explicit method of treatment" is systematic interpretation, and that the interpersonal elements are simply precursors to this critical stage of analysis. They are *"necessary but by themselves not sufficient precursor conditions* for the establishment of an effective psychoanalytic situation" (ibid., p. 194, original italics).

Nonetheless, Gitelson clearly considered the patient's attachment to the analyst as a central process for impacting psychic structures and thereby providing what he termed a "new developmental beginning" (p. 197). Of particular significance is his emphasis on Loewald's (1960) idea that patients introject the structure of their relationship with the analyst, not just aspects of the analyst's personality or psychic structure. In short, Gitelson, much like Loewald, extends the classical ego psychological view by arguing that the influence exerted by the ego is not "simply on that aspect of the ego which is ultimately accessible to interpretation in its explicit meaning" (pp. 203–204). Hence, Gitelson argues for the mutative impact of the analyst's "concern and care for the strengthening and development of the [patient's] ego" (p. 204). In this volume, although emphasizing diverse ways by which it is achieved, Spivak (Chapter Six) and Wolson (Chapter Eight) directly stress the importance of the analyst's concern and care, whereas Porter (Chapter Nine), Diamond (Chapter Ten), and Bolgar (Chapter Thirteen) do so more implicitly.

Attachment and insight: from bifurcation towards integrated perspectives

During the second half of the 20th century, numerous analysts of varying theoretical persuasions, including Balint (1949, 1968), Alexander (1956), Kohut (1971, 1977, 1984), McLaughlin (1981), Mitchell (1988, 1990, 1993, 2000a), and Aron (1991), considered insight as corollary, at best, in their appraisal of the mechanisms by which analysis achieved meaningful change. Instead, these analysts highlighted the critical importance of the relationship between analyst and patient. Consequently, the prevailing theories of curative factors and therapeutic action had become bifurcated—either *insight through interpretation* or *development through the relationship with the analyst*—was considered primary.

In contrast with this tendency towards polarization, however, British object relations theorists with their interest in the nature of pre-Oedipal development (e.g., Fairbairn, 1941, 1943, 1958; Guntrip, 1961, 1969; Winnicott, 1958b, 1965), Kleinian analysts reconceptualizing the importance of countertransference (e.g., Heimann, 1950; Money-Kyrle, 1956), and classically trained, independent thinking American analysts, such as Loewald (1960), Stone (1961), and Gitelson (1962), provided monumental steps towards bridging the gap in the longstanding debate between the power of insight and the impact of the relationship as mutative. For example, Loewald (1960) in his influential paper, "On the therapeutic action of psychoanalysis", proposed that patients identify with their analyst's mental functioning in an affectively rich manner that directly contributes to attaining insight.

It is noteworthy that today, even the most traditional of mainstream analysts, such as Abend (2007), who favours the centrality of interpretation, also accept without apparent contradiction "the power of the relationship … as contributing to therapeutic outcome" (p. 1429). In this volume, Spivak (Chapter Six), Diamond (Chapter Ten), and Wolson (Chapter Eight) each elaborate on this integrative bridge with respect to specific aspects of interpretation, the analyst's mental experience, and the analyst's relational "love" respectively, while Eagle (Chapter Three) deepens the reader's appreciation for the intrinsic linkage between self-knowledge and attachment by drawing on both psychoanalysis and philosophy.

Building bridges: one psychoanalysis or many?

Many of the major debates in psychoanalysis that dig down deep to the level of theory have had their beginning in disagreements at the level of its therapeutic action, and these discussions often have had as their basis the treatment of different clinical populations. Klein's (1932) ideas emerged in relation to a need to apply psychoanalysis to clinical work with children. Alexander and French (1946) believed that for a great number of maladjusted patients, "insight … is no magic wand" (p. 128) and in many cases, "considerable preliminary emotional readjustment is necessary before insight is possible" (p. 127). Fairbairn's (1941, 1943) object relations theory aimed to find ways of working with the inaccessible schizoid patient. Segal (1950, 1956) and Bion (1954, 1956, 1957), in working with psychotic patients, elaborated the Kleinian-based paranoid-schizoid position. Sullivan's (1953) interpersonal ideas emerging from the School of American Psychiatry sought to understand and address anxiety in the interactions of schizophrenic patients. Winnicott (1945, 1974) attempted to address primitive states of mind. And finally, Kohut's (1971, 1977) self psychology, deriving from ego psychology, was born out of a need to address shortcomings in the treatment of patients with narcissistic pathology.

Broadly speaking and employing Rangell's (2007) metaphor of a tree, we suggest that there are four main theoretical schools, at least in North America, each representing a major branch stemming from the trunk of Freud's "classical" psychoanalytic tree: namely, (1) ego psychology/conflict theory; (2) Kleinian/Bionian and the British "Middle School" object relations theory; (3) self psychology; and (4) relational, interpersonal, and intersubjectivity theory. Each offers an alternative model to that of classical analysis regarding development, pathogenesis, and therapeutic action. These divergences notwithstanding, in order to create more viable bridges between theories and to understand today's evolving perspectives on therapeutic action, certain phenomena that each school addresses and the questions they raise need to be acknowledged.

We suggest there are four nodal phenomena that provide opportunities for addressing lines of divergence and convergence between the different theoretical models. Moreover, the various schools conceptualize as well as emphasize each of these four nodal points differently. First, a nodal point of all theories is the question of *anxiety* and the strategies or modes for dealing with it. In Fairbairn's (1941, 1943, 1955) object relational theory, anxiety stems from threats to a closed intrapsychic system, which was meant to protect the person from the loss of an internalized object. To Klein (1948), anxiety stems from the primitive aggression emanating from the death drive that threatens to annihilate good and bad internalized objects and the self, whereas for Bion (1962b), primitive anxieties form in part-object relations where there is a deficit in what he terms alpha functioning, needed to metabolize "chaotic proto-mental states" or "beta" elements. In ego psychology (Brenner, 1979a; Rangell, 1989; Arlow, 1990), anxiety is a warning signal, a product of a mind in conflict. It can be elaborated as expectant punishment from within, such as guilt, or from without, such as the loss of love, loss of the object, or bodily harm for unconscious wishes deemed objectionable and/or dangerous. In Sullivan's interpersonal model (1953), anxiety stems from the fear of the disorganizing effects of the Other's anxiety, whereas in Kohut's (1971, 1977) self psychology, fragmentation anxiety ensues when self-cohesion is threatened. Each theory, in turn, prescribes particular modes of intervention that account for change.

In addition to how anxiety is defined and addressed by our different theories, a second question has to do with the relative importance given to the role of *unconscious fantasy and reality* in the development of psychopathology and illness. This key issue forms an integral part of the history of psychoanalysis beginning with Freud's abandonment of the seduction hypothesis as he wrote to Fliess in 1897 (Masson, 1985), and the important influence attributed to unconscious fantasy. Klein (1932) further emphasizes the role of phantasy to such a degree, according to Bowlby (1940, 1963), so as to nearly neglect the role of the child's external world in shaping the child's emerging personality. In contrast, Fairbairn (1955, 1963), Winnicott (1958b, 1960, 1965), and Kohut (1977) turn their focus to actual failures of the environment and stress how these failures account for trauma and deficit-based psychopathology. Interpersonalists, such as Levenson (1983), have moved further away from ideas of unconscious fantasy to a focus on interpersonal transactions in the "here and now". As Levenson (ibid.) puts it, "For the intrapsychic therapist the expansion, or regression, is vertical back in time, deeper. For the interpersonalist, the regression is horizontal, mapping wider patterns of interaction" (p. 68). In the present volume, Sobelman (Chapter Seven) pays specific attention to the role of fantasy in treatments, and contends that the patient's fantasies about how psychoanalysis cures represent pain and deprivation in the patient's earliest relationships that require analysis.

Attachment theorists (Ainsworth & Bell, 1970; Main, 1993) have also stressed the importance of real life events in the form of actual loss and/or threat of loss and separation. An important impetus for Bowlby's work (1969, 1973, 1980, 1988) was what he deemed the near complete disregard for reality that he observed in Klein's view of the infant (see Bowlby, 1958). It was the emphasis on real events, such as loss, abandonment, and actual neglect, being championed by attachment theory that accounted for much of the derision with which many psychoanalysts met Bowlby's ideas and deemed his model for the longest time as not psychoanalytic (Haartman, 2008). It is interesting to note that attachment theory had until recently been articulated as a mode for understanding infant/mother dyads and intervening at an early age to repair security of attachment; more recently, however, we see how attachment research and theory is being directly applied to psychoanalytic treatment (Steele & Steele, 1998; Mitchell, 2000a; Fonagy, 2001; Fonagy & Target, 2007).

Another major question with which each psychoanalytic school grapples has to do with the nature of patients' *resistance* to the analyst's efforts and to analytic change (Freud, 1926a, 1937). Analysts of every persuasion acknowledge that patients defend against the aims of treatment even while embracing them. In this respect, as Friedman (2007) suggests, "[A] theory of therapeutic action is just the reverse image of the theory of resistance" (p. 1655). Not every analyst, however, agrees with this approach to resistance. For example, Kohut's (1971, 1977) methods of understanding the dynamic meaning of resistance and working with it differ considerably from those of classical and conflict-based approaches. In terms of the latter, Portuges and Hollander in this volume (Chapter Four), stress the value of carefully analysing the patient's resistance as well as the analyst's counter-resistance in order to account for therapeutic action.

A fourth, and final, nodal point in the divergent theoretical models of recent years is the issue of *countertransference* and the extent to which it represents a "common ground" in psychoanalysis (Gabbard, 1995). As Gabbard notes in what he considered the "emerging area of common ground" (p. 475), most analysts today accept their *participation in* the patient's transference and recognize that their own countertransference, internal experience, and ongoing mental activities are essential in advancing the process. Likewise, Diamond (this volume, Chapter Ten) observes that this recognition has led analysts of various theoretical persuasions, including contemporary ego psychologists, British object relations theorists, modern Kleinians and Bionians, interpersonal and relational analysts, and classically trained American independents, to include countertransference-based technique to produce intrapsychic change. Of course, this inclusion or overemphasizing of countertransference can be problematic, particularly when relying on *pars pro toto* thinking (Rangell, 2007, this volume, Chapter Two). Arlow (1993b), for example, cautions against over-stressing countertransference at the expense of under-utilizing aspects of technique that he considers essential. Among these are noting and interpreting qualities of the patient's flow of associations such as gaps, contiguities, and hesitations.

For quite some time, the divide between the classical model and the British object relations models, described by Greenberg and Mitchell (1983) as the divergence between the drive/structural and the relational/structural traditions, was believed to be unbridgeable. Increasingly, however, this divide has given way to a more integrated viewpoint espoused at times by Kernberg (1979, 2001), more explicitly by Gill (1983), Sandler (1981, 1992), Wallerstein (1983), and most recently by Ellman (2010) and Eagle (2011). Today, leading analysts, such as Wallerstein (1988), Gabbard (1995), Rangell (2007), Ellman (2010), Bolognini (2011), and Eagle (2011) contend that there is a growing common ground between the diverse theoretical models as the field continues to evolve and mature. One of the most dramatic instances of this developing common ground is evidenced in the rapprochement between ego psychology and Kleinians (Schafer, 1997). Similarly, the American object relations school attempts to integrate the discoveries of the British object relationalists with classical and ego psychology (Kernberg, 2001). A different type of reconciliation has been in effect with the integration of attachment theory and traditional psychoanalysis, which historically had been at odds (Steele & Steele, 1998; Fonagy, 2001; Fonagy & Target, 2007). And even among cognitive behaviourists there has been a growing recognition that psychoanalytic principles underlie some of the positive outcomes being reported by research on cognitive behaviour therapy (Wachtel, 1977; Kazdin, 2008, 2010; Shedler, 2010).

In short, a multiple-factor model (Ellman, 2010) most likely best reflects the data of psychoanalysis wherein a unique, dialectically-based interaction is inevitably in play between endogenous and exogenous factors, drives and objects, unconscious and conscious processes, internal and external reality, self-knowledge and relationship, separation and attachment, solitude and interaction, one-person and two-person psychologies, linear and non-linear causality, past and present, and theory and experience. As the chapters in this volume make evident, the evolving perspectives of this second century of psychoanalysis expand the conversation by continuously engaging in these antinomies rather than bypassing the inherent tension and lack of certitude by neatly resolving them. This promises to deepen our understanding of the human psyche and how psychoanalysis produces transformation.

CHAPTER TWO

The aims and method of psychoanalysis a century later

Leo Rangell

In this compressed presentation, I will examine the core raison d'être of the science and profession of psychoanalysis as it has grown and developed over its first century of existence. Bursting upon the scientific scene like a thunderbolt at the turn of the 20th century, the new system of knowledge has been characterized during its entire life span by tumultuous upheavals. Through all of these, there has emerged a durable entity that I believe will maintain a permanent place in the intellectual armamentarium of man. Its goals and technique are intimately intertwined and directly derivative from its theory of understanding. I will focus on the growth and changes that have evolved in both, the theory, and the resultant aims and method derived from that.

Psychoanalysis, if we are to anthropomorphize a science and profession, after a steady evolutionary growth, has reached a new phase of its development. In terms of this longitudinal survey of its existence a century after it was born, we might venture to say it has reached the beginning of its adolescence. While this may seem jarring to many who feel it has more likely already passed its old age and has become moribund if still alive, I shall present what I feel is a more accurate and enduring description of its present condition and status.

Since this book will be composed of a group of chapters representing the individual experiences of each author, the assessment I offer will be against the background of my own personal intellectual journey. I entered the field as a candidate in an unambivalently classical Institute, the New York Psychoanalytic, in 1940–1941. This was a year after Hitler had invaded Czechoslovakia, and the year Pearl Harbor was struck, on December 7, 1941. I left New York at the end of 1942 to serve in the American Air Force during the war. After the war I returned in 1946 to the Los Angeles Psychoanalytic Institute, where I completed my candidacy and graduated in 1950. My orientation was Freudian, my most inspiring figure Otto Fenichel, whose summary work (1945b) had appeared in an earlier version during the year of my residency, and whom I was to meet later briefly at an army post.

My graduation paper, read at the Beverly Wilshire Hotel, was the last paper of that Society before a major organizational split was to take place. This had national significance in that three other similarly-defined divisions occurred during the same period in other institutes throughout the country, New York, Philadelphia, and Washington-Baltimore. In the aftermath of the charged upheaval and separation of opposing groups, I chose to continue my affiliation and theoretical outlook as a classical psychoanalyst as I understood the term. The alternative was the neo-Freudian, Franz Alexandrian position of a more active, corrective role of the analyst and presumably greater responsiveness to external, social factors in neurosogenesis.

My reasoning at that crucial moment of self-definition was to stay with me throughout my professional life. I felt in essence that the purported division of the time was an artificial one, a false dichotomy based on limited observations rather than thinking through theoretical principles. The analytic position, as I conceived it, while aiming at neutrality and objectivity, did not exclude flexibility and empathy, nor did the traditional analytic attitude downplay to any degree the inputs of the outer world. The analyst, in my view already at that time, added the scientific stance to the observer without reducing his humanness—and highlighted the intrapsychic without placing into shadow the interpersonal.

Here I already discern a growing conviction that stayed with me throughout my life-long immersion in trying to understand the workings of the mind. I am referring to the complementary series, which I feel applies across a wide swath of issues. A mechanism described by Freud (1905b) in a specific context was to become for me a quite global explanation for many if not all the conflicts of theory and praxis that were later to confront the field. In most controversies, it is not a question of all or none, but how much of every polarity applies at any point of the spectrum. In the dichotomies that were the aftermaths of these "great splits" around 1950, I felt that all analysts aim at objectivity, but they must also retain empathy. The issue in each individual case was not the presence of either one but the ratio between dual forces, how the combination in question fared.

Empirically, as I surveyed the social ambience of my professional life at that early juncture, it was the neutrality necessary for objectivity that was to me the most in peril of being lost by the splitting in process. While I felt keenly that many analysts, including admired leaders on what was called the conservative side, failed to be warm, or even likeable, I felt that the emotional wave on the so-called progressive side left little affinity for neutrality, which was too often confused with coldness. From then until now I went with what I felt were scientific principles over social relations. Already at that first crossroads, with whatever I may have gained, I also lost some friends.

My paper (1952a) at that symbolic moment of graduation was a specific demonstration of this dilemma and my attempt at its solution. In presenting a detailed clinical investigation of a patient with a symptom that could not have better called for a psychoanalytic study and treatment, the entire analytic enterprise exemplified and furthered my chosen intellectual course. The case was that of a doll phobia—not in a little girl, but a grown man in his forties. I cannot here go into details, but wish to use that experience to further this description of the overall development of psychoanalytic theory. That paper went on to win an International Clinical Essay prize, and became a much-used teaching instrument.

Its main contribution to the present theoretical theme is that I came to utilize the metaphor of a wheel as a frame to explain the clinical data. At the hub was the symptom doll. At this same centre, as the pin-point essence of the phobic reaction, however explicitly the doll figures were constructed and however creatively dressed, the qualitative characteristic focused upon in all the threatening, life-like doll-object-figures was the empty, flat, and neutral crotch. At the base of the phobia was castration anxiety.

A felicitous theoretical construct, the metaphor of the wheel said it all. It had room for every input that affected both the life course of the patient and the specific development of his central phobic symptom. The periphery of the circle was the external world; the core the doll, the concentrated symptom object. In alternative or rather overlapping terms, the hub also contained, from one of Freud's (1900) major paths, the Oedipus conflict, the centre of the neurosis and anxiety, the motive for defence (Freud, 1926a; Jones, 1920; Fenichel, 1945b). In another later addition, applicable to all cases, I added the infantile neurosis to the multiply-determined hub-core. All these aetiologic elements existed in a fused mass to provide the central fuel for the psychopathology of the patient.

Radiating spokes within the wheel represented a myriad of clinical facts, pieces of history, memories, free associations, of the transference and in life, dreams and their tributaries, leading to and coming from the central product at the hub. Each spoke was a path flowing in both directions, from the outside affecting the inner world, and from the intrapsychic to its effects on the environment and its significant objects. Confirmed experientially throughout the analysis were both Erikson's (1956) mutuality and Waelder's (1936) "multiple functions of the ego".

The main point to be derived from this early clinical reference is the inclusiveness and totality of explanatory theory, in contrast to exclusiveness or any narrow limitation. I have always consciously resisted elevating one element over all others of what is a complex system, a tendency I began to see and sense from early on, looking back at the very history of the pioneers around Freud. This analysis of an unusual but pathognomonic phobia contained and embraced the external as well as internal transference, the pregenital as much as the Oedipal and beyond, and also relationships and objects from ongoing life, the present as well as the past, the here-and-now between the analytic pair as much as the interpersonal patterns of the patient with his growing object world, and innate givens along with all later experiential inputs. To all of these, the analyst was neutral and empathic, open equidistantly to all incoming data while in affective harmony with the goals, motives, and comfort of the patient. The theory of therapy is a direct derivative of this total explanatory theory of aetiology. In terms of therapeutic action, in addition to the patient's insight into his repressed castration anxiety due to the analyst's interpretations, many other factors in combination contributed to analytic change, including the role of catharsis, the analyst's suggestions to confront the phobic object, and the introjection by the patient of the analyst's employment of secondary process logic.

Another experience that tested the subject of the exclusivity and limits of the borders of the entity of psychoanalysis came shortly thereafter, when my early participation on the national scene began by invitations to serve on panels of the American Psychoanalytic Association. After the first one, which came very quickly in 1952 on "The theory of affects" (Rangell, 1952b), the next was in 1954, a panel at the American on what was to become a repetitive subject, "Similarities and differences between psychoanalysis and dynamic psychotherapy" (1954c). As both the reporter and participant of the first such panel, my views on this pressing topic (1954b, c) were incorporated in what became one of the most thumbed-over issues of the *Journal of the American Psychoanalytic Association* in the history of that journal.

The relationship between the two closely-related procedures became the hot topic in the post-war exuberance of the practice of both. The concerns of psychoanalytic theoreticians and leaders at that time were to protect the new science from loss of its uniqueness or indeed its very identity as the fresh, suddenly-popular dynamic, psychotherapeutic modes of treatment rapidly gained momentum. As these were increasingly accepted into more austere territory, the medical schools, the intellectual public, and the seeming readiness of significant numbers in the social and psychological sciences to embrace their guiding premises, a central theme under discussion in this novel milieu became whether the two related disciplines were separate or continuous, and what constituted psychoanalysis proper (I do not mean "proper" psychoanalysis, in a pejorative sense—that is an even more difficult matter).

In the panels and discussions on the subject in that historic issue of the *Journal of the American Psychoanalytic Association*, I was one of two analysts—the other was Merton Gill—who, in comparing the two disciplines, undertook to venture a definition of psychoanalysis. Gill's (1954) definition was terse and sparse—thereby more impressive: analysis "results in the development of a regressive transference neurosis and the ultimate resolution of this neurosis by techniques of interpretation alone" (p. 775). Mine was more inclusive, or equivocal, less elegant, that analysis aimed at a resolution of the transference *and infantile neurosis*, i.e., the neurosis for which the patient had come to the analysis to begin with, and of which the transference was a replica. Both of us agreed at that time that psychoanalysis and dynamic psychotherapy, though contiguous and interdigitating, were separate disciplines. "Day is different from night, though there is dusk; and black from white, though there is grey (with no implication as to one being right or wrong, better or worse)" (Rangell, 1954c, p. 737).

The formulation in these early debates that to me most defined the line of demarcation between the two disciplines was that of Edward Bibring (1954), who described five technical procedures, and corresponding curative principles of each, that are utilized to different degrees in the two approaches. These are: suggestion, abreaction, manipulation, clarification, and interpretation. While these technical manoeuvres overlap and none are absent in any psychotherapeutic procedure, insight due to interpretation is the dominant mode in psychoanalysis, while suggestion and manipulation are strongest at the pole of the dynamic psychotherapies. All are derivative of the same psychoanalytic theory of the mind. To objections raised against the term "manipulation", Bibring states simply and forthrightly that to his mind there is no more suitable term available. This term is "used here in a completely neutral sense" (p. 745). This simple statement might well be a model for the expression of views throughout this discussion. I say this because of the very easy shift to ad hominem implications that has vexed this would-be scientific domain from the beginning.

Another significant contribution supplementing these views was that of Leo Stone, whose formulations were equally specific about the two comparative disciplines as he (1954) introduced "the widening scope" of psychoanalysis to a broader spectrum than the neuroses, such as psychosomatic cases. The composite of this cluster of opinions on the identities and relationships between the two contiguous disciplines became the dominant view into the succeeding clinical period of the 1950s and 1960s.

Such was the positive ambience at mid-century surrounding the public and professional image of psychoanalysis, a science of the mind and its derivative therapeutic technique, and the line of demarcation from its closest scientific neighbour, analytic psychotherapy. Much debated and sparsely put, this composite formulation was viewed as the standard for the understanding and treatment of human behaviour at the end of the first half, going into the second half of the "Century of Freud". This was the peak period of the superordinacy of psychoanalytic thinking, the most-accepted social, aesthetic, professional, and scientific overview of the nature of the new mental science. With this went the prevalence of psychoanalysts occupying chairs of departments of psychiatry as well as the treatment most in demand by patients, and intellectually syntonic with the vanguard of mental health practitioners.

That was "the Golden Age" of Freudian thinking and influence, propelled further by the optimism that followed the victorious Great War. It was not as if competition was absent or stifled nor that many alternative treatments had not been introduced and elicited much interest and debate. This had of course been going on since the first inklings of psychoanalysis. Where Jung, Adler, Rank, or Ferenczi introduced their dissident views early, later alternative theories occupied the scene in a continuous series, from Sullivan (1953) since the Twenties, Melanie Klein (1932) from the same period or slightly later, Horney (1937) from the Thirties and just before World War 2, and a continuous stream of debated ideas and theoretical systems in the years since.

While the 50s and 60s were the high points, in theory and excitement, the mid- and late-60s became a period of questioning, increasingly challenging the established order, and the beginning of a general decline in the standing and success of the new discipline. This, in my view and experience, was multi-determined. From one side, this was part of the 60s "student revolution", which itself was connected to the post-modern intellectual revolt against existing institutions and ideational schools. Any credo or practice that had achieved some stability and equilibrium was authoritative and therefore a target. There was often a degree of truth in this, but also a large component of fantasy and projection. In almost every discipline, the new movement was to throw out the baby with the bathwater. Psychoanalysis was no exception.

Although many look outwards to explain the increasing disillusion and decline, I believe that this external fate was at least equally determined by changing attitudes within the profession itself. Both were involved. Externally, on the intellectual scene but affecting the scientific centre as well, was the widespread, post-modern rebellion I have just mentioned against almost all established institutional structures, inside and outside academia, spearheaded by the student activism and revolution widespread through the late 60s. I saw this directly involve the Rome Congress of the IPA in 1969 where, by serendipity, during the few days before I was elected president at that congress, I was witness to the street parades against the "IP$A".

But internal to the field of psychoanalysis, a theoretical upheaval coincided exactly with the time of that same congress that was to change the intellectual landscape of the science in the United States, perhaps forever. The window through which a new theoretical wind entered the American scene, not coincidently, was in Los Angeles. I (2004) have written elsewhere and extensively documented the social milieu in which this took place, describing the interpersonal influences that played an important role over and above scientific principles. The theoretical storm that suddenly transformed the dominant American psychoanalytic conceptual frame was the arrival of British Kleinians by private invitation to the Los Angeles Psychoanalytic Institute and Society. A huge tempest ensued, with consequent fallout developments that defined the psychoanalytic scene in this country from then on.

While this historical progression was lauded by many, probably the great majority, as an indication of democracy and an open mind not present before, I will present a differing view and opinion of developing events that were to define the state of psychoanalysis for the remainder of the century and beyond. Following a distasteful period in which the welcome to the Kleinians was withdrawn in unruly fashion in favour of the rapidly-following self psychology, a gradual rearrangement ensued organizationally, with new societies and institutes emerging based on support of a new alternative theory, Kleinian, Self, or just being labelled eclectic. Excitement, separatism, often to the point of cultism, followed, even a lawsuit in a test case for a British Kleinian analyst to be included in the American Psychoanalytic Association without bias as to theory. This was separate from and preceding by over a decade the famous lawsuit in the late Eighties, differently motivated, based on the divisive medical/non-medical controversy. The result of the latter was the influx of multiple societies of analysts, such as LAISPS and others, which were to enrich psychoanalytic activity, both theory and practice, from a vast non-medical direction.

Coming back to the end of the Sixties, with this development, the scientific ambience in the United States underwent an abrupt change. Until then, the analytic world accepted, or at least lived with, a division in which the country represented, or was, the undisputed seat of what was euphemistically referred to as "ego psychology". In my opinion, that was a shortcut, or even a slogan, for a quite different orientation. American psychoanalysis, during its heyday years in mid-century, was by no means limited to the role of the ego, but was in an operative sense dedicated to what I (2007) call "total composite psychoanalytic theory". In contrast with the theoretical ambience started in Great Britain and exported through most of the analytic world, which evolved into the well-known three analytic paths, the theoretical guideline in the US, considered mainstream during that exuberant period, was the total theory as developed to that time (i.e., Freud's id, to which the ego, 1923a, and superego, 1920, had been added).

The unified national orientation of "ego psychology" in the US, in a literal and more accurate sense, was an "id-ego-superego-internal-external-world-psychoanalysis-psychosynthesis". I include psychosynthesis, which I feel has been under-appreciated or articulated as a necessary segment to complete the therapeutic aspects of the total psychoanalytic process. Analysis, a process of teasing apart, needs to be followed and completed by a re-synthesis or putting together again. With regard to external labels, I consider myself neither a contemporary Freudian nor a modern Kleinian, both of which stand on different bases and concepts of conflict than the total Freudian system. Nor am I a self psychologist or intersubjectivist, although aspects of each are contained within total Freudian theory. I regard myself as a "Developed Freudian", retaining what proved to be timeless of the original discoveries, and adhering to its subsequent findings from all alternative theories that are found equally valid and indispensible. While I believe that this term could apply to many analysts practising today—in fact most dynamic psychotherapists practise according to its central tenets—there is no official group in current scientific-political discourse that defines itself in that way.

It is important to recognize and acknowledge that the respect with which this overall orientation was received during this period was based not on authoritativeness, nor on "hegemony" or arrogance with which it has been labelled, but on the rationality and comprehensiveness of the theory dominant and practised in the United States as compared to the rest of the world. Empirically, the quite universal respect and support enjoyed by psychoanalysis in America at mid-century was based on an unspoken but appreciated knowledge that this orientation was a coalescence of all components of a total rational theory, at the core of which was an unambivalent Freudian centre. Alongside the friction around the 1938 special regional status of the American Psychoanalytic Association over the noxious and deeply divisive medical requirement adopted by the Association, a parallel major division, also controversial but in my opinion proudly defensible, was the difference in the dominant theories in the two psychoanalytic cultures.

While the debates over theory in Europe were increasingly between the Kleinian view of the British vs. the Freudian position centered in Vienna and Berlin, the stance in the United States clearly came to represent the Continental Freudian view of theory. Influenced largely by the influx from the mid-Thirties of major political refugee theoreticians (such as Hartmann, Rapaport, Waelder, Fenichel, Kris, Loewenstein, and a continuous line of contributors), the intellectual impact of these émigrés on analytic theory ironically did more for Freudian psychoanalysis in the United States than did the settling and integration of both Sigmund and Anna Freud into the British Society.

The American version of total metapsychology theory that resulted ("ego psychology" for short), besides not opening itself up to the early post-natal emphasis of the Kleinian view, also held firm in not succumbing to its own home-grown fragmentation brought about up to that time by competing theories that highlighted one part over the whole, whether the interpersonal focus of the Sullivanians, or the wider culture of Karen Horney. American psychoanalysis did not oppose any of these special emphases—whether pre-Oedipal or cultural—but contained them within its total theoretical framework, which was more complete and comprehensive than the sum of its parts.

The "Golden Age" of psychoanalysis lasted through the 50s. The theory of therapeutic action during this long and fruitful era, initiated by the beginning discoveries, but adding flesh to the initial concept with each passing decade, followed the 1954 formula of Edward Bibring. Psychoanalysis worked by the "curative principle" of insight brought about by the "technical maneuver" of interpretation. The analyst uncovers the repressed truth, conveys it coolly and in as matter-of-fact a manner as possible to the patient, who experiences a newly liberated affect associated with the repressed historical fact now come to light, and "gets better"—which I (1969) modify to "makes himself better" (the subtle distinction between the two was left to posterity to recognize and work out). In the glow of success that this idealistic sequence achieved, it could hardly be recognized how Utopian but raw and skeletal—and innocent—and partial this succession of words can be.

The necessary insight in this prevalent view was produced "by interpretation alone", in the definition used literally by Gill, who during the course of a brilliant career, generally took a number of positions to the extreme. While changing his view four or five times, he always drew a large contingent of followers to his strongly-articulated current concept (later it was to be "transference only"). Although in each period the emphasis defined the therapeutic zeitgeist, my own definition during the same time frame rendered these absolute elements more diffuse, clouded, and mixed with others. From the beginning, the initial neurosis and the patient's specific past remained as much in the forefront to be explored and understood as what transpired in "the here-and-now". Similarly, the exclusive analysis of the transference, or interpretation alone, were merged with other elements, such as suggestion and abreaction, to join in producing mutative change.

What seems like a magical expectation from just "knowing" (the patient "gets better"), only now appears as naïve and incomplete as it is. In 1971, in Vienna, towards the conclusion of my presidential address to that congress, I quoted Daniel Ellsberg as to why he came to reveal the Pentagon Papers (Rangell, 1972): "My father used to read to me a passage from the Bible which said, 'The truth will set you free'" (p. 10). Since this is what psychoanalysis is all about,

I could have ended my talk with this sentence, and it would have finished on an upswing. "However," I went on, to the surprise of the audience, "there is another truth, and that is that this is not always true. We might remember how young Sigmund Freud, at the age of 16, told his friend, regarding Oedipus Rex, that ignorance might maintain his cheerful state" (p. 10). I cannot accurately report the reaction of the audience to this additional insight.

The blissful period of how analysis works, that the patient (automatically) "gets well", held sway through the 50s and well into the 60s, when a slow state of grumbling discontent began, questioning methodology, results, and eventually theory. The aetiology of this collective mood was multiple. I have indicated the post-modern development challenging accepted wisdom on a wide front in the external intellectual culture. This was accompanied from the mid 60s through the remainder of the decade by a simultaneous disillusionment within psychoanalysis, putting its claims to the test of more critical inquiry and opening it up to new explanations, understanding, and methods.

The peak of the course and fate of the new discipline during its first century came at the end of the 60s, coinciding sharply with the time of the Rome Congress in 1969. Splits, major shifts, new paradigms evolve as a result of ideas and people, the two converging in readiness and motivation. A major ideational and demographic change in the status of the science and discipline of psychoanalysis took place in 1969–1970, coinciding with the Rome Congress and before the next one held in Vienna. This involved both Kleinian and self psychology, in different ways. I have written in depth in *My Life in Theory* (2004) about the timing, geographic locations, and complex interpersonal backgrounds of these developments. It was not an accident but a combination of powerful interpersonal as well as theoretical factors that were at the apex of events that led to the arrival of a new intense theoretical challenge into the American scene significantly through a window in Los Angeles. The initial signature of coming events was the arrival of Hanna Segal and a group of Kleinian analysts from the British Society at the private invitation of a small nucleus of analysts of the then Los Angeles Psychoanalytic Society and Institute, who had begun to introduce Kleinian theory to local analysts shortly before.

This is not to comment on the validity of any particular theory, but about the extra-Institute and acting-out nature of the sequence of events. With respect to the scientific base, the affective excitement over Kleinian theory quickly abated, as the same local individuals shortly dis-invited the visiting analysts and turned with equal vigour to proselytizing the new self psychology that had also appeared and gathered steam after that same congress. Passage from one theory to another then began to occur with regularity, each new belief, or more accurately brief slogan representing a theory, being greeted with equal ardour and excitement. One outcome in Los Angeles was that a number of analysts who had developed a genuine preference for the theories of Klein, formed the first (today perhaps the only) avowed Kleinian institute in the United States. Since this brief historical account revolves explicitly around a personal view, its validity may be judged by comparing this summary with a chapter in a book by Kirsner (2000), a psychoanalytic historian from Australia, headed "Fear and loathing in Los Angeles".

Psychoanalysis was never the same again. A flame had been lit over a parched land, starting a wildfire that had no borders and changed the national theoretical landscape for all time. It was not only in Los Angeles that frustration had been brewing. The roots of the problem existed at the beginning of the discipline and had been gaining momentum. The reach of the science had been overestimated, or wrongly or incompletely applied, in every region and location, and the fruits of its full potential missed in a mire of confusion and contradictions. Discontents were increasingly pervasive on two fronts, one the power to heal of the instrument bequeathed to us, and second, a festering disappointment in the rate of personal advance in the field.

It took a few years for the effects of the turmoil that was created to settle into a discernible next phase. After the long reign of a satisfying and respected practice based on developing Freudian theory (aka "ego psychology"), an era of pluralism set in, fuelled by developments inside and outside the field. Externally, there was the gradual long-range response that expectations had been too high, that the promised or expected returns were neither forthcoming nor reliable. Internally, for a combination of the same reasons, the deficiency of the theory, and the superimposition of interpersonal conflicts, the theory was modified, experimented with, and manipulated in efforts to achieve more satisfying results on both fronts.

A scientific conclusion that came to be widely recognized was that insight is not enough. While the lifting of repression and making the unconscious conscious was revolutionary and contributory, insight might be necessary but not sufficient, or at least was not always sufficient. A patient, who repeatedly asked "So what?" after he learned something new, stimulated me (1981a) to write my paper, "From insight to change". The patient's quarrelsome query may have been a resistance, but there was more to the question than resistance, and he spoke for many patients. "Working through" is the phrase to encompass this phase in conventional understanding. But this leaves much to comprehend. How is that accomplished?

The fact is that the intrapsychic segment from insight to reparative action can still be a conflictual and stormy one (Rangell, 1969). In many cases, there still remains as much to do analytically after interpretation as may have already been achieved. Freedom from anxiety may have come about as applied to experimental action, but not yet to concrete acts into the "real" world. Specific aetiologic backgrounds may still await effective analytic work on unconscious defences against action. A theoretical model might be the steps still necessary for the patient to confront a phobic object after insight has been won. Bibring's formula may require some modification. Suggestion, even urging, might in fact be part of the analytic work. In practice, catharsis, abreaction, and even manipulation can hardly be confined to psychotherapeutic in contrast to psychoanalytic procedures. A full life does not permit such finely tuned lines.

Upon this base of doubt, a variety of alternative theories or part-theories appeared from the 70s on, in quick succession, each commanding interest and enthusiasm for a time, each then being succeeded by another partial theory or technique, which then receded in favour of the next. I will be able to mention their contents only briefly, not to undervalue any but to place them in perspective in relation to the whole. There was self-disclosure, where the neutrality of the analyst was questioned and counteracted; a period when enactment was stressed, elevating this mode of data collection in relation to verbal associations; a two-person analysis rather than a focus upon one person analysing another; countertransference on a par with transference analysis; a changed definition of transference to include all affective reactions of the patient to the analyst, and similarly the countertransference; intersubjectivity rather than the priority of the affects of the patient; the concept of self-object, and of a patient-analyst duality, rather than a self and an object; or of the whole self or person, and an elimination of psychic systems. With some or many analysts, projective identification was also raised to the level of a theory.

Each theory had prominent proponents. To name them would face the chance of this becoming an ad hominem debate. A reason that this lurks is that some adherents of new positions switched abruptly after Anna Freud's death. Or a former president of the American Psychoanalytic Association who previously supported its theoretical position now becomes vociferous against "ego psychology", considering it dictatorial rather than an attempted view of a scientific formulation. Or a close associate of Anna Freud turns to object relations, middle-group theory in the British adjustment after her passing. The same analyst now writes, by way of a definition, "Psychoanalysis is what is practiced by psychoanalysts" (in Jiménez, 2009), which would have been quite offensive to Ms Freud.

Interestingly, Kleinian theory, probably the competitive view closest to being an alternative total theory, did not sweep this country as much as did the interpersonal or intersubjective theories, or as completely as it became dominant over all of South America and elsewhere as well. Over time, for example, it has come to make itself felt in the US as well. A recent notice in the San Francisco Society (2009), which has quite consistently been of a Freudian orientation, announces,

> A new post-graduate, neo-Kleinian Study Group, led by members of the Betty Joseph study group, will meet to focus on listening to clinical material from a neo-Kleinian perspective.... The "here and now" focus on the to and fro of the analyst/ analysand dialogue requires very careful and particular kind of listening and understanding of material.... As we work together ... a group hopefully will form with a focus on deepening, recognizing, metabolizing and containing material experienced in projective identification and countertransference, both in the analyst and in the group.

A number of groups, both older, established institutes and new groups or nascent ones still in the pre-group stages, are today interested in and open to study "neo-Kleinian" concepts, with the tacit assumption (also verbalized) that the earlier version was "crazy Kleinian", which has moved towards the rational centre. In my opinion, this involved the taking on of more Freudian conceptualizations, such as giving more emphasis to the Oedipal, with only a shadow of some of the older (excessive) Kleinian thoughts still visible.

I have been at pains to stress in previous writings that I do not oppose or dismiss the new positions taken but see their inclusion in a different light. What I dispute is the exaggerated, even extreme forms some of these deviations have taken, at least in their early stages. This was probably as true for the original discoveries as well. Certainly, neutrality was overdone by many for many years. New converts today stress they are "modern" Kleinians, or "contemporary" Freudians; the original versions of each are considered—and were in many cases—extreme interpretations of valid new insights. At a panel (1995) in which Jacobs, Natterson and Friedman, Spezzano and I participated on "Enactment", the chosen theme for the 40th anniversary celebration of the Southern California Institute, to the intersubjectivists presenting there was no self or object but only a self-object. In the discussion, the two-person social constructivist view was closely intermingled with the technique of enactment, with the spirit emphasized that there is always and only a self-object. This was considered to be the case in life and in treatment. There is no one-person alone; in the analytic dyad, never a patient alone, but always a patient-analyst unit. Nor, similarly, is there a mother or a baby but only one fused unit, which I have often heard as an interpretation of Winnicott's (1941) compassionate understanding of the mother-child bond.

Metaphors are referred to as though they are actualities. Mahler, Pine, and Bergman's (1975) separation-individuation phase is no more. I (1999) take issue with this, stating (as in a panel, 1999) the obvious, that there is also a self or person separate from the object. Similarly, Bion's (1970) recommendation that the analyst approach the patient every hour "without memory, desire, or understanding" might be acceptable as a metaphor but has been too much argued by his devoted group as if it were actuality.

In my (2007) overall view of a unitary theory, total composite psychoanalytic theory is pictured as a tree that is cumulative and consists of an ever-growing group of branches and twigs. Many of the "new" suggestions of alternative theories were there—or should have been there—from the beginning, although historically they were in fact too often masked by an over-emphasis in the new direction. Empathy, caring, for example, was too often hidden or in some cases even absent, in the zeal and momentum of the newly discovered use of the human being as an objective-observing instrument. Total Freudian theory was also always object-related: Dodd Cohen (2007), a member of LAISPS, pointed out that "Freud's baby" was object-oriented from the beginning. And in the way it was practised by at least many, Freudian treatment did not sacrifice humanness for objectivity. Freud's (1912b) admonition to be cautious about therapeutic zeal was too often taken literally—and was in retrospect made too prominent by many following Freud.

Along the way, as analysis developed and changed from taking a few months to many years, even decades, basic changes came to be visible, appropriate to changing relationships, as the bonds between the participants became more complex. Both theory and technique expanded in tandem. Enactments became a routine part of the data observed, not suddenly but gradually. An IPA panel (1967) on "Acting-out", in which I (1968) participated, took up such actions outside the analytic situation. A parallel interest as data observed was "Acting-in" (Zeligs, 1957) within the analysis. Maintaining a strictly neutral stance, or blank screen, became a subject for cartoons, and changed quickly and easily to a natural bilateral interchange. Yet in the spirit of "add, not replace", this was grafted upon, but did not replace the neutral analytic position.

Shevrin (2003) has articulated the long-term consequences of eliminating valid and often most illuminating literature of the past. Revisiting the seminal work of Rapaport, and the abandonment of his comprehensive "Structure of psychoanalytic theory: A systematizing attempt", Shevrin writes that as a result, "Psychoanalysis as a science and practice is in grave danger of conceptual rootlessness. ... The development of a cumulative body of evidence once well underway has essentially come to a halt" (p. 1019). I have suggested the same about other crucial omissions, that the present decline and malaise in psychoanalysis, of which so many, inside and outside the field, are conscious today, is furthered by the same theoretical distancing from Freud, Hartmann, Anna Freud, Fenichel, or of Mahler and other more recent contributors. It is on the collective work of all of these that a coherent, composite theoretical system, worthy of being included in the family of science, was built.

Coming from here to the central query of this book and its individual chapters, what has changed to constitute psychoanalysis today? Having addressed the core issues in 1954, and faced them again (1981b) 25 years later in 1979, what are my observations and conclusions 30 years later, in 2009? It is a worthy and challenging opportunity to comment on these. Psychoanalysis today is not the analysis of a symptom but of a life. Having put such an idea into words, it follows that of the countless patients presenting themselves to analytic therapists for ego-alien suffering and pain, a very small percentage enter to seek psychoanalysis. The analyst's technique responds accordingly, adapting his therapeutic thrust to the needs and capabilities of the particular patient, rather than to a specific psychopathological syndrome. Most patients seeking "treatment" are in the group appropriate to various forms of analytic therapy short of official psychoanalysis as a treatment modality. The psychoanalyst who undertakes the treatment and exploration of those relatively few who seek and undergo psychoanalysis for professional or intellectual or other reasons needs to orient himself to the special task.

In my total daily operations as a psychoanalyst over the years performing the range of psychotherapies, the largest number, in the 90+ percentile, are in some form of dynamic psychoanalytic psychotherapy. This stands whether or not the patient is using adjunctive methods as well, such as anti-anxiety or anti-depressive medication (obtained from any source). No concomitant activities rule out attempts at analytic understanding. One patient went to Esalen, took nude group baths, tried many treatment methods suggested in ads or the press, none of which supplanted or ruled out his analytic search. Many of the transient modes eventually came under the explanatory aegis of analytic understanding and reached natural end-points on their own.

Current developed theory, as I see and advocate it, contains changes and modifications undergone over the century in many of the areas emphasized in the new systems, but limited in a quantitative sense to a rational and sustainable degree. Total composite theory contains, in fact, almost all that is new and valid and rational in alternative theories. Some were there from the beginning; others were added or refined at later stages. Thus neutrality and objectivity are enmeshed with a degree of empathy in every appropriate analytic relationship; self-disclosure is present in every analysis; concerns for objects are as prominent as interests of the self in both analyst and patient in every analysis, although either can be hidden or distorted by defences of varied types; and identification with the analyst, or aspects of the analyst's functioning, can occur in any therapeutic procedure.

A composite of such changes and developmental progressions have changed the face of psychoanalysis, making not only psychoanalytic therapy but psychoanalysis a different breed of experience than in the past. I am not beyond coming up with a joke, or starting an hour myself, or referring to an outside event or current news. Nor is it taboo to answer a question. None of these prevent an objective stance, or deviate from the goal of expanding the patient's consciousness and aiming to enhance the mastery of his ego over his self.

For the mass of an analytic practice, as well as for the exceptions, the 1954 paper of Edward Bibring still exudes the most general illumination while specific changes have occurred as the field has been in flux. With the cumulative experience over a century of the entire span of analytic therapies, the fact is that all analytically-oriented therapies utilize all of the curative principles and techniques listed by Bibring; it is the relative proportions of each that changes in any individual case. Psychoanalysis itself, in candidates in training, or abstract thinkers so motivated, or symptom patients whose curiosity and motivations lead them to seek more, has the maximum predominance of interpretation and insight. All analytic therapies have pieces of this plus much more; there is no dearth of reassurance, suggestion, support, or manipulation. With the increasing length, depth, and goals of psychoanalysis during the course of the century, what I would attest to as a change is that even psychoanalysis does not fail to be heavily imbued with all of these accompanying mechanisms. There is no analysis lasting for years that does not contain islands of suggestion, reassurance, clarification, and support.

Psychoanalysis is active into the trunk of the theoretical tree, the hub (core) of the wheel with which I started, while it explores and makes available more than any other approach the psychic terrain of the unconscious, issues of childhood, sexual conflicts, anxieties over aggression, narcissistic wishes and urges to action, Oedipal issues, and castration anxiety. Analytic psychotherapy, however, from the briefest and most superficial to many conducted over long periods of time, may never approach conflicts over Oedipal impulses or their obverse, the anxiety of castration. While in psychoanalysis proper we are more likely to be dealing with later Oedipal issues and concomitant castration anxieties, in analytic psychotherapy pre-Oedipal and separation issues, and aggressive rather than libidinal conflicts, are more likely to be articulated and treated. Anna Freud (1976) has stated that earlier is not necessarily deeper. I have found this insight of considerable merit.

CHAPTER THREE

Classical theory, the Enlightenment Vision, and contemporary psychoanalysis

Morris N. Eagle

Introduction

There is little doubt that in important ways traditional or classical psychoanalysis is a product of what Searle (1998) referred to as the "Enlightenment Vision". The links between the Enlightenment Vision and the classical psychoanalytic conceptions of neurosis and its treatment, as well as of human nature and the relationship between the individual and society, are evident in a number of ways. Paralleling the Enlightenment perspective that goes as far back as Plato, according to the classical psychoanalytic view of human nature, we are beset by the ongoing conflict between the demands of peremptory, instinctually derived passions (id) and the voice of reality-testing and reason (ego). From this perspective, neurosis can be understood as a way of dealing with the inevitable conflict between passion and reason that is characterized by exclusion from awareness of unacceptable aspects of oneself (via repression), which leaves the individual at war with himself or herself. If neurosis is characterized by exclusion and not knowing, treatment consists in the transformation of not knowing into knowing (making the unconscious conscious through lifting repression) and thereby enabling more adaptive means of dealing with inner conflict.

Just as from an Enlightenment perspective there are irrational forces in the physical and social worlds that need to be understood and from which we need to be liberated (e.g., impersonal forces of nature; dogmatic religious authority), so, similarly, are there irrational forces in the personality that need to be understood and from which we need to be liberated. Furthermore, as is the case with the physical and social worlds, the primary constructive means of dealing with irrational forces in the personality are reason and knowledge—self-knowledge in the latter case.

Conceptions of therapeutic action

In what seemed to be a fortunate and remarkable convergence, the Enlightenment imperative to know thyself was also believed to be a clinical necessity, that is, a necessary condition for being cured. Thus, self-understanding, self-knowledge, and insights about oneself were not only autonomous Enlightenment goals and values themselves, but also the means by which clinical cure was to be achieved. Given the reality of repression and the disguised nature of the unacceptable and excluded aspects of oneself, self-knowledge and self-understanding are not inherently transparent. It becomes necessary to lift repression and undo defensive disguise. The main means of doing so is through the use of *interpretation*, which constitutes the making of the unconscious conscious—a primary goal of psychoanalytic treatment. There is also little doubt that most people who went into analysis believed—and were also led to believe—that increased self-knowledge and increased insights (e.g., into unconscious wishes, anxieties, conflicts, and defences), whatever other benefits they might bring, would relieve their neurotic distress and difficulties.

Cracks in the exclusive emphasis of insight and self-knowledge

Cracks in the above picture began to appear in various guises and contexts. It was a commonplace clinical experience that at least seeming self-knowledge and insights often did not relieve neurotic distress or alter neurotic patterns. There were a number of reactions to and attempts to account for the observation of lack of therapeutic progress despite the at least seeming acquisition of insight and self-knowledge. One such attempt consisted in positing a distinction between intellectual and emotional insight and proposing that only the latter is truly conducive to significant therapeutic change. One of the problems with this attempt is that because no systematic and independent criteria were established for intellectual and emotional insight, it was essentially a circular account: thus, if no significant change occurred, the insight was only intellectual. And how does one know that the insight was only intellectual? Because significant therapeutic change did not occur. (As we will see later in this chapter, the discussion of intellectual versus emotional insight points to an important distinction between third-person and first person self-knowledge.)

The intuition that the experience of emotion has something to do with therapeutic change constituted a primary rationale for placing a great deal of emphasis on the analysis of the transference (an emphasis that also characterizes contemporary psychoanalytic theories). In his classic paper on therapeutic action, Strachey (1934) proposed that because here-and-now transference interpretations have an emotional immediacy and are more likely to elicit emotional conviction from the patient than non-transference interpretations, they are more conducive to therapeutic change. Freud, too, suggested that "cure" did not come about through understanding alone, but also required emotional immediacy and intensity. He remarked that "When all is said and done, it is impossible to destroy anyone *in absentia* or *in effigie*" (Freud, 1912a, p. 108) and commented that psychoanalysis achieved "cures of love" (as cited in Bach, 2006), by which he meant that the patient's transference love for the analyst and his or her desire to please the analyst facilitated the patient's acceptance of the analyst's interpretations. To be noted here is that, according to Freud, it is the patient's acceptance of the analyst's interpretations that is mutative, not the patient's love itself. In other words, interpretation and insight—even if a mediating factor was now added—remained the primary agents of therapeutic action (Gitelson, 1962).

Other concepts and views were also voiced to account for the apparent failure of insight to lead to therapeutic change. In addition to the obvious appeal to *resistance*, the concept of *working-through* was introduced. That is, the patient needed to engage in a process in which repeated interpretations and the insights they produced are internalized and made an integral part of oneself. (This issue re-emerges in other contexts—third-person versus first-person self-knowledge and the transformation of id into ego—and will be pursued later in the chapter.)

Modifications of the near exclusive emphasis on interpretation and insight began to appear in the classical psychoanalytic literature, some of which were presumably made necessary by the "expanded scope" of psychoanalysis (Stone, 1954) in treating more disturbed patients. For example, Eissler (1953) suggested that modifications in psychoanalytic technique and approach—"parameters"—(e.g., support) were often necessary with more disturbed patients. However, Eissler advised, the analyst should return to the classical psychoanalytic approach as soon as possible. The clear implication in Eissler's paper is that although the introduction of "parameters" may be necessary for a period of time, interpretation and insight remain the primary agents of therapeutic action and change.

Additional expressions of a concern with factors other than interpretation and insight included the "working alliance" (Zetzel, 1956; Greenson, 1965), which was distinguished from transference and, unlike transference, was not to be subjected to analysis and interpretation. The obvious precursor to the "working alliance" concept was Freud's emphasis on positive transference, which he maintained, also need not be subject to interpretation—a controversial idea not accepted by some Freudian analysts (e.g., Brenner, 1979b). However, as important as the "working alliance" and the "unobjectionable positive transference" might be, their therapeutic role was that of a background factor that made possible and facilitated the effective operation of the "real" agents of therapeutic action, namely, interpretation and insight. Thus, one can say that (in contrast to contemporary theories) although relationship factors "infiltrated" the classical psychoanalytic literature, they were not viewed as direct therapeutic agents themselves. Their importance lay mainly in their background role in facilitating insight and self-understanding through interpretation, the direct agents of therapeutic action and change.

More serious doubts: emphasis on relationship factors

Although what I referred to above as "cracks" in the near exclusive emphasis on interpretation and insight emerged, their therapeutic primacy was, for the most part, not seriously questioned in the classical psychoanalytic literature. A shift from the exclusive emphasis on interpretation and insight was more likely to be expressed, often implicitly, in the non-classical psychoanalytic literature. For example, Winnicott's (1965) concept of the "holding environment" and his linking of "maturational processes" to a "facilitating environment" not only conceptualized therapeutic change as developmental growth, but also pointed to "facilitating" agents of change (e.g., a holding environment; transitional experiences) other than insight-producing interpretations. As another example, Fairbairn's (1952b) emphasis on the patient's experience of the analyst as a "good" object as a necessary condition for therapeutic change implicitly diluted the exalted role of interpretation and insight.

Serious doubts and scepticism regarding the special efficacy of interpretation and insight were explicitly expressed, at least in the United States, with the appearance of Alexander and French's 1946 concept of "corrective emotional experience", which was anticipated by Ferenczi and Rank as early as 1924. At the time that the concept of "corrective emotional experience" appeared, it had relatively little impact on how psychoanalytic treatment was conducted or understood. Alexander's concept was dismissed as involving, among other things, manipulation of the transference (a somewhat justified criticism), and classical analysts continued doing treatment and conceptualizing treatment in the traditional way, that is, with the primacy of interpretation and insight intact.

Further serious and systematic challenges to the therapeutic primacy of insight and self-knowledge, and therefore to the "Enlightenment Vision" of traditional psychoanalysis, arrived with the advent of self psychology and relational psychoanalysis, which had in common a de-emphasis on the special therapeutic role of insight and interpretation and an increasing emphasis on what one can broadly call *relationship factors* in treatment—not necessarily their interpretation or analysis, but relationship factors themselves. As we will see, at the core of these relationship factors is some form or other of corrective emotional experiences.

The scepticism regarding the therapeutic role of insight and self-knowledge raised the question of the degree to which the autonomous Enlightenment values of self-knowledge and self-understanding had been falsely paraded as curative agents for neurosis and other forms of psychopathology. This question did not need to be raised so long as one could maintain that Enlightenment values and clinical cure converged. From the very beginning, Freud assumed this was the case. For example, early on he rejected what one might call Janet's cure through false belief. That is, he did not adopt Janet's use of hypnotic suggestion to substitute a benevolent false memory for the hysterical patient's traumatic memory. Instead, he employed hypnosis to bring traumatic memories to consciousness in the conviction that becoming aware of them was curative. Although much altered and elaborated—free association replaced hypnosis, conflictual wishes and desires replaced traumatic memories, interpretation replaced hypnotic suggestion, and so on—the same basic assumption that informed Freud's early use of hypnosis also underlay his more mature clinical approach, namely, that bringing repressed unconscious material to conscious awareness—making the unconscious conscious—is curative.

But what if it turns out that this is not the case? Indeed, it is precisely this basic assumption that has met with much scepticism in contemporary psychoanalysis and elsewhere (see, for example, the work of Bonnano and his colleagues, e.g., 1995, and Taylor and her colleague, e.g., Taylor & Brown, 1994). In the face of this scepticism, the question that arises is the status of awareness and self-knowledge in psychoanalysis. If self-knowledge is not necessary for cure, what role, if any, does it play or should it play in the psychoanalytic context? It seems to me that Freud's disclaimers that psychoanalysis constituted a *Weltanschauung* notwithstanding, it is closely linked to an Enlightenment Weltanschauung. One can speculate that were Freud forced to accept the disjunction between the curative and the enlightening, he might well have opted for the latter. That is, he might well have concluded—to put it as directly as possible—that psychoanalysis, as he understood it, was as much, or perhaps more, a means of knowing oneself than a "treatment" of mental illness. Recall that at one point, Freud (1926b) voiced the idea that psychoanalysis' primary claim on posterity was as a theory of the human mind and a route to self-understanding rather than as a form of treatment. Indeed, this is the position recently taken by Alan Stone (1997), who suggests that rather than think of psychoanalysis as a treatment for serious mental illness, one should view it as an unmatched vehicle for discovering the "otherness" of oneself.

If one thinks of neurosis—the main arena in which psychoanalysis developed—as an expression of the human condition in civilized society rather than a form of mental illness, then it follows that psychoanalysis is not so much a treatment of mental illness but rather an examination of the human condition as it uniquely manifests itself in each individual case. From a classical psychoanalyst's perspective, the essence of neurosis lies in the inevitable inner conflicts surrounding one's anxiety and guilt-laden desires and wishes and the defences erected to deal with them. On this view, one can think of neurosis as entailing a complex network of self-deceptions, self-alienations, and compromises, including symptomatic compromises, that exact a cost, but that enable a continuation of the self-deceptions and self-alienations that maintain the kind of image of oneself that one experiences as necessary for one's functioning (see Greenwald, 1980). As novelists and playwrights have always known, there are certain things that one does not tell others and then, there are certain things that one does not tell oneself. This whole complex network of conflicts, self-deceptions, self-alienations, and compromises, in various forms, is as much a description of the human condition as it is of psychopathology or mental illness. It is as much the stuff of literature as it is of psychiatry. Hence, one might argue, as Stone (1997) does, that traditional psychoanalysis is as much an examination of the human condition and an expression of the "Enlightenment Vision" that the unexamined life is not worth living as a form of treatment for psychopathology.

The cultural-philosophical zeitgeist

The scepticism within the psychoanalytic community towards the Enlightenment belief that self-knowledge and learning truths about oneself are liberating was but one expression of larger cultural-philosophical trends. Indeed, scepticism not only regarding the therapeutic power of discovering truths about oneself, but regarding the very *possibility* of discovering or ascertaining truths of any kind, let alone looking to them for curative and emancipatory purposes, has been a feature of some trends both in contemporary psychoanalysis as well as in contemporary philosophy. Thus, in an important sense, contemporary psychoanalytic reactions to and questioning of the Freudian embeddedness in the "Enlightenment Vision" is an expression of the zeitgeist.

One of the most influential philosophical critics of the "Enlightenment Vision" has been Rorty (1991), who has attacked the idea that theories possess truth value, that they constitute "mirrors of nature". According to Rorty, theories should be viewed as accounts designed to accomplish specific pragmatic projects rather than formulations that correspond to or mirror the world as it is. In his critique of the "Enlightenment Vision", Rorty (1991) has also argued for the privileging of "solidarity" over "objectivity". He writes:

> The tradition in Western culture which centers around the notion of the search for truth, a tradition which runs from the Greek philosophers through the Enlightenment, is the clearest example of the attempt to find a sense of one's existence by turning away from solidarity to objectivity. The idea of truth as something to be pursued for its own sake, not because it will be good for oneself, or for one's real or imagined community, is the central theme of this tradition [p. 21].

There is a striking correspondence between Rorty's philosophical views and certain aspects of contemporary psychoanalysis. In particular, there is a clear parallel between the privileging of solidarity over objectivity and the trend in contemporary psychoanalysis of privileging the therapeutic relationship over self-knowledge and discovering objective truths about oneself. To the extent that the therapeutic role of understanding remains prominent in contemporary psychoanalysis, it is not primarily *self-understanding* but *feeling understood* by the other that is the main carrier of therapeutic action. That is, it is the experience of "solidarity"—in Kohut's (1984) words, the "empathic bond"—with the other that is therapeutic. This is especially evident in the self psychology conception of treatment and of therapeutic action, where the primary emphasis is not on insight and "expanded consciousness", but rather on the patient's experience of the analyst's empathic understanding, which Kohut (1984) refers to as the "basic therapeutic unit" (p. 96). As the following illustrative passages indicate, in his 1984 book, Kohut repeatedly contrasts the self psychology view of the therapeutic process with that of the classical view:

> Self psychology does not find the essence of the curative process in the cognitive sphere per se. In the terms of Freud's earlier topographic model, it does not believe that we have defined the essence of the curative process when we say that the unconscious has become conscious ... self psychology believes that the essence of the curative process is defined neither by reference to the expansion of the realm of awareness nor, at least not per se, by reference to the increased ability of the psychic apparatus to modify the drives ... self psychology does not see the essence of the curative process as lying primarily in the expansion of the domain of the ego [p. 64].
>
> But I must immediately add that ego expansion (in particular as manifested by an increase in verbal mastery) does not eventuate in every instance of cure. More significantly, even when this desirable development has indeed transpired, it is a secondary result of the basic curative alteration and must not be regarded as constituting the essence of the cure [p. 65].

But while expansion of consciousness and of verbalizable insight are often encountered in the late stages of successful analyses, some unqualified analytic successes include in the main neither of these gains. "It is in the same context—i.e., in the context of my argument against assigning curative primacy to verbalizable insight ..." (ibid., p. 217, fn. 1).

There are a variety of other ways in which contemporary psychoanalytic theories of treatment and of therapeutic action have de-emphasized the role of insight and self-understanding and have replaced it with other factors. Perhaps the most radical way is found in the writings of a number of authors, including those of Mitchell, whose scepticism is not limited to the therapeutic value of self-understanding and self-knowledge, but seems to be extended to include rejection of their very possibility. Thus, Mitchell (1998) writes that to maintain that one uncovers or discovers unconscious mental contents in the patient's mind is a mistaken view. Rather, one "interpretively constructs" the patient's mind. He also writes that although the patient's mind is "pre-existing", he or she does not come to treatment with a "pre-organized" mind. Rather, the patient's mind is organized by fluid and momentary interactions with the analyst (Mitchell, 2000b). On this view, the analyst does not so much understand the patient's mind (and convey that understanding in the service of self-knowledge and self-understanding), but rather organizes and "interpretively constructs" the patient's mind. (See Eagle, Wolitzky & Wakefield, 2001; and Eagle, Wakefield & Wolitzky, 2003, for a critique of Mitchell's position.)

From making the unconscious conscious to where id was, there shall ego be

Although, as I have argued above, classical theory places great emphasis on the therapeutic value of self-awareness and self-knowledge, Freud himself was already implicitly expressing some scepticism (long before contemporary doubts) regarding their therapeutic sufficiency. This scepticism is implicit in Freud's (1923a) replacement or at least supplementation of the psychoanalytic goal of making the unconscious conscious with "where id was, there shall ego be"—when that aphorism is understood in a particular way. Although it is often understood primarily as an outgrowth of the structural model, I will try to demonstrate that the shift from making the unconscious conscious, to "where id was, there shall ego be", reflects a distinction that, in some respects, parallels the distinction between third person and first-person self-knowledge made by some philosophers (Moran, 2001). I will then try to show that one need not have to choose between solidarity and objectivity and that important aspects of the Enlightenment Vision are compatible with and can be incorporated into the contemporary emphasis on the therapeutic relationship. Let me begin with a detour of examining the different ways that Freud's aphorism "where id was, there shall ego be" has been understood.

As Apfelbaum (1966) has noted, Freud essentially formulated two views of the relationship between the id and the ego and therefore of the meaning of "where id was, there shall ego be". According to the first view, the relationship between the id and the ego is one of "primary antagonism" (A. Freud, 1966). With its peremptory demands for gratification, its constant potential danger of overwhelming the ego with excessive excitation, and its ever-present threat of reaching consciousness and overtaking motility in the form of anti-social action, the id is a natural enemy of the ego. Hence, on this view, "where id was, there shall ego be" is interpreted as where the peremptory push for gratification of infantile wishes was, there shall greater ego control and delay be. From this perspective, positive change in treatment consists primarily in enhancement of the ego functions of delay and control. Given the timelessness of the unconscious, the drive impulses and wishes themselves—that are subject to delay and control—remain essentially unchanged. From this perspective, what mainly changes in successful treatment is not the wishes and desires one harbours, but rather how one deals with them. One can subject them to greater control and delay, one can renounce them, or in fortunate instances, one can sublimate them.

The purpose of self-knowledge—of making the unconscious conscious—on this view is, so to speak, to know whom the enemy is and find effective means of dealing with him or her. One deals with the irrational inner forces that beset one through knowledge, autonomy and control, renunciation, and transformation to social ends just as the enlightened individual would deal with irrational external forces in the same manner. To be noted here is that the "chaos, [the] cauldron full of seething excitations" (Freud, 1933, p. 73) that constitutes the id is never fully assimilated into the ego. The ego must always be on guard—just as one would have to be with any natural enemy—to deal with and ward off the potential dangers the id presents to it.

According to the alternative view one finds in Freud's writings, in health there is seamlessness between the id and the ego rather than an inherent antagonism. Indeed, at one point, Freud (1915b) suggests that rather than—or at least, in addition to—repression being instituted because of the dangerous nature of id impulses, it is repression itself that makes these impulses seem more dangerous than they in fact are. He writes that in repression:

> ... the instinctual representation develops with less interference and more profusely.... It proliferates in the dark and takes on extreme forms of expression ... (and) brighten [the patient] by giving him the picture of an extraordinary and dangerous strength of instinct [p. 149].

On this second view, the antagonistic relationship between the id and the ego is more a product of psychopathology rather than a natural state of affairs. According to this perspective, the fear of the id could only come about in one of two ways: (1) A constitutionally weak ego experiences id demands (as well as other demands) as more than it can cope with and therefore, as dangerous, and (2) Id impulses are experienced as dangerous because they are associated with the "danger situations" of loss of the object, loss of the object's love, castration threats, and superego condemnation (Freud, 1923a). In other words, the antagonism between id and ego is environmentally induced rather than inherent.

From this latter perspective, the aims of treatment are not limited to enhancement of the ego functions of delay and control. Rather, as Friedman (1991) puts it, the treatment brings the good news that the "danger situations" are no longer dangerous and that aspects of oneself that are associated with these "danger situations" are also no longer dangerous and therefore need not be disavowed as alien contents. "Where id was, there shall ego be" can now be interpreted, not as where instinctual demands were, there shall greater ego control and delay be, but rather as where disowned and impersonal "it" was, there shall the personal owned "I" be. One can now gain knowledge of the disavowed aspects of oneself, not as one needs to know the whereabouts of an enemy, but for the purpose of avowing and assimilating them into one's personal identity—so that one's sense of "I" is expanded to include these hitherto disavowed aspects.

Despite the early therapeutic claims attributed to bringing unconscious material to awareness, it became clear to Freud that simply rendering unconscious contents conscious was not sufficient for lasting therapeutic improvement. One of the main reasons that simply making the unconscious conscious—for example, via hypnosis—is not sufficient for significant therapeutic change is that the unconscious material made conscious is not necessarily *integrated* into the individual's personality. Normally when an idea or feeling is in consciousness, it is experienced as *my* idea or feeling. Consciousness and personal ownership normally go together. However, this is not always the case. Simply because an idea or feeling is experienced consciously does not preclude the possibility that it will be experienced as an ego-alien "it". For example, someone may have a fully conscious obsessive thought that is experienced as an ego-alien "it". Indeed, the very language employed to describe the experience—"it keeps occurring to me" rather than "I think"—reflects its "not me" status.

Third-person versus first-person self-knowledge

Let me now focus on the purpose of taking this detour—tracing the different meanings of "where id was, there shall ego be". I want to suggest that when one understands id and ego closer to their original German meaning (das Es and das Ich) as impersonal "it" and personal "I", the distinction between "it" and "I" parallel, in certain respects, the distinction between third-person versus first-person knowledge (although, of course, Freud did not use these terms). Further, Freud was in effect acknowledging that while third-person knowledge may be useful to the individual, it is not sufficient for lasting therapeutic change and must be supplemented by first-person knowledge.

What does one mean by third-person versus first-person self-knowledge and how is that distinction relevant to therapeutic change? In contrast to third-person knowledge, which is based on observational evidence and inference, first-person knowledge is characterized by immediacy and its non-observational and non-inferential nature (Moran, 2001). One can become conscious of something about oneself in the sense of acquiring knowledge about oneself the way one would acquire knowledge about a third person. For example, one can learn something about some aspect of oneself through observations of one's behaviour and through inference from those observations or through an interpretation "that makes sense". However, one could acquire the same knowledge were the observations, inferences, and interpretation made about a third person. The knowledge that one acquires about oneself in this manner is not essentially different from the kind of knowledge one acquires about another person. That is, if I infer my beliefs and desires based on observations of my behaviour—either that I or my analyst make—I am acquiring knowledge about myself in the same way that I would acquire knowledge about another person.

Although there are occasions when one does so, normally one does not acquire knowledge about oneself in this way. For example, normally I do not observe my behaviour and then infer that I want to go to the library. I just know, non-inferentially and non-observationally, that I want to go to the library to get a particular book. Indeed, if I regularly learned about my wants and desires only through inferences based on observational evidence from my behaviour, one would have good reason to view this as an extreme form of intellectualization and pathological self-alienation or what Moran (2001) refers to as "estrangement".

One can now begin to understand why third-person knowledge of oneself is most frequently not sufficient for therapeutic change. Such knowledge may continue to have an impersonal "it" status, not necessarily in the sense of being ego-alien, but in the sense of not being fully integrated into one's first-person sense of who one is. One remains essentially the same person, having acquired additional information about oneself the way one would acquire information about a third person.

According to the logic of the replacement or at least supplementation of making the unconscious conscious, with where id was, there shall ego be, the problem in neurosis is not simply that (because of repression) one does not *know* enough about oneself, but also that there are aspects of oneself (wishes, desires, anxieties, etc.) that, because they are not integrated into one's personality, exert deleterious influences on one's psychic functioning. This central idea was there from the beginning of psychoanalysis and remains at the core of the classical conception of neurosis. It also remains at the core of some later conceptions of psychopathology—for example, Fairbairn's (1952b) formulation that unintegrated internalized objects (rather than instinctual wishes and desires) produce "splitting of the ego" (pp. 8–10). No wonder that Fairbairn urged that psychoanalytic theory go "back to hysteria" (p. 92).

For self-knowledge to lead to "deep" change, it must be integrated into one's sense of who one is—that is, it must become first-person knowledge. The aspects of oneself that hitherto had an impersonal "it" status need to become transferred into a personal "I", with the consequence not only that the personality becomes more unified, but also that the realm of the self or ego becomes enlarged and one's sense of agency becomes strengthened (Schafer, 1984).

Dichotomy between insight and therapeutic relationship

How does this kind of change come about? It is in response to this question that one can see the possibilities of integrating solidarity with objectivity and of finding a place for the Enlightenment values of insight and self-knowledge in the contemporary emphasis on the therapeutic relationship. To exploit these possibilities requires dissolving the usual dichotomy between the role of the therapeutic relationship—its provision of corrective emotional experiences—and of interpretation and insight.

The dichotomy between the two breaks down in light of the following considerations. Interpretation and insight do not take place in an interpersonal vacuum, but rather in the context of an ongoing relationship. Indeed, many interpretations and ensuing insights have to do with that relationship. We know that from early on, representations and models of ourselves and of the interpersonal world are acquired in repeated interactions with parental figures (e.g., Stern's, 1985, Representations of Interactions Generalized or RIGs; Bowlby's, 1973, Internal Working Models). We also know that exploration and knowledge of both our physical and social worlds are facilitated by the availability of a secure base. Indeed, the therapeutic situation is, or should be, a quintessential example of exploration and acquisition of self-knowledge in the context of a secure base (Bowlby, 1988a). In the therapeutic context, one can say that one gains one-person knowledge through a two-person process. That is, one acquires greater self-understanding and objectivity towards oneself in the context of solidarity with the other.

Also, corrective emotional experiences can implicitly impart insight and self-knowledge—what Lyons-Ruth et al. (1998) refer to as "implicit rational knowing"—and interpretation and insight themselves can constitute corrective emotional experiences. As Mitchell (1998) has observed, an interpretation is a complex relational event. It is not as if there are relational experiences and then another class of non-relational interventions that we call interpretations. For offering and receiving interpretations are themselves complex relational experiences. As a function of its content, timing, tone, as well as the attitude conveyed, an interpretation may be experienced by the patient as a repetition of negative parental behaviour or may elicit the corrective emotional experience of feeling deeply understood. When the latter occurs, an interpretation may as likely generate solidarity as objectivity.

The range of possibilities in how an intervention is received and experienced by the patient is not limited to interpretations, but applies to all interventions. For example, an intervention that is intended to be supportive may be experienced by the patient as condescending or an intervention intended to be empathic may be experienced as intrusive. The point is that it makes little sense to dichotomize between, on the one hand, a class of non-interpretive relational factors that presumably provide a corrective emotional experience and, on the other hand, a class of interpretive interventions that provide something else such as awareness and insight. That is so because, to repeat, interpretations can constitute corrective emotional experiences.

It should be noted that one consequence of the dissolution of the dichotomy between interpretation—insight and the therapeutic relationship—and corrective emotional experience is that it renders quite fuzzy and casts doubt on the concept of "transference cure". According to the traditional psychoanalytic perspective, it is only the "gold standard" of insight brought about by interpretation that leads to lasting change. Changes that are primarily a function of non-interpretive factors are viewed as mere "transference cures" which, because they are unaccompanied by increased awareness, insight, and self-knowledge, are presumably not lasting and do not serve as protection against again succumbing to neurosis in the future, when the therapeutic relationship is terminated. However, if corrective emotional experiences can generate insight and self-knowledge and if interpretation and insight can constitute corrective emotional experiences, then the distinction between "transference cure" and non-transference cure becomes exceedingly difficult to establish (see Eagle, 1993).

When Freud identified "cures of love" (Bach, 2006) as an important factor in psychoanalytic treatment, he was giving voice to the intuition that the therapeutic relationship constituted a critical aspect of the treatment. However, in focusing exclusively on its role in facilitating the patient's acceptance of the analyst's interpretation, Freud was degrading the importance of both the therapeutic relationship and of interpretation and was excessively dichotomizing between the two. With regard to the first point, were the reception and therapeutic impact of an interpretation solely or primarily a matter of a "cure of love", that is, of the patient's desire to please the analyst and comply with his or her implicit expectations, we would be looking at the spectre of suggestion that Freud was so intent on refuting. In such a case, it would be difficult to distinguish suggestion and compliance from insight and awareness. It would also be difficult to distinguish "cures of love" from the supposed insubstantial "transference cure". After all, acceptance of an interpretation motivated mainly by desire to please may occur in the absence of any awareness and insight. Furthermore, such acceptance may be virtually independent of the content or accuracy of the interpretation, that is, whether or not it "tallies with what is real [in the patient]" (Freud, 1917, p. 452)—which, according to Freud, distinguishes psychoanalytic interpretation from mere suggestion.

Although an interpretation is a "relational event", the relational context is not restricted to the patient's desire to please—or displease— the analyst. It includes much more than that. For, although the relational context may influence how an interpretation is "received" and the therapeutic impact it is likely to have, one would expect—by Freud's own account—that other factors, primarily to what degree the interpretation "tallies with what is real [in the patient]" (ibid., p. 452), would equally influence its therapeutic impact. Without the inclusion of this latter factor, namely, this "goodness of fit" between the analyst's interpretation and the patient's conscious or preconscious experience, we are looking at pure and simple suggestion.

In short, that interpretation takes place in a relational context does not mean that properties of the interpretation itself—its content, tone, and timing—do not matter. However, and perhaps most important, whatever insight and awareness are generated by interpretations are not a matter of disembodied content that stands by itself, but rather are experienced *in and through* the patient-therapist relationship. That is what makes it a relational event. Further, an interpretation that generates insight and awareness contributes both to *self-understanding and self-knowledge* as well as to *feeling understood* by another. That, too, is what makes it a relational event. In other words, viewing interpretation as a relational event makes it clear that whatever insight and awareness are generated by an interpretation entail, in Rorty's (1991) terms, both solidarity—feeling understood—and objectivity—self-understanding.

Therapeutic alliance

In discussing the role of the therapeutic relationship, one needs to make reference to research on the therapeutic alliance. One of the most consistent findings in psychotherapy research is that the strength of the therapeutic alliance is the single best predictor of treatment outcome (Baldwin, Wampold & Imel, 2007; Horvath & Symonds, 1991; Martin et al., 2000). Furthermore, a poor therapeutic alliance predicts increased dropout from treatment (e.g., Siqueland et al., 2002; Johansson & Eklund, 2006). The fact that these findings cut across different therapeutic approaches with presumably different specific therapeutic techniques has led many observers to conclude that the main curative factor in virtually all types of therapy is the therapeutic relationship (e.g., Lambert & Barley, 2001).

It should be noted, however, that although a strong therapeutic alliance is *consistently* related to therapeutic outcome, its contribution to outcome has been a modest one. It is important not to confuse consistency with size of contribution to outcome. For the modesty of its contribution suggests that factors other than alliance contribute to therapeutic outcome. Furthermore, I know of at least one study, dealing with drug abuse (Barber et al., 2001) in which the strength of the alliance was *not* a significant predictor of outcome and in which it was *negatively* correlated with therapy retention in cognitive therapy.

In the present context, the important question is, to the degree that it does, how does the therapeutic alliance influence therapeutic outcome? Through what processes and mechanisms? The ways in which psychotherapy researchers have grappled with these (and similar) questions can serve as a model for how to carefully address the role of relationship factors in treatment. Although, as noted, the quality of the therapeutic alliance is the single best predictor of psychotherapy outcome, one should not necessarily assume that it always functions as a direct causal factor. As Kazdin (2007) has observed, the patient's experience of a stronger therapeutic alliance may be the *effect* of other therapeutic processes. For example, the experience of symptom relief or reduced anxiety following, say, an empathic and accurate interpretation, may strengthen the patient's sense of a collaborative relationship, an affective bond with the therapist, and the feeling that he or she and the therapist agree on the same treatment goals. The patient's experience of a strengthened therapeutic alliance may then, in turn, facilitate the patient's ability to benefit from other interventions (e.g., empathic understanding; interpretations). In other words, I am suggesting what one might call a causal network or circular causal chain in which the therapeutic alliance can be understood as both an effect of other therapeutic processes as well as a causal agent that (1) facilitates other therapeutic processes, and (2) is itself directly linked to therapeutic outcome.

Although therapeutic alliance may predict outcome, and although it is plausible that experiences associated with a strong therapeutic alliance would be healing, its role as a direct causal agent is still not established. One possibility is that the link between therapeutic alliance and outcome is at least partly due to a third common factor. For example, Kazdin (2007) has shown that the patient's baseline functioning accounts for part of the therapeutic alliance. In other words, a pre-treatment "healthier" patient may both have a better prognosis and also be more likely to form and experience a stronger therapeutic alliance. And to complicate matters even further, one reason for the better prognosis may be the patient's greater capacity for forming and experiencing a stronger therapeutic alliance and for benefiting from therapeutic interventions (e.g., interpretations). In short, the research on therapeutic alliance does not provide support for the idea that it is the therapeutic relationship, plain and simple, that accounts for positive therapeutic outcome.

Therapeutic change without interpretation

In the above, I have argued that as a relational event, interpretation itself may constitute a corrective emotional experience. However, ever since Alexander and French (1946) introduced the concept of corrective emotional experience, the argument has been made that therapeutic change can occur without explicit interpretation of any kind, simply by virtue of one form or another of a corrective emotional experience. Examples here include Alexander and French's (1946) proposal that therapeutic change can occur as a function of the therapist behaving differently from parental figures; Kohut's (1984) claim that empathic understanding itself is curative without "verbalizable insight"; and the evidence presented by Weiss and Sampson and their colleagues (1986) demonstrating therapeutic change can occur by virtue of the analyst passing tests presented by the patient, without any interpretation at all.

Also, some contemporary theorists have indeed argued that interpretation and increased awareness and self-knowledge are relatively powerless to alter deeper engrained representations that "may never become symbolically coded" (Lyons-Ruth, 1998, p. 284). One of the emphases in contemporary psychoanalytic theories is on what cognitive psychologists have referred to as "procedural knowledge". The term refers to "rule-based representations of how to proceed, of how to do things" and "may never become symbolically coded" (Lyons-Ruth et al., 1998, p. 284). They operate much like motor skills (e.g., riding a bicycle) in that they are based on non-verbal implicit procedures rather than on explicit declarative knowledge—hence the term "procedural knowledge". In the interpersonal context, procedural knowledge can be thought of as "knowing how to do things with others" (ibid., p. 284) or "implicit relational knowing". Stern's (1985) concept of Representations of Interactions Generalized (RIGs) and Bowlby's (1973) Internal Working Models (IWMs) serve as good examples of "implicit relational knowing". They are based on abstracting out invariant features of repeated interactions with caregivers. That they are formed early in life is suggested by the evidence that by one year of age, the infant has already developed an attachment pattern (secure, avoidant-dismissive, or anxious-resistant) that is relatively resistant to change. Changes in this domain of "procedural knowledge", it is argued, are brought about not by interpretation and insight, but by "moments of meeting" between the patient and therapist, that is, by non-interpretive interactions between the two. It will be recognized that all the above factors essentially constitute variants of corrective emotional experiences.

If therapeutic change can occur simply as a function of various kinds of therapeutic interactions, without explicit interpretation and without enhanced insight and self-knowledge; and further, if there is little or no evidence that such change is less substantial and more fleeting, how does one justify any meaningful link between psychoanalysis and the Enlightenment Vision? I believe an answer to this question is already present in the above discussion of the false dichotomy between insight and corrective emotional experience. Let me elaborate. That therapeutic change can occur through corrective emotional experiences, without explicit interpretation and "verbalizable insight" does not rule out the possibility—in my view, likelihood—that corrective emotional experiences themselves can generate enhanced insight and self-knowledge, even if they are not explicitly verbalized. Consider, for example, Alexander and French's

(1946) claim that the fact that the therapist's behaviour is different from that of parental figures is itself therapeutic. Why would that be so? What processes are involved?

One possibility, relying primarily on conditioning theory, is that the therapist's "non-parental" behaviour serves to "*extinguish*" the patient's conditioned responses and expectations (e.g., of being rejected, of being judged, of being punished). However, unless one is content with an account limited to automatic conditioned responses, which can occur in lower and even decorticate animals, one surely has good reason to believe that implicit cognitive and affective processes are involved in the acquisition, extinction, and alteration of an individual's *expectations*, even if these expectations have not been verbalized or made explicit. Further, once one acknowledges that an individual's representations and expectations are involved, one is in the realm of knowledge structures, even if these structures are implicit ones having more to do with praxis than with theoretical knowledge. The patient whose expectations of being judged and punished have been altered through corrective emotional experiences now has a different knowledge structure, which, if one were to state it explicitly and formally, would go as follows: "It is not the case that all parental figures will judge and punish me." Borrowing Lyons-Ruth's (1998) language, one would say that the patient's "implicit relational knowing" has been modified. Or, in the language of Merleau-Ponty (1962) the patient's "background structure" has been altered. The important point to note here is that the acquisition and alteration of knowledge are involved, even if the knowledge is of an implicit and procedural kind. As noted earlier, this kind of knowledge is similar to acquiring a motor skill, such as learning how to ride a bicycle. That I may not be able to describe explicitly how I ride a bicycle does not mean that I do not have a knowledge structure of some kind.

I would also propose that corrective emotional experiences may constitute *implicit or "silent" interpretations* that, like explicit interpretations, may generate insights and self-knowledge. For example, when the analyst is non-judgmental and non-punitive but rather empathic, he or she is making the implicit interpretation: "Not all significant figures are judgmental and punitive." Furthermore, at least in certain circumstances, such implicit and "silent" interpretations may be more mutative than explicit ones insofar as they are embodied and "enacted" rather than merely verbalized. Thus, complementing the patient's acquisition of implicit insight and knowledge are the therapist's implicit and "silent" interpretations.

Even in the case of explicit verbalized interpretations, the patient is "receiving" and reacting to both the semantic verbal content and extra-linguistic features such as tone—what a jazz musician friend of mine referred to as "the music in the voice". Thus, accompanying explicit verbalized interpretations are implicit and "silent" interpretations that communicate aspects of the analyst's attitudes of which he or she may be unaware and which are likely to influence how the explicit interpretation is understood and received. Ideally, the explicit verbal content of an interpretation and the implicit communication will be congruent. However, that is not always the case. For example, an analyst may offer an interpretation with "benevolent" content in an indifferent or harsh and judgmental tone. What is the interpretation here? One can say that there are two contradictory interpretations being given, the explicit semantic one and the implicit paralinguistic one.

The issues become even more complex. Up to this point, I have taken for granted Alexander and French's (1946)—and others'—assumptions that when the therapist behaves differently from parental figures, that is, non-judgmentally, non-punitively, or empathically, the patient *experiences* him or her as non-judgmental or non-punitive or empathic. But this assumption ignores the power of the patient's early schemas and representations to assimilate new experiences to these early schemas and representations and thereby to subjectively render them as versions of old experiences. To put it simply, merely because a therapist behaves or tries to behave non-judgmentally, does not necessarily mean that the patient will *experience* him or her in that way. Rather, the patient may experience the therapist in accord with early schemas and representations, and, in addition, may be especially sensitive to cues, including non-verbal cues, that give credence to and support that experience and may also behave in ways that "call for" (Strupp & Binder, 1984) or tend to elicit therapist behaviours that conform to the patient's early schemas.

These considerations suggest that therapeutic action and interaction are not likely to be only or primarily a matter of the therapist behaving differently from parental figures. What may also be required are explicit interpretations regarding the patient's assimilative tendencies—his or her tendency to, in Fairbairn's (1958) words, "press-gang" the therapist into old and familiar roles as well as the communication of any interpretations in a manner and style that does not "feed" the patient's assimilative tendencies. The latter, of course, requires a good deal of awareness of one's attitudes and countertransference reactions. Finally, the explicit interpretations of what I am referring to as the patient's assimilative tendencies, that is, the patient's transference reactions, presented in a tone and manner that do not provide support for these assimilative tendencies, themselves may constitute a corrective emotional experience.

Let me review and relate the above discussion to a main theme of this chapter—the role of insight and self-knowledge in contemporary psychoanalysis.

1. I have tried to show that a central aspect of the trajectory from classical to contemporary psychoanalytic theories is an increasing scepticism towards the therapeutic sufficiency—or perhaps even therapeutic value—of interpretation, insight, and the Enlightenment values of self-knowledge accompanied by an increasing emphasis on the therapeutic relationship and corrective emotional experiences. Psychoanalysis has moved, in Rorty's (1991) words, from the primacy of "objectivity" to the primacy of "solidarity".

2. I have pointed to the distinction between third-person and first-person self-knowledge and have argued that it is the latter rather than the former that is generally associated with therapeutic change. I have also suggested that Freud's shift from making the unconscious conscious to where id was, there shall ego be—when the latter is interpreted as where the impersonal and disavowed "it" was, there shall the personal and avowed "I" be—implicitly entails the distinction between third-person and first-person self-knowledge.

3. I have argued that first-person self-knowledge is more likely to be acquired in the context of a therapeutic relationship and further, that the dichotomy between interpretation, insight, and self-knowledge, on the one hand, and therapeutic relationship and corrective emotional experience, on the other, is an unwarranted one.

4. I have suggested that corrective emotional experiences can constitute implicit and "silent" interpretations and can generate implicit insights and self-knowledge.
5. I have suggested that explicit interpretations may be especially important in relation to the patient's tendency to assimilate new experiences into old schemas and representations.

Putting the above points together, the following conclusions seem warranted:

1. If one recognizes the distinction between third-person and first-person self-knowledge and if one broadens the concept of self-knowledge to include implicit or tacit knowledge (see Polanyi, 1967), the link between psychoanalysis and the Enlightenment Vision can be retained.
2. Because in the analytic situation, first-person self-knowledge is acquired in and through the therapeutic relationship, one need not choose between "objectivity" and "solidarity". Rather, one recognizes that in the relational context, the self-knowledge the patient acquires is likely to entail the experience of *both* greater "objectivity" and greater "solidarity".

Different conceptions of psychopathology

Because this chapter deals with the issue of therapeutic action, I have said little about the question of how psychopathology is understood. However, I want to note that the relative emphasis on interpretation in classical theory versus the therapeutic relationship in contemporary theories correspond, in part, to different conceptions of psychopathology. According to classical theory, psychopathology is conceptualized primarily in terms of conflict between aspects of one's self (e.g., wishes, desires) that have defensively been disowned and been given an "it" status and one's sense of who one is. However, in some contemporary theories, psychopathology is understood as the product of maladaptive representations acquired early in life and in other contemporary theories psychopathology is characterized in terms of self-defects. Thus, with regard to the former, the unconscious status of maladaptive representations and interactional "rules" is not primarily a function of repression and other defences, but rather of the fact that they were acquired non-verbally early in life. As for the latter, insofar as defects rather than inner conflicts are emphasized, the role of interpretation is minimized.

Given these different conceptions regarding the nature of psychopathology, it is no surprise that conceptions of therapeutic goals and therapeutic action also differ. For example, making the unconscious conscious has different meanings in the two different contexts. Whereas, in the classical context, it refers to becoming aware of one's hitherto unconscious defences, anxieties, conflicts, wishes, and fantasies following the lifting of repression, in the contemporary context in which procedural knowledge is highlighted, making the unconscious conscious has little to do with undoing repression of wishes and desires, but rather refers to making explicit the implicit "rules" and expectations underlying one's interactional patterns and representations of self and other.

Another way to contrast classical with contemporary views is to note that at the core of neurosis is the existence of ego-alien aspects of oneself (e.g., wishes, desires, fantasies) that are in conflict with and remain unintegrated into one's personality and one's sense of who one is, whereas in contemporary theories, the focus is on early internalization of maladaptive representations and "rules" that are not necessarily experienced as ego-alien, but often constitute implicit ego-syntonic aspects of one's sense of who one is. Given this latter conception of psychopathology, the goal of treatment could hardly be described as where the ego-alien "it" was, there shall the ego-syntonic ("I") be. Indeed, the appropriate goal of treatment would seem to be precisely the opposite of the classical view, namely: the transformation of (maladaptive) aspects of oneself that are experienced as ego-syntonic so that they are experienced as ego-alien—quite the opposite of where "it" was, there shall "I" be. One is reminded here of Fairbairn's (1952b) emphasis on the need in treatment for the patient to "exorcise" the internalized "bad" object, that is, to disown what was defensively and maladaptively made part of oneself. Whereas in classical theory, a primary task in treatment is for the patient to avow and own the wishes and desires he or she defensively disowned and disavowed, for Fairbairn a primary task in treatment is to help the patient disown and "dissolve" his or her "devotion" and "obstinate attachment" to internalized objects.

From its earliest period, psychoanalytic theory thought of neurotic psychopathology as the consequence of defensively relegating aspects of oneself (e.g., traumatic memories, conflictual wishes) to the status of a "foreign body" inhabiting one's personality. Hence, the therapeutic task of psychoanalysis was to help the patient become aware of and integrate these disowned aspects—in Stone's (1997) words, the "otherness of oneself"—into the personality. Given this framework, the lines between psychoanalysis and the Enlightenment Vision are quite evident. However, as we have seen, this is no longer the contemporary psychoanalytic framework for understanding psychopathology.

And here is where the links between psychoanalysis and the Enlightenment Vision are less evident and more complex. On the one hand, one can analogize between the individual's unexamined and unquestioned early acquisition of implicit "rules" and representations and the engrained unquestioned and unexamined assumptions handed down by, say, dogmatic religious authority. In both cases, the Enlightenment task is to emancipate oneself from the "irrational" representations and "rules" that one has internalized and taken for granted. So, in that sense, contemporary psychoanalysis continues to have Enlightenment emancipatory goals. However, in an apparent departure from at least certain elements of the Enlightenment Vision, we are also told that self-awareness and self-knowledge, that is, simply examining and becoming aware of the implicit "rules" and representations that restrict one's life, will not be sufficient to change them. That is, the truth—or at least, the truth alone—will not necessarily set one free. In Rorty's (1991) terms, objectivity will not suffice. Also required are new relational corrective emotional experiences that are capable of altering and replacing these "rules" and representations. However, as I have tried to show, these corrective emotional experiences often do generate implicit knowledge. In that sense, knowledge of some kind is instrumental in therapeutic change and the connection between the Enlightenment Vision and psychoanalysis remains somewhat intact. In Rorty's (1991) terms, self-knowledge and objectivity are maximally therapeutic, when they are pursued in the context of solidarity, of new corrective relational experiences.

Final comments

That self-knowledge, particularly third-person self-knowledge, may not be sufficient for therapeutic change does not, in my view, justify the position taken by some contemporary theorists that genuine self-knowledge is not possible, and that all that can be offered in psychoanalytic treatment consists entirely in fashioning coherent narratives, so-called "narrative truth", "aesthetic fictions", "interpretive constructions", "retellings" of one's life, new perspectives, and products of the analyst's "irreducible subjectivity" (Renik, 1993a). Not only does this position constitute a radical break with any trace of the Enlightenment Vision, but in my view it also constitutes a radical break with what defines and is most worth preserving of the psychoanalytic project.

I believe that there are limits to what one can meaningfully view as psychoanalytic. Although these limits may be difficult to define, they have something to do with historical continuity and core axiomatic propositions and assumptions. So, let us say that what is called contemporary psychoanalytic treatment had nothing to do with such matters as inner conflict, transference, unconscious motivation, defences, enhanced self-awareness, agency, self-understanding, and so on, but consisted entirely in attempts to provide corrective emotional experiences through, say, unconditional positive regard (Rogers, 1951). Would one continue to view that approach and its underlying theoretical basis as psychoanalytic—even if the external trappings of psychoanalytic institutes, psychoanalytic training, and so on remained in place? As I am sure is evident, my own view is that the fate of psychoanalysis is linked, in one form or another, to the fate of the Enlightenment Vision.

SECTION II

CONFLICT, FANTASY, AND INSIGHT
IN THERAPEUTIC ACTION

CHAPTER FOUR

The therapeutic action of resistance analysis: interpersonalizing and socializing Paul Gray's close process attention technique

Stephen Howard Portuges and Nancy Caro Hollander

When we began to do the research for this paper on the therapeutic action of resistance analysis, we had to take into account how our theoretical differences would influence our respective reading and understanding of the material. Portuges, whose psychoanalytic research has focused on Freudian conflict theory, wanted to evaluate Paul Gray's unique ideas about the analysis of resistance as an important strategy for therapeutic change. Hollander, whose research and clinical orientation integrates object relations, relational psychoanalysis, and trauma theory, was intrigued about how Gray's treatment model could be applied to psychoanalytic orientations beyond contemporary ego psychology. We struggled to integrate what were often conflicting ideas about Gray's "close process attention" technique, which arrives at the investigation of transference by emphasizing the analysis of resistance in order to promote therapeutic change. Ultimately, we found a way to incorporate relational and intersubjective ideas in a framework that seeks to understand how social reality is mentally registered and manifested during treatment. We believe that in so doing, we have developed a way of making Gray's analysis of transference, defence, and resistance consonant with our shared psychoanalytic perspective.

We begin by exploring the phenomenon of patients' psychological resistance to psychoanalytic examination. In its paradigmatic form, whenever patients have difficulties saying what comes to their minds, analysts, as they listen with "evenly suspended attention", are to help them overcome obstacles on the path of continued self-exploration. This was Freud's conception of resistance, the cogency and shortcomings of which we will evaluate. Then, after identifying contemporary conceptions of resistance, we will describe Paul Gray's theory of close process attention, a radical and innovative psychoanalytic method that seriously challenges the way most psychoanalysts listen to, and treat, their patients. One of us teaches Gray's method of resistance analysis to psychoanalytic candidates and graduate students in psychology and we both use our respective versions of it with those patients we think it will benefit. We are both critical of what we take to be its weaknesses. After identifying some of the limitations of Gray's important contribution to clinical technique we go on to discuss how Gray's version of resistance analysis can be enhanced by having analysts pay close attention to their influence on the formation and expression of patients' thoughts. We conclude the paper by discussing the problematic issue of analysts' resistance to showing patients how important components of social reality like class, ethnicity, and gender are represented and reproduced in the psychoanalytic exchange.

Freud's conception of resistance analysis

As psychoanalysis matured and became a unique psychological treatment for neurosis and character disorders, Freud relied on his developing knowledge of the dynamics of defence and resistance to articulate the psychoanalytic treatment method. Between 1900 and 1920, Freud's topographically-based formulations about resistance, interspersed throughout his writings, were linked to transference. In one of his most succinct ways of connecting them, he referred to three aspects of their complex relationship that were at once identical, oppositional, and mutually protective. Nowhere is this clearer than in his 1919 brief paper called "Lines of Advance in Psychoanalytic Therapy", when he wrote:

> We have formulated our task as [psychoanalysts] thus: to bring
> to the patient's knowledge the ... repressed impulses existing in
> him, and ... to uncover the resistances that oppose this exten-
> sion of his knowledge about himself. Does the uncovering of
> these resistances guarantee that they will also be overcome? Cer-
> tainly not always; but our hope is to achieve this by exploiting
> the patient's transference to the person of the [psychoanalyst], so
> as to induce him to adopt our conviction of the inexpediency of
> the repressive process established in childhood and of the impos-
> sibility of conducting life on the pleasure principle [p. 159].

This statement of the relationship between resistance and transference reflects Freud's thinking that the emergence of the patient's
transference is dependent on the analyst's elucidation of the
patient's self-imposed ignorance of forbidden object-related libidinal or aggressive wishes. Even in this early version of the story,
Freud's psychoanalytic method aimed to have the patient recognize
that s/he had involuntarily sequestered something without knowing it. When these hidden ways of self-protection were challenged,
s/he either automatically opposed efforts to surface the knowledge
and the methods for keeping them secluded or became terribly
frightened, depressed, and ultimately ill when these habitual methods of self-defence failed to fulfil their function. "Resistance" was
the name Freud gave to this unconscious oppositional activity and,
technically, resistance was to be overcome. Indications of resistance
were sometimes visible to both analyst and analysand:

> The objective sign of this resistance is that [a patient's] asso-
> ciations fail or depart widely from the topic that is being dealt
> with. He may also recognize the resistance subjectively by the
> fact that he has distressing feelings when he approaches the
> topic. But this last sign may also be absent [Freud, 1933, p. 68].

In the Freudian lexicon, resistance keeps the patient from realizing
that s/he has minimized the threat associated with knowing about
the dynamics of desire. Freud's talking cure threatened to name the
desire, its objects, the defensive methods used to camouflage them,
and the reticence to become aware of these mental phenomena. Thus,
only derivatives—shadows of what must not be known—eventually

come to be revealed through the unique form of interpretive reflection that is psychoanalysis. As the threat of self-discovery increases, as the psychoanalytic relationship develops, desire's echoes are silently transferred to "the person of the analyst", again hidden from the patient's view, disguised as if to avoid self-incrimination. The transference protects the patient from recognizing the actual source of his or her frustrated desire by keeping the knowledge of *what* has been transferred and the *fact* of transference itself from consciousness. Whatever else it may be, transference, as Freud (1938a) clearly recognized, is also resistance, the ultimate impediment to the psychoanalytic goal of removing barriers to the patient's extended self-discovery and simultaneously a potential means of facilitating that discovery. Periodically, transference emerges as the object of the analytic couple's reflective gaze and, from time to time, becomes the vehicle through which self-knowledge can be reconfigured. Through psychoanalytically mediated self-observation, resistance analysis, when transference is its object, can help to transform self-deception into self-understanding.

With the emergence of his structural model of mind and the signal theory of anxiety, Freud's ideas about the psychotherapeutic treatment of resistance and transference were now discussed in terms that focused the analyst's attention on the dynamic relationship among the mental agencies id, ego, and superego (cf. Freud, 1923a, 1926a, 1933). In one of his final references to the appearance of resistance in the psychoanalytic setting, Freud stressed that:

> In our therapeutic work we constantly *alternate between the id and the ego, analysing now a fragment of the one and now of the other.* In the one case our aim is to bring a part of the id into consciousness and in the other to correct something in the ego. *The crux of the matter is that the mechanisms of defence against former dangers recur in analysis in the shape of resistances to cure.* The consequence is that the ego's attitude to the cure itself is that of defence against a new danger .... We see then that *there really is a* resistance *to the discovery of resistances* ... [1937, pp. 393–394, italics added].

The patient's unrecognized struggles against the recurrence of childhood catastrophic threats emerge as battles against the analyst's interpretive methods, and insight is obscured by the ego's reluctance to perceive its own self-deceiving manoeuvres. Since Freud also realized that resistance is endemic to free association and a dialectical twin to transference, its analysis became central to effecting therapeutic change. In linking resistance and transference for the last time in his posthumously published *Outline of Psychoanalysis*, Freud remarked:

> If we succeed ... in enlightening the patient on the *true nature* of the phenomena of transference, we shall have struck a powerful weapon out of the hand of his resistance and shall have converted dangers into gains [1938a, p. 177, italics added].

But even as his ideas about psychoanalytic technique matured, his thinking about the "true nature" of transference (and by implication, resistance) was inconsistent. For example, when he wrote in 1937 about alternating between id and ego analysis, between drive-derivative and defence interpretation, he was still straddling contradictory clinical implications of his topographical *and* structural conceptions of the mind. Topographic psychoanalysis would have the analyst making direct interpretations of dynamically unconscious, libidinally-infused ideation and thereby skirting the defensive operations. Topographic analysis necessarily reinforced the patient's reliance on the analyst's authority about the validity of the interpretation, since whatever the analyst believed s/he knew was for the patient unknowable and beyond the patient's direct access. Interventions based on the structural model, on the other hand, would focus the patient's attention on surface (i.e., conscious) manifestations of resistance that the patient could independently observe.

Freud's ideas about resistance and transference remain influential in the theorizing of subsequent generations of psychoanalysts. For Melanie Klein, resistance was "the manifestation of a negative transference" (Hinshelwood, 1989, p. 418). When the resistance was interpreted as anxious avoidance of some feature of the therapeutic relationship whose genetic source was parental, the patient's anxiety was allegedly relieved and the positive transference reinstated (Hinshelwood, 1989). Ronald Fairbairn (1952b) believed that resistance in treatment was due to the patient's "devotion to his repressed objects, ... which is all the more difficult to overcome because these objects are bad and he is afraid of their release from the unconscious" (p. 73). Similarly, more than 40 years later, Ogden (1986) argued that resistance was to be understood as a reflection of the patient's difficulty in letting go of pathological attachments to "unconscious internal object relationships" (p. 165). Concurring with Weinshel's (1984) emphasis on resistance as "the clinical unit of the psychoanalytic process" (p. 69), Boesky (1990), a contemporary Freudian who exemplifies a trend towards recognizing the interactive aspects of psychoanalysis, thinks of resistance as a

> ... joint creation of patient and analyst ... to which the analyst inadvertently contributes in every successful analysis as an unavoidable expression of the [analyst's] essential emotional participation in the ... psychoanalytic process ... [p. 573].

Malin's summary of Kohut's self psychological approach suggests that resistance emerges when the patient feels "a need to safeguard the self" because he or she fears that the vulnerable deficient self will be exposed (Malin, 1993, p. 506). Stolorow, Brandchaft, and Atwood's intersubjective perspective sees "resistance ... *always* being evoked by some quality or activity of the analyst" (Stolorow et al., 1987, p. 14, italics added). Resistance is stimulated by those psychoanalytic couple's interactions that evoke "... the impending recurrence of traumatic developmental failure" (Stolorow, Atwood & Brandchaft, 1994, p. 10) and is most likely brought about by the analyst's mis-atunement that threatens collapse or deterioration of a therapeutic self-object function.

When Edgar Levenson (1987b) recognizes that, beyond its intrapsychic function, resistance is also directed against the analyst, he is inter-personalizing the patient's struggle. Bromberg (1995) develops the relational aspect of resistance even further. He argues that the patient's therapeutic development requires an encounter with the analyst so that the reciprocal process of opposition and confirmation may proceed inter-subjectively. Bromberg sees resistance in the psychoanalytic setting as an enactment that protects the patient's self-continuity. Although he dislikes the term, he nevertheless thinks that resistance does not simply oppose insight but "rather is an intrinsic aspect of the growth dialectic that makes clinical psychoanalysis possible" (Bromberg, 1995, pp. 176–177). Donnel B. Stern (2003) has another name for resistance. He calls it "dissociation", the evidence for which he "note[s] as absences, gaps, contradictions, stereotypes, repetitions, and dead spots in the material" (p. 99).

Most contemporary psychoanalysts who continue to see the analysis of resistance as a central aspect of psychoanalytic work converge on the idea that *overcoming* resistance was an early Freudian wish that could not achieve its aim of inducing patients to suppress resistance's contamination of free association. It is now clear from the vantage point of his own theory that Freud's implicit demand to "stop resisting" was at best paradoxical and at worst contradictory: overcoming resistance means taking conscious control of unconscious processes through an act of will. Were that possible, psychoanalytic treatment would become fundamentally irrelevant. In whatever way and by whomever they believe it is produced, most psychoanalysts realize that resistance is the compromised form of free association whose analysis is a potentially transformative aspect of therapeutic action. Rather than only frustrating the analyst's therapeutic efforts and the patient's self-discovery, resistance

> ... preserve[s] psychically vital states of autonomy, identity, and self-cohesion from potentially destabilizing impingements. As such, resistances embody desperate psychological imperatives imbued with unconscious infantile misconceptions ... any behavior or attitude can serve the purposes of resistance only until an analyst finds the technical resources to exploit its other relevant meanings. If this occurs, rather than impede the analyst's efforts, resistive phenomena further the analyst's intentions by announcing and defining crucial areas of meaning that must receive specific elaboration [Adler & Bachant, 1998, pp. 454–455].

However, some psychoanalysts neither recognize nor endorse the importance of Freud's resistance theory, even though their transference-based treatment conceptions presuppose it. Others openly oppose the concept on theoretical grounds. Interestingly enough, both of these perspectives were represented in a recent report of a panel on resistance (Samberg, 2004). According to the panel reporter, Eslee Samberg (2004), David Tuckett, who at the time was the co-editor of the *International Journal of Psychoanalysis*, began his contribution by saying that he was "not accustomed to using the concept of resistance as such in his work and that he had perhaps preconsciously treated it as an historically outdated concept" (p. 245). Tuckett argued for "a more complex set of ideas about the difficulties in bringing about psychic change and [of] the need for the analyst to attend to the total transference situation" (p. 245). He noted that he was most interested "in the impact of interpretation on the patient's unconscious fantasies and affective experience" and said that he viewed "the aim of interpretation as facilitating a deepening capacity for symbolic representation and affective experience in place of unconscious repetition and avoidance" (p. 245).

Tuckett then illustrated his theory of therapeutic action by discussing his treatment of a woman he believed was obstructing the analysis. He described her efforts to make him ineffective by being "silen[t], forget[ful], pseudo-stupid … and [expressing] resentment" (p. 246), which he regarded as subtle patterns of negation. He experienced her impediments to his interventions with "a general sense of frustration" and astutely talked about enacting his countertransference by "showing off, making premature interpretations, over-intellectualizing and becoming over-aggressive" (p. 246). Conceptualizing her symptoms as defences against anxiety and shame about her wish to feel close to him, he viewed her attacks as envy-driven transference repetitions whose cure required interpretation and working through.

There is an implicit conception of resistance embedded in Tuckett's transference interpretations and in what he calls his "countertransference enactment". However, since he does not acknowledge the significance of resistance and counter-resistance analysis in his theory of technique, he cannot be expected to consistently recognize the signs or symptoms of either in the psychoanalytic setting. Furthermore, since his working model privileges interpreting transference-based, affectively-impregnated unconscious fantasy, his management of the patient's resistance to the emergence of the very transference he wants to interpret would not occupy a prominent place among his intervention tactics. What remains unrecognized in Tuckett's assessment and treatment of his patient's provocative stance was a means of enlisting her self-observational skills to identify her reluctance to say *that* she was having difficulty telling him what was coming to her mind. Similarly, it might have been possible for him to wonder if she was aware of this very difficulty that identifies resistance. In either case, he would have been thereby better able to help her understand why she was having the problem he viewed as obstructing his way of helping her change. As Tuckett's patient resisted becoming conscious of her transference attitudes towards him, Tuckett persisted in trying to have her see what she was not yet ready to recognize or acknowledge: her emotional reliance on her analyst. In the discussion that followed his presentation, Tuckett asserted that "resistance is a universal phenomenon that starts out as an unconscious phenomenon and becomes a relationship phenomenon" (p. 247). However, without a working model for analysing either the patient's transference resistance or her resistance to becoming aware of it, Tuckett would have to become frustrated with what he could only experience as his patient's obstinate refusal to swallow his transference elixir. The relationship phenomenon that followed had him feeling obliged to counter-attack.

If David Tuckett is among those analysts who believe that the concept of resistance is outdated, it can be said that Daniel Stern stands for those who think it wrong and useless. In his contribution to the resistance symposium, Stern did not discuss his work with patients. He nevertheless unequivocally questioned "the validity and usefulness of the resistance concept" (Samberg, 2004, p. 247), asserting that it applies only to what he calls "explicit" knowledge. Although he believes that explicit knowledge—"symbolic, verbal, declarative, and reflectively conscious" (ibid.)—is the only form of human understanding capable of becoming dynamically unconscious, much of human experience, he claims, is "implicit, non-symbolic, non-verbal, procedural, not-reflectively conscious knowledge encompassing how to be with others ... [and] will never become explicit or transposable into words" (ibid.). For Stern, implicit knowledge and its corollary "implicit relational knowing" are therefore not only beyond resistance analysis but beyond interpretation of any sort. Elsewhere he argues that his perspective points psychoanalysis towards interventions other than interpretation as the main vehicles of psychological change (cf. Stern, 2004).

In contrast to such important objections to the concept of resistance, we continue to believe along with Freud that, if adequately applied during treatment, resistance analysis can facilitate therapeutic action and psychological change by engaging the patient's active collaboration in the psychoanalytic process. Indeed, the psychoanalytic setting (and to a lesser extent the psychoanalytic psychotherapeutic setting) affords both analyst and patient the opportunity to learn about the function and genesis of mental operations in the face of conflict. Whether its immediate source is intrapsychic, interpersonal, or both, conflict is a ubiquitous feature of mental life. The compromises that people form to resolve conflict inevitably arise in the psychoanalytic situation (cf. Brenner, 1984, 1994), typically as observable signs of some disturbance in the relationship, often in the patient's inhibited or otherwise distorted thought or speech. Sometimes the reluctance represents a transference reaction from a registered but repressed incident in the patient's life. At other times, it may serve to enact, express, or symbolize otherwise inexpressible fantasies. Reluctance to verbalize forbidden ideas or wishes, whose content is derivative of a childhood trauma, is a manifest form of unconscious resistance (Kris, 1990). Conflict has been a major focus of the development of clinical psychoanalytic technique. Freud's signal theory of anxiety showed how conflict-producing wishes typically arouse two forms of mental opposition: negative affects (anxiety, depressive feeling, guilt, and shame) and camouflaging manoeuvres or defences that minimize the affect's impact by distorting the forbidden association to the wish (Freud, 1926a). What is most important about the role of negative affects in mental life is that their ideational content typically contains disguised or unrecognized forms of one or more of what Freud called the dangers or traumas of childhood (1926a). These childhood calamities all involve some form of threatened or actual injury to the mind or body, the loss of an important person, the withdrawal of their needed love, and the threat of self-punishment. When these threats and the defensive manoeuvres they accompany are transferred from the childhood context to the analytic situation, the patient involuntarily seeks to minimize the danger and experiences the manifestation of this resistance as reluctance to think, feel, speak, or otherwise know the content of these constituents of conflict. When enactments of reluctance to say what comes to mind occur, the *hypothetical constructs* conflict, transference and resistance become *observable phenomena* in the analytic setting.

Paul Gray's model of close process attention

Among those most closely identified with contemporary Freudian conflict theory, Paul Gray's technique makes one of the most original and detailed technical contributions to the analysis of resistance as the vehicle for therapeutic action (Busch, 1994, 1995, 2009). Gray believes it is most useful when working with patients suffering from neurotic conflicts whose defences inhibit them from knowing about and being able to make adaptive use of libidinal or aggressive drive derivatives.

Gray (1996) calls attention to what he believes are problems with traditional psychoanalysis which relies on analysts becoming aware of their own "free associations" to patient material, finding "creative ways of resonating to their own unconscious" and making interpretations of the patient's unconscious fantasy (pp. 92–93). He argues that interpretations of patients' dynamically unconscious material makes the analyst appear to be the "only one who knows" and fosters compliance through the transfer of the patient's (parental) authority to the analyst (Gray, 1987). Consequently, he thinks that rather than making "deep interpretations", it is necessary to stay on the surface, close to the moment at which ruptures inevitably occur in the patient's free associative activity. These breaks signal the operation of defences the analyst's interventions can help the patient observe, recognize, and analyze.[1]

Against Freud, Gray (1982) cautions that depending on the positive transference "as the vehicle for *influencing* the patient's participation in the analytic process … [retains an] authoritarian element" that inhibits the ego's autonomy and the patient's self-analytic capacity (p. 630). It is important to note that Gray's use of the term "authoritarian" is not hyperbole but rather an intentional critique of a typically unrecognized tendency among psychoanalysts of all persuasions to engage in a kind of psychoanalytic mind reading that reinforces an unwarranted belief for both members of the dyad in the analyst's indubitable knowledge about the patient's unconscious. Gray argues that instead of encouraging the patient to develop his or her self-observing and self-analytic capacity, regardless of how sensitively the interpretation is delivered:

> [The authoritarian] analyst … does not invite the analysand to use his observing ego to share the analyst's perception of the data … [and] is apt to be experienced by the patient as an authority, [instead of] treat[ing] the patient's observing ego as of potentially equal value to his own [1982, p. 643].

These admonitions about the analyst's interpretive strategy are based on what Gray (1982) has called a "developmental lag" in psychoanalytic technique. Despite the fact that the technical implications of the structural theory focused psychoanalytic interpretation on the ego's defensive activity, the lag occurred because analysts continued to base their interpretations on the topographic idea that the patient's knowledge of dynamically unconscious (id) contents would make the "unconscious conscious" and would eventually be curative once they were lived in the transference. Gray (1991) believes that this traditional psychoanalytic technique affords analysts certain gratifications, which include the satisfaction entailed in making interpretations that are "brilliant" and the pleasure accompanying expressions of sublimated aggression that disturb patients' defended equilibrium (pp. 91–92).[2]

Understanding the reluctance to abandon such gratifications, Gray nonetheless rejects these "deep interpretations" of id-based drive derivatives in favour of interventions that focus on the ego's defensive activity manifest in the patient's resistances to the free associative process. Gray's appreciation of the technical implications of Freud's structural model leads him to argue that these resistances to free association must themselves become the object of psychoanalytic understanding to fully capture the role of the ego in the resistance process. When Freud prepared patients for psychoanalysis, he enjoined them to say whatever went through their minds and not to yield to their own self-criticism by withholding thoughts they felt to be irrelevant or objectionable. He further instructed them to "… never forget that you have promised to be absolutely honest, and never leave anything out because, for some reason or other, it is unpleasant to tell it" (Freud, 1913, p. 135). Freud's intention was to have patients *overcome* resistance; Gray wants to collaborate with them to *analyse* that resistance (Gray, 1991).

A fundamentally important difference between *traditional psychoanalysis* and the method of close process attention is that resistances are *not* viewed as an obstacle to free association; rather, the method of free association is seen as the vehicle through which resistances become the focus of the analytic dyad's mutual interest in the patient's gradual acceptance of his or her thoughts once they have become conscious (Kris, 1990). In recognition of the painful affective experience inherent in the prospect of "saying whatever comes to mind", close process analysis alerts patients to the impossibility of the task (Busch, 1995, p. 55). So, for example, at the outset of psychoanalysis, Gray orients patients to his psychoanalytic approach by explaining that he will be helping them "*toward* free association", which will inevitably be interrupted by certain "interferences and obstacles", i.e., resistances, to saying what comes to mind.

> I point out that it is precisely the study of these interferences and obstacles to putting the [patient's self-] observations into words that provides us with greater access to what is now out of reach and which contributes to the patient's problems; and that the *nature of the obstacles* to free associations will be intimately connected with the *nature of the problems* or conflicts that brought the patient to treatment [Gray, 1994b, p. 69, original italics].[3]

These modifications of Freud's instructional procedure are critically important to the conduct of psychoanalysis. For patients, the free associative procedure constitutes a paradox in which they consent to follow an instruction that cannot be followed. For analysts, among other things, these instructions oblige an acute attentiveness to disturbances in the patient's attempts to speak freely in the analytic setting and a focus on signs of probable conflict signalled by observable and reportable alterations in the flow of the patient's thought and communications. Silences, inappropriate affect, obvious avoidance of topics, rituals, lateness, missing hours, or not paying, are typical indications that, among other things, the patient may be *showing* what he or she is troubled about *telling*. It should be noted that Gray (1993) emphasizes verbal material as the psychoanalytic data because he believes that "… it is their verbalizations that we can best use to document and share our observations" (p. 326; see also Gray, 1996).

Here is an example of a close process intervention from Davison, Pray and Bristol (1990, p. 603) that shows the patient defending himself shortly after expressing an aggressive idea about wanting to hurt someone. Note that the analyst's comments are descriptive, on the "surface" of the patient's mind, and point to the sudden change in his language and feelings. In this case, the patient's expression of a drive-defence sequence is noted in the intervention and is followed by what Gray calls a re-externalization of the transference of authority.

Patient: *I am so angry with Betty I could strangle her ... [he elaborated*
          for a while, then he became hesitant] ... on the other hand she
          has many fine qualities, etc.

Analyst: *Now you are focused on her fine qualities, a moment before you*
          were experiencing very different feelings, then your feelings
          shifted. Can you see what happened here?

Patient: *I was afraid you would think I was a brute for feeling so angry*
          at her.

Aimed at helping patients improve their capacity to observe their own intrapsychic activity, Gray describes how he first listens for signs of a derivative of an aggressive or sexual wish in patients' narratives and then pays careful attention to the appearance of changes in the content or the context of subsequent material. Gray believes that these narrative changes are an indication of an (unconscious) ego-based defensive operation initiated automatically to prevent forbidden aggressive or sexual wishes access to consciousness or to diminish the intensity of negative affects these wishes would otherwise stimulate. In his innovative psychoanalytic technique, Gray carefully applies Freud's recognition of the ego's capacity to observe itself. He also believes that patients are aware of some aspect of their altered narrative, whether manifest as increased discomfort in the analytic setting, as a reflexive self-critical comment about some aspect of what they have just said, or as a reaction to whatever the analyst did or did not say. Consequently, once having identified a wish-defence sequence, Gray interprets the *conscious* manifestations of patients' resistance to speaking freely by addressing their awareness of some aspect of their conflicted associative thought and speech process. Gray tries to avoid burdening his interpretive intervention with whatever he might believe is unconscious about the conflicted sequence, even though he may know its theoretical role in the production of the compromised association.

Gray (1990) makes a point of indicating that close process attention intends to "reduce the patient's *potential* for anxiety" by identifying derivatives of "unconscious infantile fears" and decreasing "... the patient's need for symptomatic regression" (p. 1085). He explains that his modification of traditional psychoanalytic procedure can be thought of as a recursive three-phase process in which phase specific interventions contribute in complementary ways to therapeutic action (Gray, 1993). In the first phase, Gray listens for a sign of a drive derivative emerging into consciousness in the patient's narrative, which is typically followed by a change in its content or context. This change is understood as an unconscious defensive manoeuvre to reduce discomfort about exposing conflicted wishes. Gray maintains that since this process is observable to both members of the psychoanalytic dyad, the analyst can intervene by bringing the patient's attention to it in the form of an observation (such as "I noticed you stopped talking") or an inquiry ("Did you notice something just there that felt unsafe …?"). He believes that this first phase of close process attention helps patients to become familiar with the *fact* of their resistances and recognize that escape from anxiety is a generic motivational condition.

In the second phase, using the patient's conflicted discourse, Gray begins to elucidate the drive-derivative/defence sequence. He notes that the success of this phase depends on the analyst's sensitivity to the patient's capacity to be receptive at the moment of the intervention, which entails an awareness of what the patient knows and understands about why the analyst is communicating these particular observations. The challenge for the analyst is not to overwhelm the patient's ego as s/he does the work of re-contacting a tolerable degree of the drive derivative and of recognizing that the conflict over revealing it motivated a defensive measure. When insight is achieved, the patient learns about "his [or her] capacity for ego strength through the experience of gradually, autonomously exercising his control over the impulses being reclaimed" (Gray, 1990, p. 100). Gray helps the patient learn to tolerate the appearance of objectionable wishes without being automatically and involuntarily obliged to distort their meaning to appease a hypercritical superego. Once the patient is reliably able to identify that something has stimulated defensive activity, the analysis of the meaning of the resistance, the final phase of close process attention, can proceed.

Phase three focuses on the ego's superego functions and the patient's transference of childhood images of parental authority re-externalized onto the analyst. Gray assumes that conflicts about speaking to the analyst are motivated by a fantasy that doing so would entail an important risk, whose clarification becomes a major part of the psychoanalytic work. In this phase, Gray (1993) believes the patient is ready to examine the ego's defensive use of the analyst that either inhibits free expression when the analyst is experienced as judgmental or facilitates compliance via fantasies of the analyst's affectionate approval.

> Ultimately the analyst can ... demonstrate how the pre[-] super-
> ego perceptions of the parental authorities ... resurrected in the
> analytic situation ... include, and contain, due to projection, the
> instinctual wishes and impulses that the child needed to control
> [p. 334].

From Gray's perspective, reducing patients' anxiety potential requires a collaborative engagement between analyst and patient that has the analyst shift from a traditional, evenly suspended psychoanalytic listening and intervening strategy to one that closely guides the psychoanalytic couple's interest in investigating patients' troubled communication efforts as they emerge in the psychoanalytic setting.

This close process attention model of psychoanalytic treatment recognizes that the psychodynamics of transferred authority include both aggressive and libidinal wishes. Gray (2000) notes that certain defensive patterns, "... particularly transference defenses associated with what traditionally is regarded as the superego" (p. 230), are especially aroused by conflicted aggression. He goes on to argue that when the analyst listens with "evenly-hovering attention", s/he often bypasses the identification and treatment of these aggression-prohibiting (transference) defences. Gray believes that when the analyst uses the traditional listening technique s/he may fail to pay close enough attention to the patient's transference-idealization that all too often functions as a defence against "access to conflicted aggression" (ibid., p. 229). Gray sees this traditional analytic listening perspective as a form of counter-resistance to the recognition and analysis of hostile transferences that keeps patients from becoming more fully aware of how, when, and why they turn their conflicted aggression against themselves. The possibility that patients might eventually be able to choose more adaptive strategies for the management of aggression is thereby thwarted rather than facilitated. Gray also believes that the analysis of conflicted aggression that close process attention technique encourages opens the way for patients to bear the frustrations of unrequited erotic longings for the analyst. Thus, close process analysis of aggression should result in greater access to sexual passions as well. Gray (1973) also maintains that the analysis of conflicted aggression is more demanding on the analyst than the analysis of erotic transferences: "I believe that the analyst is faced with a qualitatively different task in achieving neutrality in the face of verbalized aggression as compared with verbalized erotic wishes" (p. 477) and goes on to say that the qualities required to achieve this "neutrality" are not emphasized sufficiently in analytic training. Thus, Gray (2000) ultimately summarizes his thinking on drive derivative analysis in stating: "Although I am not promoting the analysis of conflicted aggression as an exclusive technique, I would be gratified to see it given at least equal opportunity" (p. 231).[4]

There is some controversy about which patients are able to benefit from Gray's innovation. We noted earlier that Gray (1982) views close process attention as being most appropriate for patients suffering from inhibitions due to neurotic conflict who can sustain the cognitive and experiential aspects of this psychoanalytic method without having to rely exclusively on the internalization processes that any successful psychoanalysis provides (p. 644). Nevertheless, he believes that the benignly authoritative roles assumed by traditional analysts may be necessary for many patients "… for whom consistent defense analysis would be too burdensome", because of their tendency or need for incorporative or internalizing identifications. He lists among such patients those "… with narcissistic disorders, borderline conditions, some very severe neuroses, most children, and many adolescents" (Gray, 1982, p. 643; see also Gray, 2000).

Among other analysts using close process methodology, Paniagua (1991, 2001) and White (2006) think that this "two-tier classification of patients" is unrealistic, since dissociative as well as repressive defences are found "in all of our patients" (see White, 2006). Hutchinson (1996) has suggested the application of close process attention to patients suffering from primitive mental states and impulse disorders as long as the analyst is careful not to disrupt defences needed to sustain psychological functioning. In such cases, the analyst must monitor the "affective temperature" of the words that describe drive derivatives and should intervene when a defence mobilized to protect against a drive derivative is demonstrable but not intense enough to provoke a rigid defense (ibid., p. 147). He argues that certain patients with impulse disorders have difficulty adaptively protecting themselves, so that attempts to help the patient reduce the severity of a "harsh superego" could go astray without first strengthening the ego's ability to otherwise ward off the intensity of either libidinal or aggressive drive derivatives (Hutchinson, 1996). On the other hand, Davison et al. (1990) point out that when patients are entrenched in a regressed transference experience, the primacy of their disturbing mental states precludes the more demanding effort of paying attention to their defensive processes. They subsequently point out that in the absence of further research, some patients, for reasons not yet understood, may simply not be able to use the technique (Davison et al., 1996).

Interpersonalizing close process analysis

While we believe that close process attention is a useful method that contributes to therapeutic action, we think the model has important limitations that can be transcended by elucidating and explicating the analyst's impact on the formation and expression of the patient's thought and action in the psychoanalytic situation. Gray tried to correct what he saw as problematic features of traditional psychoanalysis that rely on overcoming resistance to free association via "deep interpretations" of unconscious mental activity and the analysis of countertransference as a method by which the analyst could also know the mind of the patient. For Gray, the analyst's countertransference appears to have been reconfigured to mean the analyst's resistance to analysing the patient's resistance. Moreover, to keep the attention of the analyst close to the patient's intrapsychic process, he argued that responding to considerations of external reality in the patient's narrative served defensive purposes for both patient and analyst. The model regards the analyst's considerations of external reality in the patient's associations as a counter-resistance to dealing with the patient's psychic reality in general and as a protection against the intensity of the patient's drive derivatives directed at the analyst in particular. We think that by excluding the relevance of the analyst's self-observational work (beyond the analyst's counter-resistance) and external (i.e., social) reality from the treatment model, Gray limits the significance of the analyst's and patient's unique psychological, social, and ideological characteristics that are determinants (however unformulated) of the psychoanalytic process in which they are both engaged (Hollander, 2009a, 2010; Portuges, 2004, 2005; Hollander & Gutwill, 2006).

Although it is beyond the scope of this chapter to elaborate the social and ideological components of mind, we have created the following clinical scenario as a heuristic device to show how the analyst's psychology affects the psychoanalytic treatment process in a way that close process attention does not take into account.

The patient is a 39-year-old African-American, working class woman who came to psychoanalysis as a control case suffering from a depressed mood about not being able to conceive. She has been in psychoanalysis for three years and is now in the second trimester of her first pregnancy, just having learned of the positive results of her amniocentesis. The analyst is a 44-year-old childless Caucasian woman who is having difficulty getting pregnant. She has just experienced her second failed *in vitro* fertilization procedure.

Patient: *The baby is fine! I am so relieved and happy about the test, I could hardly wait to tell my boss when I got off the phone with the doctor.*

Analyst: *[Audible sigh.]*

Patient: *Um … [pause] I don't know, she didn't seem all that excited. I sure wish she had been a little more enthusiastic …. I started to feel irritated and thought "She has three kids and a live-in housekeeper." [pause]. I don't know. She works so hard. She must have been exhausted.*

Analyst: *You paused after sounding so excited about the good news and began speaking critically about your boss's lack of enthusiasm. Then there was a change in your voice and you spoke positively about her. Did you notice something that seemed risky or unsafe about what you were telling me?*

Patient: *Yes. I was thinking about how I must have seemed to you when I made that crack about her three kids and the support she has that I don't. I sounded too pissed-off and I tried to cover it up and … there is something else. When I said how excited I was to find out about the baby, I heard you sigh and I thought I had upset you.*

Analyst: Oh. I didn't realize I had sighed. [pause] So you were angry
about your boss's reaction to your good news, then you felt
distressed about the intensity of your criticism of her. Now you
are concerned that I was disturbed by your good news.

This brief vignette illustrates the analyst making interventions consonant with Gray's close process attention technique. It also depicts a patient who has developed a reasonable degree of non-punitive, self-observational and self-analytic skill, a central goal of the model and an indication that the technique has contributed to therapeutic action. The analyst's first intervention emerges as a result of her perception of the patient's aggressive drive derivative and the patient's apparent reluctance to continue as she forms a defensive reaction against the expression of her anger (boss's lack of enthusiasm is rationalized as her being tired after working hard). The object of the analyst's intervention is the patient's affective shift from anger to apparent empathy, a reaction formation against her conflicted aggressive wish. The analyst's second intervention is based on her view that the patient has unconsciously inhibited her aggressive reaction to the analyst's sigh and transferred a compromised version of it to the analyst ("… I thought I had upset you"). As their exchange comes to an end, the analyst is encouraging the patient to continue exploring her projection that constrains and disguises her transferred aggression.

We see here the contributions to therapeutic action of the close process technique and, from our perspective, we encounter what we have come to believe is its major weakness as well. This analyst's exclusive focus on the patient's intrapsychic dynamics forecloses her ability to think about *her* unintended impact on the patient. The close process analyst is theoretically limited from contemplating *in vivo*, let alone paying close attention to, the ways in which her own thoughts and feelings about the patient's communication are regularly conveyed, however subtly or inadvertently. We think it reasonable to infer from what we have said about the analyst's frustrated wish to bear a child that her sigh upon hearing her patient succeed where she has failed is understandably experienced by the patient as a communication, a perplexing interpretation, to which the patient responds by inhibiting her narrative (she pauses immediately upon hearing the sigh and then the affective component of her narrative changes from irritation to compassion). However, as the analyst follows Paul Gray's guidelines for conducting close process resistance analysis, her exclusive focus on the patient's intrapsychic process does not call for the integration of the interpersonal effect of what she also knows to be true: the patient has what she still desires. Although it is hard to believe that this fact would not influence what the analyst feels and would not emerge, however enigmatically, in what s/he says or how s/he says it, Gray would argue that the analyst ought to be able to successfully bypass her own state of mind to continue her psychoanalytic work, whose goal is to help the patient recognize and deal with inhibited aggression in a more sublimated adaptive manner.

Many psychoanalysts have recognized that psychoanalytic neutrality, the principle that Gray believes must guide his method, is an unattainable pseudo-ideal (Hoffman, 1996; Hollander, 2009b; Portuges, 2009; Renik, 1996; Stolorow, 1990). In our view, it is important for numerous reasons that analysts recognize and acknowledge when and how their thoughts, feelings, or actions affect the patient, not the least important of which is their obligation to do no harm. We believe psychoanalysis ought to provide both patient and analyst the opportunity to recognize and find ways that are ultimately respectful of their relationship to constructively deal with their differences and with the psychoanalytic reasons for the errors they make about one another. In whatever ways psychoanalysts' theories guide the integration of their mistakes, misperceptions, and misunderstandings into what they tell their patients, the ongoing analysis of their inevitable enactments ought to be conscientiously represented in their intervention strategy. Their willingness to do so helps patients develop autonomous observational skills, improve their reality testing, and facilitate their becoming less dependent on the very superego-based transference of authority that Gray's writings have illuminated. We believe that *interpersonalizing* Gray's close process method by encouraging analysts to identify their impact on the patient's mind and to integrate their own self-reflective observations into their therapeutic practices could significantly enhance its use-value for all psychoanalysts, no matter their psychoanalytic perspective. With this important interpersonalizing modification in mind, if, as Freud suggested, resistance and transference analysis are the *sine qua non* of our clinical discipline, Gray's ideas about how to listen and how to talk to patients warrants our most careful consideration.

Socializing close process analysis

Further, we want to offer an additional critique of Paul Gray's theory related to its explicit elimination of external reality from psychoanalytic consideration. From our perspective, adherence to this technical precept leaves the influence of social factors out of the psychoanalytic contemplation of its practitioners. We believe that this theoretical exclusion compromises Gray's method as it does any clinical practice that rejects or diminishes the fact that social reality is formative in the production and reproduction of psychic life. Knowledge of social reality begins in infancy and is mandated through the family, the church, the schools, the public and professional media, and the state via culturally normative principles or ideologies that successfully explain how the social world works and how it *ought* to be. These systematic schemes of ideas impose important political principles, moral values, and beliefs that qualify the developing child as a subject, organizing and locating him or her in the social order. Since social reality infiltrates psychic reality, psychoanalysis is weakened by its exclusion from theories of the mind's structure, psychopathology, and remediation. Even though representations of the social world figured prominently in the making of the Freudian mind, reality was most often construed to mean that which is mentally registered, determined largely on an individual basis by the quality of the resolution of Oedipal struggles or other dynamic organizers, and preceded by the qualifier "psychic". This solitary-mind perspective of psychic reality was a genuine contribution to the ontology of irrationality and to the explanation of certain otherwise unintelligible states of mind like dreams, parapraxes, and the formation of symptoms. At the same time, a problematic consequence of this "one-person psychology" was to subvert the psychoanalytic recognition of the ideological influence of political, social, and economic forces on psychological development and its manifestation in the clinical setting.

This mote in the psychoanalytic eye is most clearly demonstrated in our clinical illustration. Recall that this analyst is theoretically mandated to pay close attention only to the patient's intrapsychic process, and neither member of the dyad has or is likely to explicitly recognize, let alone take up, the influences of their different class or ethnic/racial positions in the social order. The analyst is a white middle class professional, whose African-American working class patient has twice resentfully referred to her boss's privileged social position that permits the boss to employ a professional caregiver for her children's welfare. These are derivatives of the patient's recognition of the social structuring of her relationship with her boss and a potentially displaced reference to that of her relationship with her analyst (she speaks only about the boss's privileged position when she has reason to know about the analyst's as well). While the psychological basis of the displacement is likely to be recognized by the close process analyst, its social foundation cannot be uncovered.

However, Gray's is but one version of the "keep social reality out of the psychoanalytic investigation thesis" which we believe has characterized the history of clinical psychoanalysis. Even for analysts who do not practise close process resistance analysis, their attitudes and values about class and race are embedded in, and for different reasons sequestered in an enactment of psychosocial resistance that escapes recognition. Too often the social determinants of the psychoanalytic exchange have been firewalled, so that neither analyst nor patient can speak about them. Here for example are four factors that can keep the analyst from realizing that social forces have entered the psychoanalytic frame and from developing adaptive ways of dealing with them.

- Following the psychoanalytic interpretive principle that references to social reality in the patient's narrative are to be regarded only as stand-ins for some aspect of the analyst-patient relationship or more generally as symbols for conflicted developments in the patient's history.
- The analyst's anxiety about breaching the convention of silence on controversial and contested conflict-laden social issues lest the civility that disguises the unresolved history and current realities of asymmetrical class, racial, and gendered relations will be ruptured in the clinical setting.
- Being concerned about proselytizing the patient's social values and political perspectives.
- Thinking that taking up the real differences emerging from their different locations in the social order will sabotage the possibility of sustaining a working alliance.

Social reality becomes part of human character and pathology through the incorporation and integration of hegemonic ideological elements that constitute the unconscious social holding environment for a patient's beliefs, attitudes, and values. This integration renders human mentation social-psychological in nature. By taking up these social-psychological beliefs, attitudes, and values only as psychological aspects of self, love, and work, clinical psychoanalysis resists conceptualizing the patient as a social subject and citizen. This psychoanalytic separation of psychic reality from its social roots is a form of collective false consciousness, a psychosocial resistance. This resistance keeps psychoanalysts from examining how the asymmetries of class, race, and gendered power relations are reproduced as hegemonic attitudes and values. Consequently, hegemonic values remain invisible and infiltrate the psychoanalytic process without the possibility of their becoming either conscious or contested. We need only remember that psychoanalysis thrives in democratic culture in order to recognize that the important issues of social justice, democratic participation, and the obligations of citizenship ought to be included as legitimate objects of psychoanalytic scrutiny.

Précis

In this paper, we have examined patients' resistance to knowing more about themselves during psychoanalytic treatment. After illustrating variations in conceptualizations of resistance among psychoanalytic orientations, we synthesized the important and clinically valuable contributions of Paul Gray's theory and technique of resistance analysis and highlighted its role in therapeutic action. Finally, we offered our critique of the limitations of Gray's method and went on to suggest how it, as well as any other psychoanalytic technique that relies on reciprocal self-reflection to achieve its aims, would be enhanced by including not only interpersonal but social factors in the conceptual framework of psychic reality and its clinical treatment.

Notes

1. It is important to recognize that Gray equates resistance with manifestations of defence that emerge as a result of the psychoanalytic

procedure. "I believe that such a theoretical perspective, though not exhaustive, is practical in comprehending and observing resistance during the analytic process" (Gray, 1994b, p. 72).

2. Converging on Gray's understanding from a radically different philosophical perspective, Jacques Derrida, the postmodernist founder of deconstruction, identifies the analyst's interpretive pleasures in the following way:

> To analyze anything whatsoever, anyone whatsoever, for anyone whatsoever, would mean saying to the other: choose my solution, prefer my solution, take my solution, love my solution; you will be in the truth if you do not resist my solution [Derrida, 1998, p. 9].

3. Gray's technical advice to analysts is to base their interventions on difficulties involving the patient's linguistic communications rather than on other actions in the session. For a critical perspective on this issue, see Roughton (1995) and Busch (2009).

4. Gray's theory of mind and technical emphasis on the importance of analysing derivatives of aggression contrast sharply with Melanie Klein's, for whom aggression is a manifestation of the death instinct's sadistic and envious destructiveness that inevitably becomes manifest in the negative (aggressive) transference. In the Kleinian tradition, interpreting the negative transference is central to reducing patients' phantastic anxieties about self or object annihilation (Klein, 1957; Rosenfeld, 1971).

CHAPTER FIVE

From ego psychology to modern conflict theory

Christopher Christian

The ways and means by which psychoanalysis achieves meaningful change remain as poorly understood today as they did two decades ago, when Fonagy (1982) made a similar observation. Although we have been able to systematically show that psychodynamic psychotherapy is effective, despite difficulties in disseminating those facts (Shedler, 2010), we have had more difficulties in understanding the therapeutic action by which either psychodynamic psychotherapy or psychoanalysis achieves its effects. In an issue of *The Psychoanalytic Quarterly*, devoted in its entirety to the question of therapeutic action, Smith (2007) drew attention to the fact that therapeutic action is often discussed at different levels of abstraction making comparisons between different schools difficult. On one level are our theories of pathogenesis; on another are our theories of how the mind works; then there are a number of ideas about what the analyst does; and at another level still is the role of the analyst as a person effecting change.

In this chapter, I review the history of ego psychology and its role in the development of the centrality of conflict in psychoanalytic theory and practice. I then go on to examine modern conflict theory from the four angles proposed by Smith with a particular focus on the work of Charles Brenner with the purpose of elucidating the mechanisms by which modern conflict theory is thought to effect therapeutic change. This, in turn, can facilitate comparisons between modern conflict theory and other clinical models, including some described in the current volume (e.g., Paul Gray's model discussed by Portuges and Hollander, 2011, in the preceding chapter).

The following brief historical overview will help situate modern conflict theory within the field of psychoanalysis in general, and ego psychology in particular. In 1923, in his seminal paper "The Ego and the Id" (1923a), Freud presented his final model of the mind in the form of the tripartite structure of id, ego, and superego. This paper, along with "Inhibitions, symptoms and anxiety" (1926a), would be the springboard for what would become known as ego psychology. Whereas the psychoanalyst's role in treatment began with a focus on uncovering repressed unconscious content that was thought to be at the heart of a patient's symptoms, without regard to the patient's defences, ego psychology would shift the analyst's attention to the mechanisms by which such content became unconscious and how it remained so. Going forward, analysing the ego's role in defence would be placed front and centre of psychoanalytic technique (A. Freud, 1936; Waelder, 1936; Fenichel, 1941b).

Initially, and for many years, defence was defined only in terms of repression. Over time, and as ego psychology evolved, a series of defence mechanisms would be itemized, including regression, reaction-formation, isolation, undoing, projection, introjection, turning against the self, and reversal into the opposite. Many of these defences had been outlined by Freud (1900, 1905b, 1924). However, it was Anna Freud (1936), in her important monograph *The Ego and the Mechanisms of Defense*, who expounded upon the intricacies of these defence mechanisms with sensitively written clinical vignettes illustrating their origins and functions.

It is easy to lose sight of the profound impact that Anna Freud's brief monograph had on the field of psychoanalysis. According to Young-Bruehl (2002), *The Ego and the Mechanisms of Defense* was one of two "systematic works of the 1930s [that] were understood by all Freudians to be the key elaborations of the structural theory" (p. 757).[1] Wallerstein (1984) considered *The Ego and the Mechanisms of Defense* as "the foundation piece of the whole of the modern era of ego psychology and of how we collectively understand and practice psychoanalysis" and "perhaps the single most widely read book in our professional literature" (p. 66).

Although Anna Freud would go on to establish herself in London in 1938, it would be in America that her work took hold wherein ego psychology would become the dominant psychoanalytic paradigm for over three decades. At the forefront of what Young-Bruehl (2002) refers to as the "hegemony of ego psychology" was Heinz Hartmann. In his work, Hartmann (1939a) would expand the role of the ego as a mental structure by emphasizing how the ego was not only tied to conflict and pathological functioning, with a role circumscribed to mobilizing defences; but in addition, the ego would have at its disposal energy that, while stemming from aggressive and sexual drives, could be desexualized and de-aggressivized by a process that he would describe as *neutralization*. According to Hartmann, the ego could operate within a *conflict-free sphere*. Examples of ego-operations within this conflict-free sphere were psychological capacities like intelligence, cognition, memory, planning, etc. In this way, Hartmann sought to define psychoanalysis as a general psychology and not just as a theory of psychopathology and its treatment. Hartmann (1939a) would also introduce the term *average expectable environment* to emphasize the relevance of reality in facilitating adaptation. Thus, the ego was not limited to its role in conflict vis-à-vis the id and the superego, warding off impulses and avoiding guilt and self-punishment, but would also operate to find ways to gratify impulses, as made possible by the opportunities afforded by the person's social milieu.

By the 1940s, the Hartmann era had begun, launching what Bergman (1997) has described as "one of the most productive periods in the history of psychoanalysis" (p. 71). Behind Hartmann's ascendance, both in the American Psychoanalytic Association and at the New York Psychoanalytic Society and Institute, was the hope that psychoanalysis would be made more scientific, and that by doing so, it would avoid some of the problems attendant to the splintering factions in Europe, where psychoanalysis had to contend with the ever-present risk of becoming an ideology rather than a so-called true science (Makari, 2008). Critics contended that if psychoanalysis was to be valued on the same plane as any other field of science, it behoved analysts to spell out their methodology and the general laws upon which this new science relied, and to delineate where and how analysis fitted with other sciences including developmental biology, psychology, and sociology.

A major challenge confronting Hartmann's project for a scientific psychology was the pressing need to organize and reconcile significant differences and contradictions that remained in the large corpus of Freud's work. Important allies in this endeavour (at least initially) would be found in Merton Gill (1954), David Rapaport (1959), Rapaport & Gill (1959), George Klein (1969), and Robert Holt (1976), as they attempted to systematize a comprehensive general theory of psychoanalysis, as well as modernize Freud's metapsychology.[2] Ultimately, the project for a scientific psychology would languish, partly due to the fact that there was an absence of any kind of structure that would allow the numerous constructs being developed by ego psychologists to be operationalized, formulated into testable hypotheses, and then tested empirically. As with any other science, a general theory of psychoanalysis had to be "testable by methods other than those by which the initial evidence for it was obtained" (Rapaport, 1959, p. 116).

Although it is hard to imagine how psychoanalysis could ever become a *general psychology* when it remained isolated from the rest of psychology as a field, the fact is that numerous attempts to develop research into conflict, pre-conscious and unconscious mentation, and other tenets of psychoanalytic theory, were met with indifference or outright hostility by the psychoanalytic community (Fonagy, 1982). This attitude may have had its early roots in Freud's own views on psychoanalytic experimentation, expressed in his oft-cited response to a letter from American psychologist, Saul Rosenzsweig (1934), who wrote to Freud about his experiments confirming some of Freud's ideas on repression. Freud's retort:

> I have examined your experimental studies of the verification of the psychoanalytic assertions with interest. I cannot put much value on these confirmations because the wealth of reliable observations (from the clinical situation) on which these assertions rest, make them independent of experimental verification. Still, it can do no harm [Freud, as cited in Grunbaum, 1984, p. 1].

Despite the risks that such an attitude posed for the future of psychoanalysis and its place as a natural science, a place that Freud

(1938b) persistently sought to secure,[3] we see to this day remnants of this antagonism to research, perhaps most recently articulated by Irwin Hoffman (2007) to a standing ovation at a meeting of the American Psychoanalytic Association, and in a recently published article in the journal of the same organization (2009), where he declared that the "nonobjectivist hermeneutic paradigm" (p. 1043) is best suited to psychoanalysis and that empirical research "is potentially *damaging* both to the development of our understanding of the analytic process itself and to the quality of our clinical work" (p. 1043, italics added).

Many psychoanalysts single-mindedly subscribed, and still do, to the view that the means for testing psychoanalytic tenets was through the method of psychoanalysis itself[4]—an impossible feat, most would agree, along the lines of the Kantian eye attempting to see itself. For these and undoubtedly other reasons psychoanalysis remained divorced from the University, precluding any programmatic research that would test and refine the theories that ego psychology was formulating.[5] Today, universities have, by and large, purged psychoanalysis from their departments and their curricula (Bornstein, 2001, 2002). In fact, the graduate student interested in psychoanalysis is more likely to find the subject discussed in comparative literature than in the psychology courses. Psychoanalysis has met the same fate in medical schools. As Leon Hoffman (2010) recently noted, "In a mere 40 years the number of psychoanalysts in key academic psychiatric positions declined by almost fourfold" (p. 21).

In addition to the lack of formal structures for developing a research programme, many have pointed to the difficulties in Hartmann's writings themselves as a major culprit (Apfelbaum, 1962; Rangell, 1985; Busch, 1993; Brenner, 2002), marked, as they were, by an absence of clinical vignettes to illustrate clinical application and lacking the experience-near language of the clinical setting. Although this style may have been partly due to Hartmann's quest to define general laws of psychoanalysis, the net result was a metapsychology that seemed divorced from clinical practice. As Rangell (1985) points out, many regard Hartmann's work with "mild interest and considerable ambivalence" and his "formulations on ego autonomy, are looked upon askance" (p. 154). Some go as far as to claim that Hartmann's conceptual framework may have had "a *deleterious* effect on clinical theory and technique" (Busch, 1993, p. 164, italics added), as the importance of the ego, clinically speaking, was pushed aside for more abstract theorizing, that in "forsaking clinical examples, has left a generation of analysts in awe of Hartmann's intellectual powers, while shaking their heads when considering its relevance to their last patient" (p. 164). Makari (2008), in his fascinating review of the history of psychoanalysis, recently iterated a similar opinion, stating that the "*I* psychology with its connection to lived experience mutated into an abstract, impersonal ego psychology in Hartmann's hands" (p. 483).[6]

By the 1970s, the dominant status of ego psychology would be challenged by a growing pluralism in American psychoanalysis. As Schafer (1970) points out, a cultural shift made the type of grand over-arching narrative that Hartmann sought to attain run counter to postmodern notions of relativity, deconstructionism, hermeneutics, and gender theory that were being embraced in psychoanalysis by the likes of Stern (1989), Elliot and Spezzano (1996), and Irwin Hoffman, (1992, 1998). A similar linguistic turn was taking hold in other fields, as structuralism, with its emphasis on mechanisms and foundationalism, gave way to post-structuralism, privileging processes, and interactions, while denouncing the idea of apparatuses.

Within ego psychology, important reassessments of psychoanalysis centered on the work of Charles Brenner, who would go on to redefine ego psychology sometimes in the form of modest "addendums" to Freud's theories, and at others, with sweeping changes. Brenner's writings had a simplicity (for some too simplistic) and clarity that was a far cry, and for some, a welcome relief, from the complex metapsychology of Hartmann and his collaborators. Brenner's style would be characterized by an emphasis on a language that was experience-near and directly tied to clinical work.[7] Brenner's, as well as Arlow's (1969, 1979, 1996) influence, according to Marcus (1999):

> was so great that compromise formation theory swept American ego psychology. It did so in part because it was easier to comprehend than the approaches of Hartmann, Jacobson, Schafer or Loewald, and seemed closer to clinical phenomena. By the 1970s it was dominant. In fact, it captured the term American ego psychology, which became synonymous with conflict and compromise formation [p. 845].

Brenner would move ego psychology away from intellectual and abstruse constructs, particularly energic ones, and define a different ego psychology from that of Hartmann—one, that through its clear postulates, based on observational clinical evidence with sound ecological validity could, as Leon Hoffman (2008) has written, "significantly move the psychoanalytic enterprise towards a more systematic empirical base" (p. 1018) and, by doing so, perhaps succeed where the work of Hartmann, Kris and Lowenstein (1949) had not.

The impetus for one of Brenner's most important reappraisals would be Anna Freud's (1936) monograph, *The Ego and the Mechanisms of Defense*. Specifically, the idea of mechanisms posed problems because, as Brenner (1992) saw it, the term *mechanisms* gave the false impression that there were mental activities and processes of the mind that worked solely and exclusively in the service of defence. It was more accurate and less confusing to appreciate the fact that any mental activity or "ego functioning can be used defensively" (Brenner, 1992, p. 373). Brenner would illustrate his points with elegant and simple examples. Throughout a series of clear and lucid writings spanning more than five decades, he would show again and again (1959, 1982, and 2008) how defences were as varied and extensive as the range of mental activities and could only be defined in terms of their mitigating effects on "unpleasurable" affects such as anxiety and depression.

A second tenet of psychoanalysis that Brenner (1975, 1979, 1992) would challenge revolved around Freud's theory of signal anxiety. In Freud's first theory of anxiety, anxiety was understood as the product of undischarged or improperly discharged tension resulting from the accumulation of libido, which was transformed and given outlet in the form of anxiety. Freud (1894) thought that this toxic damming up of libido, the "sum of excitation", was capable of causing physical damage to the organism. Fenichel (1945a), in an explanation that, given our advances in neuroscience, would seem oversimplified by our standards, described it as follows:

> Where the instinctual need is not adequately satisfied, the chemical alteration connected with the gratification of the drive is lacking and disturbances in the chemistry of the organism result. Undischarged excitement results in an abnormal

quality and quantity of hormones and thus in alterations in
physiological functions [p. 295].

Freud's second theory of anxiety (1926a) revised these energic models with a theory of *signal anxiety*, in which he proposed that anxiety originated when repressed impulses were threatening to emerge
into consciousness and the danger of an intrapsychic nature was
sensed. On these occasions, the ego would send anxiety as a "signal
and prevent such a situation from occurring" (Freud, 1926a, p. 135).
Brenner's (1975, 1979b, 1992) revision would contend that not only
anxiety, but in fact any dysphoric affect (including feelings of guilt,
shame, and misery) could be used as a signal by the ego to bolster
defences. As he put it:

> Anxiety is not the only affect that can trigger defense and
> conflict. Unpleasure of any sort can do so if it is intense enough.
> The unpleasure may be anxiety, but it may also be a different
> variety of unpleasure, what I have proposed to call depressive
> affect [1992, p. 372].

These were not minor addendums to Freud's theories of psychic
functioning but, Brenner's disclaimers notwithstanding (1953a),
they were in fact substantial modifications with far reaching implications, including how the analyst attends to clinical material, what
counts as clinical evidence, and the claims that the analyst can make
about psychic life generally speaking. As an aside, it is important to
keep in mind that disagreements in psychoanalysis and revisions of
psychoanalytic theory and techniques historically lead to splintering within, and defections from, what is considered "mainstream"
psychoanalysis. The "heretics" this time were well known and well
respected analysts whose influence loomed large. Brenner and
Arlow were postulating radical revisions of ego psychology within
the "classical" or "Freudian" perspective and within the bastion of
classical psychoanalysis, as the New York Psychoanalytic Institute
was branded by its critics (Malcolm, 1982).

Considering the history of psychoanalysis and psychoanalytic
institutes, Brenner's revisions were met by critics from within ego
psychology camps with little resistance. Bergmann (1997) believes

that following the controversial discussions between Anna Freud and Melanie Klein (King & Steiner, 1991), a new, more tolerant attitude towards dissent had taken hold in psychoanalysis that allowed space for *the modifier*—an advocate of major changes whose views, nonetheless, did not lead to expulsion or desertion from psychoanalytic institutions, but rather, over time, led to important developments in the field. According to Bergmann (1997), "Modifiers threaten the continuity of psychoanalysis and create controversies but they also keep psychoanalysis alive and are a source of creative ideas. Melanie Klein, Heinz Hartmann, and Heinz Kohut are examples" (p. 82). In this illustrious list Brenner could, in time, claim a rightful place.

Arlow (1972), like Brenner, did not fear being explicit in his criticism of the curriculum in psychoanalytic institutes. For example, he stated in 1972 that, "among the learned disciplines we must be unique in the practice of using basic texts, most of which are 50 years old" (p. 557). He believed there was a cultural lag in all departments of psychoeducation. Gray (1982), borrowing Arlow's term, made similar observations ten years later, noting that there was a "developmental lag" in reference to what he believed was a "reluctance to apply certain ego concepts to the method of psychoanalytic technique" (p. 639).

Brenner, for his part, would continue his revision of psychoanalysis with an eye to clarifying terms and challenging established language, and by 1994 he would spell out what was perhaps his most contentious idea after what he himself described as intensely conflicted feelings about doing so. He would develop a paper in which he concluded that it was time, as Boesky (1994) summarized it, to "seriously consider abandoning the concepts of id, ego, and superego because these terms erroneously separate and disconnect the components of conflict in the human mind" (p. 509). In Brenner's (1994) words:

> My doubts concern the questions whether the facts as we know them today support the theory that there is a structure or agency of the mind, the id, that consists of drive derivatives; that is separate from another agency of the mind, the ego, which has other functions, including defense; and that both are separate from another structure, the superego [p. 474].

It is axiomatic in New York Freudian circles that when Brenner writes a paper, psychoanalysis loses a term! Perhaps a more sympathetic assessment would be that by reducing the use of special terminology, Brenner was able to move psychoanalytic theories forward. *Modern conflict theory*, a term Brenner credits to Abend (2007), would be defined by its emphasis on intrapsychic conflict and compromise formations. The components of a compromise formation are: (1) an *objectionable wish or thought* that is challenged on moral grounds; moreover, these frustrated wishes or thoughts are derivatives of sexual and aggressive wishes originating from childhood; (2) *unpleasure* originating from the strictures that oppose the wish, and a fear of punishment *that results in conflict*; and (3) *attempts at an intrapsychic compromise*, whereby the person attempts to gratify these derivatives of the forbidden childhood wishes, without incurring too much cost in the form of unpleasure.

What is perhaps more radical, and can potentially move Brenner's conflict theory into the mainstream of general psychology, is that the theory accounted for more than just psychopathology, to include the understanding that so-called "normal behaviours" are also a product of conflict and compromise formation. Brenner would go on to carefully provide examples of vocational choices, hobbies, and partner selection among other things, as products of conflict and compromise formation. He noted (1982) that, "[T]here is no sharp line that separates what is normal from what is pathological in psychic life" (p. 150). In fact, the difference between pathology and "normal behaviour" was not the absence of conflict but rather the degree to which the compromise formations allowed for a maximum of gratification with a minimum of unpleasure. In this way, Brenner's ideas challenged Hartmann's (1939a) most accepted tenet of "a conflict free sphere". Brenner (2002) argued:

> Mental health does not mean absence of conflict, much less "neutralization" of drive energies. The idea that conflict is a sign of pathology in mental life, and that in normal adults it is replaced by judgmental repudiation, stems from Freud. Hartmann took it from Freud and carried it to a clearly invalid extreme [p. 336].

A brief clinical example from my own practice will perhaps illustrate how these revised ideas help clarify a wider range of clinical phenomena. The patient, a woman in her early 30s, sought analysis because of anxiety, depression, and difficulties in her relationship with her fiancé. Regarding the latter, she explained that she found it hard to be faithful to him. She scrutinized everyone she met who she regarded in fantasy as a potential suitor, while believing that she could give herself over to whoever showed an interest in her. She brought up as an aside that she also had problems in her career as an actress. She was frequently told by teachers and colleagues that her acting was *stilted*. Although she seemed to consider her problems in her relationship as a separate issue from her problems as an actress, in our analytic work we came to appreciate how these two issues were connected.

The stilted acting was fruitfully understood in terms of compromise formation as follows: in her life, the patient struggled with sexual impulses that she found objectionable, shameful, and guilt-inducing and to which she would respond by becoming self-critical and then depressed. As an actress, when she played roles in which she portrayed women in the throes of passion, she became anxious, worried at an unconscious level that these roles betrayed her own illicit passions. Here, the stilted acting, by no means a pathological symptom, could nonetheless be understood as the result of conflict and compromise formation whereby the patient sought to convince the audience, and more importantly herself, that she was only *acting*, so as not to expose her true personal conflicted feelings. Furthermore, the poor reviews she received, which caused her much distress, served as atonement for her unacceptable feelings, and had the effect of diminishing her unconscious guilt for the gratification, albeit partial, of any sexual wishes that she derived from acting.

To the extent that psychoanalysis is successful, patients change during the course of their treatment. To use Brenner's terminology, they derive more pleasure from *satisfying their pleasure-seeking wishes* without undue unpleasure, as they are less neurotically intrapunitive about having the wishes in the first place. Moreover, since they are less threatened by neurotic anxiety, misery, guilt, or shame about gratifying wishes associated with sexual or aggressive feelings originating in childhood, they are less compelled to automatically defend themselves against what they can now realize are unrealistic beliefs about their consequences. In so doing, they have become more reality-oriented because they are less compelled to confuse moral standards from childhood with adult judgments about the propriety of their desires as adults.

In the course of an analysis, it would be erroneous to think that conflicts disappear, or that defences disappear, or for that matter that defences become more mature. Psychoanalysis does not purport to eliminate intrapsychic conflict. From the viewpoint of modern conflict theory, the wishes that give rise to neurotic symptoms do not change nor are they relinquished. Brenner (2002) acknowledges, and tries to help the patient understand, that wishes of childhood origin persist throughout the person's life. What does change during the course of an analysis and, for that matter, during the course of a life, is the balance between the various intrapsychic components of conflict and the derivative forms in which the wishes of childhood origin are gratified. The shift in their arrangement is what gives rise to more adaptive compromise formations. By "more adaptive" what is meant is that the new compromise formations allow for a refined gratification of wishes, with less unpleasure. In the case briefly discussed above, one could expect that in the course of her analysis, the patient would derive more satisfaction from her acting, experience less inhibition, decrease self-punishment in the form of guilt and depression, and, not least of all, the patient might actually see an improvement in her acting skills.

The seat of therapeutic action in modern conflict theory, therefore, is on the compromise formations as a whole (including elucidating the nature of the wish, the attendant displeasure, issues of morality, and the defences employed). Operating within this framework has the advantage of grounding the analyst's work close to the data reported by the patient, relying very concretely on what is observable in the room with a patient and made evident by the patient's communication and free associations. As the analyst listens to the patient, he makes explicit the connections that had been left only implicit by the patient between one utterance and another. This, in turn, allows the analyst to show the patient the elements of conflict and compromise formation that are laid bare by the material that has unfolded (Arlow, 1993b, 1996). This close process attention has the effect, as Gray (2000) argues, to remove the mystery of where the analyst's formulations come from and reduce the view of the analyst as working far ahead of the patient.

Brenner has described his views on how the analyst works in a number of writings (1976, 1982, 1987, 1996), which can be summarized as follows: as the analyst listens to the patient's material, the analyst develops *conjectures* about the nature of the patient's conflicts and, over time, once the evidence is available, puts forth these conjectures to the patient following *a line of interpretation* that is refined, or discarded and replaced in response to new material made available in the course of treatment. In this process, the use of dreams plays an important role, as do slips of the tongue, associations, induced countertransference experiences, enactments, and any other material that works its way into the hour. Brenner (1982) stressed that dreams were undoubtedly important in analysis, but no more or less so than anything else the patient talks about or otherwise makes known during the analytic hour, including the patient's motivation for reporting a dream. Likewise, transference is ubiquitous and its interpretation is essential in psychoanalysis, but so is the interpretation of extra-transferential material. Strachey's (1934) idea that transference interpretations are the only ones that are *truly* mutative in treatment has been a precept in psychoanalysis that has defied critical scrutiny. As Brenner (1969) contends:

> Some analysts appear to have drawn the conclusion that to be truly effective analytically, an interpretation must be a transference interpretation. Carried to its logical extreme, this means that if, for example, a patient comes to an analytic hour upset because of news of the sudden death or illness of a close relative, what one looks for and interprets to the patient is the transference aspect of his reaction to the news. One looks for evidence of death wishes toward the analyst, or of guilt about such wishes, or of anger that the analyst permitted such a thing to happen, and so on [p. 348].

In short, all evidence of how the patient's mind works is examined and put forth to the patient.

Therapeutic action: four levels of abstraction

Let us return to Smith's (2007) four levels of abstraction in our assessment of therapeutic action underlying modern conflict theory, and consider each level, beginning with the theory of pathogenesis.

A. Theory of pathogenesis

The corpus of Brenner's work, spanning from 1950 to the writing of his memoirs published posthumously in 2009, unequivocally affords a central place to conflict and compromise formation in normal mental functioning as well as in symptom formation. Among these conflicts, the most critical are those over the "sexual and aggressive wishes that characterize mental life during the period from 3 to 6 years of age" (Brenner, 2002, p. 35). These wishes are of primary lasting impact because they elicit the most intense fears of the unpleasures that are associated with their gratification, either in fact or in fantasy. The feared consequences are the situations of danger enumerated by Freud (1926a), and referred to by Brenner (1982) as the calamities of childhood. They include loss of the object, loss of the object's love, castration or bodily damage, "and the various aspects of superego punishment subsumed under the headings of punishment, guilt, remorse, self-injury and penance" (pp. 163–164).

B. Theory of mind

The theory of how the mind works, Smith's (2007) second level of abstraction, can also be subsumed under the term compromise formations. The wishes of childhood origins and the unpleasure associated with them give rise to thoughts, actions, symptoms, fantasies, etc., that are multiply determined and seek to satisfy the different components of conflict. Through compromise formations, a person attempts to obtain as much gratification of these wishes without eliciting too much unpleasure, typically in the form of anxiety or depressive affects, excessive feelings of guilt, or incurring external consequences (such as punishment). Symptoms and mental illness are compromise formations that are less adaptive, while so-called normal behaviours are compromise formations that are more adaptive: where the issue of adaptiveness is relative to the extent to which a compromise formation gratifies a wish with minimum incurrence of unpleasure.

Brenner often stated that his conclusions about the advantages of using conflict and compromise formations to understand and describe mental functioning were drawn from what he deemed to be the "best available relevant data" in the field of psychoanalysis. His preference for this phrasing, "the best available data" (1959, 1982, 1993, 1996, 1998, 2000), indicated an openness to revising his conclusions as called for by more convincing evidence. Thus, he stated (1993):

> There is no such thing as ultimate reality or final truth in sci-
> ence. Every generalisation, whether one calls it an hypothesis,
> a theory, or a law, is never more than provisional. It is the best
> guess one can make at present, and this is as true for physics or
> chemistry as it is for psychoanalysis [p. 1192].

This was also the charitable attitude by which Brenner (1969) asse-ssed Freud's conclusions, which he believed were based on the best data available to him at the time: "[T]he data available from the application of the psychoanalytic method seemed to Freud to be best explained by the structural theory" (p. 49). The latter was a model that Brenner defended as the most fitting for explaining mental phe-nomenon, but which he was willing to revise.

C. Ideas about what the analyst does

This leads to the third level of abstraction enumerated by Smith (2007): namely, what the analyst does. In light of Brenner's theory of pathogenesis and his ideas about how the mind works, it follows that the main aim of the analyst is to make the nature of the patient's compromise formations known to the patient. In Brenner's (1995) words, "The more insight the patient has into the wishes and con-flicts that have given rise to pathological symptoms, the more likely it is that those symptoms will recede or disappear and that normal compromise formations will appear in their place" (p. 415). In the course of the treatment, the analyst listens, forms conjectures about the nature of the patient's conflicts and compromise formations, and communicates these to the patient following a line of interpretation so as to make them as self-evident to the patient as possible.

Ideally, through interpretation, the analyst seeks to address the components of the compromise formation *in toto*. In actual practice, however, these different components are interpreted and analysed as they surface separately in the course of any treatment and as their relation to other components of the compromise formation become clear. At times the focus of the analyst's interpretation will be on defence, at other times it will be on anxiety and its origins; and at other times still there will be a focus on reconstructing and elucidating the wishes and thoughts of childhood origin. The patient's affects, their quality, intensity, their congruity and incongruity with content, provide critical information about the nature and equilibrium of the components of the compromise formations at which the patient has arrived. Ideally, the relationship between these components are delineated and used to help the patient understand how his or her mind works, the ways in which the patient obfuscates or avoids this self-understanding, and the motivations he or she has for doing so.

And herein lies a fundamental difference between Benner's app-roach and that taken by Paul Gray (1996, 2000), a contemporary ego psychologist (see Portuges & Hollander, 2011, Chapter Four in this volume). For Gray, the childhood drive derivatives that Brenner considers an essential part of every compromise formation are like an air balloon submerged under water, and kept there by the oppos-ing force of the ego in the form of resistance. Once the resistance is removed, the repressed id contents will surface without a need for genetic reconstruction (the means by which the analyst elucidates, to the extent possible, the nature of the wishes of childhood origins and drive derivatives). Gray (1996) writes:

> Since my theoretical stance is one of choosing to believe that there are no unconscious id forces "drawing down" mental elements from above, my working hypothesis, on which my technique depends, is that consistent, detailed analysis of the resistances against specific drive derivatives will *itself* allow gradual, analytically sufficient ego assimilation of the warded off mental elements as they are able to move less fearfully into consciousness [p. 101].

In this respect, the role of the analyst is circumscribed to a focus on defence. By contrast, Brenner (1976, 1982) believed that the analyst needed to formulate conjectures about childhood drive derivatives and communicate these to the patient as interpretations. From Brenner's perspective, one cannot assume that the drive deriva-tives will surface on their own. Just as it is important for the ana-lyst to develop conjectures about the patient's anxiety and defences, so it is also important for the analyst to develop conjectures about the origins of the drive derivatives that elicited the anxiety being defended against. These conjectures are refined over time, based on the information that becomes available in the course of treatment, as well as on the analyst's theories of normal childhood development, understanding of Oedipal issues, and other dynamics.

D. The analyst as a person

Finally there is the issue of the analyst as a person effecting change. In reference to the personal qualities of the analyst as an agent of change, the issue of countertransference inevitably becomes germane. In addition to Brenner's views on countertransference, I will discuss his views on the therapeutic alliance and on the authority of the analyst.

To begin with, Brenner gave no special weight to countertransference in the psychoanalytic process (the term only comes up in five of more than 90 papers that he published), and most of what he has to say on the subject was contained in a brief but incisive paper titled, "Countertransference as compromise formation" (Brenner, 1985). The central argument in this paper, which emanates directly from Brenner's ideas on transference, can be summarized as follows: compromise formation is a ubiquitous part of mental functioning. Like the patient, an analyst's thoughts, behaviours, and even choice of profession are the products of conflict and compromise formations. When the balance in the components of the analyst's compromise formations becomes disturbed in his or her work with a patient, we refer to it as countertransference. As you might expect, some patients will upset this balance, at which point the analyst benefits from trying to understand how and why, using introspection, consultation with colleagues, and/or personal analysis. Brenner does not argue with the commonly held view that countertransference can inform treatment. However, he disagrees with the idea that countertransference is, as Kleinians would have it, "the ego function that makes analysis possible" (Brenner, 1985, p. 156) or for that matter with those who make the concept *synonymous* with intuition or empathy.

Brenner (1979b) was wary of the notion that a therapeutic alliance was a *precondition* for a successful analysis. He believed that too strong an emphasis on the establishment and maintenance of a therapeutic alliance was in fact contraindicated on the grounds that it posed a similar problem to that posed by not analysing the so-called unobjectionable positive transference (Freud, 1912b). The idea of enlisting the patient's cooperation by appealing to his or her rational, reasonable, mature part in order to overcome resistance neglects the complex mixture of ambivalent feelings with which every patient approaches treatment—an ambivalence that Brenner believed was best analysed and not influenced by suggestion or manipulation. Furthermore, as Abend (1996) put it, "[W]hat passes for a benign, positive, and productive transference attitude, rather than function-ing to help overcome resistance, as Freud had believed, actually serves as a crucial resistance against the emergence of important analytic material" (pp. 219–220).

The patient's so-called cooperativeness is no less important to understand than is his or her lack thereof. For example, in a paper on sibling rivalry, I (Christian, 2007) attempted to show how one analysand's *cooperativeness* in treatment represented a critical famil-ial re-enactment of her need to be a model child, determined by an unconscious fantasy of being a replacement child; that is, one who could compensate her parents for the loss of their only son. The ana-lyst's humaneness, a core value stressed by the literature on ther-apeutic alliance, is made explicit through the process of the work itself and over time, where the analyst communicates an interest in all and everything that the patient is feeling and thinking.

Perhaps the most discordant position, as it relates to the per-son of the analyst as an agent of change, has to do with Brenner's views on the issue of the authority of the analyst. This is an espe-cially polemical issue in a zeitgeist that emphasizes egalitarianism, co-construction of meaning, a two-person psychology, and where the term *client* has replaced the term *patient*, ostensibly avoiding the latter term's pejorative connotations. Brenner's position, most clearly articulated in his 1996 paper "The Nature of Knowledge and the Limits of Authority in Psychoanalysis", is that the analyst, by virtue of training, experience, and personal analysis, is in a "much better position to understand the nature and origin of a patient's conflicts than is the patient" (p. 26).

Critics, particularly those from the hermeneutic tradition, such as Mitchell (1998), argue that the analyst can never make claims to know whatever is in the patient's mind because these contents "are knowable both to the analyst and to the patient *only* through an active process of composing and arranging them" (p. 17, italics added). The mind, Mitchell (1998) believes, is "understood only through a process of interpretive construction" (p. 16). As Eagle (2003) points out, there is certainly value in Mitchell's position to the extent that it challenges authoritarian notions in psychoanalysis, according to which the analyst is seen as having "virtually infallible access to the Truth about the patient's mind" or that there is, in fact, "one canonical truth to be arrived at" (p. 415). However, as Eagle elaborates, "[I]t is one thing to reject the claims of infallible access to the truth about the patient's mind and another thing to reject altogether the possibility that one can reliably infer certain truths about the patient's mind … as if there were no stable organization prior to and independent of these interactions [those between patient and analyst]" (p. 416). Brenner (1996) contended that the conjectures at which the analyst arrives are provisional and subject to revision as the available evidence supports their correctness or fails to do so. However, the patient could not be expected to be the final arbiter of their correctness.

Critiques of modern conflict theory

Some, including Boesky (1994), have argued that conflict theory is simply another level of abstraction adding little to the utility already afforded by the structural theory of id, ego, and superego. Boesky (1994) argues that the components of compromise formations, drive derivatives, unpleasurable affects, defences, and moral considerations are just as much "psychic structures as are the three major agencies of the Freudian psychic apparatus, but they are on a lower level of abstraction" (p. 511). Conflict and compromise formations are abstractions, undoubtedly, but carry with them less of the anachronistic baggage that encumbered the meanings of id, ego, and superego (themselves translations that departed significantly from Freud's original terms in German). As Holt (1989) points out, these structures are "extremely difficult to use without reifications or personification" (p. 211), which he believes leads clinicians to "lose sight of the fact that in the end it is the patient who talks, dreams, and acts in the real world, not his ego, superego, or id, or some coalition of these soul-like entities" (p. 211).

Other criticisms of Brenner's model are captured succinctly by Ellman (2005), and have to do with an alleged lack of emphasis that modern conflict theory places on the relationship between analyst and analysand: "Brenner's version of analysis does not focus on the analytic relationship but rather stresses interpretive efforts" (p. 463), thus, encouraging in the analyst a narrow and unyielding focus on conflict and compromise formations at the expense of the analyst's empathic attunement with the patient. Ellman (2005) argues "[I]f the analyst is consistently concerned with what is the unexpressed aspect of the hypothetical compromise formation, the analyst is distinctly in the wrong analytic space" (p. 462). Bolognini (2001) espouses a similar position:

> [T]he analyst's exclusive focus on "what lies behind" overt mental contents can be just as unproductive, resulting in a loss of contact with the vast part of the patient—the very part with which the analyst is engaged in the process of gaining access to deeper, unexplored areas [p. 455].

Ellman goes on to reason that it is only when a patient can trust the analyst that transference will make itself manifest and then amenable to interpretation; and that, if the analyst is listening for elements of conflict and compromise formation in the patient's material, then the analyst cannot create a state of mind that allows him or her to experience the patient's emotions more fully, a critical precondition for analytic trust. Ellman's viewpoint is a valuable caution against the futility of working too schematically with patients. Yet his ideas also overlap with the views of those who give emphasis to the therapeutic alliance as a *precondition* for treatment (Greenson, 1965; Zetzel, 1956, 1965). In both cases, modern conflict theory would regard the lack of a therapeutic alliance, or the lack of trust, as manifestations of the transference that needs to be analysed. Yet, to do so does not and should not disable the analyst's capacity for engaged and empathic attunement. The notion that the analyst's listening for conflict and compromise formation is *by necessity* experienced by the patient as a lack of involvement with the patient's affective state, discounts the equally plausible scenario that this stance in the analyst can be experienced by the patient, over time, as an attitude of caring, dedicated and involved listening, in which case what determines one reaction as compared to the other has to do with patient's history and transference. Many, myself included, would argue that it is *only* by listening through a particular theoretical framework that the analyst is able to reach relatively unavailable aspects of the patient's psychic life and in turn help the patient understand him or herself more fully.

Lastly, modern conflict theory has also been criticized on the basis of oversimplifying mental functioning. If everything is conflict and compromise formation, then what is left? The idea that modern conflict theory oversimplifies mental functioning is, in my view, an oversimplification of modern conflict theory, considering the infinite ways in which a person can experience pleasure and unpleasure and the infinite ways in which unpleasure can be defended against. As Smith (2008) points out, when carried to its logical extent, all pleasure, unpleasure, defences, and self punishment are "themselves compromise formations, each in turn made up of the individual components of conflict" (p. 59). This may account for Brenner's belief that conflict and the need for compromise formations is never exhausted, potentially making analysis an infinite regress. As Smith (2008) puts it,

> Brenner's modifications, then, while eliminating the more abstract terminology and in this sense, simplifying the theory of mind, make the analyst's task considerably more complex, as he or she is no longer able to rest on the identification of id, ego, or superego functioning in their separate domains [p. 59].

Some concluding thoughts

The history of psychoanalysis shows evidence of a kind of religious fervour with which psychoanalysts have clung to their ideas, a fervour that generated a dangerous orthodoxy that arbitrated what was, and what was not, psychoanalysis, as well as who could, and who could not, call him or herself a *real* analyst. How does one judge objectively whether Adler's practice was or was not psychoanalytic?—or that of Jung or Rank? Although in some important respects we have come a long way from such a constraining orthodoxy and from the politics of exclusion (Richards, 1999), it is not difficult to find its vestiges within and between psychoanalytic institutes. So much so, that even "a giant of American psychoanalysis" (Smith, 2008, p. 705) like Brenner would, nonetheless, be uncertain as to whether he should voice his conviction about what he believed was the outlived usefulness of the structural theory. In light of such political risks, Brenner showed a type of moral fortitude that may be difficult to appreciate from a vantage point removed from the ideological wars raging in psychoanalysis that persist to this day, marked by rigid theoretical allegiances that inevitably stifle growth. In this respect, I was struck by Brenner's uncharacteristic personal note in which he acknowledged his own conflicts in giving up the structural theory and the amount of time it took for him to express his revisions openly. In one of his last papers, Brenner (2002) disclosed:

> It was no easy matter for me to consider giving up the famil-iar and useful concepts of id, ego, and superego. It took me a dozen years to convince myself that it is valid and useful to do so. Even then, I doubt if I should have expressed this con-clusion so directly in the public forum without encouragement from my colleagues, Drs Yale Kramer and Arnold D. Richards (Brenner, 1994, p. 473, fn.). It has become evident to me dur-ing the course of the years that have elapsed since I published my first paper on the subject (Brenner, 1994) that most of my analytic colleagues are today as reluctant to discard the con-cepts under discussion as I myself was for many years. I am convinced that my own reluctance was due to the continuing influence of conflicts arising from childhood sexual and aggres-sive wishes. It was important to me to continue to believe in the concepts of ego, superego, and id, even in the face of what seems to me now to be convincing evidence that those concepts constitute an invalid theory [pp. 415–416].

Among those analysts who currently subscribe to modern conflict theory, few and only the most insular would dispute the impor-tance of attending to countertransference as a potential source of information about the patient; and to ruptures and repairs of the therapeutic alliance (without needing to elevate the construct to the status of an orienting principle in treatment); and to Oedipal *as well as* pre-Oedipal development.

The history of ego psychology makes it clear that psychoanaly-sis has nothing to gain, and much to lose, by remaining insulated and divorced from other branches of science. The political charade behind the so-called evidenced-based treatments notwithstanding, it is critical that psychoanalysis, through interdisciplinary work, engage in research that can continue to expand its unparallelled explanatory value of human behaviour and mental functioning. To this end, the clear language of modern conflict theory readily lends itself to the formulation and testing of basic tenets about psychic life.

In my experience, the advantages that modern conflict theory brings to the practice of psychoanalysis rest upon the ways in which this approach orients the analyst in listening to, and making sense of, material that is part and parcel of every clinical hour: wishes, thoughts, feelings, the unpleasure related to these, and the infinite ways in which a person attempts to reduce unpleasure, all the while remaining unaware of how said unpleasure ties in with other elements to form part of long-standing conflicts and compromise formations. By communicating this understanding to the analysand (i.e., by interpreting), the analyst manages to "destabilize the equilibrium of forces in conflict" (Arlow & Brenner, 1990, p. 679) and by doing so, throws into bold relief the components of compromise formations. In the process, there is a broadening in the range of the patient's awareness of the essence of his conflicts, the irrational nature of his anxieties, and the outworn need and usefulness of his automatic defences. It is this process of increasing insight that, to my mind, is mutative in psychoanalysis—an insight that expands a patient's options and brings his mode of operating in the world closer in line with the reality of his *present time* and the exigencies of his social milieu.

In all, there is a clarity that modern conflict theory brings to clinical practice—a clarity that I believe exists because, in some essential respects, the model reflects, as Brenner was apt to say, how the mind works.

Notes

1. The other one was Heinz Hartmann's (1939a) *Ego Psychology and the Problem of Adaptation*.
2. George Klein and Robert Holt would go on to forcefully challenge the scientific basis of psychoanalysis, sparking, according to historian Nathan Hale (1995), the "crisis" of psychoanalysis in the United States.

3. "Psychology, too, is a natural science. What else can it be?" (Freud, 1938b, p. 282).

4. See Shulman (1990) for an important critique of this position.

5. Research is not required by candidates to complete their analytic training (Shulman, 1990).

6. Notwithstanding these dire assessments of the current relevance of Hartmann's work, his ideas, especially the emphasis placed on the "average expectable environment", are clearly represented, even if not always acknowledged, in attachment theory, and most current theories of child development in which the child's relation to his or her immediate environment, particularly the mother, is emphasized as a key determinant in the infant's growth and maturation. In a re-appraisal of Hartmann's work as it relates to adaptive processes in child development, Linda Mayes (1994) stressed how Hartmann's ideas "turned the psychoanalytic eye back to the experiential world and the individual's capacities to cope appropriately and advanta-geously with his environment" (p. 13). In her view (Mayes, 1994), Hartmann's theory of adaptation has the potential to bring "psy-choanalysis close not only to a general theory of psychology, but … to a more integrated theory of development and would allow psychoanalysis to become a 'general developmental psychology'" (p. 17).

7. It is estimated that Brenner's classic book, *An Elementary Textbook of Psychoanalysis* (1953b), has sold over one million copies (Stepansky, 2010).

CHAPTER SIX

The interpretive act: returning freedom and agency to a beleaguered ego

Alan P. Spivak

> A layman will no doubt find it hard to understand how pathological disorders of the body and mind can be eliminated by "mere" words.
>
> —Freud (1905c, p. 283)

> What the patient needs is not a rational reworking of unconscious infantile fantasies; what the patient needs is a revitalization and expansion of his own capacity to generate experiences that feel real, meaningful, and valuable.
>
> —Mitchell (1993, p. 24)

Freud introduced interpretation into psychoanalysis as the central agent for deciphering and communicating the meaning of dreams (1900). Once he realized that the dynamic structure of neurosis is similar to that of dreams, Freud extended its purview, making it the primary vehicle to unlock the unconscious meaning of any and all analytical material. By this move, interpretation was elevated to the status of *primus inter pares* for effecting psychic growth by psychoanalytic means. The phrase "to analyse" now was synonymous with "to interpret". For most analysts today, interpretive activity remains primary, elemental, and indispensable. But in some current writings, interpretation has lost pride of place to factors in the analytic process that once were considered ancillary or preparatory. This alternative view holds that various emotional experiences mediated through relationship are the primary facilitators of change, and that insight derived via interpretation is either unnecessary or, at best, icing on the cake. At the extreme of this position resides scepticism about the power of "mere" words, at least those of the analyst, to influence psychopathology. The scepticism echoes that of the lay persons to whom Freud alluded in the above quotation.

In this chapter, I argue that to polarize, as agents of change, interpretation with emotional or relational experience is to create a false dichotomy. Indeed, interpretation is the vehicle most likely to elicit the vitality and meaningfulness that Mitchell (1993), a major figure in the relational movement, opts for in the above quotation. But even more, I propose that interpretation sets in motion a process that fosters the psychic integration of such experience. Devoid of integration, poignant emotional moments, at best, linger in the mind as raw memories. They do not necessarily transform into stabilizing sources of ongoing inner vitality, the *sine qua non* of structural change. Without interpretation to elicit them, through analysis of defence, many emotional moments would likely never occur in the consulting room. Furthermore, without interpretation to unfold their meaning, many that do take place would offer a cathartic release but would not evolve into psychic growth. Let us remember that it was the limitations of cathartic methods that inspired Freud to invent psychoanalysis.

The problem of insight

Viewed historically, the first purpose assigned to interpretation was the attainment of cognitive insight (Freud, 1900). This conceptualization, soon rejected as sterile, gradually evolved into the term "emotional insight" (Fenichel, 1941a; Martin, 1952; Richfield, 1954; Valenstein, 1981). In my view, neither concept sufficiently captures the complexity of what takes place in the mind of the analysand upon hearing the words of the analyst. The achievement of psychic transformation cannot be divorced from the process in which it is embedded. It is neither cognitive nor emotional insight alone, but the experience of being listened to and understood by another, in a way that is completely unique, that promotes growth. The question to be addressed here is what constitutes this uniqueness.

"Psychoanalytically" evoked psychic development, as I shall elaborate, is a distinctive achievement, tied inexorably to a method that has parallels, but no equivalency, either in ordinary life experience or in other treatment modalities. It begins with the analysand recognizing diverse and opposing constituents of his mind being brought together in the mind of another. It is this that then allows the fissures to be brought together (i.e., integrated) in the analysand's own mind. This initial stage in a complex process spawns a powerful experience of immediacy which, in and of itself, provokes growth. One's experience of self, to a degree, is enlarged at once! Similarly, symptoms of anxiety and depression may be relieved immediately, even if temporarily. When all goes well, the working through process that follows, itself furthered by interpretive activity, consolidates the gain, fostering an ongoing dialectic of reflection and elaboration that can be continued indefinitely in self-analysis.

Over time a variety of gains, of various proportions, derive from effective interpretations, including: (1) an experience of a more integrated self; (2) diminishment of anxiety; (3) reduction of omnipotence; (4) emotional containment; and (5) an increase in reflectiveness. The mental reorganization behind these observables operates silently and out of sight (see also Arlow 1979; Loewenstein 1951).

Goals of analysis

In today's marketplace numerous modalities abound for treating symptoms of mental dysfunction, each heralding successes. For psychoanalysis to justify its therapeutic relevance, given the time and expense it requires, it must bring something more to the table. Of course we feel that it does. Psychoanalysis distinguishes itself by addressing the fundament underlying symptoms that is left untouched when the latter are relieved by other means. This remainder is the state of alienation that is derivative of unconscious fantasies defended against by splits and repressions. Analysis, uniquely, heals by fostering easier access among the various constituents of mind. In so doing, it increases the capacity to bear experience without relying on excessive defence. Alienation gradually is replaced by an expanded sense of personal agency; an elasticity of the personality; and a psychosomatic authenticity. These gains combine to relieve a beleaguered ego, experienced as overwhelmed by forces beyond its control.

In essence, experiencing one's inner life more fully and bearing the knowledge replaces disavowing aspects of self and experience. Put still another way, analysis strengthens the ego's capacity to face inner truth and tolerate psychic pain, supported by another who, to a degree, simultaneously shares the experience non-intrusively. Analysis provides the optimal opportunity for a person to stretch himself to his maximum capacities, to feel the fullness of emotional life, and to increase freedom and creativity of thought.

Complications for a theory of analytic action

Any attempt to theorize analytic action is challenged by the fact that, often, change takes place that does not fit the proposed theory. "Spontaneous" symptom relief or emotional reliving may occur without insight, simply on the basis of freely associating to a relatively silent analyst. Or an analysand may achieve his own insights, with the analyst serving as a background presence. Winnicott (1968a) termed this analytic function "holding". Poland (2000) describes it as "witnessing". Sometimes highly intellectual insight, despite the bad press it consistently receives within analytic theorizing, is followed by improvement. We may valorize transference interpretations, but some patients improve when mostly extra-transference interpretations are given. Whether those of us who hold a scientific bent like it or not, theories of analytic action are *not* forged in the crucible of rigorous scientific investigation. Rather they derive from an individual analyst's theory of psychopathology along with his personal experience, which includes trial and error. A theory is not confirmed just because others hold it. It is simply a shared belief. When it is held by a large number of colleagues it constitutes a belief system. Neither beliefs nor belief systems, however alluring, constitute scientific validation. In what follows I offer my understanding, i.e., belief, pertaining to several key contributions to analytic action, with emphasis on the pivotal role played by interpretation.

Potential space

The core of the analytic process consists in the analyst creating and maintaining an ambiguity that is particularly reflected in the transference. The ambiguity constitutes an intermediate area of experience requiring of the analysand a capacity for transitional relatedness. The patient is asked to suspend disbelief and to deal with a paradoxical reality in which his experience of the transference is both real and unreal, both past and present. The patient must be able to tolerate, sometimes briefly, often for considerable time, not knowing the reality of his experience. In Freudian language we denote the phenomenon by the temporal term regression (Freud, 1900). In the Winnicottian (1968b) domain we stamp it with a spatial metaphor, potential space.

In order for the ambiguity to be maintained, the analyst must do nothing to reduce it. Despite internal pressures that inevitably emerge in every analysis to foreclose the space, by giving affirmation, direct signs of love, advice, or validation, and despite pressures from the patient, commonly operating through projective identification, the analyst must himself bear the ambiguity until he is able to achieve understanding and then convey it to the patient.

That the ambiguity of the analytic space is essential to the process and must be preserved at all cost can best be understood by contrasting it with the formation of symptoms and pathological character. These develop to bind excessive anxiety or dysphoria. Once established, they are as if frozen. Similarly, the person is frozen in time as primary process merges past, present, and future into the timelessness of the unconscious, holding them there, as though with the gravitational force of a black hole. As the analytic process unfolds, the analysand is returned, through his associations and enactments in the transference, to an approximation of the original state of mind that stimulated the pathological resolutions. The interplay of regression and ambiguity, two attributes of potential space, puts in doubt much of what the analysand has long held fast as certainties. During the course of the work, the repetition compulsion activates the internal world of the patient, requiring unconscious fantasies, drives, and internal objects to be externalized into the transference and the external world. We recognize psychoanalytic structural change by means of the interpretation and working through of these key constituents of mind.

To summarize, by combining notions of Freud and Winnicott, one can say that analysis relocates the symptom into potential space where fixed cathexes can be remobilized to allow access to the playful, paradoxical qualities of primary process. The sequence is not without its hazards, in that an already overwhelmed ego may be re-traumatized on the path to repair. That the analysand hovers between trauma and repair while on the couch is an unavoidable risk within the process.

The interpretive act

The interpretive moment parallels the mother living the baby's experience and meeting its "first gesture" with recognition (Winnicott, 1941). The words, the emotion, the expressiveness must reflect that the analyst knows and feels first hand where the patient lives. Ultimately the intrapsychic impact of analytic action resides in the realization that one is being recognized and understood by another. It entails the patient experiencing through the interpretation that the analyst has fully immersed himself, surely in the patient's conscious experience, but even more in his psychic reality, i.e., his unconscious. Two processes of empathic immersion intertwine to promote the analyst's lived knowledge of the patient's unconscious: first, projective identification (Klein, 1946) and secondly, trial identification (Fliess, 1942). The latter distinguishes itself from the former in that the analyst matches the patient's communications with elements from his own history. The analyst finds in himself an emotional experience analogous to that of the patient. Unlike projective identification there is no "taking in" of another's experience.

When knowledge of the analysand's unconscious is attained through projective identification, sometimes described as the "colonization" of the analyst's mind (Grotstein, 2005), it may produce an identity diffusion that can be difficult for the analyst to bear. De M'Uzan (1994) uses the term "paradoxical thought" in response to the patient's intrusion into his psyche. Though the analyst is at high risk he is also positioned with optimal mutative potential. As Godbout (2005) suggests, "The interpretation made at such moments has all the more chance of reaching the patient since it will have, so to speak, emerged from her, that is, from the infiltration of the analyst's mental functioning" p. 83).

How the analyst uses his mental and emotional resources, however derived, and communicates them to the patient is strikingly important. The interpretation must be an authentic response. An interpretation deriving from either of the two sources of empathic immersion differs from the transmission of knowledge derived from other means, such as theoretical resonance, in that its essence is both explanatory and revelatory. In this immersion the analyst has no authority or expertise outside his capacity to transport himself to another's psychic reality, to bear what he experiences during his visit, to process it through his own psychic system, and then to communicate to the patient what he found. There is a convergence with Bion's (1962a) model of the infant's anxieties being returned to him in a tolerable form through the mother's reverie. The mother must be able to receive, tolerate, and make sense of her infant's raw experiences. When a patient recently said to me "I can see you are suffering too", she accurately perceived that I was deeply moved by being immersed in her painful working-through of mourning the violent death of her husband. As Godbout (2004) puts it "… the event of 'suffering pain' begins by being divided up between two parties. One's experience of pain or frustration is suffered by the other, and progressively will this dynamic be internalized" (p. 1130). This is conveyed by tone of voice and gesture.

Loewald (1975) as well emphasized the vital role played by the analyst's emotional resources in giving the patient access to his own: "Interpretations of this kind explicate for the patient what he then discovers to have always known somehow, but in the absence of its recognition and explication by the analyst such knowledge could not be acknowledged and grasped" (p. 286).

Conventional explanations result in *knowledge of* self but not in *being* one's self. For an interpretation to be used it must stimulate an admixture of surprise, relief, injury, excitement, and some degree of *immediate* recognition. "Ordinary" knowledge often requires some amount of work to comprehend. Analytically derived recognition differs in that, at the point of acceptance, even when blocked initially by massive resistance, it is experienced as a self-evident truth. Psychic work both precedes and follows this moment. I shall elaborate on this point later. The immediacy of the changed and highly charged relation to oneself has inspired such moments with the familiar designations of "Aha" or "Eureka". The realization of correctness or truth, the intrapsychic component, typically stands out in bold relief from the interpersonal influence that mediated it. When it does not, the latter must be addressed so that suggestive influence does not supersede the experience of psychic truth.

While immersion in the analysand's internal world is essential, no less essential is the alterity, the other-mindedness, of the analyst. It is the associations having been processed and integrated through the latter's unique and separate psychic system, which of necessity slightly alters their meaning, that makes the recognition both unique and familiar. It is the *alterity* of the analyst that enhances the element of surprise so essential to vitalizing the experience and elevating it beyond a simple mirroring. As the analyst organizes the material through his own metaphor, he provides a new experience not simply a new edition (Schafer, 1983). The analysand then makes creative use of the analyst's interpretive metaphor. A bit of anxiety accompanies the process. LaMothe (2001) describes this aspect of the process as paralleling a certain aspect of play with a baby, which as he states it, is "… as though an unselected object is presented to a baby, it awakens and evokes" (p. 326).

The experience of gaining direct knowledge of something that is simultaneously new and old is analogous to being told the answer to a puzzle or the secret of a magic trick, in that it appears so astonishingly obvious once revealed, that often one is awestruck by not having solved it before without help. This is because the solution, namely a "truth", was always there lurking in plain sight. It is exactly this that Freud (1905b) had in mind when he said that knowing is re-knowing, adding that, "The finding of an object is in fact a re-finding of it" (p. 221).

When the insight (truth, recognition, gestalt) has emerged from a resonance within the analyst, whose voice and tone reflect that he has heard various influences within the patient, each making its own claim for notice, and that he has integrated them through his own psychic system, an emotional connectedness between the members of the dyad can reach extraordinary depth and poignancy for each.

In a similar vein, it is paradoxical that the analyst best expresses his emotional availability to the patient, through no self-conscious effort other than offering his understanding.

By contrast, if the analyst speaks from some place in himself that is not the result of his unconscious being in tune with that of the other as, for example, when speaking from application of a theoretical premise, the recipient hears but a lecture. He may be narcissistically wounded or, at the other pole of response, symptomatically relieved, but he is not authentically touched, that is, he does not experience a direct sense of truth. He comprehends, but he is not enlivened as no integration of psyche and soma has been achieved.

The usual response to pain is evasion. The content of the interpretation asks of the analysand to bear the pain. The analyst's tact, emotional availability, and personal integration assist the analysand in doing so. The confluence of these elements leads to an immediate bit of transformation.

While many truths and insights of secondary importance will be gained, over time the core of the patient's past experiences will be recreated and re-enacted with all of the defensive operations that accompany them. Defences are as welcome in the analysis as are feelings and desire. In fact, it is essential that defences and their manifestations in resistances not be short-circuited by the analyst's offer of a more benign relationship (Langs, 1975).

Sander (1992), in speaking of the healing moment, refers to Winnicott's (1971c) description in his book, *Therapeutic Consultations in Child Psychiatry*, where Winnicott uses the term "sacred moments" to describe those critical developmental happenings "when the child becomes aware that another is aware of what he is aware of within himself" (Sander, 1992, p. 583). These single sessions produced changes that lasted for years. Moments paralleling these experiences occur in psychoanalytic treatment as well. In fact, healing moments are everyday occurrences in response to interpretive work. They are reflected in near instantaneous alterations in mood, somatic manifestation, associative fluidity, and interpersonal connectedness, often accompanied by an extraordinarily poignant intimacy between patient and analyst. After such occasions each participant, much as a lover who hates parting, may dread the approaching end of the hour.

To sum up, the ultimate objective of the analysis is that the patient be better able to bear being and knowing himself, which includes, as A. Sandler (1984) discussed, becoming on friendly terms with the various aspects of his inner world. Therefore one must reject any short-term seductions that could preclude this growth and development. As Bion (1970) has claimed, it is only by facing emotional truth that analytic growth can occur. Relational influence alone, devoid of truth that is unfolded by interpretation, or discovered on one's own, permits or promotes evasion. Interpretation, devoid of human sensitivity and compassion, is sterile and cannot be used.

Reflection versus experience

In what is one of the most quoted papers in the psychoanalytic literature outside Freud's writings, Strachey (1934) speaks to the effects of the mutative interpretation, which for him always is made within the transference. Interestingly, only once does he use the word insight to describe the results of the process. His emphasis, in what he calls the first phase, is on the *experience* of the transference and its interpretation, that is, on the effects of being understood by another. For Strachey, the cognitive and the interpersonal go together part and parcel, much as I am suggesting here. However, my emphasis, while including the priority Strachey gives to experiencing the transference, is on the immediate experience of *any* interpretation, including the extra-transference interpretation. In contrast to Strachey, I do not feel it necessary to engage in what he terms the "second phase" of interpretation designed to show external reality to the patient. In my experience, describing the patient's psychic reality in an experience-near way is sufficient to remove the motive for projection, as it reduces the omnipotence of the impulse. Additionally, showing reality to the patient carries with it the undesirable hazard of infantilizing the patient through the assumption that the analyst is the authority on what is reality and what is not.

In my experience, and in contrast to Strachey's view, extra-transference interpretations can have significant mutative effect (see also Couch, 2002). However, there is no doubt that transference interpretations have the advantage of demonstrating *in vivo* that the analysand's words and enactments are *not* destructively omnipotent. I am in agreement with Etchegoyen (1983) that this helps build psychic structure and integration. Furthermore, the interpretation of destructive omnipotence whether it be in the form of envy or hatred enables the object to be "used" (Winnicott, 1969). The interpretation constitutes containment as Bion (1962a) described it and has the advantage over Winnicott's (1968a) silent holding of more overtly and reliably communicating that the analyst has not been made ill or been destroyed. This is so because silent holding sometimes is experienced fantastically or quasi-delusionally as evidence of a destroyed analyst, of passive aggressive retaliation, or of masochistic surrender (see also Bion, 1970). In other words, there is no guarantee how the patient is processing the holding, and consequently, it behoves the analyst to try to understand the analysand's interpretation of it and convey to him in words the unconscious meaning. In fact, the analyst's interpretation of the unconscious meaning of the holding, which may be quite at odds with the conscious experience, can be a key to unlock and work through the patient's defensive compliance to the analytic method. This, in turn, may critically facilitate accessing and working through fundamental elements of the patient's characterological surface falseness, should it exist.

Controversies between the relative merits of immediate experience in the analytic hour versus cognitive insight have been waged periodically throughout the history of psychoanalysis. The classic literature debate occurred between Reik (1948) and Fenichel (1941b). Reik believed that classical technique insufficiently emphasized the role of the analyst's capacity for spontaneity, intuition, and openness to surprise, while Fenichel stressed the importance of a disciplined technique that applies systematically what the analyst already knows. The current emphasis, particularly emanating from modern conflict theory (Abend, 2007; Brenner, 2002; Gray, 1990) and attachment theory (Fonagy, 1999; Target & Fonagy, 1996), is on learning about one's mind and upon reflection as a conscious cognitive process. While I am by no means challenging the value of these goals and accompanying processes, I cannot help but think that the pendulum may have swung too far in the cognitive direction (see also Diamond, 2011, Chapter Ten in this volume). After all, Freud (1912a) recommended to analysts a listening stance in which secondary process mentation is replaced by listening receptively to their unconscious. He similarly recommended that patients be discouraged from engaging in usual modes of cognition: "Always expect to find something new" (Freud, 1912b); moreover, he suggested that analysts refrain from asking the patient to "collect" memories or "think over" something, adding that "Mental activities such as thinking something over or concentrating the attention, solve none of the riddles of a neurosis" (ibid., p. 119).

While one may readily, and for good reason, think of Winnicott as the analyst who stressed playing as a part of the analytic attitude, it is noteworthy that in several technical papers it was Freud who introduced play, playfulness, and the "game" of psychoanalysis. Freud speaks of the "rules of the game" (1913, p. 121) and of the analytic process thereby set in motion as bringing about a "loosening" up of the patient. Freud (1914c) refers to transference as a "playground" (p. 153) in which there is "almost complete freedom" (see Kwawer, 1998).

Suggestion and other technical seductions

Throughout his work Freud was conflicted about the value of suggestion as a technical tool (see Freud, 1905c). On the one hand, he was clearly recommending its use when he urged the physician to apply all the powers of persuasion to influence the patient. He believed that the positive transference was a force for inducing receptiveness to the content of interpretation. Thus, he was in effect using the patient's love for the analyst to gain the status of a beneficent authority, thereby stacking the deck to promote the patient accepting his declarative interpretive statements (Freud, 1912a, p. 106). On the other hand, Freud (1912b, p. 118; 1913, p. 143) ultimately leaned towards discarding personal influence, with the exception of the use of tact, contenting himself to rely more upon the content of interpretation to move the analysis forward. It is noteworthy, however, that Freud never fully abandoned suggestion.

Subsequent to Freud, analytic discourse has become polarized with respect to the value of suggestion and other forms of interpersonal influence mediated by either non-verbal or verbal supportive interventions (Friedman, 1978). In contrast to Freud's ambivalent relation to suggestion, for example, contemporary Freudians, ego-psychologists, and Kleinians are virtually allergic to technical procedures that do not ultimately lead to understanding of unconscious meaning. Cure through suggestion, reassurance, or the current fashion, "analytic love" is suspect (see for example, Bach, 2006). Since these methods can so easily and dramatically elicit emotion, the sheer drama and, often, interpersonal closeness, can mislead an analyst into believing that resistance has been overcome and lasting change will follow. Since I believe that the ultimate objective of the analysis is that the patient is better able to bear *knowing, experiencing*, and *reflecting* upon the fullest range of his psychic life, I too reject the allure of these seductions. They short-circuit the process that requires of the analysand to tolerate the widest spectrum of his internal world.

Suggestion operates by the analyst installing himself in the super-ego of the analysand. From that lofty and biased position it reinforces defence rather than lifts repression or nurtures sublimation, an indicant of psychic growth. In current practice, given the attention paid to the primacy of splitting and dissociation within psychopathological states, we might say that suggestion dominates one component of the mind at the expense of part or parts of the personality from which the ego maintains distance. Whatever gains may be achieved, either temporarily or even long term, a splitting in the personality is reinforced and rigidified. Accordingly, the patient pays the piper a hefty sum.

If, for example, love is offered to the patient in the form of directly telling the patient that the analyst does care, value, or feels love for him, self-condemnation is diminished and narcissism is feted. But since the process reinforces the patient's defensive system (i.e., resistances) and is largely devoid of conscious awareness and reflection, the patient's alienation from body and self is maintained. Love or support when given directly acts like a balm or a drug. It promotes positive transference while typically attenuating conscious access to negative transference and requiring of the analysand neither mourning nor facing unpleasantness. Since psychic work is not required, ego mastery of difficult-to-bear experience is not achieved. An offer of love detached from interpretive understanding transports rather than transforms. That is, it deflects attention from psychic pain, allowing a vulnerability to remain unnoticed and unrepaired. From this vantage point cure through love, "transference cure", is a countertransference cure. The direct application of love as a clinical technique must be distinguished from an analyst's genuinely loving feelings, which may emerge spontaneously in the course of analytic work, as a facet of appreciating and empathizing intimately with the inner world of another. In fact interpretive understanding conveyed through the medium of these feelings can have an enhanced mutative potency.

Analytic neutrality

An essential element of therapeutic action is the analyst lending his even-handedness towards the inner life of the analysand, who has lost or never attained his own. The absence is reflected in symptoms and rigid traits of character. One part of the mind, perhaps the super-ego or a bad object, has achieved dominion over others. In effect, the analyst helps the analysand either to restore, or to create for the first time, objectivity with respect to his internal world. The result is an increased capacity to bear psychic pain and subsequently to reflect upon his mind.

It follows from this point of view that neutrality and analytic empathy, often posed as antagonists, actually are convergent analytic stances. This is so because empathy involves hearing in the analysand's communications the various "voices" in the inner world which simultaneously make claims upon him. Neutrality, for its part, involves a willingness to listen to all claims without siding in the conflict. When an analyst loses his neutrality, he simultaneously has lost his empathy. In writing of generative empathy, Schafer (1959) seems to refer to a similar process. As he states, understanding leads to an immersion in the inner world of another and is a new object. This definition differs from Kohut's empathy in that it includes the total situation of the inner world, an ability to hold the multiple self states, conflicts and points of view of the patient's inner world and convey it or an aspect of it, including what the patient can use. Bolognini (1997) also considers empathy, which he distinguishes from "empathism" (p. 279), to be an immersion in more than just the patient's self experience. Empathy experiences the tugs from within a larger spectrum of another's psychic life, including inner objects in conflict.

I am in accord with Etchegoyen (1983) who suggests that when an analyst loses his neutrality, through the pulls of the countertransference, as is likely to happen at various moments in every analysis, "… his eventual interpretation not only corrects the misunderstanding, but also 'cures' the analyst of his momentary countertransferential conflict. This is so because every time one interprets, one recovers oneself as an analyst in so far as one returns to the patient what in fact belongs to him" (p. 448).

Godbout (2005) helps to clarify what is essential about analytic neutrality by linking it to intrapsychic change:

> To us, as to many others, this mutation of mental functioning is what specifies a truly psychoanalytic approach in comparison to other psychotherapies. We do not want the analysand to come out of analysis with yet another internal object, even the "good" one, which had always been missed (but which would be only temporarily opposed to the introjects already in place and would end up "taking over" as soon as the analyst were no longer available to "correct" the patient's emotional experiences). We do not want to encumber the patient's ego with yet another ideal governing her life and maintaining conditions of dissatisfaction. These are all factors of alienation from one's subjective desire and freedom, to the profit of an other. Instead, we wish to promote an aptitude of the ego to symbolically integrate on its own what affects it—thus making the patient an analysand rather than an "analyzed," a nuance that is more than just politically correct when its full meaning is restored. The principle of the analyst's neutrality, rightly criticized when it pretends to be absolute, conserves in our view its value and even its necessity in relation to this project of dis-alienation [p. 81].

When the analyst "lives" the patient's conflictedness through his countertransference, and then reflects upon it, he is maximally positioned to identify what the patient cannot yet bear knowing (see also Porter, 2011, Chapter Nine in this volume). The ensuing interpretation enables the analysand more fully to experience the richness of his mind and his emotions as they are expressed in various symbols and disguises.

If the analyst validates the patient's perception of a significant other instead of waiting to understand the unconscious dynamic behind the perception, regardless of the patient's initial response, the analyst makes things more difficult because he is siding with only one side of the intrapsychic conflict. As Etchegoyen et al. (1987) remind us,

... in the first place no explicit statement can solve an unconscious conflict; secondly, because by showing himself as a "good" superego the analyst is perpetuating the conflict; and thirdly, because the patient will perceive the analyst's error and, in consequence, his poor professional performance will perpetuate the vicious circle in which she moves [p. 58].

As Reich (1933) noted, interpretations have an injurious component since they sting the analysand's narcissism by reminding him that he is not fully in control of his mind. I would add that an interpretation also threatens to be narcissistically wounding because it requires acceptance of the analyst's alterity. For this reason, typically the more fragile patient, as well as the less fragile at especially vulnerable moments, will benefit from an interpretive stance which begins with an affirmative statement showing the patient that the analyst, having aligned his perspective with his own, can see that his behaviour makes good sense, that it serves adaptation (see Schafer, 1983). At such moments the analyst is allowing a "therapeutic symbiosis" (Searles, 1973). But if the analyst uses this line of interpreting exclusively and does not eventually move to anxiety producing interpretations that reach to the core of the analysand's difficulties, splitting will be encouraged, mourning avoided, and the analyst will become problematically installed as an ideal object rather than a good one.

The experience of receiving a "good" interpretation

A 16-year-old girl, who at the age of five had traumatically witnessed her babysitter being molested by a burglar who had broken into her home through a bedroom window, was being seen in psychoanalytic psychotherapy. While, for a time, the child's subsequent development appeared to proceed normally, as an early adolescent, the bright girl suddenly developed a learning disorder as her grades dropped to barely passing. One day she was telling me that in recent months, whenever she sat in her room trying to study, she would soon find herself staring out of the window daydreaming. When I asked her (i.e., interpreted) if she thought that maybe she was looking out of the window to be sure no one was breaking in, she was utterly startled, but pleased. "Why didn't I think of that?

Why didn't I think of that?" she exclaimed with surprise, envy, and delight as she instantly recognized her unconscious anxiety having been revealed to her.

The girl's response to the interpretation consists of several elements. First, the content was something that she already knew, but that she did not know she knew. Secondly, her reaction of surprise is the "Aha" of one who has misplaced a familiar object and then is dismayed to find that it has been in plain sight all along. And finally, from an intersubjective perspective, the girl acknowledged and accepted enthusiastically, albeit ambivalently that she had been recognized by another. The ambivalence resides in the barb to her narcissism, attendant upon being required to acknowledge both that she has an unconscious and that someone else could glimpse a bit of it before she herself could. In accord with the paradoxical nature of transitional phenomena as described by Winnicott (1953), knowledge of herself was both given to her from the outside, and yet was already there to be found. This view accords well with Freud's (1905b) postulate: "The finding of an object is in fact a refinding of it" (p. 221).

Up to this point I have limited myself to considering interpretations that are quickly accepted. Of course, an interpretation may provoke innumerable responses other than initial receptivity and use. If it is ill-timed the patient may feel humiliatingly exposed. He then is "found out", *not* found. The analysand experiences the analyst saying, "Gotcha!" An interpretation initially can be felt to be a phallic penetration, a gift, a feeding, making a baby together, etc. But when the moment arrives that it can be accepted for what the analyst had intended, the interpretation is commonly experienced as having been recognized or found. This is just as true when the interpretation is of a resistance.

In addition to the *content* and its *mode* of delivery, the interpretation tells the patient that the silence that preceded it was not a waste, but was filled by *the analyst's deep participation* in coming to understand that which now is being communicated. It may greatly increase belief in the power of the analysis to reach the depths of the patient's mental and emotional life. The various other meanings constitute either veridical perceptions of the analyst's countertransference or the projection of some internal object of the patient. Interpreting the *intersubjective experience* is the next order of business to follow the interpretation of *content*. Not to follow up an interpretation of content with an exploration of the intersubjective meaning is to squander a valuable opportunity. This is so because attending to the disparity between what the analysand heard and what the analyst intended enables cues to be gleaned to the influence of an internal object responsible for distorting the meaning (see also Faimberg, 1996). Consistent interpretation of these distortions is a powerful tool for the analysis of character and of the compulsion to repeat.

The alimentary canal metaphor

An interpretation has commonly been construed in metaphor as something that, when accepted, "goes inside" or "is taken in" (see Bion, 1962a). But one might ask how can this be so? How can an interpretation be a feeding if, as Freud (1905c) maintained, everything the analysand needs to know already is inside. In accordance with Freud's view and with what I have previously argued and demonstrated in the example above, I propose that interpretive content is not an idea to munch on, taste, and digest, as are other more familiar forms of knowledge. What does go "inside", however, is the *emotional link to the analyst*. The goodness of the analyst, the positive transference, becomes internalized (Langs, 1985; see also Loewald, 1960). The analyst, with his interpretation, finds what is there to be found. He does not feed. While, as I have noted above (see pp. 136–138), by means of a multitude of unconscious fantasies an analysand can make of the interpretation any number of experiences, but at the point the analysand can use the interpretation for what the analyst intended, acknowledging what already is "inside", the analysand feels recognized, seen, understood, but rarely fed.

The analysand's response to the interpretation begins when he detects that the analyst is about to speak. Bodily posture, quality of breathing, facial expression cue the analyst that the initial response is one of welcoming, surprise, guardedness, fear, etc. As the words and meaning are received, one can observe the analysand's initial expressions intensify or relax, indicating that he is monitoring the interpretation as threat or relief. Although milder forms of response may appear on the surface, at a more primitive level, induced by the regressive pull of the analysis, possibly to the schizoid-paranoid position, the patient may be assessing some variant of, "Is he my friend or is he my enemy?"

The analyst is challenged to wind his way between many potential obstacles among which two are most common: first, if he interprets too quickly, he intrudes into potential space and disrupts a vital process; second, if he waits too long, he colludes with resistance. The analyst's dual charge is to accept the "moment of hesitation" (Winnicott, 1941; i.e., to hold and contain), while preparing to "seize" the moment (i.e., to interpret).

Invitation to interpret

Freud (1913) recommended that the analysand should lead at every step in the analysis. Shor (1974) applied this idea to the timing of interpretations. He suggested that an interpretation should be made only upon the invitation of the patient. I would extend this notion to include implicit invitations. Explicit and implicit invitations are consistent with "the first gesture" of Winnicott (1941), which alludes to the baby or child, in relation to the mother, initiating the movement within a dyad. The patient may signal this invitation quite silently and unconsciously, as when through an enactment he may test the analyst, hoping to see his response.

Kleinian analysts are keen to emphasize the separateness of analyst and patient, as they describe the difficulties that arise in making interpretations with patients who are intolerant of them (Britton, 1989; Caper, 1997; Feldman, 1993). By contrast, self psychologists contend that many patients need the analyst to be experienced, not as separate, but as an extension of the self, as a selfobject (Kohut, 1971, 1977; Ornstein & Ornstein, 2005).

The concept of potential space, with its inherent ambiguity, bridges the dichotomy between these schools of thought by converting the ambiguity to a paradox and dialectic. It suggests an analytic stance that keeps open whether, at any given moment, the analyst is separate, at one with the patient, or both at once. It allows the patient the illusion of oneness until the patient, himself, signals that he is ready to experience, by means of interpretation, the separate mind of the analyst, that is, his subjectivity. For some patients separateness cannot be tolerated until they have first immersed themselves in a prolonged illusion of oneness. Accordingly, for a long time the analyst may be used as a background figure, the environmental mother of Winnicott (1968a). At such times no interpretation is needed, and can even be detrimental as it is experienced as a toxic intrusion.

Since the affective link to the analyst takes place in potential space, any approach by the analyst that does not recognize and appreciate the transitional quality risks traumatizing the patient with inter- pretations that can only be experienced as assaults. The interpret- ing analyst will be experienced as a sniper, a pedantic educator, a preacher, etc. The analysand will strive to protect himself with his customary defences. To adapt Winnicott's (1941) famous meta- phor, if through the interpretation the patient sees only the analyst's "face" (i.e., his otherness) instead of himself reflected there, he will have to adapt to the analyst, rather than participate in creating his experience of understanding.

An interpretation creates a weaning from an unconscious belief or conviction that protects a crucial self-object tie, including one to a bad object. According to Ogden (1985b), the premature objecti- fication or discovery of the mother as object, as distinct from the environmental mother, leads to the establishment of an omnipo- tent internal object mother. In my opinion this is less likely to occur if the analyst's attitude to the analysand is to find and recognize, rather than to feed interpretations. If the latter attitude prevails, the patient cannot "generate the space in which he lives" (Ogden, 1985a, p. 356). Defensively, he may become omnipotent himself, turning the tables on the analyst by not needing him, outdoing him, or by becoming pseudo-independent. This stance can tempt both par- ticipants into power dynamics wherein the analyst, in the counter- transference, is lulled into using interpretation to defeat the patient's omnipotence. The analysand also can take the defensive route of pseudo-compliance or pseudo-identification. That is, he can defeat the analyst by "joining" him. But since the joining is done by way of a split in the ego, a defeat of the analyst is also a defeat of himself.

Destabilization: the road to vitality

It is not the depth of the unconscious being accessed that is the transformative issue at any interpretive moment, as that can vary considerably, rather it is the "aliveness" of what is being touched. A key to the work, therefore, is the analyst tracking vitality within the hour: for Freud (1905b) aliveness springs from drive derivatives; whereas for Winnicott (1941) the "first gesture", the linking of psyche and soma, is where the patient lives and is the well-spring of his animation. Anxiety may prompt vitality to be secured for safekeeping by being buried or otherwise hidden in defence. In this case the analyst will find aliveness in the hour masquerading in strong resistances, even as deadness. Accordingly, the most affect-less hours, with corresponding countertransference boredom or fatigue, may signify desperate efforts of the analysand to hide vitality that unconsciously is believed to be too dangerous to expose. It is crucially important for the analyst to distinguish this dynamic from one in which an excruciatingly vulnerable "empty" or "depleted" self, the product of a deficit rather than defence, is being exposed. Making this distinction may be no easy matter as the one may be disguised as the other.

Over time, however, interpretive depth, defined as bringing to light core unconscious fantasies and wishes underlying maladaptive and repetitive actions, matters mightily and must be reached to maximize structural change and ensure its stability. Since interpretation interrupts a steady state, it first works by destabilizing. It is the destabilizing impact that helps to vitalize the experience. As Schlesinger (1995) reminds us, the analysand attempts continually to reanimate the neurosis in the analysis while interpretation aims to subvert it.

Some interpretations, at first glance, do not appear to destabilize but rather to integrate what the analysand has just described and emotionally to relieve him, inasmuch as puzzling feelings and behaviour can suddenly make sense. The patient initially feels well understood and empowered. The destabilization may only show up when an attempt to move to action based on the insight provokes anxiety and reactivates defence. The analysand, unconsciously, is attempting to re-establish the *status quo ante*. Often, only a careful monitoring will reveal that an actual transformation has indeed occurred. What is required at these times is a follow-up interpretation that will re-expose the person to the truth of his internal situation, that is to the psychic alteration that leaves him feeling excited and vulnerable (Schlesinger, 1995). An example is in order.

A 63-year-old divorced woman had had many years of psychotherapy with a therapist in another state for symptoms of life-long depression. Several years after moving to Los Angeles she began analysis with me, severely depressed with serious suicidal thoughts. Her despondent feelings were organized around the belief that the future was bleak. She could see ahead only an old age with financial concerns, no man in her life, and living in a city that she did not like. After six months of analysis her depression had responded to my interpretations and had been replaced with intermittent periods of good cheer, as she felt better prepared to face the same difficult future that she earlier had anticipated. Her associations in the two weeks prior to the hour of my focus here were rather upbeat with tentative plans for how she could improve her financial and social life. At the start of the session in question, she appeared happy, relaxed, playful, and looking younger and more alluring than usual.

The patient reported a dream in which she was in a room with a young teenager in a red dress. The girl seemed cold so she offered her the grey wrap that she was wearing. The red dress reminded her of the menstrual blood of a teenager, which she believes is much redder than that of an older woman. She thought the dream symbolized her lost sexuality, vitality, and opportunities of youth, as she began, once more, to speak pessimistically about the future. But now her affect did not match her words. Informed by my countertransference responses to her engaging feminine appearance and her affect, and recalling the recent optimistic mood and playful affect of recent sessions, both of which contrasted with her unconvincing pessimism, I reminded her that she had put her grey wrap around the girl. I then interpreted that in so doing she seemed to have found and joined up with the girl's youthful sexuality, rather than to have lost it. Namely, she blended the grey of her hair and of her mood with the violent red of sexuality. (Essentially, my interpretations challenged the pessimism she applied defensively to her associations).

The patient responded animatedly that she knew this was true and wondered why she had not seen it herself. I interpreted that perhaps she was afraid of the implications of once again seeing herself as an attractive and appealing woman. This in turn led to memories of a very painful rejection by a lover several years earlier, which soon led to core memories of herself, as a little girl, losing her father's love to a baby brother.

It appeared that the interpretive work of the previous months had resulted in a re-finding of her sexual self and enthusiasm for life. However, the returned libido brought with it fears of rejection, present and past, along with unconscious guilt for seductive intent towards a married lover, her father from the past, and me in the transference. The compromise formation resulted in associations of retreat. The follow-up interpretations, that is, my comments that drew attention to her retreat and its defensive function, helped stall the retreat and move the analysis forward, as they brought to light unconscious masochism that could be further addressed by analytic work, rather than become enacted.

In the session the patient said that several times in her previous therapy she had made the intellectual link between rejection by father and lover, and depression, but that the knowledge had "made no difference". She was very curious why she responded so emotionally in this hour, feeling that an "old" insight was now moving her deeply and tearfully. She eventually said, "It is my relationship with you that is making the difference. You are with me. I can tell that you care. I never really felt that way in my other therapy." She went on to explain that whenever she tested my emotional availability, she found it present. In accord with what I have said earlier in this essay, emotional availability was not offered to her by my having adopted a purposeful stance. It was derived by deep immersion over time in her inner world and it accompanied my interpretations, spontaneously, without deliberate intent.

This brief vignette illustrates that an interpretation can shed light on an unconscious conflict that is screened rather than revealed in the patient's narrative. The patient, who consciously was feeling and looking better as a result of our analytic collaboration, consciously believed herself to be unconflicted about her desire to relieve her depression and pessimism. But unconsciously she was made anxious and guilty by the gratifications that now, as she could see, potentially were available to her should she express her analytic growth by taking action in the outer world. She, therefore, defensively, began to retreat by taking comfort in pessimism and a return to a depressive-masochistic outlook, since they spared her Oedipal guilt and mourning should her hopefulness continue. The interpretive work put her in touch with this inner truth, as it focused on the unconscious conflict. That my interpretations were expressed in experience-near terms and, in part, were derived from an empathic immersion in her inner world, helped her to feel that I was with her. The seamless combination of truth and humanity opened up the possibility for a life-long dynamic finally to be worked through and significantly attenuated or possibly resolved.

Discussion

Throughout this chapter I have cautioned against settling for conceptualizations of analytic growth that minimize understanding in favour of relationship, holding, emotion, or other experiences provided to the patient that are designated "beyond interpretation". In taking this position, implicitly, I have been arguing for what I consider to be the key feature of an analytic attitude that best affords the opportunity to facilitate psychic change to the fullest extent possible. I have endeavoured to show that interpretive work is not merely the giving of insight, cognitive or emotional, but a very human experience of profoundly understanding another. That it is the unconscious that is being understood makes the experience for the analysand uniquely psychoanalytic. Interpretation encourages a focus on all components of the patient's mind and facilitates a strengthening of the ego and a greater sense of agency. It vitalizes the ego by undoing defence and giving access to instinctual and emotional life. When it is derived from the analyst's resonance in the analysand's unconscious, the interpretation provides an integrating experience while simultaneously elevating the patient's understanding beyond a simple mirroring. The well-rounded focus of interpretive activity also helps to prevent the analytic process being limited to a *pars pro toto* activity.

CHAPTER SEVEN

Back to the future: the curative fantasy in psychoanalysis

Linda Sobelman

ack to the Future, a popular 1985 movie directed by Robert
Zameckis, tells the story of an adolescent boy struggling to
come to terms with his feelings about his family, with his
anxieties about his own worth and abilities, and with what these
portend for his future.

Marty McFly, the lead character, views his father as an ineffec-
tual, passive loser and his mother as dowdy and prudish. Marty
fears that he will follow in his parents' footsteps and be unsuccess-
ful in his own life. Indeed, in the early scenes of the movie, Marty is
shown suffering a series of humiliating defeats that seem to justify
his fears.

In a later scene, Marty meets up with Doc, his adult mentor-
friend, an eccentric inventor who has developed a time machine.
Through the accidental use of this machine, Marty is transported
back in time to the year his parents met, when they were Marty's
current age. By means of a series of ingenious interventions, Marty
transforms his timid father into a brave hero, enabling his father to
triumph over the town bully, win his mother's love, and achieve status and respect in the eyes of the community. When Marty returns to
present time, he now views his parents as successful, sexually vital,

145

and happy. Marty's father has become the ideal parental figure with whom Marty can identify.

Thus, by reinventing his past, Marty is able to alter his present circumstances, and, by extension, to create greater possibilities for his future.

Bick (1990) presents a cogent analysis of *Back to the Future* as depicting the resurgence of Oedipal conflicts of the adolescent's second separation-individuation phase of development in the form of an elaborate family romance fantasy.

The concept of the family romance was developed by Freud (1909) to describe one of the ways children cope with inevitable disappointments with their parents. In this fantasy, the child imagines himself to have different, more desirable parents, the specifics varying with the nature of each child's individual discontents.

Although *Back to the Future* presents the re-emergence of Oedipal conflicts during adolescence, family romance fantasies incorporate wishes arising from all levels of development. At the pre-Oedipal level, the core of the fantasy is a wish to restore the idealized omnipotent parents of infancy. The family romance is a universal fantasy, employed throughout life to assuage narcissistic injuries and to regulate self-esteem.

Bick's analysis of *Back to the Future* emphasizes the universality of the family romance, and the developmentally- and age-appropriate fantasies of its hero. But family romance fantasies can also play a particular role in psychopathology, both in terms of the persistence and intensity of such fantasies as well as their manifestation in symptoms and in defensive character structure. Once patients enter treatment, family romance fantasies create a "transference readiness" (Frosch, 1959) that contributes to the process as well as the content of transference in the treatment situation.

It does not take much of an imaginative leap to envisage the character of Doc in *Back to the Future* as representing a fantasy of the analyst as the magical healer who enables the patient to actualize his family romance.

Embedded in our patients' transference wishes are conscious and unconscious beliefs about the genesis of their difficulties and the conditions necessary for cure. In this curative fantasy, the patient seeks in the person of the analyst a replacement for the disappointing objects of childhood. The wish is for the analyst to be an idealized parent, compensating for deficiencies in the actual parents (real or imagined), thereby providing an optimal medium for growth.

A recurrent debate in the history of psychoanalytic clinical theory involves the appropriate therapeutic stance of the analyst in response to the patient's transference wishes. Parallel to patients' beliefs, analysts' theories of pathogenesis and the nature of therapeutic action underlie these positions. Two different examples of theoretical approaches to the understanding of patients' curative fantasies follow. The first demonstrates a drive-conflict view, while the second presents a self psychology view of patients' unconscious fantasies of cure. By examining these different models, we can clarify some of the dimensions that characterize the two poles of this debate.

In his discussion of "Unconscious Fantasy and Theories of Cure", Abend (1979) presents a drive-conflict approach to the handling of such fantasies. He describes curative fantasies as derivatives of unconscious wishes for the fulfilment of childhood libidinal desires. The fantasies correspond to the typical sexual theories of childhood in connection with these libidinal wishes. The patient seeks satisfaction of the infantile instinctual wishes in the transference. Curative fantasies, according to Abend, are ubiquitous in analysis and impact the patient's motivation for change. The effect of curative fantasies on the patient's responsiveness to analytic influence may be either positive or negative.

According to Abend, the basis for our patients' curative fantasies is the belief that their problems are the product of parental failures and deficiencies. Their hope is that psychoanalytic cure will be achieved through the analyst's acceptance of the legitimacy of their wishes, tolerance of the need for catharsis of suppressed affects such as frustration and rage, and gratification of the underlying libidinal needs.

Abend (1979) acknowledges that, at times, patients' complaints about their parents are justified and that legitimate developmental needs for instinctual satisfactions have indeed been frustrated. In these cases, nevertheless, Abend believes that the retrospective fantasy serves compromise functions. It both communicates and disguises the patient's wish for other, unrealistic infantile libidinal gratifications. These must be analysed and renounced in order to effect a cure.

Abend cautions that analysts themselves are not immune to the unconscious appeal of such fantasies of cure. He suggests that this appeal contributes to the recurrent popularity of analytic theories of cure analogous to those of our patients. Among these, he cites Alexander's (1950, 1954) advocacy of corrective emotional experiences in treatment and Winnicott's (1956) suggestion that, particularly with more disturbed patients, gratification of the patient's needs can bring about a necessary developmental shift, creating the opportunity for the evolution of the patient's ego.

Self psychology is the recent heir to the theories of cure that place emphasis on the necessity for the analyst to provide a new, more self-facilitating relational experience in order to promote patients' growth. Adherents to this approach claim allegiance to the work of Balint (1968), Ferenczi (1932), Kohut (1971, 1977, 1984), and Winnicott (1965, 1971b, 1975).

Ornstein and Ornstein (1977; Ornstein, A., 1995) explore the concept of the curative fantasy from the vantage point of self psychology. They describe the patient's curative fantasy as closely related to Kohut's notion of selfobject transferences, perhaps best described as an aspect of such transferences. It involves an inner conviction that development cannot proceed unless certain needs which were unmet in the past are now fulfilled. Selfobject transferences, on the other hand, always include the repetition of the consequences of early pathogenic relationships. In essence, selfobject transferences reflect the curative fantasy that has been repeatedly frustrated.

The Ornsteins believe that most theories of the therapeutic action of psychoanalysis focus too narrowly on pathology. In other words, most theories of cure correspond to theories of pathogenesis, with the aim being to reverse the process of illness. With the concept of the curative fantasy, the Ornsteins refocus our attention on the natural inherent tendency of the individual towards growth and development.

The notion of a natural healing tendency is, of course, not exclusive to self psychology. Implicit in Freud's dictum "Where id was, there ego shall be" (1933, p. 80), for example, is the idea of the inherent integrative capacities of the ego. Analysis, in Freud's model, frees the libido from infantile fixations and regressions, allowing its reintegration through adherence to the reality principle at a higher, more mature level. The ego's integrative capacity is viewed as a natural by-product of the conflict resolution. But the emphasis in Freud's model is on those attempts at conflict resolution that have resulted in psychopathology, and the need for infantile wishes and gratifications to be renounced in order for more mature outcomes to be possible.

In the self psychology model, the wishes expressed in the curative fantasy represent legitimate developmental needs. Although those needs may be expressed in primitive ways (concretely or in a demanding manner, for example) the task of the therapist is to identify and remobilize the wished-for experience, and to facilitate the patient's self-acceptance of the legitimacy of those needs. Responsiveness to the patient's ego needs is given primary importance, and the analysis of conflict and compromise assumes a secondary role.

Thus we see two very different interpretations of the patient's curative fantasy. In the self psychology model, the curative fantasy represents the patient's hopes for a "new beginning" (Balint, 1968). In the drive-conflict model, the curative fantasy is a reflection of the pathological process itself. As a compromise formation, it gives expression to unconscious wishes for instinctual gratification, all the while disguising them in a rationalized form.

These different models give rise to two contrasting approaches to the transference/countertransference matrix. The conflict model focuses on the patient's tendency to view the analyst in terms of past, pathogenic object relationships. The self psychology model, while also addressing these past relationships, emphasizes the patient's hopes for a relationship with the analyst as a new, wished-for, health-promoting figure.

Adherents of the self psychology model point to the danger of the conflict-oriented therapist retraumatizing the patient in a manner that parallels the original parental failure by rejecting the legitimacy of the patient's needs. Drive-conflict therapists, on the other hand, view the self psychological therapist as colluding with the patient's defences and failing to address the unconscious sexual and aggressive conflicts underlying the maladaptive compromise formations.

Each of these critiques has merit. The drive-conflict model, as outlined by Abend, minimizes the extent to which the patient's clinging to infantile instinctual wishes may reflect a fixation or regression due to parental failure and deprivation of legitimate need. The self psychology model, on the other hand, minimizes the patient's role in actively clinging to, and recreating, a pathological mode of relating in the present.

The debate between the drive-conflict model and the developmental-arrest model has assumed different guises over the decades (e.g., Ferenczi's, 1920, active therapy; Alexander's, 1950, 1954; Alexander & French's, 1946, corrective emotional experience; Winnicott's, 1954b, ego need vs. id wish; Kohut's, 1971, deficit vs. conflict). The tone of the discussions has often been contentious and polarizing. Frequently, proponents of one approach have over-simplified the position of the other and set up a straw man to attack. Nevertheless, the debate has ultimately proved productive, as the merits of the various challenges are recognized and attempts are made to refashion theory to accommodate the new insights that result. Both contemporary conflict theory and self psychological theory have evolved and profited from these discussions. In many respects, polarization between the two approaches has softened.

Abend returns to the topic of therapeutic action and the role of patients' unconscious curative fantasies in recent writings (2002, 2007). In his 2002 article, he reviews the same cases presented in his earlier discussion of curative fantasies (1979). His purpose in revisiting these cases, apart from reasserting the importance for the outcome of treatment of attending to the patient's curative fantasies, is to caution against abandoning the traditional analytic stance of neutrality. Abend (2002) contends that attention to resistance analysis and unconscious conflicts about change in doing "the ordinary work of analysis" (p. 222) will suffice to address patients' fantasies about the conditions necessary to promote growth. Nevertheless, in his re-examination of these earlier presented cases, as in his more general discussion of modern conflict theory (2007), the influence of the earlier debates is evident.

Defining the goal of analysis as the resolution of the transference neurosis, Abend points out, is a legacy of early Freudian theory that has outlived its usefulness. Brenner's (1976) reformulation of conflict theory acknowledges the persistence of instinctual conflict throughout life. Conflict is still defined as arising from the tension between unconscious libidinal and aggressive wishes striving for gratification on the one hand, and the child's defensive efforts to avoid anticipated danger by concealing or modifying those wishes on the other hand. But now, the goal of analysis is conceived of as an alteration of the compromise formation to allow for the greater satisfaction of such wishes, while incurring a lesser degree of discomfort.

Gone is the emphasis on the need to renounce infantile wishes with its associated implication of the illegitimacy of those wishes. A less adversarial stance is also evident in the approach to resistance. More emphasis is given to the role of actual experience in determining the nature of resistance. The patient's fear of real or imagined danger in the present, as well as the real and imagined experiences of childhood that formed the patient's defences is to be explored. Thus, the reasons the patient felt, and continues to feel the need for defence are empathically examined rather than confronted in a challenging manner.

In recent decades, the drive model has lost its position of dominance in psychoanalytic thinking. At present, most contemporary psychoanalytic models incorporate some version of object relational theory (Greenberg & Mitchell, 1983). The individual is viewed as inherently object-seeking; desire is understood to derive meaning from the context of relationships with others; the internal world is conceived of in terms of internal objects and object relations.

Building on his earlier examination of object relations theories in psychoanalysis (Greenberg & Mitchell, 1983), Mitchell (1988, 1993) has described an emerging third theoretical model that falls within the relational perspective. This paradigm, which he calls the relational-conflict model, integrates commonalities among interpersonal, object relations, and self psychological theories. According to Mitchell (1988), in the view of the relational-conflict model,

> ... disturbances in early relationships with caretakers are understood to seriously distort subsequent relatedness, not by freezing infantile needs in place, but by setting in motion a complex process through which the child builds an interpersonal world (a world of object relations) from what is available [p. 289].

The emphasis on object relational needs as the units of study rather than drives places these theories in accord with self psychology. At the same time, however, relational-conflict theorists raise objections to the self psychology model that are, in some important respects, similar to those of the drive-conflict theorists. Ultimately, these points of debate have implications for our understanding of patients' transference wishes. Thus, for me, the appropriate therapeutic response to a patient's curative fantasies remains a central issue.

Like the drive theorists before them, relational-conflict theorists emphasize the patient's tendency to organize present relationships in terms of familiar pathogenic relationship patterns from the past. Attention is drawn to the patient's propensity to create negative self-fulfilling prophecies and the mechanisms by which this is accomplished (i.e., selective attention; eliciting familiar if painful responses from others via projective identification). In the analytic setting, such self-fulfilling prophecies take the form of enactments in which the analyst is induced to take on a complementary role to the patient in repeating painful relational patterns from the patient's history.

The drive model and the relational-conflict model are also similar in the centrality accorded the role of conflict in the organization of the personality. Conflict is, however, defined differently in the two models. The drive model posits tension between wishes and defences erected against the emergence of those wishes. For the relational-conflict theorist, relationships are inherently conflictual in that the wish for connection exists in a dialectic tension with the wish for individuation. At another level, conflict exists between discordant identifications with aspects of significant others. Both models, however, view the process of change as inevitably conflictual for the patient because clinging to old, familiar solutions reduces anxiety and provides security even as it produces pain and frustration.

Thus, both the drive model and the relational-conflict model point to a neglect of the role of conflict and minimization of the importance of defence analysis in Kohut's (1971, 1977) original self psychology model. In response to these challenges, self psychology has also been undergoing changes.

A number of self psychologists have recognized the need to expand the theoretical model to attend more adequately to the defensive aspects of character and to account more fully for the persistence of resistance to change. To some extent, self psychology has always recognized the patient's defensive responses by viewing them as reflecting a fear of retraumatization by unresponsive others. But this formulation has not gone far enough in explaining pathological character structure and the consequent attachment to old solutions.

Newman (1988, 1999, 2007) is prominent among those self psychologists who are attempting such a revision. He believes that Kohut's model, in its emphasis on thwarted needs for mirroring and idealization, minimizes the importance of a second aspect of selfobject need, that of affect regulation.

According to Kohut's model, empathic failure on the part of early caregivers leads to reactions of disappointment and rage. Over time, in response to the ongoing fear of retraumatization, the frustrated needs go underground and, thereafter, are expressed in split-off or symptomatic form. Character, in this model, is seen as conveying ongoing selfobject hunger, that is, it is a reflection of unmet developmental needs and longings. In analysis, selfobject hunger becomes manifest in mirroring and idealizing transferences. Therapeutic action occurs through the repeated process of inevitable empathic disruptions and their repair by means of the analyst's understanding and interpretation. This repeated process enables the patient to understand the ongoing need for selfobjects as well as to gradually internalize the analyst's function.

The expansion proposed by Newman emphasizes the fate of the affects in the face of cumulative empathic failure. He points out that a second stage of empathic failure occurs when the parent who was initially misattuned to the child's needs is then unable to respond in a soothing, containing manner to the child's affective reaction of disappointment, withdrawal, or rage. Over time, in addition to fearing disappointment of the original needs, the child comes to dread the re-emergence of his unintegrated affect states. In this model, character pathology, in addition to conveying selfobject hunger, is also a reflection of the patient's restitutive structure designed to avoid the awareness of feared affect states.

With the increased emphasis he places on the dread of unintegrated affects in the development of pathological character, Newman reconciles the self psychology model and the relational-conflict model in some important respects. Greater attention is paid to the repetitive aspects of character when the patient's fear of remobilized emotions of disappointment and rage is taken into account. Newman acknowledges that the transition from object relating to object usage is more difficult to attain in such cases and requires a different form of engagement on the part of the analyst than that suggested by Kohut or Winnicott.

Specifically, Newman points to the inevitability of transference/countertransference enactments and the importance of the analyst's affective engagement in these exchanges. Patients with protective pathological character structures repetitively interact with others in ways that maintain distance in order to avoid the possibility of disappointment with its dangerous emotional sequelae. In analysis, these repetitive relational patterns inevitably result in transference/countertransference enactments.

In the course of an enactment, the patient induces feelings in the analyst that result in the analyst reacting to the patient in a manner that parallels the parent's original failure. However one views the conscious or unconscious motivation of the patient (whether it be a test of the analyst's ability to respond in a new, more attuned manner, or as a negative self-fulfilling prophecy, or as a combination of both), the effect on the analyst is the same. At some point, in spite of our best intentions, we will react to the patient's treatment of us as untrustworthy, self-centered, or inadequate. We become hurt, angry, or despairing and respond to our patient with anger or withdrawal.

The occurrence of this empathic rupture results in the eruption of the warded off negative emotions. The analyst's capacity to emerge safely from his countertransference reaction, to survive the patient's intense negative reaction to his failure, and to re-establish affective engagement with the patient is the agent of cure. For those patients who have not had the sustained experience of a caretaker's ability to withstand and contain intense affects, the analyst's provision of a containing function becomes essential.

Although increased attention to the repetitive aspects of transference softens the polarity between the developmental-arrest and the relational-conflict approaches to a considerable degree, a significant area of disagreement remains.

In Newman's self psychology model, interpretation of the patient's active role in co-creating enactments is given one-sided attention. The patients' cuing of the analyst as to the wished-for response is acknowledged. This is, of course, the meaning of the curative fantasy. The patient's role in actively repressing his deeper needs and his motivation for doing so in the dread of reactivating unintegrated affects is examined. But the patient's need to recreate pathological relationship patterns, the consequent pressure he exerts on others to enact the complementary role in his familiar but disappointing drama, and his selective attention to the other's reactions, which confirms his self-fulfilling prophecies, is insufficiently addressed with the patient.

In the traditional self psychology model, the neglect of the patient's active role in inducing negative reactions in the analyst follows from the injunction that the analyst must maintain an empathic focus on the patient's point of view and avoid any intervention that the patient might experience as critical. This includes the caution against countertransference disclosure, as it could coerce premature awareness of and compliance with the analyst's perspective. According to this view, the analyst must contain his countertransference until the patient has achieved a stable sense of self. This suggests that judicious countertransference disclosure may have a place during the later phases of treatment. At this time, after the patient has acquired a cohesive self, the exploration of the mutual impact of patient and analyst can play a significant role.

These cautions are well-founded. Nevertheless, there are potential pitfalls in this approach. One danger, of course, is that "later" never comes. A rationale must be developed and technical strategies devised for its implementation that are consistent with the overall theoretical model. Otherwise, a shift to the examination of the patient's impact on others will feel discordant to both patient and analyst and is unlikely to be successful.

Bollas's (1983) discussion of the expressive uses of the countertransference exemplifies the kind of rationale and technical strategy that is required. He argues that by selectively disclosing some aspects of his subjective state of mind to the patient for mutual observation and analysis, the analyst helps to link the patient with split-off parts of himself. Occasional indirect use of the countertransference from the beginning of the analysis provides a gradual way to introduce the analyst's subjectivity so that the eventual direct expression of the analyst's experience of being the object of the patient will not be traumatic.

An equally significant problem is the possibility that the treatment will reinforce splitting. In the safety of the empathic analytic setting, the patient will dismantle his defensive posture and access warded off affects and needs. Outside the consulting room, however, the patient may well continue to provoke negative reactions in others. Without awareness of his impact on others, he will continue to blame the other for the disappointing interaction. This will reinforce the patient's belief in the need to protect himself from these dangerous figures. Unless the patient's impact on others is addressed, he is likely to interpret his own anger as reactive and justified, while at the same time he will interpret the anger of others as unprovoked and unjustified.

In his exploration of the analyst's affective participation in nego-tiating enactments, Newman concedes a legitimate place for vari-ous forms of countertransference disclosure. But in his examination of the benefits of such affective engagement, Newman stops short of endorsing its potential for enhancing the patient's awareness of his role in creating the enactment. On the contrary, Newman is con-sistent throughout his writing in cautioning the analyst to accept responsibility for the enactment and to avoid placing responsibility on the patient.

In Newman's (2007) view, much like Kohut's (1984), the critical mechanism of therapeutic action lies in the analyst's provision of missing maternal functions. Whereas Kohut emphasized the role of the analyst in meeting selfobject needs for mirroring and idealiza-tion, Newman adds the analyst's role in providing affect regulation and holding.

In the relational-conflict model, the role of provision is less central, while interpretation is given greater emphasis. In a sense, this dis-tinction can be seen as reviving the familiar debate as to the rela-tive importance of insight versus relationship in promoting change. But in the relationship-conflict model, insight and relationship are viewed as inevitably intertwined.

In the course of an enactment, the pathogenic relationship to the early caretaker is mirrored by the interaction between patient and analyst, but with a crucial difference. Unlike the original experience, the impact of the enactment on both participants can be examined and understood. The analyst invites a collaborative spirit of joint inquiry into the process by which the enactment occurred and a mutual effort to discover a new way of relating.

By experiencing and then analysing their joint participation in an enactment, the patient and the analyst create a new relationship to one another. This new relationship includes the ability to appreciate the differences between the patient's experience and the analyst's experience as potentially enriching and deepening the relationship between them.

What does the relationship-conflict model have to say about the patient's curative fantasy, the conscious or unconscious wishes with which the patient enters treatment? Unlike the self psychology model, the patient's hopes are not seen as an infallible guide to the patient's needs. Contrary to the drive model, the patient's hopes are not seen as derivatives of infantile instinctual impulses that must be renounced. According to Mitchell (1993), the hopes the patient brings to treatment are always partially right and partially wrong. As he puts it:

> The patient's initial hopes are always a complex blend of wishes and needs, hopes fashioned from pain, frustration, longing, laced with restoration, magical transformation, and retribution [p. 228].

Through the repeated experience of patient and analyst mutually creating new ways of relating to one another, and coming to understand the meaning of that process, the patient's hopes gradually transform. New possibilities for relating constantly emerge, and new ways of understanding those possibilities develop.

Case example

Ray explained his reason for seeking treatment at age 35 as his failure to achieve career success despite his belief that he was brilliant and talented. In each of the several disparate career paths he had attempted, Ray had no difficulty attracting the attention of powerful people and obtaining promising jobs. Repeatedly, however, Ray would alienate his bosses and/or co-workers, eventually either getting fired or having to leave in disgrace.

As a child, Ray had been a pawn in his parents' battles with each other. Ray had allied with his narcissistic father who favoured him. In doing so, he felt that he had lost the love of his depressed mother, who had withdrawn from the competition in defeat. She maintained closeness to Ray's three younger sisters, who sided with her.

Now, in work settings, Ray desperately strove to be the favoured, brilliant child. He alienated co-workers with his competitive behaviour. With bosses, he craved constant accolades, becoming demanding and resentful if these were not forthcoming. Often, he would attempt to form an alliance by pitting one powerful person against another (as he had done with his parents). This strategy generally backfired, leaving Ray feeling betrayed and abandoned by both.

What was Ray's curative fantasy when he entered analysis? He hoped that, unlike his mother, I could withstand rejection from him without withdrawing my love. Even more important to Ray was that I prove able to tolerate the rageful attacks that would follow my occasional defensive reactions. Ray's mother had typically responded to his anger with retaliatory outbursts, setting off an escalating negative spiral. Over time, their relationship had become one of mutual distance and mistrust.

Tolerating the transformations of self experience induced by Ray's interactional pressure was frequently painful and difficult. In trial identification with negative aspects of his relationship with his mother, I experienced myself at various times as: hurt and angry at Ray's rejection of me, defensively denying my anger, emotionally withdrawing from Ray and rejecting him, wanting to take him down a few pegs from his grandiose self-experience, and wanting to cruelly retaliate against him for his attacks on me.

During our several years of work together, Ray and I came to understand his initial curative fantasy as "partially right and partially wrong". Ray did, indeed, need me to survive his anger while maintaining a caring, empathic connection with him. But Ray's (and my) understanding of containment and survival enlarged to include the awareness that by setting limits on his attacks I was, in essence, providing a form of containment that his depressed mother had been unable to muster (Newman, 1999). Through my occasional partial acting out of countertransference anger (Carpy, 1989), Ray had the experience that anger can enhance mutual understanding and respect rather than necessarily threatening a relationship.

Ray also came to see that his fear of others' withdrawal from him dominated his experience of relationships and, ultimately, his way of constructing relationships. My interpretations of his beliefs about my countertransference were mutative in implicitly acknowledging and appreciating the validity of his perceptions (Hoffman, 1983). At the same time, these exchanges also countered his reflexive tendency to selectively focus on others' anger and to globalize by concluding that momentary anger means withdrawal and hatred.

Ultimately, we identified the centrality of Ray's wish to make significant others into the image of a perfect parent. This followed from his belief that he had to go "back to the future" to create a more perfect self, as he believed that only this would ensure love.

Conclusion

The curative fantasies with which our patients enter treatment reflect their experience of pain and deprivation in their early relationships with parents. The fantasies express their sense of what was missing in those relationships and what they believe they still require for healing those early wounds.

We are repeatedly pressed by our patients to identify with the disappointing parent who failed them and asked to somehow find a way to respond differently. And we have to repeatedly bear the pain of our patients' reactions of rage and withdrawal in response to our inevitable failures to do so.

Treatment is engaged with what is most meaningful to our patients to the extent that we can tolerate trying on the roles that we are assigned in our patients' fantasies (Sandler, 1976). The outcome of treatment is not determined, however, by our ability to become the wished-for parent. Rather, change is dependent on our ability to set in motion a complex process of mutual exploration. Through this process our patients come to understand the active role they play in creating and maintaining their experiences of themselves and others. They come to understand the layers of defence they have developed in response to early frustration, and how these defences prevent the gratification of needs even as they act to protect them.

Ultimately, the extent to which we are able to establish this mutative process determines the extent to which our patients are able to experience time as moving forward to a hopeful future rather than endlessly repeating the pain and frustration of the past.

SECTION III

RELATIONAL EXPERIENCE AND MUTATIVE DYNAMICS

CHAPTER EIGHT

The seminal therapeutic influence of analytic love: a pluralistic perspective

Peter Wolson

On December 6, 1906, in a letter to Carl Jung, Freud wrote,

> It would not have escaped you that our cures come about through attaching the libido reigning in the subconscious (transference) .... Where this fails, the patient will not make the effort or else does not listen when we translate his material to him. It is in essence a cure through love. Moreover, it is transference that provides the strongest proof, the only unassailable one, for the relationship of neurosis to love [McGuire, 1974, p. 185].

In addition, Bach (2006, p. 125) noted that Freud told the Vienna Psychoanalytic Society shortly after writing the Jung letter, "Our cures are cures of love," and he mentioned to a colleague, Max Eitington, that "the secret of therapy is to cure through love" (Grotjahn, 1967, p. 445). As indicated in the letter to Jung cited above, Freud believed it was necessary for the patient to love the analyst through the attachment of libido in the transference, but did he also mean that the analyst needed to love the patient, and for the patient to experience the analyst's love, in order to be cured? A number of

163

writers (Loewald, 1960; Lear, 1990; Bach, 2006) believe that Freud intended the latter, and have cited the 1906 letter as evidence.

Clearly there are numerous forms of therapeutic action described in the evolving theories of psychoanalysis. These include: awareness and abreaction; structural conflict resolution; object relational conflict resolution; self and internal object acquisition and differentiation; strengthening self constancy and object constancy; sublimation; adaptation; cultivation of an observing ego; and reparation of psychological deficits. This paper shows how the analyst's love, in its multiple conscious and unconscious expressions and the patient's experience of it, is a pervasive, underlying mutative agent that contributes significantly to the forms of psychic change listed above. This is largely unacknowledged by most psychoanalytic theoreticians.

The seminal therapeutic role of analytic love

Love is a saturated term with considerable surplus meaning. Since it could potentially be confusing, why employ it? The main reasons are contained in: (1) Freud's overarching theory of the libidinal basis of human motivation; (2) his psychosexual theory of development, and (3) transference analysis.

According to classical Freudian (1920) theory, love, Eros, represents the primary instinctual motivation for human behaviour and the prolongation of the species. The title of Jonathan Lear's (1990) book, *Love and Its Place in Nature: A Philosophical Interpretation of Freudian Psychoanalysis*, reflects this central organizing principle.

The basic premise of Freud's (1905b, 1923b) psychosexual theory is that the child's psychological development, the creation of its internal world, depends on how it negotiates the psychosexual stages: oral, anal, phallic-Oedipal, latency, and genital, each of which, with perhaps the exception of latency, expresses a different erotogenic form of love. The outcome of this developmental process, whether healthy or neurotic, is largely determined by the child's relationship to parental love objects under the influence of its psychobiological drives. For example, at the oral stage, love mainly involves processes of oral dependency on mother and developing the general ability to "take in" and "spit out" from having had a responsive, attuned, nurturing mother who provides an emotional atmosphere of safety, reliability, and trustworthiness. During the anal stage, it entails power, control, mastery, and submission concerning the child's anal impulses in relation to a parental authority who, ideally, teaches the child impulse control in a calm, balanced, loving fashion without excessive discipline, harshness, or laxity. The result of this experience determines the child's capacity "to hold on" and "let go" of its affects, impulses, thoughts, and objects and to relate to and learn from authority figures without undue conflict. In the phallic-Oedipal phase, love assumes a romantic form and entails competition, success, failure, and jealousy fuelled by sexual and aggressive drives in relation to the parental couple. Working through this stage influences the ability to take initiative without fear of castration or guilt. Kohut (1977) believed that this occurs naturally when the parents respond to the child's Oedipal rivalry lovingly, as a developmental achievement, rather than becoming threatened by it. During the latency stage, love involves peer identification, twinship, and the ability to achieve and work with others (Erikson, 1950; Sarnoff, 1976). Peer group love is essential to successfully negotiate this stage. The child manages these crucial stages, which involve different forms of love, through processes of introjection, projection, internalization, and identification, and the result is highly dependent on the experiences of parental love.

The extent and quality of parental overindulgence and/or frustration at each stage can result in psychosexual fixations and defensive processes (Freud, 1905a; Fenichel, 1945b) and/or developmental arrests (Kohut, 1971). These become influential psychodynamic constituents of the patient's internal world. In my view, it would seem that the obverse would also be true. The extent to which parents have been lovingly attuned and appropriately responsive at each developmental stage, and not abusive, depriving, and neglectful, would contribute to the psychological health of the child. Of course, this result could be limited by the child's psychobiological predispositions. The analyst's clinical norms for healthy parenting at each psychosexual stage might provide a template for the form of love that was lacking or deformed and that is therapeutically coveted and, to varying degrees, needed by the patient. My view has been influenced by the writings of Ferenczi (1932), Alexander (1950), Winnicott (1960), Bion (1963), Kohut (1971, 1977, 1984), Loewald (1960), Lear (1990) and Bach (2006).

Clearly, the term "love" is not used in any idealized sense with hate split off from its meaning. In its deepest unconscious expression, love is often inextricably involved with hate, especially in relation to parental love objects at each psychosexual stage. It is when hate infiltrates and dominates one's internal love relations that the most virulent splitting and adhesive internal conflicts ensue.

Historically, analysts have minimized the therapeutic impact of their interaction with patients, except for acknowledging its role in providing a necessary facilitating background for interpretive work, a working alliance (Greenson, 1965). The general consensus has been that therapeutic action derives from seminal insights communicated through interpretations of unconscious processes. With the growing prominence of object relations theory, self psychology, intersubjectivity, interpersonal analysis, relational analysis, and attachment theory, the psychoanalytic literature has increasingly recognized the therapeutic influence of the analyst as a new, reparative object (Loewald, 1960) in addition to the therapeutic function of insight (Kohut, 1971, 1977, 1984; Greenberg & Mitchell, 1983; Mitchell & Aron, 1999; Renik, 1993b; Eagle, 1993).

It is precisely because of the quality and depth of the analytic experience for both patient and analyst that the term "love" seems most appropriate as a core agent of psychic change. In my opinion, the effectiveness of psychoanalysis, as distinct from other forms of psychotherapy, is based upon working through psychological conflicts and repairing psychological deficits, during which time the patient experiences the analyst in the transference as the embodiment of his or her internal love objects—parental imagos or self representations (narcissistic love)—and the analyst similarly experiences the patient as representing internal love objects and self representations.

Transformation through analytic love unfolds because the object relational, drive-defence, and self-oriented psychodynamics that constitute the structures of the patient's and analyst's internal worlds, have been forged from relationships with significant loved ones from childhood, as indicated above. Through psychoanalysis, these conflicted, drive influenced internal love relationships become enacted, repaired, and resolved in the transference, as I will subsequently discuss in the section on "The Relational Unconscious"

(p. 182). Recently, the therapeutic importance of analytic love has been emphasized in two significant works by Sheldon Bach (1994, 2006).

The therapeutic action of analytic love: a pluralistic perspective

In discussing therapeutic action, we must ask ourselves, "What within the human psyche needs to change?" The following is a limited review of the major mutative factors involving analytic love in the pluralistic evolution of psychoanalytic theories. It is important to stress that the manifestations of analytic love noted below, with few exceptions (Ferenczi, 1932; Loewald, 1960; Lear, 1990; Bach, 1994, 2006; Natterson, 2003), reflect my viewpoint and not that of the theoretician. The majority of these theorists did not acknowledge analytic love as a mutative agent.

1. *The classical topographic model—making the unconscious conscious*

In the original topographic model (Freud, 1900), the mutative analytic task was to uncover repressed memories and unconscious drive derivatives. The patient's awareness of forbidden sexual wishes contained in repressed memories was facilitated by the analyst's interpretations. By recalling such buried memories, the patient would often experience an abreactive discharge of pent-up libido, therapeutic insight, and the diminution of neurotic symptoms. To achieve this goal, analysts relied heavily on dream analysis, "the royal road to the unconscious", which became known as "id analysis". The clinical use of understanding the various levels of awareness involved in the topographic model addressed the vital psychological function of exposing, expressing, and integrating the repressed neurosis-inducing unconscious libidinal motives into the preconscious and conscious psyche.

In my opinion, this result was, in part, achieved through the analyst's love by fostering an extremely safe, non-judgmental atmosphere in which the patient could risk becoming aware of, exposing, and confessing what had been so traumatic. Analytic love could be inferred from Freud's (1912a) notion of the "unobjectionable positive transference" (p. 105). The patient, even while feeling threatened, needed to trust the analyst, like a wise parental caretaker who knew what was best. Later Freud (1913) spoke of the therapeutic use of analytic authority to increase the suggestive power of interpretations. The analyst implicitly reassured the patient that becoming aware of psychologically dangerous memories was not only something the analyst could bear but would also relieve psychic pain. This caring perspective reduced the danger of traumatic memories and facilitated self-integration and relief from neurotic symptoms. In addition, the analyst functioned as a caring mentor figure, teaching the patient how to explore the unconscious meaning of dreams for symptom relief.

Uncovering unconscious drive derivatives and repressed memories as well as unconscious object relational conflicts remains a major form of therapeutic action today. In this process, the patient's associations are thought to be an intermixture of reality, unconscious fantasies, wishes, and defences. Consequently, therapeutic action has depended on the analyst's understanding of the patient's psychic reality.

From this perspective, patients experience external and internal reality subjectively, through their unique psychodynamic lenses, which have been forged in childhood largely through internalizing experiences with parental figures while being influenced by sexual and aggressive drives. Some analysts now believe that the patient's psychological history is largely co-created through analytic exploration by both patient and analyst. Multiple historical narratives are postulated and altered during the course of analysis (Schafer, 1983; Spence, 1982). Ultimately, this evolving, co-created narrative serves as a container through which the patient's strengthened observing ego can put intrapsychic problems into a more realistic perspective.

In my view, the analyst's willingness to privilege the patient's psychic reality, and co-create historical narratives that are emotionally securing and meaningful, is an empathic manifestation of analytic love. Steingart (1995) believes that the analyst ultimately needs to love the patient's psychic reality in order to be effective. This is certainly difficult with patients whom the analyst dislikes or feels repulsed by. But it is the analyst's efforts to see the world from the subjective viewpoint of the patient, which often lead to respecting and loving patients who might have initially repelled the analyst. Understanding a patient's need to manifest noxious, off-putting behaviour can obviously help overcome countertransference revulsion. However, sometimes the rejection of a patient has more to do with countertransference reactions in the narrow sense. Patients ultimately need to feel that their analyst, who often represents their primary love objects in the transference, appreciates and loves them in order for them to love themselves and others. To remain emotionally withholding or detached in the service of a misguided interpretation of analytic neutrality has been iatrogenically damaging for many patients and colleagues who have told me of feeling deeply wounded by such misattuned analytic attitudes. In the transference role of the "bad" object, the withdrawn, detached analyst might be merely repeating and reinforcing the rejecting behaviour of the internal "bad" parental objects, leading to failed analyses. In my opinion, such analysts have often confused therapeutic neutrality with emotional withholding, indifference, or unresponsiveness rather than maintaining the sufficient degree of objective listening that is necessary to be clinically discerning and responsive.

2. *Conflict resolution and transference—the classical structural model*
Through insight-inducing interpretations, the analyst therapeutically modulates conflicts between the id, ego, and superego, resulting in structural change that entails a therapeutic alteration in the relative strength and balance of these mental entities as they dynamically affect one another (Freud, 1923a). As in the topographic model, interpreting unconscious ideas, affects, and drive derivatives remains a crucial part of this process, but the task has become more complicated. It now involves uncovering and illuminating conflicts between unconscious drives and the defences mobilized against them, often under the sway of a judgmental superego.

The concept of analytic love can be thought of as generally comprising two dimensions—namely, a paternal and a maternal type. In the context of Freud's basic rules of neutrality, anonymity, and abstinence, classical analysts who employ insight-inducing interpretations are expressing both types of analytic love. In the analytic interaction, the patient is treated as a separate human being with his or her own source of initiative. By not overtly guiding, reassuring, counselling, or judging, and exclusively focusing on interpretations of the psychodynamics of the patient's internal world, the analyst is implicitly supporting autonomy and independence. In this one-person, intrapsychic psychology, the analyst supplies insightful understanding, and it is the responsibility of the patient to use or not use those insights to resolve internal conflicts. Analytic love expressed in this relational interaction through neutrality, abstinence, and anonymity resembles a type of fatherly discipline, implicitly expecting and encouraging the patient to be self-reliant. The classical analyst is inclined to believe that direct provision will tend to infantilize and reinforce regressive psychopathology, although there are some notable exceptions, such as the need to use "parameters" in certain cases.

A more maternal form of analytic love can occur when the analyst interprets deeply and correctly and the patient feels profoundly understood. Through this analytic attunement, the patient's ego is validated and seen, which can strengthen self-cohesion, self-esteem, and self-confidence. Moreover, the analyst's insights might be experienced as "food for thought", as a loving feeding experience, or used for guidance. In the latter sense, interpretations might be perceived as a form of parental mentoring. The patient might then identify with and internalize the analyst, relying upon this parental imago for security, encouragement, and direction in coping with problems of living.

In Freudian analysis, the analyst becomes the repository of transference as the patient regresses while lying on the couch during four or more sessions per week. Through interpretations of resistance and transference, the analyst helps the patient work through the transference neurosis by differentiating between projected transference imagos and the realistic perception of the analyst (cf. Strachey, 1934). In this way, the past is differentiated from the present and neurotic compromise formations involving id, ego, and superego become structurally altered and modified. Ultimately, this is intended to result in an amelioration of symptoms and the resolution of the transference neurosis (Freud, 1912a).

Analytic love is reflected in the analyst's willingness to interact with the patient this deeply, to safely talk about the way the patient feels about the analyst, and to bear and contain the patient's love and hate and try to understand its unconscious meaning without defensively retaliating. To compassionately understand the patient's disappointment or hatred towards the analyst, while representing the bad parental imago, is an act of kindness and generosity that many patients have never experienced with either their parents or other significant objects. Such analytic love can modulate patients' anger towards parental imagos, fostering the mature acceptance of parental limitations (in effect, the limitations of reality) and ambivalence, while strengthening the ego.

In contrast to Freud's (1912b) emphasis on the therapeutic importance of analytic neutrality, anonymity, and abstinence, Ferenczi (1932), originally a classical Freudian, came to believe that insight alone could not resolve neurosis without the patient's experience of a curative analytic relationship. With Freud as his analyst, Ferenczi became convinced that the neutral but authoritarian stance of the so-called objective Freudian analyst was anti-therapeutic, often fostering a masochistic submission to authority. He advocated the need for the analyst to be more egalitarian, expressive, and gratifying. The analyst, in effect, needed to be a better, more loving parental figure than the patient's parents had been. Ferenczi (1932) considered the "bad" parenting and deficient or misguided love responsible for the patient's neurosis. Consequently, he advocated the importance of the analyst accepting guilt by proxy (Thompson, 1943) for the psychologically damaging parenting projected by the patient in the transference. He believed that the analyst's empathic understanding and assumption of responsibility had the mutative effect of transforming the pathological parental imago into a more benevolent one, thereby resolving the neurotic conflict. Kohut (1971, 1977) later employed a similar method in his analytic approach to self disorders.

For patients like Ferenczi's, struggling with authoritarian superegos, the Freudian model might lead to iatrogenic failure, since the authoritarian interaction of this model might repeat and reinforce the object relational dynamics of the patient's internal conflict with a harsh superego, and provide no "corrective" experience other than an intellectual understanding of the internal conflict. This would be especially true if the analyst's personality was authoritarian.

Influenced by Ferenczi (1932), Alexander (Alexander & French, 1946) conceptualized the patient's experience of effective classical analysis as a "corrective emotional experience". He thought that the classical analyst's understanding interpretations of the patient's state of mind, which were in stark contrast to the often rejecting, neglectful, abusive, and/or overindulgent childhood parental imagos projected onto the analyst in the transference, provided a reparative therapeutic experience. In his opinion, this relational experience, which included the analyst's interpretations rather than verbal insight alone, led to structural change. In effect, Alexander believed that analysis was a corrective provision of analytic love, even though other analysts, like Eissler (1950), were highly critical of this viewpoint. The therapeutic action of provision and relational experience will be addressed further in my discussion of Winnicott, Bion, Kohut, Stolorow, and Mitchell.

3. *Ego psychology, adaptation, sublimation and the cultivation of an observing ego*

Ego psychology postulated a conflict-free sphere of the ego from birth. While retaining the topographic and structural models, instead of describing human beings as motivated solely by drives, ego psychologists believed that babies are born with a genetic capacity for adaptation and sublimation in addition to other ego functions and needs. The main theorists, such as Anna Freud (1966–1980) and Heinz Hartmann, Ernst Kris, and Rudolph Lowenstein (1946), focused on the goal of transforming conflict-laden libidinal energy into neutralized, sublimated energy and strengthening the ego through defence analysis rather than id analysis. In their opinion, this increased the ego's capacity to tolerate and contain sexual and aggressive drive derivatives (see Gray, 1994a, for an example of a contemporary ego psychology approach). With interpretive focus on adaptive ego functions, such as intelligence, motility, etc. and the secondary gain from defences, patients could feel more understood. This emphasis on adaptation suggested a more maternal, empathic form of analytic love, which Kohut (1971, 1977, 1984), in his development of self psychology, incorporated in his technique of "experience-near" interpretations; that is, interpreting empathically from the patient's subjective viewpoint. He was convinced that this validating clinical process would strengthen the self-structure by increasing self-esteem and overcoming intransigent neurotic patterns in contrast to the classic technique of "experience-distant" interpretations that treated the patient impersonally as an object of scientific investigation.

Since character was conceptualized as drive-defence constellations embedded in the patient's "psychic flesh", so to speak, defence analysis often constituted character analysis by changing neurotic personality structures into more adaptive configurations. Through analysing the transference neurosis, the harshness of the superego would become modulated as the patient identified with the analyst's benevolent understanding and transformative insights about the origins, secondary gains, and adverse influences of character-ological defences (Strachey, 1934). In addition, structural change was thought to occur through the modulation of pathological compromise formations, the acquisition of more adaptive compromise formations (Brenner, 2002), and the cultivation of a perceptive observing ego (Gray, 1994a), which the patient could eventually employ in self-analysis. In these instances, I believe that identification with the analyst's loving, understanding attitude towards the patient permitted the patient to look upon himself more lovingly instead of through the eyes of a harsh superego. Loewald (1960) thought that identification with a new, reparative object was the primary mutative agent.

4. *Developmental ego psychology: self and object strengthening and differentiation*
While Freud's developmental theory identified psychosexual stages related to phase-specific erotogenic zones, it did not emphasize phases of self and object differentiation. However, in his paper, "On Narcissism", Freud (1914a) discussed the formation and differentiation of the self-structure from internal objects. Moreover, one can see how separation-individuation can occur at each psychosexual phase of development. During the early oral phase, for example, the baby introjects and assimilates what it likes, which becomes part of its self (ego), and projects and evacuates what is aversive through the purified pleasure ego (Fenichel, 1945b). Thus, the first semblance of the "other", or external reality, is perceived as bad. Through "good-enough" mothering, maturation, and the replacement of the pleasure principle by the reality principle (i.e., the baby's growing need for real milk rather than fantasy milk), the baby begins to perceive mother as a trustworthy, loving object. Similarly, self and object differentiation occurs when the child is able to independently regulate its capacity to "hold on" and "let go" during the anal phase with the help of loving parental guidance, and ultimately becomes capable of tolerating separation from mother and father in the resolution of the Oedipus complex. When this occurs, the child is able to allow

mother and father to be, both literally and metaphorically speaking, in intercourse sequestered behind the bedroom door while relying upon itself for the first time. The therapeutic action of separation-individuation in the psychosexual model occurs as the dynamics of each developmental phase are manifested in the transference and worked through.

In contrast to Freud (1905a, 1914a), Mahler and her colleagues (Mahler, Pine & Bergman, 1975) directly focused on the importance of separation-individuation from an ego psychology perspective based upon observational studies with children. Both Freud (1905a, 1914a, 1923b) and Mahler et al. (1975) concluded that the construction of the self and of internal objects must be acquired in childhood through necessary developmental experiences with parental figures while under the influence of instinctual drives. In other words, the existence and development of the self-structure and internal objects are not psychobiological givens. For patients who lack self and/or object constancy, as manifested in borderline disorders, the therapeutic action of psychoanalysis facilitates the cultivation and strengthening of self-representations and object-representations. Mahler's theory of separation-individuation at the rapprochement sub-phase of development is highly useful in treating patients who have not successfully negotiated this phase and consequently lack self constancy and object constancy. For these patients, the mother has typically been absent, neglectful, abusive, indulgent, and/or too possessive, which has impeded the process of self and object differentiation.

Like the toddler with its mother, as the patient vacillates back and forth between intimacy with the analyst, which potentially threatens the loss of self (ego boundaries) through merger, and between autonomy (separating from the analyst), which threatens object loss and abandonment, the analyst strengthens the patient's self-structure and object representations by remaining a consistent, stable object; on the one hand, supporting the patient's need for closeness and refuelling like a reliable, loving mother, and on the other, validating the patient's need for autonomy and separation like a strong, encouraging father. In response to these forms of maternal and paternal analytic love, the patient acquires greater self and object constancy, develops firmer ego boundaries and becomes more individuated and self-reliant. Thus, the creation and development of psychic structure, self and object representations, is a vital existential dimension of therapeutic action in psychoanalysis (Wolson, 2005), facilitated by analytic love.

5. *Object relations theory (Klein and the British independent school)— object relations conflict resolution and the fostering of healthy dependency*

In the object relations model, the main conflicts are between self representations and internal objects (Klein, 1975a, b; Balint, 1968; Bion, 1977; Fairbairn, 1952a; Guntrip, 1969; Racker, 1968; Rayner, 1991; Spillius, 2007). The topographic model and the structural model are retained, but the primary human motive is no longer libidinal; that is, to experience pleasure and avoid unpleasure. Instead, it is to find a love object. This is graphically illustrated in Bion's (1963) theory of the baby's innate preconception of the nipple as its primordial part object, the love for the mother. According to Bion (1963), internal object relational conflicts derive from the psychological and environmental difficulties in fulfilling the baby's genetic need to depend on its mother for nurture.

In contrast to the psychosexually more advanced phallocentric and triadic Oedipal theory of Freudian psychoanalysis, the object relations model is matrocentric, dyadic, and largely pre-Oedipal, focusing on mother and baby. It emphasizes pre-Oedipal oral, anal, and infantile Oedipal (i.e., an earlier pre-Oedipal rendition according to Kleinian theory) object libidinal problems of dependency, aggression, and primitive defences. From the Kleinian perspective, aggression, a manifestation of the death instinct, contributes more to psychopathology than do the sexual drives (Klein, 1975a, b; Spillius, 2007). Consequently, the clinical focus is on modulating envy, rage, and greed and working through the primitive defences of splitting, idealization, devaluation, contempt, projective identification, and archaic guilt in the cultivation of healthy dependency. The basic assumption is that mother-baby dependency conflicts underlie all others and that mental disintegration is at the root of psychoneuroses (Bion, 1977). Therefore, focusing on primitive mental states is assumed to achieve the deepest psychological effects with all patients, even neurotics.

Many Kleinians work exclusively in the transference believing that this will lead to the deepest structural changes (Joseph, 1989).

In my view, their willingness to constantly engage the patient interpersonally and intimately is an act of analytic love. Instead of always conceptualizing countertransference in the narrow sense, as a barrier to good analytic work (Freud, 1910b, p. 145), British independents and Kleinians (although Klein herself did not) also use countertransference therapeutically, as a diagnostic barometer of the patient's internal world and as a visceral means of understanding the patient's projective identifications. Racker's (1968) conceptualizations of concordant and complementary countertransference reactions are therapeutically helpful in this respect. This utilization of countertransference has contributed to analytic effectiveness in the treatment of patients across the diagnostic spectrum and has been embraced by psychoanalysts of diverse persuasions (see, for example, Diamond, 2011, Chapter Ten in this volume; Porter, 2011, Chapter Nine, this volume). In these respects, Kleinians have increased the analyst's capacity to empathically comprehend the patient's inner world.

Resolving internal object relational conflicts for Kleinians has been exclusively through intrapsychic interpretations which are intended to help patients understand the way their minds work, not through relational experience (although, what they interpret are the patient's thoughts and feelings as they relate to the analyst in the transference). Thus, while making interpretations to foster healthy dependency, interpretively confronting primitive aggressive impulses and defences is a more fatherly form of analytic love, implicitly encouraging separation and independence. The "fatherly" analyst helps the patient take responsibility for devaluing, defensive attacks to ward off healthy dependency and aggressive projective identifications to deny, disown, displace, and project the experience of possessing their own independent minds.

The British independents are more flexible on this issue, with some, such as Winnicott (1960) and Rayner (1991), accepting relational experience as therapeutic. The developmental model of separation-individuation within object relations theory can be deduced from the Kleinian constructs of the paranoid-schizoid position (Klein, 1946) and the depressive position (Klein, 1935, 1940). The former represents a psychotic lack of differentiation. In contrast, the depressive position is a reaction to separation as the baby becomes capable of perceiving mother as an independent, whole object. The baby's catastrophic loss of omnipotent control over the vital maternal object motivates it to destroy her in fantasy, which results in guilt and subsequent depression. Recovery always involves experiences of reparation for damaging the maternal love object. Understanding the dynamics of the aggressive drive, envy, greed, projective identification, guilt, and reparation, in addition to how paranoid-schizoid dynamics can defend against anxieties of the depressive position and vice versa, is especially beneficial with patients who struggle with primitive object relations.

The analytic love inherent in the Kleinian model lies in the attempt to make contact with and flush out the patient's deepest, primitive anxieties and foster relief through understanding in the transference. It should be noted that for some highly defended patients, bypassing the defences by interpreting what is thought to be the source of the deepest underlying anxiety might be the best way to therapeutically influence them. But when doing so, the analyst must not only be particularly sensitive to the possibility of being wrong, but also to fostering a masochistic submission to an idealized, "mind-reading" authority figure (Gray, 1994a; see also Portuges & Hollander, 2011, Chapter Four in this volume).

Some Kleinians, like the late Herbert Rosenfeld (1987) and Betty Joseph (1989), became increasingly aware of this possibility and have adjusted their technique to accommodate the patient's readiness to receive interpretations, and in this sense, have become more lovingly attuned. Rosenfeld (1987) even suggested that some patients need ego-strengthening through non-verbal relational interventions as a precursor to interpretations. In fact, in his last book, *Impasse and Interpretation*, Rosenfeld (1987) conceptualized the analytic process relationally as a two-sided interaction and not as the one-person psychology of traditional Kleinian theory. Betty Joseph (1989) has studied all aspects and interventions in the analytic interaction contributing to psychic change, not just interpretations. Thus, in addition to the mutative function of insight, these Kleinians appear to be exploring the therapeutic impact of relational experience in addition to their general acceptance of identification with the analyst resulting from the experience of effective interpretations (Strachey, 1934).

6. Repairing deficits in psychic structure—Winnicott, Bion, and Kohut
Winnicott (1951, 1960), a member of the British independent school, proposed that patients who have not experienced sufficiently "good enough mothering" that would allow them to use transitional objects and transitional phenomena to create internal objects, need the analyst to provide a reparative "holding environment", like a loving mother. This construct assumes that the non-verbal relational experience of the analyst as well as verbal interpretive "holding" have essential therapeutic value for these patients, resulting in the internalization of objects and the creation of an inner world of object relations. The patient's capacity to make therapeutic use of transitional objects is not merely a function of insight, but also of the patient's experience of the analyst's participation, which includes the interpreting and non-interpreting analyst.

Winnicott (1958a) made invaluable therapeutic contributions to patients deficient in the capacity to be alone and who lacked the necessary developmental experience of having been able to effectively impact their mother to fulfill their vital needs. He stressed the importance of the analyst's capacity to tolerate and survive the patient's destructiveness, in my opinion a basic expression of maternal love, which is necessary to resolve ambivalence towards the projected maternal imago and ultimately internalize a trustworthy, soothing maternal object.

The therapeutic value of provision is also evident in Bion's (1963) construct of "containment". In this model, the analyst receives the patient's projected, indigestible "beta" elements for therapeutic containment. Through experiencing, bearing, and understanding these primitive parts of the patient's mind, the analyst transforms them into what Bion labelled "alpha" elements, that is, interpretations which the patient can assimilate, digest, and grow from. Bionians maintain that the mutative effect of this experience occurs through insight, not through relational experience. However, Bion (1963) has described the containment process as an experience of toxic oral or anal evacuation by the patient and palliative nurturing by the analyst. In this process, the analyst is often portrayed as providing a therapeutically healthy feeding experience, like a loving, nurturing mother. The therapeutic interpretation is perceived as assimilated maternal "food for thought" for a sick analytic baby, which suggests that relational experience of the ingested interpretation plays a primary therapeutic role in containment. It is virtually impossible to distinguish the patient's relational experience of the interpreting analyst from the patient's transformative insight due to the analyst's accurate understanding. The relational experience and the insight are inextricably intertwined, although the patient might benefit from the relational experience and the insight to different degrees and in different ways. .

In contrast, Kohut's (1971, 1977, 1984) self psychology describes specific developmentally vital forms of relational provision in its focus on repairing narcissistic deficits. At the time he proposed this theory, analysts were having great difficulty treating narcissistic patients because the latter seemed incapable of libidinal transferences involving dependency on the analyst. Consequently, many analysts, beginning with Freud (1914a), believed that narcissistic patients could not be analysed. But Kohut discovered the "selfobject transference", which was based on the patient's narcissistic need for the analyst to provide a selfobject function, an activity that strengthened the patient's self-structure rather than worked through an internal conflict between drive derivatives and defences. When responded to as a selfobject, the analyst represented a missing part of the patient's self-structure, a vital loving function that had not been provided in childhood, resulting in a developmental arrest at the stage of selfobject deficiency. Kohut believed that maternal, paternal, and sibling selfobject experiences, such as mirroring, idealization, and twinship were necessary for the healthy development of the self to resume. In my view, vital selfobject experiences are narcissistic forms of love.

Confronted by a selfobject transference, the analyst needed to diagnose the patient's selfobject need. For example, the patient might display grandiose exhibitionism, monopolizing the hour without interest in the analyst, provoking the analyst to attend to his every gesture. This would suggest a selfobject need for the analyst to mirror the patient due to the lack of parental mirroring in early childhood. By diagnosing and explaining this need and analysing ruptures in the experience of mirroring (optimal frustration) during the transference—that is, disruptions of the self-selfobject continuity, the analyst facilitated a "transmuting of internalizations" (Kohut, 1971) that strengthened the self-structure. In addition to "optimal frustration", Bacal (1985), a contemporary self psychologist, proposed that the analyst's "optimal responsiveness" would also strengthen the self-structure. Evidence of self-strengthening could be observed in the patient's stronger sense of identity, greater self-esteem, and increased ambition. Selfobject analyses of twinship transferences also strengthened the self in these ways whereas selfobject analyses of idealization facilitated the development of a sense of direction and goals (Kohut, 1971; Wolf, 1988). Through these forms of analytic selfobject love, the self-structure became stronger and more cohesive.

Like Ferenczi, Kohut (1971, 1977, 1984) advocated that analysts take responsibility for parental failures (i.e., in Kohut's view, parental selfobject failures) in the transference, privileging the patient's psychic reality. This made the process of psychoanalysis less authoritarian and more relational than classical psychoanalysis, ego psychology, and Kleinian analysis. Instead of adopting the clinical attitude of the latter traditional theories that the patient's transference constituted distortions resulting from internal conflicts from childhood, Kohut believed that it was therapeutically necessary to affirm the patient's psychic reality through empathic attunement and "experience-near" interpretations. He warned that interpreting the selfobject transferences of narcissistically vulnerable patients as neurotic distortions would wound them further. In my view, this change in technique expressed a more maternal form of analytic love.

Kohut's great contribution to psychoanalytic therapeutic action was making the analysis of deficit as important as the analysis of internal conflict and providing an extensive diagnostic assortment of selfobject needs and selfobject transferences for analysts to choose from. Prior to Kohut, with the exception of Winnicott's (1960) "holding" and Bion's (1963) "containment", there was no psychoanalytic theory that acknowledged the pervasiveness of psychological deficit related to developmental arrests. Instead of having to rely upon the limited constructs of "holding" and "containing", analysts now had the capacity to diagnose a wide variety of developmentally acquired selfobject deficits, such as mirroring, twinship, idealization, and the selfobject transferences associated with them. This list has been expanded to include the selfobject needs and transferences of merger, effectiveness, and adversity (Wolf, 1988). I would add to the list the "need to be needed", which is so vital for a sense of belonging. All these selfobject needs require different forms of analytic love through understanding and empathic responsiveness, to repair the related deficits.

It should be noted that psychological deficit and internal conflict are inextricably interwoven. For example, a mother responding to her baby's oral needs with the attuned, timely provision of the desired milk is simultaneously nurturing the baby libidinally and also providing responsive mirroring. The responsive feeding validates the baby's self-esteem, making it feel special and entitled to ingest the milk it desires. Thus, a withholding, non-nurturing mother is predisposing her baby to internal conflict over frustrated oral dependency needs as well as a psychological deficit from the lack of attuned mirroring. An analyst's interpretations and emotional responses to the patient are similarly intertwined, simultaneously providing a deep understanding of internal conflicts and an attuned, empathic responsiveness that can strengthen the self-structure.

8. Intersubjective, interpersonal and relational models: reparative relational experience

In self psychology, the analyst's acceptance of responsibility for the self-selfobject rupture in the transference made the traditional psychoanalytic community more receptive to the therapeutic value of relational experience within traditional psychoanalytic circles. Since self psychology lacked a theory of object relatedness, Stolorow transformed his self psychology orientation into a theory of intersubjectivity (Stolorow, Brandchaft & Atwood, 1987). Intersubjective theory expanded psychoanalysis from a one person, intrapsychic model to a two person dyadic model. It hypothesized that the unconscious psychodynamics of both patient and analyst influenced each other in the analytic process. The gradual acceptance of this theory among traditional psychoanalysts stimulated their interest in the writings of Interpersonal Psychoanalysts, such as Levenson (1987a). Members of the interpersonal school had been historically rejected as psychoanalysts by traditional Freudians due to their non-acceptance of libido theory.

Interpersonal theory posited that the influence of the social environment—parents, society, and culture—is what causes mental problems instead of biological sexual and aggressive drives (Levenson, 1987a). The interpersonalists viewed the combined effects of insight-inducing interpretations and interpersonal experience as the primary mutative factors in psychoanalysis. Greenberg and Mitchell (1983) integrated interpersonal theory into traditional psychoanalysis through the rubric of "relational analysis", by including any object relations theory, such as Fairbairn's and Winnicott's, with the exception of those containing instinct-based drive theories, like Klein's. This was because "drive" was not interpersonally determined.

The therapeutic importance of interpersonal maternal attunement in Stern's infant research (1985), of self-validation and emotional responsiveness in neurological studies on brain growth in children (Schore, 1994, 2002, 2003), and of psychobiological modes of attachment described by Siegel (1999), have profound implications for the transformative influence of analytic love on brain development and mental functioning.

9. The relational unconscious

In the relational unconscious, transference and countertransference provoke a continual unconscious intersubjective enactment of a co-created infantile drama emanating from the internal worlds of analyst and analysand (Friedman & Natterson, 1999; Varga, 2005) in which a form of vital parental loving is at stake (Wolson, 2006). This definition differs from Davies (1996) and Gerson's (2004) original conceptions of the relational unconscious, which, while stressing the clinical importance of intersubjective enactments, do not subscribe to the presence of a "continuous" relational enactment with analytic love at its core.

In working with the relational unconscious, the analyst needs to become aware of its observable manifestations to maximize its therapeutic utility. By understanding the influence of the patient's transference pressure on the analyst as well as how the analyst might be affecting the patient, the analyst is able to infer more accurately what he or she is embodying that the patient is therapeutically needing, such as a type of fathering or mothering that was lacking in childhood or a stronger superego that is needed for drive regulation, or a displaced self-representation through which the patient can work through narcissistic issues, or a needed selfobject function. The analyst is unconsciously drawn into enacting these roles through the stimulus pull of the transference/countertransference interaction (Sandler, 1976).

At times, the analyst is actually experiencing and behaviourally expressing the living embodiment of the patient's internal mother, for example. And similarly, the patient might actually feel and behave like the analyst's internal father. Through the patient's experience and understanding of this enacted analytic relationship, conflicted internal object relations and drive-defence conflicts are worked through and developmental arrests repaired.

For example, a therapist became drowsy, on the verge of falling asleep, as her patient, whom she increasingly despised, talked on and on in a circuitous fashion as if the therapist was not present. In supervision, the therapist reported that the patient reminded her of her narcissistic mother who treated her like a self-extension, ignoring her existence. The patient also struggled with a narcissistic, self-centered maternal imago who showed no interest in her. In the transference, she angrily dominated the narcissistic therapist mother with her self-centered talking, to make sure she would be heard. The therapist realized she was unconsciously enacting the patient's disinterested mother through her drowsiness, which simultaneously represented retaliating against her own narcissistic mother embodied by the patient. In supervision, the therapist became aware that she needed to overcome her drowsiness and anger in order to provide the patient with the therapeutic attentiveness, empathy, and insightful understanding that she had always lacked.

Although one could critique the therapist for not having sufficiently worked through her countertransference in the narrow sense, I believe this was the therapeutic "lightning in the bottle". As the embodiment of the "bad" narcissistic mother, the therapist needed to accept her responsibility for failing the patient, to fight her drowsiness and rage, and become more maternally attuned. This would, in effect, give the patient an opportunity to experience her "bad" narcissistic mother, in the form of the therapist, struggling to become empathically caring towards her. Over time, this would potentially transform her self-centered maternal imago into a loving one, diminish her narcissistic vulnerability and rage, and strengthen her self-structure.

In order for the therapist to facilitate this therapeutic experience, she had to work through her rage towards her own narcissistic mother now embodied by the patient. In other words, in the analytic interaction with her patient, she needed to become an empathic, understanding therapist to her own mother, whom she despised. As she could increasingly understand why the patient was having to monopolize the session and ignore her, the therapist felt more loving and accepting, not only towards her patient, but towards her own internal mother. In turn, the patient for the first time felt understood and seen by her narcissistic therapist mother, and her narcissistic rage diminished. Eventually, the therapist was able to interpret the enacted dynamics between them, helping the patient clearly see how her mind worked. This understanding graphically defined and clarified this transformative relational experience, thereby cognitively reinforcing the changes in psychic structure.

As this vignette illustrates, in the reciprocal interactive chemistry of the relational unconscious, the analyst attempts to discern through introspection the most therapeutic clinical response, whether it be an interpretation or some other intervention. By tolerating and embracing patients' demands, attacks, rejections, neglect, dependency, and/or love and helping patients understand what is motivating them to feel, think, and behave as they do, the analyst often responds more understandingly and therefore, in effect, more lovingly from the patient's perspective, than the patient expects from projected parental imagos. This is especially true of the analyst's attuned, insightful interpretations, which are often in positive contrast to the projected, harsh, neglectful, or abusive parental imagos and self representations. The combined, intertwined experience of insight with relational caring facilitates conflict resolution, the gradual modulation of the "bad" internal objects and the integration and strengthening of the patient's self-structure. This, of course, is similar to what Strachey (1934) said three-quarters of a century ago. However, he did not address the reciprocal transference/countertransference enactment in the relational unconscious with the therapeutic agency of analytic love at its mutative core.

Conclusion

Clearly, the concept of analytic love is complex. It is not a simplistic, polarized notion that excludes analytic hate. It includes the full range of the analyst's reactions and clinical attitudes towards the patient. It pervades virtually everything that an analyst does that is therapeutic. I strongly believe that analysts need to know, accept, and embrace analytic love as a core mechanism of therapeutic action in order to achieve the best results. This is because patients need to feel and believe that their analysts love them, as Ferenczi maintained (Thompson, 1943). They can only know this if the analyst conveys love through effective interventions. I believe that the patient's projection of wished-for analytic love needs realistic confirmation for it to result in psychic change.

The form of analytic love depends upon the patient's psychodynamics. Some require the more maternal, pre-Oedipal Winnicottian or Kohutian love; others, the more fatherly love of classical Freudians, ego psychologists, or Kleinians. And many require varying combinations of each type, suggesting the importance of a pluralistic perspective (Pine, 1988; Bernardi, 1992; Pulver, 1993).

In summary, at its mutative best, psychoanalysis facilitates the patient's unconscious drive-defence and object relational conflict-resolution, self integration, and reparation of psychological deficits through the loving relational experience of insight-inducing interpretations and non-verbal holding, containing, and selfobject functions in the continuous intersubjective, interpersonal transference/countertransference interaction.

CHAPTER NINE

The analyst's subjective experience: holding environment and container of projections

Peggy Porter

I will begin with the wisp of a memory: a beautiful young woman from another culture—a first session, a beginning rapport, a painful topic. Her rapid blinking of eyes and almost impercep- tible turning away from me, her quick fanning of the air in front of her face. I knew she was fighting tears.

But here is my point: I also knew with some certainty that I must not appear to notice. (I knew this before I consciously realized she did not *want* me to notice.) I remember glancing involuntarily at the tissue box on the table, quickly glancing away, making the unaccus- tomed effort to sit completely still and silent until she could regain her composure. I felt we were both working to "contain" the moment, to move beyond it. I remember wondering if I should "do something" after all. This all occurred within the space of seconds, and it was an atypical reaction for me to a patient's being close to tears. Weeks later, when this woman finally allowed herself to cry openly, she told me how devastating it would have been for her on that first day if she had, in her words, "lost face in front of a stranger".

We know that this kind of unconscious transmission does occur between people—not only between patients and their analysts— and after the fact one can speculate about how such a transmission is sent or received, used or not used, or what actually happened, as I do now. For example, in the above instance, if I had tried to formulate my patient's experience without reference to my own receptive experience of her meta-message, I would have focused on how she seemed to be protecting herself against showing me her tears. If I had then tried to interpret her "resistance" (however empathically I might have done so), I think I would have been taking something away from her, in the process that Bollas (1987) has called "extractive introjection" (p. 158). More than that, I would have been showing her that I was incapable of receiving, or was perhaps dismissing, her more important unconscious-to-unconscious communication to me to stay back—that she was not ready. I would have been intruding. In any case, I do not think an interpretation would have been particularly useful at that point— or what Strachey (1934) has called "mutative" (p. 142)—because, although it would have been immediate to the situation, my patient had not as yet developed any significant transference to me. Instead, she would now have had good reason to feel unsafe with me, perhaps invaded. It was a first session—it was just too soon. Fortunately I sensed her more important meta-message to me, and it stopped me.

I take this kind of unconscious-to-unconscious communication as a given phenomenon, and I base my analytic work on it. I know that the accurate reception of this kind of wordless communication will eventually become background "holding" for my patient—an essential part of Winnicott's "total environmental provision" (1960, p. 588). I will also rely on my internal experiencing in other aspects of the work—for example, to understand when something is being projected onto me, to contain it, and eventually to bring it back to my patient. I try to be vulnerable to whatever receptive capabilities may be available to me at a given moment. I know this will mean staying open to my own emotional, visceral, proprioceptive, and mental responses—very possibly in that order—as well as simultaneously trying to remain open to similar processes in my patient.

I believe it is a great paradox of psychoanalytic work that when I focus most fully on my own conscious and unconscious experiencing in the moment, I am at the same time placing myself most fully at the service of my patient. As Bollas (1987) has said, "in order to find the patient, we must look for him within ourselves" (p. 202).

It is well known that in the first 50 or 60 years of psychoanalysis, until about the middle of the last century, the psychoanalytic transferences were studied; the psychoanalytic countertransferences usually were not. In an odd iteration of the now mostly discredited "ontogeny recapitulates phylogeny", it seems to me that we as individual analysts *do* often follow the same developmental path as has been followed widely within our field: we initially learn to focus on our patients' material—their dreams, transferences, and resistances—and only after that, as we become more comfortable with ourselves in our roles and through our own analyses, we begin to attend to our own internal experiencing in the countertransference (see, for example, Diamond, Chapter Ten in this volume; Helscher, Chapter Eleven, this volume). We come to trust our own emotional, visceral, and proprioceptive experiences—which, although they may not make sense on the surface of it—upon reflection, often make *better* sense than whatever was being verbally communicated at the time.

This process will be different with each person, and with each patient-analyst pair. Whenever real psychoanalytic work ensues, there is a powerful affective and interactive exchange that can only occur between these two particular people at this particular time in their lives—each coming to it with all their own non-verbal and verbal experiences and responses—both conscious and unconscious—and their own separate internal worlds and objects as they have existed up until that particular moment in their lives. Little (1951) acknowledges something similar when she says of the patient-analyst relationship:

> It will always include something which is specific to both the individual patient and the individual analyst. That is, every countertransference is different from every other, as every transference is different, and it varies within itself from day to day, according to variations in both patient and analyst and the outside world [p. 33].

In the same paper, she adds that the analyst's ability to access his own experiencing—or, as she expresses it, "the analyst's attitude to his own id impulses"—"will still vary in him from day to day, according to the stresses and strains to which he is exposed" (p. 38).

It is this ability to access our own experiencing for use in the analytic interaction that we hope will continue to increase throughout our entire professional lives. As an early teacher of mine expressed it, "There's no completing the curriculum" (J. Warkentin, personal communication, 1975).

When a patient and analyst engage deeply in a psychoanalytic process, the interaction which occurs in this particular patient-analyst pair will have a lasting impact on the lives of *both* participants. Although the analyst will treat other patients, and the patient may eventually work with other analysts, the particular therapeutic action of this one and only psychoanalysis between these two unique people will never be replicated.

In this chapter, I begin by searching out a few pertinent antecedents for this particular view of the analyst's role as an *interacting* (receptive, holding, nurturing, and containing), *countertransferring* subjectivity interacting with another transferring subjectivity. This material will be familiar to many, but may provide some conceptual roots of what is often learned through personal experience (e.g., the apprenticeship one experiences through supervision and training analyses). Secondly, I will then exemplify the analyst's use of her subjective interactivity with her patient through an instance where countertransference was used to identify, contain, and work with the patient's projective identification and introjection. Finally, I will end with a focus on the analyst's subjective position, which I believe must underlie all others if the patient is to thrive.

In preparing this brief review, I am again reminded of how far we have come, how quickly, in the first hundred years of psychoanalysis. As noted above, during the first half of the last century there was little attention paid to the analyst's countertransference, with a few notable exceptions (e.g., Winnicott, 1949). In general the actual interaction between analyst and patient was not studied, although again with exceptions (see below). The middle years of the last century seem to have brought a new burst of creative activity to the scene, though, and many of the ideas offered at that time still inform our understanding today about the analyst's use of her own experiencing in her work (Heimann, 1950; Little, 1951; Racker, 1953).

Early antecedent: on re-examining the "telephone metaphor"

In his "Recommendations to Physicians Practising Psycho-Analysis", Freud (1912b) acknowledges a necessary *reciprocity* between analyst and patient when he states that the doctor's "evenly-suspended attention" (p. 111) is *"the necessary counterpart* to the demand made on the patient that he should communicate everything that occurs to him" (p. 112, italics added). In the same paper, Freud uses the "telephone metaphor"—that the doctor "must turn his own unconscious like a receptive organ towards the transmitting unconscious of the patient" (p. 115). But while acknowledging the need for the analyst's unconscious reception of the patient's unconscious transmission, he says the analyst should "put aside all his feelings" and that this "emotional coldness ... creates the most advantageous conditions for both parties" (p. 115). Thus he seems to be advocating the use of the analyst's unconscious reception of the patient's unconscious transmission through intellectual means alone. In what seems an impossibility, he appears to be suggesting that the reception should occur without the use of the analyst's affect. In another paradox in the same paper, he states that the doctor must allow himself to be "taken by surprise" (p. 114), but again, presumably, by *intellectual* surprise only.

On the other hand, while Langs (1981, p. 359) has credited Strachey (1934) with being the first to examine the implications of an interactional approach, it seems to me that here Freud *is* recommending an interactional approach—the analyst's reception of the patient's transmission, and then the analyst's returning this information to the patient as late as "a year and a day" later (p. 112).

Antecedent: Strachey's interactional approach

Unlike Freud, in James Strachey's classic paper "The Nature of the Therapeutic Action of Psychoanalysis" (1934), he recognizes the analyst's affective therapeutic interaction with the patient through the analyst's acceptance of the patient's projections and his returning of them in more benign form for the patient's introjection. He here acknowledges the role of the *"real* analyst" (italics added), who is "less aggressive" (p. 143) than the imago projected onto him by the patient. Strachey states, "[We] find ourselves involved in an actual and immediate situation, in which we and the patient are the principal characters" (p. 132), and that it is this very immediacy in the transference that allows for "mutative" (p. 142) interpretations. But he also explicitly acknowledges the real analyst's "occasional feelings of utter disorientation" (p. 127), and references Melanie

Klein, who said that the analyst must overcome a "quite special internal difficulty" in order to give an interpretation at the exact moment the patient's id-energy is most alive and focused on the analyst (Strachey, p. 158). He states further that the analyst "is exposing himself to some great danger in doing so" (p. 159), and "such a moment must above all others put to the test his relations with his own unconscious impulses" (p. 159). Nevertheless, although the analyst may be experiencing great affect, he is to react to it with an "absence of behavior" (p. 149).

Heimann, Racker, the Kleinians, and the constructive uses of countertransference

When Paula Heimann presented her groundbreaking paper "On Counter-transference" at the 16th International Psycho-Analytical Congress in 1949 (published 1950), Leo Berman (1949) had just published his own paper, which probably better represented the views of orthodox psychoanalysts at that time (prior to the early 1950s). Berman made the now classic distinction between the ordinary, reasonable, and appropriate reactions of the analyst as a person, and his "countertransference", which he defined as "the analyst's reactions to the patient as though the patient were an important figure in the analyst's past life" (p. 159)—that is, he actually looked at "countertransference" as the analyst's own "transference", now focused on the patient. According to Berman, the "ordinary" reactions could be potentially helpful; the "countertransference" could not.

But during what was to become a pivotal period in psychoanalysis—the middle of the 20th century, and especially the early 1950s—Heimann was the first of several to make no such distinction between ordinary and countertransferential feelings of the analyst: she not only defined "countertransference" to include *all* the responses of the analyst to the patient (both conscious and unconscious); she also viewed all these responses as *potentially constructive.*

Heimann (1950) specifically stressed the "*relationship* between two persons", (p. 81), and said that if the analyst tries to work without consulting his feelings, his interpretations are "poor" (p. 82). As she stated:

Our basic assumption is that the analyst's unconscious understands that of his patient. This rapport on the deep level comes to the surface in the form of feelings which the analyst notices in responses to his patient, in his "countertransference" [p. 82].

Heimann (ibid.) further wrote:

There will be stretches in the analytic work when the analyst ... does not register his feelings as a problem, because they are in accord with the meaning he understands. But often the emotions roused in him are much nearer to the heart of the matter than his reasoning, or, to put it in other words, his unconscious perception of the patient's unconscious is more acute and in advance of his conscious conception of the situation [p. 82].

Heimann's view of countertransference as including *all* the responses of the analyst was shared by Little (1951), Racker (1953), and other Kleinians, and remains the view that is most widely held today.

It is actually Racker's work, though, that has seemed most influential in the literature on countertransference (1968). Although this work is already familiar, I want to comment briefly on the concepts of "concordant" and "complementary" countertransference: I have found "concordant" countertransference (p. 134), in which I identify myself with a part of my patient's personality (ego with ego, a given feeling with a given feeling), to be relatively uncomplicated compared to "complementary" countertransference, in which I identify with some one of the patient's internal objects.

As Racker expressed it: "The complementary identifications are produced by the fact that the patient treats the analyst as an internal (projected) object, and in consequence the analyst feels treated as such; that is, he identifies himself with this object" (p. 135).

In this type of countertransference the analyst may find herself in a quasi-adversarial, competitive, seductive, or otherwise challenging role with her patient, and must be especially attuned to her own subjective responses. For example, the patient may be experiencing himself as a criticized little boy and experiencing me, the analyst, as the critical mother. In this case, a problem exists if I "take that on", actually feel critical, and—here is the problematic part—*enact my criticism towards the patient* rather than reflect on it, and use it to understand and interpret my patient's experience. If I act without reflection I become yet another one of an endless repetition of people who have responded to the patient's "pull" for whatever that particular complementary response might be: in this example, criticism, but in other cases it could be competition, envy, or another un-empathic response. Racker (1953) states "that to the degree to which the analyst fails in the concordant identifications and rejects them certain complementary identifications become intensified" (p. 135), which leads me to wonder if, with better empathy, these complementary identifications could be avoided altogether, or in contrast, as I believe, they are in fact necessary for the work but must be used with great care. This idea will be explored further in a vignette at the end of this chapter.

The emphasis on the use of the analyst's own experiencing in the analytic interaction—as indicated above, an emphasis which was first adopted by the Kleinians in the 1950s—continues to be the perspective which seems most widely held today by analysts of all orientations (see Diamond, Chapter Ten in this volume).

Two subjectivities interacting

Writing in a recent issue of the *International Journal of Psychoanalysis*, and expressing views he considers relevant to the contemporary Kleinians, contemporary Freudians, British independent analysts, and some of the French school as well as some current Bionians, according to Blass's (2010) introduction, Busch (2010) states the following:

> With the greater appreciation and acceptance of the analyst's countertransference as an inevitable and integral part of analysis, we have been able to reach an understanding of the depths of the unconscious in a way that was previously unimaginable. It has become clear that this is a primary way the unconscious is communicated to the analyst during treatment [p. 29].

This again assumes an analyst who is willing to look at her own countertransference—both her conscious and unconscious responses, or what Racker (1968) would call her countertransference thoughts and countertransference positions (pp. 143–144)—and who can then think about and *contain* them.

Heimann (1950) noted the tendency of feelings to impel towards actions, and the need for containment. Modell (1991) writes, "[U]nlike in ordinary life, we discipline ourselves to inhibit our affective responses but not our affective perceptions" (p. 18). According to Racker (1968), what makes for objectivity is the analyst's ability to make himself (his own subjectivity and countertransference) the object of his continuous observation and analysis (p. 132). Many analysts today would say that, partly as a consequence of internalizing this stance and being able to contain one's feelings—to *be* the analyst who can contain and think about her own experiences—the patient is enabled to think about *his* own internal experience, and to show the same curiosity previously evident in his analyst (see also Diamond, Helscher, Chapters Ten and Eleven, this volume).

It is now generally accepted that the analyst's use and containment of her receptive and interactive experiencing is not only a powerful and positive tool, but also an essential process for a successful psychoanalysis. The analyst needs to use her whole person in her work—her entire being as she experiences it—and she needs to do this regardless of, *and especially when*, her experiencing does not seem to match what is being said or done in the session. This position of course presupposes the analyst will continue to do her own analytic "work" throughout her career—at least "on and off all the rest of her professional life" (Warkentin, 1975). As Racker (1968) points out, we "are still children and neurotics as well as adults and analysts (p. 130).

Analyst's use of subjectivity in instance of "splitting" and projective identification

In a previous paper, Firman and I (Firman & Kaplan [Porter], 1978), quoted the following brief definitions, which will be pertinent to the subsequent clinical vignette:

> The term "splitting," as used by the psychoanalytic school of Melanie Klein, refers to a normal defensive operation of the early (infantile) ego, in which a part of the self is "split off" and projected into an external object. Through the process of

> projective identification, the external project is then seen as
> having acquired the characteristics of the projected part of the
> self; or the self may become identified with the object of the
> projection (Malin & Grotstein, 1966; Segal, 1964) [p. 291].

Besides being a defensive operation, however, projective identification is also a normal way of relating to objects, which persists into mature adulthood (Malin & Grotstein, ibid.).

Further, Modell (1991) sees projective identification as "a process whereby specific elements of the patient's inner affective constellation are communicated to the therapist without the patient's conscious intent" (p. 18). When splitting is occurring, the analyst needs all her receptive and interactive subjectivity to actually experience whatever is being projected onto her, and to experience her own identification with that part of the patient that is being projected. As Modell says, "… sometimes the patient communicates by means of actions that induce in the therapist the very same affective response that the patient experienced as a child" (pp. 18–19).

In a recent presentation with Kalish-Weiss (Porter & Kalish-Weiss, 2008), I discussed how the analyst can use her countertransference in three ways: (1) to identify that a split *is* occurring; (2) to make the split-off aspect conscious and relevant to the patient so that it can eventually be integrated; and (3) to use the processes of projective identification and/or enactment which occur as a way of clarifying and "fleshing out" the details and history of the split, so that reintegration can eventually occur.

In the vignette presented below, I believe that by recognizing my own identification with the patient's projected vulnerability, I was able to help him recognize *his* own identification with an aggressive internal object who *hated* his vulnerability. He had to recognize that part of himself as well as the part he was trying to project, so that he could eventually bring both parts together and heal this particular split within. In this process, both the patient and I had to endure our own painful internal experiences in order to learn more about his internal object world.

According to N. Oberman (personal communication, 2010), split-off aspects of the psyche function rather autonomously, and the patient may move easily into and out of them *without any awareness* of what he/she is doing. Oberman has stated his belief that these splits almost invariably represent an unconscious identification with an aspect of a patient's internalized parental figure. In the vignette below, the patient had indeed moved into a split-off aspect of his psyche without conscious awareness of what he was doing, though in every other way his reality testing was fine. I, on the other hand, had a strong reaction in the countertransference to what was happening, in an instance of the type of "complementary" countertransference defined by Racker (1968).

The case of Andrew

A few years ago I was working with "Andrew", a friendly young professional, in a four-times-a-week psychoanalysis. Initially somewhat depressed, after two years Andrew felt he was getting his life back on track both personally and professionally. Then something happened which would tax our individual subjectivities as well as the strength of our relationship.

In the second year of our work together, Andrew experienced a loss due to a close friend's job change that would take the friend out of the country. Although Andrew claimed to be happy for his friend, who had wanted this job, and although he used his analysis appropriately to talk about his various feelings of sadness, loss, and even envy, he nevertheless began to present himself to me in a way I had never seen.

Rather than the outgoing and friendly young man I usually found in my shared waiting room, sometimes interacting with another patient if another patient happened to be present, I found a different Andrew.

On a given Thursday, when I went into the waiting room to get him, I had a brief sense of not even recognizing my own patient. Rather than the polite, open faced young man I usually found, I saw that he was sitting apart, with clenched lips, arms crossed over his chest, and a look that could only be described as "contemptuous". When he saw me he seemed to "sneer", and abruptly pushed past me in what felt like a deliberately provocative manner.

When I tried to encourage Andrew to tell me what was going on, he said he "did not want to talk", and brushed off my interpretations regarding his evident pain. When I said I wanted to understand, he said he did not want to be understood. After 30 minutes of mostly silence, he said he was going to leave now, got up off the couch, and left the session 15 minutes early, as I continued to sit in my chair, surprised by this sudden action he had never taken before. It felt to me as if he were being deliberately rude.

On Friday he called and left a message cancelling his appointment for that day. He gave no reason, but did say he would see me on Monday, which was our next regularly scheduled meeting. I found myself thinking quite a lot over the weekend about what was happening. Was he attempting to leave me as he had been left? But when I had interpreted something similar to him on Thursday, he had scornfully pushed it away.

On Monday he again appeared to frown with distaste towards me in the waiting room, in spite of the presence of another patient, which would normally have inhibited this behaviour on the part of this self-aware young man. He again fended off my efforts to understand and/or interpret his anger. He said he was thinking of "taking a break" from his analysis, and derided my interpretation that he was disappointed in me—that all our work on "relating" had nevertheless failed to keep his friend in town. He responded by saying analysis was useless.

On Tuesday Andrew again appeared to look at me with derision as he brushed past me into my office and flopped onto the couch. He again said he did not see the point of this work, and had decided he really *did* want to quit.

After a few minutes of silence, I asked him very gently if he was aware of his physical/facial presentation to me since Thursday. Although he said he was not, I detected a flicker of interest. I described as non-judgmentally as I could what I thought I had been seeing—the tight, down-turned mouth, what appeared to be a contemptuous stare—and asked him if he could possibly be aware of the feelings connected with those physical expressions. He said he might be able to do so. After a few moments, he said he thought his face might be reflecting his depression.

At this point I shared my belief (based on my internal experience as "recipient") that what I had been seeing was not just depression and anger, but what also appeared to be contempt—what appeared to be a *scornful* frown. Since he seemed to accept this, I pressed ahead, and asked who in his life had shown him this look. He seemed puzzled. I then asked which of his parents had shown him this look. At first he thought neither of them had, but then in a kind of "ah-ha" moment, he said there *was* a "particular look" which his mother would get, which everybody in the family would know meant she was very displeased.

Andrew and I then teased out together how he had felt when he had seen this look on his mother's face directed at him. He said he had always felt he was not doing enough, and I noted to myself my own similar feelings of not doing enough this past week for Andrew. He said that the look had had the effect of making him work harder and harder, and I again noted to myself how much time I had spent over the last few days "working harder" on this case in my own mind. I said perhaps he had wanted *me* to work harder, and he said "definitely". We then talked about what *kind* of not doing enough had elicited this look from his mother. After considerable work, Andrew realized that it was when he did not look good (polished, charming), and did not reflect well on his mother. I again thought how I felt that I had not been looking so good to Andrew over the past few days. I privately realized I had been identified with Andrew's projection of his vulnerable, inept, not-doing-enough little self—and feeling increasingly desperate to figure out what to do.

Meanwhile, as Andrew reflected on the historical details, he came to realize that at one point he had consciously decided to identify with his mother's contempt rather than to be the recipient of it, as his brother had been. We were further able to clarify Andrew's ideas about when and why his mother had used contempt as a defence, and her own social fears—and on a deeper level, fears of being unlovable—that lay behind it. We talked about how Andrew had also taken on some of these same fears, which were now activated by the loss of his friend.

As Andrew talked, his mood changed, and though he left the session still sad and still somewhat angry that I had no "magic", he no longer appeared scornful.

Discussion
I think the first step in working with this kind of split is to identify its presence. As with many other analytic processes, this identification of a split is often initiated through the analyst's own countertransferential feelings in response to it, which she can then use to help her patient also recognize its presence. In this particular instance, the "split" might be said to involve the manic defence, which some (e.g.,

Winnicott, 1935) have thought to be particularly difficult to work with because "by the very nature of the manic defence we should expect to be unable to get to know it directly through introspection, at the moment when that defence is operative" (p. 132). But sometimes, as in this case, pointing out the physical, non-verbal manifestations of this defence can help make it more workable, helping the patient recognize the "not-me-ness" of what is happening (see also Kalish, Chapter Twelve in this volume). It is then possible to tease out the identification represented by the previously split-off aspect of the psyche. Parenthetically, when "stumped", I operate on the hypothesis that the split-off aspect probably represents an identification with an aspect of an internalized parental figure.

It is then possible to make the historical details conscious to the patient and known to the analyst, and this is done partly through using the patient's own memories, and also partly through using the analyst's own subjective experiences of having been identified with the patient's projections. With this kind of back-and-forth movement between patient and analyst, they may begin to speculate about the "reality" of what may have occurred with the actual historical figure and in the patient's early experience. It is then necessary to help the patient reintegrate the previously split-off aspect of his psyche into his overall psyche, and to reintroject his projection. Finally it is important for analyst and patient, together, to reintegrate the analytic resonance—the subjective "psyche" of their relationship.

Conclusion

I want to end by focusing on the analyst's subjective response, which I believe must underlie all of her (or his) other responses if the patient is to thrive. Like Heimann (1950) and many others, I believe all the analyst's receptive, interactive, and countertransferential reactions are potentially useful when examined, and I have given an example of how this may be so in the case of projective identification. But it is the analyst's *willingness to use all her responses in the service of her patient* that is essential, and that allows her to provide what Winnicott (1960) called a safe "holding environment" for her patient's growth. She has to be able to sustain this willingness, even in the face of the moment-to-moment messiness of many good analytic hours, and continue to offer this "environmental provision" for her patient no matter what else is going on, because as Modell (1976, p. 290) has said, "To have a childhood requires the presence of a holding environment." When all is going well, the analyst will find herself in a state very similar to that described by Winnicott (1960, pp. 593–594), in which the mother is identified with her baby and is able to "achieve a very powerful sense of what the baby needs", which allows her to understand, and allows her patient to *feel* understood, as he experiences with her his memories, joys, and pain—perhaps for the first time. With a sufficient period of holding through understanding—and, as H. Bolgar (personal communication, 2010) has said, "… realizing that sometimes holding means 'letting go'"— I believe the patient, like Winnicott's infant (1960), can resume his own natural urge towards growth and integration.

SECTION IV

MENTAL EXPERIENCE
AND THERAPEUTIC ACTION:
UNCONSCIOUS COMMUNICATION,
INTERNALIZATION, AND NON-VERBAL
PROCESSES

The impact of the mind of the analyst: from unconscious processes to intrapsychic change

Michael J. Diamond

"I just dropped in to see what condition my condition was in."

—Pop song lyric (Newbury, 1967)

Since beginning to train as a psychoanalytic clinician more than 30 years ago, I have tried to understand how the various psychoanalytic theories of mind and clinical technique create the conditions for therapeutic change. During my formative years of psychoanalytic practice, particularly when working with more regressed and disturbed patients, I experienced in an immediate way the patient's stubborn resistances, challenges, and character-based defensive operations, each contributing to my countertransference and accompanying subjective experiences. As a novice psychoanalyst, these experiences seemed like obstacles preventing me from getting through to my patients.

I sought ways to generate meaningful change through these "stalemates" (see Diamond, 1989). Simultaneously, I was beginning to recognize my fluctuating internal experience with each unique patient. As a result, I realized how the tripartite model of training, particularly the significance of a deeply engaged, personal psychoanalysis, is essential for conducting psychoanalytic treatment. In learning how to be more open to my emotional and mental life, I was progressing from a psychotherapist to becoming a psychoanalyst. Now, decades later, I am still learning my way along this path.

I became profoundly aware of the value of unconscious communication and the therapeutic significance of tuning in to my mental activities with my first supervised psychoanalytic case. The patient, a depressed man with a manic character style, married his long-time girlfriend shortly after my wife gave birth to our first child. During a lengthy silence when he was sullen and withdrawn, I had a fantasy of walking with my infant daughter on a pedestrian crossing. As a car was approaching rapidly, I imagined clutching her in my arms while leaping onto the vehicle in order to keep her out of harm's way. However, the moving vehicle struck her. I felt enormous pain and helplessness visualizing my beloved daughter injured, before realizing that I was only fantasizing while seated with my silent patient.

Two sessions later, the patient revealed that he had been frequenting gay bathhouses that were breeding grounds for AIDS. With my supervisor's help, I recognized that my fantasy reflected an unconscious concordant identification (Racker, 1968) with my patient, who was unable to protect what was most precious to him given his manic penchant to mow down almost anything in his path. Indeed, he was engaging in unprotected sex that threatened his new wife and himself. Partly through recognizing my inter-psychic participation in receiving his unconsciously murderous sado-masochism through projective identification, I began to grasp what I would subsequently discover is essential in working psychoanalytically.

Over time, my internal experiences increasingly became an "object" of my analytic scrutiny, even when enacted with my patients. This culminated several years later in publishing a paper (Diamond, 1997) about my work with traumatized, dissociative patients who needed their embodied, pre-symbolized experience to reside within me for therapeutic containment and understanding. My comprehension of their primitive mental operations could only deepen because of experiencing and learning to use my intense, at times disturbing, and quite varied internal experience. Necessity being the mother of invention, I had to learn to trust and capably employ my own mind as an analytic "object" to facilitate mutative change.

The analyst's recognition and utilization of his/her mental activities, including the unconscious, somatized, and less self-reflectively accessible derivatives, comprise what I mean by *analytic mind use*. An analyst's effective interventions (including symbolizing and representational interpretations, containing processes, as well as clarifying, reflective, elaborating, and validating comments), which help patients understand their internal life and live it more fully, originate from the skilful use of mental experience. I believe that such mind use by the analyst is the driving force leading to mutative action.[1]

In this chapter, I illuminate this proposition in several ways: (1) by clarifying what I mean by mind and *analytic mind use* while placing the latter in historical context; (2) by considering its function in therapeutic action; and (3) by describing the nature of the analyst's psychic activity when using mental experience to understand the patient's unconscious (and preconscious) inner life. I will begin by considering the function of analytic mind use in therapeutic action.

The analyst's mind use as the foundation of therapeutic action

Speaking of therapeutic action in psychoanalysis in the singular as *the* therapeutic action is misleading inasmuch as mutative change occurs in myriad ways and depends on many factors, including the patient's unconscious theory of change, the analyst's use of theory and technical proficiency, and the nature of the patient's psychic functioning in combination with that of the analyst. Though various psychoanalytic schools favour diverse aims, they converge in stressing the significance of change pertaining to patients' mental experience (including accompanying bodily manifestations). In today's "emerging area of common ground" (Gabbard, 1995, p. 475), most analysts acknowledge the significance of accepting their *participation in* the patient's transference and recognize that their own ongoing mental activities, countertransference, subjectivity, and intra- as well as inter-psychic experience are essential in advancing the process. Contemporary analysts of differing persuasions, including ego psychologists (Busch, 2010), British independent/object relations theorists (Carpy, 1989; Parsons, 2006, 2009), modern Kleinians/Bionians (Caper, 1992, 2009; Mitrani, 2001), Italian Bionians (Ferro, 2008, 2009), intersubjective/interpersonal relational analysts (Aron, 2000; Spezzano, 2007), and the Hans Loewald (1960) influenced, so-called American independents (Lear, 2003; Chodorow, 2004; Ogden, 1997, 2005), have argued persuasively that psychoanalysis brings about psychological development both by discovering new information about oneself, but more significantly, by creating a *new way of relating* to one's mind.

In my view, the essence of psychoanalytic action develops out of the patient's unconscious (and at times, conscious) experience of the analyst's ongoing mental effort to draw on the experience of being with the patient in a way that fosters the patient's psychological development. By tuning in to their own minds and striving to make sense of their unique experience when centered on the patient, analysts attempt to make contact with and understand what might be occurring in their patient's largely unconscious inner world (as it often becomes manifest in the analyst's ongoing mental activities). When this occurs, patients have what Joseph (1975) called, "the experience of being understood as opposed to 'getting' understanding" (p. 79, original italics omitted). This departs sharply from an analyst's attempt to simply make the patient feel better, rid a patient of unwanted feelings, symptoms, or parts of the self, and/or provide clever, theoretically-based interpretations that are removed from meaningful engagement with the patient.

Thus, I contend that the mainstay of the therapeutic action rests in *the analyst's ability to relate to her/his mind in a way that is psychoanalytic*, and subsequently utilize what s/he is able to intuit or infer to better understand the patient. This factor transcends particular theoretical schools, prevailing intrapsychic, interpsychic, and intersubjective concepts, and specific technical interventions. Of course, however, the "what" and "way" analysts listen to their patients, as well as "how" they couch their interpretive comments, are impacted by theory, analytic identity, and affiliations.

It is the analyst's unique *psychic activity or mind use* in relationship to the patient, which includes analyst-patient reciprocal identifications, that is the constant factor in the complex process of therapeutic action. In short, mutative change, while manifestly tied to the analyst's active interpretive, affirmative, and containing interventions, ultimately rests on analysts' ability to create, recognize, and utilize their receptive and active as well as regressive and progressive unconscious and conscious mental functioning in affinity with the patient's unconscious functioning and thereby allow the patient to (unconsciously) *use* the analyst's mental activities.

The idea that the analyst uses her/his mind in particular ways in order to understand the patient has a long tradition, beginning with Freud (1912b) and elaborated for the next generation by Theodore Reik (1948) by way of "listening with the third ear". The patient's unconscious perception of the analyst's unconscious "deep inner attitude" was later considered to be the decisive, "common denominator" for analytic change (Nacht, 1963). More recently, Bolognini (2004) has stated that analytic effectiveness requires "an analyst well tuned in to himself before anything else" (p. 350); Parsons (2006) insisted that the most emotionally crucial interventions spring from the analyst's unconscious psychic work; and Ellman (2010) has claimed that for treatment to progress, "patients have to feel themselves alive in the other's (analyst's) mind" (p. 592). Others from a contemporary developmental, neurobiological perspective suggest that patients who as infants were lacking a mother's mind to organize their ongoing experience, require the use of the analyst's mind both as an implicit *stimulus* for psychological growth and as a *model* for identification (e.g., Beebe & Lachmann, 1994; Fonagy, Target & Gergely, 2000; Schore, 2001).

As the current IPA president, Claudio Laks Eizirik (2010) asserted, the analyst's mind is "more and more an object of (analytic) interest" (p. 374) despite the divergent ways of being analysts in today's pluralistic culture. He emphasized that only so long as we are in closer emotional contact with our minds are we able to be in closer emotional contact with our patients. Indeed, our minds are "the tools through which psychoanalysis is applied to each patient" (Spezzano, 2007, p. 1580) and our analytic listening is *not* just to our patient and the co-created analytic field or "third" (Ogden, 1994) that stems from two permeable psychic apparatuses meeting in analytic, "interpsychic" space (Bolognini, 2004, 2011), but also to how each is experienced within our own internal mental activities.

I expand on this tradition by emphasizing that when the patient unconsciously experiences and identifies with the analyst's inner psychic work geared towards more deeply understanding the patient, something rather mysterious happens, resulting in the patient's learning a new way to relate to his/her own mind. Few patients consciously recognize this internalization process; thus, the apparent mystery. However, such internalization becomes evident when patients allude to feeling that their analyst is "inside" them so that patients "analyse" themselves just as their analyst does.

Because successful analytic work requires the analyst to be in emotional contact with the patient—specifically with the patient's unconscious—*analytic mind use* often operates unconsciously outside the analyst's (and patient's) conscious awareness. The analyst's attending to his/her mental activities, however, often becomes more conscious when unable to gain, or when losing emotional contact with the patient. When the analyst experiences difficulties maintaining an *analytic attitude* or understanding what is happening in the *analytic process* over lengthy time periods, becoming more conscious of one's mental experience can be vital in overcoming the problem.

The psychoanalytic meaning of "mind"

The term "mind" requires clarification because it is used psychoanalytically in many ways. I conceive of mind as *the psychic representation of the processing brain* in its myriad functions dealing with external and internal stimulation, including sensory-bodily as well as imagistic and verbal associative thought processes.[2]

Psychoanalytically, *mind* is also linked with both *psyche* and *soul*, and is distinguished by its *dynamically unconscious* processes. "*Psyche*" is a Greek word that Strachey, in translating Freud's (1905c) Germanic writings, translated as "mind" (p. 283), though it similarly translates as "*Seele*" or "soul". Hence, "*psychische Behandlung*", originally translated as "psychical treatment", also represents *soul treatment* (Bettleheim, 1983; Caper, 2009). In contrast to its religious connotation, our work as analysts involves *soul* when mind is understood, in line with John Stuart Mill's (1843) conclusion, as "that which *feels*" (p. 24, italics added).[3]

From a pragmatic standpoint, mind as an object (of observation and inquiry) entails a *splitting operation* wherein one part of the psyche (i.e., typically the conscious ego in Freud's psychic apparatus) separates in order to *observe* the other, fundamentally autonomous and mainly unconscious portion that is *experienced* through its more conscious or preconscious derivatives. These latter mental activities of the mind include emotions, sensations, images, fantasies, ideas, verbal associations, and constructions, as well as theories and hypotheses as to what might be happening. Moreover, the observing part of the psyche ideally needs to assume an attitude that recognizes and accepts the autonomous, sovereign nature of these mental events that can only be experienced rather than controlled. Thus, as analysts, we must attain and retain a perspective towards both our own and our patients' mental events that recognizes their fundamental autonomy, sovereignty, and uncontrollability yet, paradoxically, privileges causation. To be sure, the analyst's mental operations require considerable cognitive flexibility based on a special combination of immersion, detachment, mobility, acceptance of paradox, and letting one's mind play with associations to its internal processes.

The analyst's mental use of unconscious communication

It was Freud who first drew attention to the central role of the analyst's mental activity and how to employ it. He recommended (1912b) that the analyst "must turn his own unconscious like a receptive organ towards the transmitting unconscious of the patient" (p. 115). Since the analyst is most concerned with the patient's unconscious, he believed that by tuning our unconscious to that of the patient, we place ourselves in the most advantageous position to interpret or otherwise intervene. The aim is to allow the patient's unconscious to impact the analyst's unconscious and then observe the conscious mental and emotional experiences that ensue.[4] The analyst then reflects upon these conscious mental experiences, or what analysts today mainly conceive as "totalistic" countertransference, and attempts to understand their meaning with respect to the patient's inner life. This entails maintaining an internal potential space wherein the patient's unconscious and/or infantile life can come alive within the analyst's "hunches, feeling states, passing images, fantasies, and imagined interpretive interventions" (Bollas, 1983, p. 3)—a "countertransference readiness" that partly determines "the analyst's ability to analyze" (Loewald, 1986, p. 286).

How to understand and use the meaning of the analyst's inner experience remains controversial. Indeed, this has been conceptualized historically in three main ways: initially, in line with the *intrapsychic* viewpoint, continuing with the *intersubjective*, and most recently, introducing the *interpsychic* perspective—each contributing something vital to contemporary analytic technique.

Speaking *intrapsychically*, most analysts agree on the idea of a generative, therapeutic split. For example, Arlow (1979) offers the seminal classical, ego psychology perspective wherein the patient's *identification with* the analyst's split between the observing and experiencing ego is considered a critical factor in the therapeutic effect of psychoanalysis (e.g., Strachey, 1934; Sterba, 1934). This involves the patient's *internalizing* the "analytic introject" or "analytic function", which I discuss as the "analytic object", as the analyst engages in continuing shifts from unconscious trial identifications with the patient to withdrawal and objective evaluations of the identification (Arlow, 1979).

Intersubjectively, Aron's (2000) relational concept of "self-reflexivity" or "reflexive self-awareness", wherein subjectivity develops through the perception of oneself in another person's mind (Benjamin, 1999), is considered the basis for the analyst's (as well as for the patient's) participation.[5] This perspective emphasizes the ability to *maintain the tension and move smoothly between* subjective self-awareness, in which one is totally immersed yet aware of oneself as an agent or the subject of one's own thoughts and actions, and objective self-awareness, which involves taking oneself as the object of one's thoughts, feelings, or actions yet without experiencing the sense of agency or being the distinct centre.

The *interpsychic*, mainly European viewpoint prevalent in France and Italy and discussed by Bolognini (2004, 2011), also important in South America among the River Plate group (Brown, 2010, 2011) influenced by Klein, Bion, and field theory (e.g., de Leon de Bernardi, 2000; Barranger & Barranger, 2008), addresses the ubiquitous joint functioning and reciprocal influences of two minds or "psychisms (meeting) in the analytic space" (Bolognini, 2004, p. 347). The two psychic apparatuses create a level of high permeability based on communicative projective identifications that require the analyst to have "faith in the practicability of dialogue with internal worlds" (ibid., p. 350). By focusing on the realm of interpenetration or cohabitation of the two minds in normative, "companionable, cooperative fusion" (Bolognini, 2011, p. 69), this perspective encompasses both the intrapsychic and the intersubjective while usually keeping the patient in the central position within the analyst's mind. Hence, the focus is on what is conscious and unconscious, mind and body, internal and external, present and past.

In sum, current work in this area continues the tradition of Freud (1933), Sterba (1934), and Arlow (1979) in describing the split between an *observing* and *experiencing ego* that privileges a "therapeutic dissociation" (Sterba, 1934, p. 119), while adding that the processes involved are intrapsychic, intersubjective, and interpsychic. The focus is on affectivity as much as on cognition, and always involves a "meeting of minds" (Aron, 2000, p. 685), the "interpenetration of affect states" (Ellman, 2010, p. 646), "two communicating intrapsychic worlds" (Brown, 2010, p. 669), and the "superimposition or coalescence of two minds" (Bolognini, 2011, p. 69).

The interpsychic nature of the analyst's mind

There is today a broad consensus that the analytic enterprise is *both* a one-person and a two-person psychology requiring an intrapsychic and bi-personal model. As Bolognini (2011) states, "[T]he intra- and inter-psychic dialectic is one of the recurrent themes of contemporary psychoanalysis" (p. 100). In this zeitgeist, where "[T]o some extent analyst and analysand lose themselves as separate individuals" (Gabbard, 2009, p. 587), many analysts accept the analyst's participation in the patient's transference, recognize that countertransference is ubiquitous, and view enactments as common while frequently useful in advancing the process (Gabbard, 1995; Bolognini, 2004; see also Chapters Eight, Nine, and Eleven by Wolson, Porter, and Helscher, respectively, this volume). What is inevitable, as Caper (1992) suggests, is the analyst's "entering into the fray" with the patient and then, using his/her mind to figure out the nature of the fray. In helping to establish the technical importance of this understanding, Bollas (1983) argued that analysts should use themselves more directly by employing "this form of countertransference experiencing for eventual knowing" (p. 34). To do so, an analyst needs to be "well tuned in to himself before anything else, and then to the patient's internal world … so … it is possible to transmit combined verbal/sensory elements from within the analyst to within the patient" (Bolognini, 2004, p. 350).

Countertransference as an interpsychic element within the analyst's mind

The development of two key concepts, *projective identification* and *countertransference enactment*, led to today's convergence on the therapeutic significance of the analyst's attitude to countertransference (Gabbard, 1995). Kleinian analysts were first to state that countertransference inexorably involves an interactive element within the analyst's mind (Heimann, 1950; Money-Kyrle, 1956). Little (1951) also highlighted the roles played by introjection and projection, and Searles (1975), Bollas (1983), and Pick (1985) elaborated on the patient's unconscious sensitivities and perceptions of the analyst during the unconscious communicative interaction.

Faimberg's (1992) term, "the countertransference position", illuminates the multiple determinants impinging upon the analyst that must be attended to in order to overcome the resistances to hearing something that arouses displeasure and thus will require additional psychical labour. Consistent with my thinking about the analyst's psychic work, the "countertransference position" is dialectically determined. Therefore, each analyst must refrain from simply supposing a one-to-one correspondence between what goes on in his psychic reality and what is in the patient's mind (though perhaps disavowed or projected outwards). Instead, analysts can use their awareness of their experience as a "point of departure" (ibid.) for exploring the complexity of the clinical situation—in short, one of many "royal" roads towards, rather than a direct representation of, either the patient's disavowed psychic experience or the co-created primitive realms of shared experience in the bi-personal field. In any event, the analyst's experience depends on many factors including the patient's verbal and non-verbal expressions (see Kalish, Chapter Twelve in this volume), and the analyst's own evoked psychic functioning, transferences, as well as personal characteristics, analytic affiliations, and theoretical positions (e.g., Faimberg, 1992).

A brief vignette

The interpsychic complexities are illustrated by my work with one patient, Ms B, who had an overriding sense of feeling isolated and empty while fearing destructive intrusion. Throughout many of our earlier sessions, my mind wandered aimlessly while I experienced the isolating silence as anxiety provoking as I struggled to bear my feelings of uselessness and self-doubt. I could not explain this by simply positing a straightforward correlation between my psychical absence and that of the patient's. Despite my discomfort, I often had reveries of creative activities such as recalling my own solitary efforts as a lonely two- or three-year-old to master the names of different automobiles, an endeavour that seemed quite removed from anything going on inside Ms B or seemingly between us. Nonetheless, rather than reflecting her anxious isolation, Ms B's apparent affective non-appearance neither indicated her genuine absence nor a straightforward projection of an anxiously disengaged mother (for me to complementarily identify with) nor an inadequate self (to concordantly experience).

In time, I came to learn that Ms B's ostensible absence reflected her need to create a psychic bubble in our analytic space that would prevent my intruding upon her and thereby drawing her prematurely into the (my) world. This bubble would enable her to be "alone in my presence" yet "go on being" (Winnicott, 1958a, 1960). Thus, our seeming disconnection instead represented Ms B's archaic longing to find a mother-analyst who, while managing her own narcissistic equilibrium, could creatively wait with Ms B and remain sufficiently present until the infant-her was ready to appear in the transference as the prematurely intruded upon, nascent self from long ago.

Without understanding why it was necessary, though nonetheless frequently reminded both by my intuitive sense of needing to wait and by Ms B's anger as to how easily my words might intrude to prevent any psychic movement, I was mostly able to contain my anxious feelings of isolation and analytic ineptitude. I was able to do so partly by wondering about my particular reveries, memories, and emotions, until I could eventually recognize my concern about prematurely pushing her out of the bubble by demanding that she communicate verbally. In working analytically with my own mental experience, I learned to wait until able to understand and interpret Ms B's transference experience of being prematurely impinged upon as she once was as a premature, forceps-delivered baby, who became a failure-to-thrive infant, a toilet-trained six-month-old who later developed encopresis, and subsequently an overly-compliant, somatically distressed child. As a result of interpretations stemming from this understanding combined with recalling my own early compensatory, creative vehicle-naming activities in the context of my *not* intruding upon her (while representing an impinging transference imago), Ms B soon began to experience an expanded sense of psychic space and significant freedom to engage in her own creative, insight-generating activities. But perhaps most significant was her identification with my *mind use* of giving myself the time and space to better understand my own internal reactions and how they both might reflect upon as well as impact her inner world. Thus, she became less constricted and riddled with persecutory anxieties, and more benignly able to seek self-understanding.

The therapeutic action of the analyst's mind use: insight and internalization

Among its major mutative functions, psychoanalytic work assists the analysand to forge a better, richer, and more creative *relationship with one's mind*. My contention as to the role played by the analyst's relationship to her/his ongoing mental activities as the driving force of therapeutic action aligns with Loewald's (1960) emphasis on the centrality of interactional processes to modify intrapsychic structure and object relations (see also Lear, 2003). Loewald (1960), depicted as both an "intersubjectivist ego psychologist" as well as the initiator of "the American independent" tradition (Chodorow, 2004), argued that mutative change occurs through "the *internalization of an interaction process*, not simply internalization of objects" (p. 251, italics added). This implies that internalizing the analyst's relationship to his/her own mind in an effort to understand the patient significantly impacts patients.

In my view, the analyst's *mind use* operates as a core therapeutic agent partially due to the fact that the patient *internalizes* a greater capacity to maintain significant self-insight by observing (unconsciously and/or consciously) the analyst's struggle to attend to, regulate, and utilize his/her mind.[6] The analyst unconsciously demonstrates his mind in action through a stance towards his own mental activity that facilitates *understanding the patient's unconscious mental processes*. In other words, by finding and implicitly communicating that there is an ongoing space for the patient in the analyst's mind, and despite the analyst's experiences of intense affect and anxiety, strong impulses to act, confusion or even chaos, boredom or deadness, as well as the storms occurring during projective identification processes, what is crucial is that the patient comes to *sense the analyst's ongoing efforts towards analytic mind use* in order to facilitate a deepening of the patient's understanding and integration. This is evident, for example, when a patient tells her analyst that she thought about how the analyst might think about the patient's intensely conflicted feelings, impulses to act, or her dream, and, as a result, begins to sort out what might be going on. I believe that effective understanding of the patient's unconscious is most likely when analysts use their minds to explore how they mentally co-exist with their patients in this uniquely analytic way. Consequently, the patient's enhanced insight can then accrue directly from the analyst's interpretive comments as well as more indirectly when patients are stimulated to deepen their own self-understanding through identification with the analyst's mind use during the interaction itself.

The latter, more indirect means to mutative change is particularly well stated within the British independent tradition that views patients as enabled to discover something in themselves as a result of being in a particular analytic relationship with an analyst who is working at that same sort of discovery in his/her own self—an interactive experience that Winnicott (1971a) suggested creates mutative "cross-identifications". By demonstrating to the patient a relationship to his own subjectivity, the analyst becomes a "subject" within the analytic process and welcomes the patient's observation of some of his self-reflective functioning (Bollas, 1983). In Parsons' (2009) view, "[U]nless an analyst treats himself or herself in the same way that he or she is treating the patient, nothing psychoanalytic at all will happen between them" (p. 224).

Mind use as process: distinguishing psychoanalysis from psychoanalytic psychotherapy
One way of distinguishing psychoanalysis proper from psychoanalytically-based psychotherapy is that psychoanalysis is mainly concerned with developing "a way of knowing oneself" through the capacity for self-analysis (Busch, 2010; see also Portuges & Hollander, Chapter Four in this volume). However, rather than a bifurcated ideal, in reality a continuum exists between the two—what might appear as psychoanalytic psychotherapy may actually involve a genuine psychoanalytic process and vice versa. Nonetheless, at the pole where most analysts would consider

psychoanalysis, both patient and analyst achieve a "discovery and rediscovery of one's own mind and a coming to terms with it" (Levin, 2010, p. 98). In psychoanalysis, the process or way of knowing is as important as what is known.

I believe that what is essential to and distinctive about the practice of psychoanalysis (versus other forms of psychotherapy) is that analysts, in appreciating the permeability and reciprocity between two unconscious minds interacting, adopt a *specific state of mind* that involves taking their own mental activities as an object of analytic scrutiny. The difference is evident within the analytic process, regardless of session frequency and couch use, by observing the patient and analyst's greater *opportunity, space,* and *responsibility* for taking one's mind as an object of self-reflection. I believe that the customary analytic frame, conditions, and attitude evolved, at least in part, to afford analysts a greater sense of reflective, creative space from which to view their internal experience as "data" with which intrapsychically to work, regress, and play (cf. Winnicott, 1971b).

The nature of the analyst's psychic work

Models of psychoanalysis can be distinguished by the significance attributed to, and the use made of, occurrences in the analyst's mind that go beyond associations and conceptual linkages to include the analyst's reverie, dreaming, images connected to what is happening in the analytic relationship, affects, bodily sensations, and negative capability (Ogden, 1997, 2005; Ferro, 2009; Brown, 2011). Advancements in intersubjectivity theory and psychoanalytic field theory, as well as Bionian and neo-Kleinian developments, help us to recognize that the analyst's mental life is, to use Ferro's (2009) felicitous term, "the principal working instrument" (p. 219) and, consequently, recurring awareness on the part of the analyst as well as maintenance of his/her mental life is necessary. To remain alert to what arouses us emotionally, intellectually, and somatically requires considerable psychic effort involving our unconscious. How are we to understand the nature of this psychic work?

Foremost in working with our minds analytically, we need to attend to our mental activities *in the service of* understanding the patient and, thus, there is always an *ethical aspect* to our analytic examination of our own psychical functioning in relation to a particular patient.

The essence of our work conceivably concerns the question of *how to be a psychoanalyst with each unique patient*. In continually discovering the emotional role or position that we find ourselves in, we analyse what a given role means to our patient (e.g., Sandler, 1976; Bollas, 1987; Faimberg, 1992). This entails neither being an historian, sociologist, politician, social worker, psychiatrist, friend, lover, surrogate parent, mentor, or the like but rather to understand the proclivity to enact the role.

Relating to our own mind as the psychoanalytic fourth
As psychoanalysts, we need to keep listening to our own associations, images, fantasies, reveries, dreams, feelings, and inner conflicts—that is, to remain *analytically minded*. From a Loewaldian position (Lear, 2003), therapeutic action entails an ongoing process of developing and deepening ourselves as analysts.

The ability to relate to one's mind throughout the psychoanalytic process should *not* be taken lightly, particularly since we are more or less conscious of our mental experience at any given moment. It is incumbent upon us as analysts to create the requisite inner reflective space that makes use of what has been stimulated in ourselves in order to understand our patients and their unconscious transferences. Though implicit from Freud onwards, I consider the patient's chiefly unconscious observation of the analyst's self-reflexive relationship to his/her own mind as a subjective object that the analyst uses to further the analytic process—a veritable "analytic fourth", in addition to the unconscious impact of the patient, the analyst, and the co-constructed analytic field or "third".

The analyst's observing and experiencing ego
As noted, Freud (1912b) implicitly distinguished between the *observing ego* and the *experiencing ego* in the analyst (see also Sterba, 1934; Arlow, 1979). However, identifying with this more detached, observing ego can serve purposes of both *introspective reflection* and *defensive avoidance* of emotion. In fact, there has been a tendency in psychoanalysis during most of its first century, towards overvaluing the analyst's intellectual, observing ego while regarding the affective, experiencing ego as more problematic. Recently however, this tendency is being actively countered by the work of more independent and contemporary analytic thinkers ranging from Loewald,

Winnicott, and Racker to Bion, Ogden, Gabbard, Aron, Ferro, and Bolognini, each emphasizing the significance of the analyst's emotional engagement—the essence of which reflects relating to one's own mind in terms of "the subjective use of objectivity" (Lear, 2003, p. 46).

Levin (2010) reminds us that it is easy to assume that skilled analysts inexorably operate as stable, unproblematic observers of affectively-laden mental experience whereas actually, analytic "observing" revolves around the indeterminacy of one's position and the sovereign nature of mental events that can only be lived through rather than controlled. Observations about our own minds are always limited, since contact with our mind is inherently emotionally evocative, indirect, complex, and partial. We can only read cues about ourselves and then form opinions about them, which we must approach with intrinsic doubt, just as there must be inherent doubt as to our interpretations or opinions when inferring another's internal state (see Spivak, Chapter Six in this volume). The optimal analytic attitude requires a tolerance for uncertainty or meaninglessness as well as the ability to bear our need for coherence without prematurely closing our minds (cf. Bion, 1970; Caper, 1992, 2009; Levin, 2010). In fact, one unique achievement of psychoanalysis may well be to hold simultaneously the "capacity to *observe without understanding*" (Caper, 2009, p. 11, italics added) alongside the ability to stand behind *what is known*.

Obstacles to the analyst's mind use and recovering an analytic mind
Therapeutic action unfolds quite naturally when the frame is sufficiently stable, the analyst's analytic attitude is basically maintained, and the analytic process is operating effectively. However, interference in the analyst's analytic mind causes analytic movement to come to a standstill and the mutative process to cease. Consequently, the analyst's task then becomes one of recovering the ability to "analyse" in the broadest sense, which requires making *interpretations* involving symbolizing, representing, linking, understanding, bringing the unconscious closer to consciousness as well as identifying repressed, disassociated, and/or disavowed aspects of the patient; *holding and containing* pre-symbolized and/or unbearable experience; and *recognition* in the form of reflecting, mirroring, and validating as well as elaborating and affirming the patient's sense

of meaning. Regaining this ability requires the analyst to attend to her/his own mind, particularly when realizing that s/he is *not* using it effectively at particular times during the session. This involves *recovering or recuperating* after finding oneself lost and no longer in an analytic frame of mind.

There are potentially *three* major *obstacles* to accessing one's analytic mind at various moments during an analysis that emerge within the analyst. First, there are obstacles stemming directly from *the patient*, such as massive projective identification, severe dissociation, attacks on linking, and negative therapeutic reactions. Second, there are obstacles stemming more from *the analyst*, including problematic concordant and complementary identifications; extreme countertransference reactions of empathy, anxiety, rage, envy, erotic feeling, etc. (i.e., sinking or drowning in the countertransference); specific transferences to the patient or countertransference, including narcissistic needs to feel included or recognized (perhaps as brilliant, insightful, or compassionate), an over-investment in theory and a need to conceptualize or rationally know with certitude, and over-identifying with one's own associations and personal issues stemming from life concerns; and, also, the analyst's personal resistance to analysis and dealing with unconscious processes.[7] Finally, there are *dyadic* obstacles residing in the analytic "field" (Barranger & Barranger, 2008; Ferro & Basile, 2009), which include: collusive defensive processes and resistances to analysis; reciprocal fears of engagement; bulwarks and impasses in the "third" (e.g., chaos, stagnation, etc.); and seduction as well as corruption involving boundary confusions, crossings, and violations.

The necessity of recovering one's analytic mind

A fundamental attribute of the psychoanalytic process is that analysts are continually being *pulled out of* their analytic attitude and identity by emotional forces originating in their patients, themselves, or by the co-created interpsychic field. It is then necessary for the analyst to regain her/his analytic attitude, state of mind, and identity by recognizing the emotional position that s/he has been drawn into, such as the role of medicating psychiatrist, didactic psychologist, or resourceful social worker. While losing our analytic attitude is inevitable and at times even useful, with analytic experience we come to accept such recurring mind loss as intrinsic to being an analyst while attaining greater conviction and confidence that we will be able to regain the necessary attitude soon enough (see also Caper, 2009).

In doing psychoanalysis, we are constantly shaping ourselves as psychoanalysts and thus, by bringing ourselves back to the activity of being a psychoanalyst, we are always "in the process of *becoming* an analyst" (Lear, 2003, p. 32, italics added), thereby preserving ourselves as an "internal analytic object" (Wille, 2008) for our patients to introject. This requires commitment to a psychoanalytic stance whereby we take "responsibility for maintaining the analysis as an analysis" (Bollas, 1989, p. 56). Our essential responsibility to *reconstitute* our analytic mind in relation to the patient's material necessitates that we continually re-create an internal space with the working process to do so. As a result of such reconstitution, at times facilitated by supervision or consultation, the analyst's *analytic mind* can become the source for therapeutic action.

Sustaining the necessary tension in the analyst's mind
What makes it particularly difficult for the analyst to use his/her mind analytically is that it requires sustaining an inherent and creative *tension* between relying on his/her *unconscious* mind and simultaneously doing what must be *consciously* done, including establishing and maintaining the frame, listening and following the affects of the session, deciphering the patient's unconscious schemas, linking the patient's material to theoretical ideas, and making interpretive as well as affirmative comments and then assessing how the patient responds to them. Both analyst and patient experience this tension since each is called upon to surrender to the sovereignty of what's occurring in their inner worlds (see Parsons, 2006). For the analyst, this conceding control and loss of contact with one's mind is familiar in the dialectic of mind use wherein consciousness of mind is lost and regained in oscillating fashion.

Navigating this internal tension requires considerable humility as well as psychic freedom, which involves, as Ferenczi noted (1919), "constant oscillation between the free play of phantasy and critical scrutiny [that] pre-supposes a freedom and uninhibited motility of psychic excitation" (p. 189). Yet analysts must find ways to sustain this tension in order to bring the necessary analytic mind to the experience at hand. To observe our own experience with a patient tests the limits of our "ability to tolerate insecurity" (Caper, 2009, p. 88) as well as our capacity to permit our minds to indulge in "playful inventiveness" (Cooper, 1986). Nonetheless, practised analysts basically do both through creating and maintaining an open, reflective, and playful space that, for the most part, neither leads to premature action, typically in the form of authoritative interpretations that defend against the anxiety of uncertainty, nor excessive inaction preventing either the exposure of not knowing or the dangers of conflict and aggression (Bion, 1970; Winnicott, 1971b; Spivak, Chapter Six, this volume).

Viewing technique: essential factors in the analyst's mind use

From a technical perspective, the analyst strives to create an *inner receptive and reflective space* in order to examine her/his mental experience through both the calm and storms of analytic work. This requires considerable intrapsychic work and interpsychic awareness, not only to help formulate our interventions, but oftentimes to enable us specifically *not* to interpret or intervene directly, and instead contain and withhold the impulse to intervene until it is most useful for the patient.

In this penultimate section, I briefly discuss *four* central processes pertaining to the analyst's intrapsychic work in the service of mutative action. I believe analysts actively use their mental experience in these essential ways: (1) allowing for *regression in ego functioning*; (2) *taking one's own mind as an object*, including its manifestation in the analytic third; (3) *utilizing more developed ego functions* for self-reflexivity and self-analysis; and (4) *containing internal experience*, including bearing uncertainty and tolerating intense affective states.

1. Allowing for regression in ego functioning: the analytic instrument

A rather mythological perspective on the analyst's use of his mind initially dominated clinical theory from Freud onward, as evidenced in Isakower's (1963; also 1992) radical notion of "the analyzing instrument". Employing a concrete view of this inner process, Isakower argued that "the analyzing instrument" of the well-analysed analyst would enable the correct interpretation to appear automatically in the analyst's mind in the form of a free association—that is, through the analyst's intuitive process, the correct interpretation would arise consciously (just as a derivative of an unconscious instinctual impulse would appear in the patient's mind).

Balter, Lothane, and Spencer (1980) offered a more nuanced approach, stressing the "mutual ego regression" for patient and analyst that, like Ogden's (1994) co-constructed "third" and Bolognini's (2004, 2011) "interpsychic" field, enables the "analyzing instrument" to be created and subsequently facilitate therapeutic action. Thus, the "analyzing instrument" is fundamentally bi-personal wherein the analyst's activated mental state is in rapport with a counterpart in the patient. The interpenetrating states of mind become paramount and the analyst is encouraged to let his mind run free to approach both his own internal activities and the patient's communications with "evenly hovering attention" (Isakower, 1963).[8]

To utilize the analyst's ego-subsystem that is termed the "analyzing instrument" or "internal analytic object" (Wille, 2008), *two* essential features allow for accessing of preconscious material: first, the concentration of attention on inner psychic processes; and second, the suspension of critical attitudes towards the emerging psychic material. The idea then is to "to catch the drift of the patient's unconscious with his own unconscious" (Freud, 1922, p. 239), via a limited "regression in the analyst's ego-functioning" that is related to *trial identifications* (Arlow, 1979), as well as relaxing into *interpsychic communication* (Bolognini, 2004, 2011), states of *reverie* (Bion, 1970; Ogden, 1997), and *play* (Winnicott, 1971b; Sanville, 1991).

Consequently, three cognitive-affective activities establish the analyst's required state of mind: (1) the relaxed concentration of *attention upon the analysand's communications*; (2) the imaginative focus of *attention upon the analyst's own internal perceptions*; and (3) the *suspension of critical activity* regarding these objects of the analyst's attention, requiring what Bolognini (2004) refers to as "… 'trustful resignation' in the extraordinary paradoxical nature of our work" (p. 353). Thus, the analyst's *regression in ego functioning* in the service of utilizing interpsychic communication, thereby can make receptivity towards, and identification with the analysand more productive.

2. *Taking one's mind as an object, including its manifestation*
   in the analytic third
Most patients, at least during a significant portion of their analysis, create a transference/countertransference environment largely favourable to the analyst's analytic state of mind, rendering the patient's internal experience sufficiently accessible. However, at

other times, particularly when working with more disturbed patients or with more primitive mental states in any patient, the patient's existence is represented through the analyst's moods, emotions, impulses, and thoughts, and at these times the analyst needs "to *take himself as the object* of interest, insight, and quite possibly of 'cure'" (Bollas, 1983, p. 1, italics added).

One way to take up the mind's relationship to itself is to consider the mind as an "object" contained within a mental field that we call the internal world or psyche. Bion (1959) argues that we need to attend to the action of the mind on itself as it experiences itself (while in the process of receiving environmental input). Bollas (1983) takes this a step further in recommending that the analyst approach himself "as the Other patient", and function as a "transformational object" (Bollas, 1979). Considerable mutative action can thereby occur through a form of unconscious identification in which one part of the self functions as the source of material and another part functions as the analyst (see also Searles, 1975; Bollas, 1983; Levin, 2010).

When an analyst experiences being unable to make contact over a period of time, it becomes absolutely essential for him to use his mind to seek his "missing" patient. Analysts spontaneously tend to tune in to their minds when they find themselves out of synch with their patients. Typically this happens when they are unable to understand the nature of the process occurring between the patient and themselves. There may be an emotional disconnection, an overwhelming emotional experience, an ongoing impasse, or complete bafflement as to what the patient is trying to convey. Consequently, the analyst can no longer think (and link). Such disjunctions often precede nascent understanding since they motivate us to attend better to our own minds in order to reconstitute ourselves. In fact, it is through this inevitable and recurring losing and regaining of our analytic understanding that we engage with ourselves in this self-reflexive way (that I've termed "the analytic fourth"), which creates "a triangular space within the analytic relationship in which thinking becomes possible" (Aron, 2000, p. 684).

In taking one's mind as an object, Ogden (1994) introduced the concept of "the analytic third" that serves to demonstrate what the analytic pair co-create. The "third" as an object, including the analyst's acceptance and use of her/his "apparently self-absorbed (narcissistic) ramblings" (p. 8), is a particularly useful vehicle for understanding the analysand's conscious and unconscious experience. Our reveries do *not* simply reflect "inattentiveness, narcissistic self-involvement, [or] unresolved emotional conflict" (p. 12), but rather are important technical tools facilitating therapeutic action through understanding the patient. In short, all the analyst's psychological activities, particularly his/her reveries, represent symbolic and sensation-based (proto-symbolic) forms given to the analysand's unarticulated experience that take shape in the analytic third. Ogden (2005) views the analyst's task over time "to become aware of, and to verbally symbolize for himself, his experiences in and of the analytic third" (p. 7). Viewing the emotional experience occurring within the bi-personal field, he notes that it is often of a "subjugating nature" wherein neither member of the analytic pair can think about what is occurring unconsciously between them nor do the psychological work with that experience.

For example, with another patient, Mr N, I would often find myself lost to my associations about my life plans, pleasurable upcoming activities, such as a film or meal, or an exciting idea about a paper I needed to write. I observed that this mostly occurred when he was detailing his manifest conflict about needing to discipline his teenage son yet fearing the son's wrath. My interpretations pertaining to his aggression-related conflicts, both within and outside the transference, led nowhere and, though the lack of emotional engagement between us was clear, I was unable to think more deeply about it.

After many sessions characterized by these sorts of "disconnects", I began to note how my thinking about my own life activities seemed to occur when Mr N himself seemed so cut off from any experience of vitality in the analysis itself. In eventually thinking about our co-created "third", I could see that he was approaching me as a "parenting expert"—a veritable "Dr Phil"—to teach him how to set limits with his son, perhaps in order to find some way to be involved with me without experiencing being emotionally dependent. In being uncomfortable with assuming such a didactic role, I increasingly became psychically absent and unable to think about what was unconsciously going on between us. Consequently, in spurning the parenting expert role and without realizing, I found myself drawn to finding something "alive" in other passions of mine. There was an emotional "deadness" in this co-created affective detachment, so that only by eventually tuning in to what was taking shape within our "subjugating third" in which I actively participated, and subsequently by limiting our collusive disconnect from analytic work, could I begin to address interpretively the deadness concealing Mr N's tremendous anxiety and underlying anger about feeling emotionally dependent on me.

3. Utilizing more developed ego functions for self-reflexivity and self-analysis

The mental functions described as "insightfulness" (Sugarman, 2006), "self-reflexivity", or "reflexive self-awareness" (Aron, 2000)—which are often termed "mentalization", "reflective functioning", "insighting", and "theory of mind" (see Fonagy & Target, 1996, 1998; Mayes & Cohen, 1996)—involve *consciously* reflecting on one's mind working in all its complexity in order to promote mental mastery or self-regulation (which many contemporary attachment-oriented analysts consider to be *the* curative factor). Sugarman (2006) argued that through the interactive process of insightfulness, the relationship with the analyst becomes integrated with the facilitation of the patient's mentalizing and thus patients attain or retain the symbolic level of mental functioning. Ferro (2008, 2009), in a more poetic turn privileging the significance of the analyst's *unconscious*, takes this up in terms of developing the "instruments for thinking thoughts", which offers "instead of a psychoanalysis of contents and memories, … a psychoanalysis that gives priority to the development of the apparatuses for dreaming, feeling, and thinking" (2009, p. 214).

Self-analysis is a more inclusive concept than self-reflexivity and is generally considered the end-stage of a developmental process that occurs in psychoanalysis. In fact, working through a patient's resistance to self-analysis is regarded as an important feature of the termination process. However, perhaps erroneously, it is assumed that an analyst is already skilled in using self-analysis, and thus can employ the requisite psychological processes to explore her/his own mental experience when analysing a patient. But what specific psychological processes are actually involved in self-analysis?

According to Busch (2010), the psychological processes involved move sequentially from: (1) *self-observation*, where one sees his/her thoughts as mental events; to (2) *self-reflection*, wherein one's thoughts are not only viewed as mental events but associative strings are noticed, related as mental events, and held in mind long enough to be reflected upon; to (3) *self-inquiry*, in which a particular space in one's mind is created where a capacity to play with ideas exists as a basis for self-expression; and finally to (4) *self-analysis*, wherein the above three processes are used to achieve effective understanding that is "relieving … or surprising …, but, probably most importantly, not frightening" (ibid., p. 27). In short, this self-analytic process speaks to a state of mind involving specific ego functions that are carried out in the privacy of one's own mind and are used by the analyst to flesh out a deeper understanding of her/his mental experience in order to further understand the patient.

4. *Containing internal experience, including bearing uncertainty and tolerating intense affective states*
In taking one's own mind as an object of analytic interest and action, analysts need to develop the capacity to bear and value the necessary uncertainty in the analytic process as well as to contain intense affective states. In terms of the former, there are frequently long periods of "not knowing" or existing for a long time in an unknowable region. Bion (1970) drew attention to Keats's (1817) notion of "negative capability" that involves developing a new analytic capability wherein the analyst actively places him- or herself in the position of *not* knowing in order to receive what remains unknown.[9]

This waiting in the context of not knowing is also captured by the English word "abide", which means enduring without yielding. It entails the analyst's "staying power" (Schafer, 1983), yet goes beyond to require more active psychic work in order to enter a reflective mental state wherein the anxiety of not knowing and "the unpleasure generated … by what the patient rejects of himself as unpleasant" (Faimberg, 1992, p. 545) is sufficiently tolerated for the analyst to get her/his bearings in relation to what as yet has no representation. This necessitates, as Caper (2009) argues, tolerating "a healthy state of darkness" to eventually find one's way "back into the patient's unconscious" (p. 11). Likewise, analysts need to perceive their patients through the veil of their own preconceptions and theories, that is, remaining "*ignorant* long enough to have new experiences of a patient from which one may learn" (ibid., p. 12, italics added).

The idea of the analyst's containment or embracing affectively-laden as well as bodily, sensory-based internal experience is widely accepted as a technical precept and is increasingly understood as a significant aspect of analytic mutative action.[10] It may require substantial psychic labour to contain or embrace intense, emotionally driven mental experience let alone uncertainty, yet in doing so, as Bion (1962a, 1967, 1976) suggests in analogizing to infants with their mothers, the analyst's calm reverie in his/her *maternal* reception of the patient's chaotic mental ("beta") products that are returned in a form that can be thought about, symbolized, and "metabolized" (i.e., the analyst's *alpha function*), establishes a "containing object" in the patient's mind that enables learning from experience.

Analysts have the difficult task of performing a balancing act between experiencing the full disturbance of the patient's transference and responding with interpretation that does *not* convey disturbing anxiety (Pick, 1985). During those times when analysis proceeds well enough, the analyst may have the luxury of an emotional involvement that allows for mental space as well. However, when more primitive states of mind are operating, as when working with more disturbed patients, or when dealing with highly charged, evocative sexuality or aggression, one or the other pole may dominate for some time. The analyst's psychic work involves going beyond empathic attunement to the patient's conscious feeling state. The analyst must be able to introject unconscious aspects of the patient's inner world that resonate with those elements of his own.

Consequently, how the analyst undertakes the emotional experience or "takes the transference" (Mitrani, 2001) becomes critical. In Kleinian terminology, the process entails "digesting, formulating, and communicating" the meaning of the experience interpretively. The challenge is to understand the patient's infantile aspects, but also to be willing to experience unpleasant conflict and even "to feel like a baby" (ibid., p. 1099). The analyst's effectiveness rests on the extent to which s/he works through the process internally in the act of intervening (Pick, 1985). As most analysts know, this work tends to occur privately and over time, often in our associations, dreams, and reveries.

Accordingly, the patient's mind develops by consistently experiencing contact with the analyst's "containing function" over a lengthy period of time (Carpy, 1989). In addition, the analyst, through living in and reflecting upon the patient's "conflictedness", is in the best position to identify and interpret what the patient is yet unable to bear knowing (Spivak, Chapter Six in this volume; see also LaMothe, 2001; Porter, Chapter Nine, this volume).

The fundamental and mutative nature of such containment emerges out of the patient's experience of, as well as unconscious identification with, the analyst's unconscious mind—what Spezzano (2007) described as finding a "home" in the mind of the analyst where one can exist as an internal object. In this respect, the analyst is called upon to use her/his mind in order to help to grow the patient's mind, and as a result, the patient may unconsciously recognize this in the analyst's way of functioning. As the British independent analyst, Denis Carpy (1989) persuasively argues, therapeutic action resides in the analyst's containment of intense countertransference affect, fantasy, and impulse in the context of being *impacted by* the patient's projected material and inevitably acting it out albeit in partial, rather subtle ways. Such *partial* acting out might then occur through the analyst's wording of an interpretation, tone of voice, unconscious non-verbal behaviour, or even in the type of interpretation chosen. By dint of the analyst's restrained enactment, the patient is able to recognize impacting the analyst but, similar to a good enough mother, the analyst struggles to tolerate the experience and by acts of renunciation, keeps the patient (like the infant) from being overwhelmed by the premature aggressive or sexualized return of the projected material.

What is essentially mutative is that the analyst is being affected by what is projected, yet is doing the necessary psychic work of struggling to endure and understand it, thereby evidencing that the patient's projection is essentially tolerable (see also Winnicott, 1949). Arguably, mutative change occurs as a result of the gradual process of identification with and introjection of the analyst's *mind use function* as a containing object stemming primarily from the non-verbal interaction with the patient. Change in the patient's psychic structure thereby ensues through this gradual non-verbal process involving the internalization of a complex intersubjective, interpsychic relationship (see also Eagle, Chapter Three in this volume, who refers to this as a "new corrective relational experience").

In sum, four processes are in play vis-à-vis the containing analyst: (1) the patient needs to *perceive the analyst's psychic effort* and unconscious mind in action; (2) the patient needs to see *the analyst as impacted* by his/her intense and/or disavowed affect; (3) the patient needs to see that *the analyst does* not *defensively have to disavow* his own intense affect; and (4) the patient needs to see that, much like the "good enough" mother (or father), *the analyst struggles to tolerate* the experience of hate, terror, envy, anxiety, sex, and love as well as other intense, disavowed or projected affect, and then communicate the meaning of the patient's experience in an effort to be most helpful. Thus, as a result of these four interacting processes over the course of analytic treatment, a patient becomes able both to re-introject previously intolerable parts of the self, and internalize the capacity to contain intense experience as a result of observing the analyst's struggle to do so.

Conclusion: analytic mind use as the vehicle for therapeutic action

As a result of the role played by the analyst's relationship to his/her own mental activities, as well as the fundamental processes that the analyst must consciously and unconsciously engage in throughout a psychoanalysis, patients become better able to develop their own mind use. In contrast to thinking about mutative action in terms of the more artificial distinction between *insight or ego/structural development* in opposition to *relational or attachment factors*, I emphasize that the analyst's unique use of her/his mind, while serving as both a transference and new object, provides the driving force for patients to become better able *to integrate* the significant facilitation of their mental functioning both to *understand* themselves better and to *internalize* the mutative facets of their relationship with the analyst.

As Loewald (1960) propounded a half century ago, the analyst must move beyond the patient's mental state to go a step further by offering a different yet experientially appropriate perspective of a more "mature" object. Thus, a difference between the analyst's mental integration and that of the patient potentially enables the analyst to utilize his/her mental experience to develop, maintain, and recover the necessary analytic stance in order to understand the patient and establish the conditions for the patient to identify with and take in the analyst's mind use. This requires discipline and faith in interpsychic dialogue in the context of an open, emotionally engaged unconscious participation in the analytic dyad. It is the analyst's more relaxed capacity to traverse this dialectic with its inherent dynamic tension that necessitates a level of maturity on the analyst's part whereby his/her mind use can benefit the patient. The lyrical words of William Wordsworth (1807) aptly suggest the essence of the analyst's mind use in this interactive, mutative dynamic that helps our patients to achieve a higher level of mental functioning (pp. 320–321):

> More skilful in self-knowledge, even more pure,
> As tempted more; more able to endure,
> As more exposed to suffering and distress;
> Thence, also, more alive to tenderness.

Notes

1. It is noteworthy that I have chosen to focus on a single inclusive factor among many to serve as the foundation leading to therapeutic action in psychoanalysis. My heuristic goal to further analytic thinking will require ongoing synthesis particularly at the meeting points of psychoanalysis, philosophy of science, neuroscience, and other disciplines concerned with the human mind. There is a danger, however, that such a focus on the analyst's mental experience, taken to an extreme, can lead away from the psychology of the patient and centre instead on the analyst or the dyadic process (cf. Chodorow, 2010). In addition, this centering on the analyst's internal experience runs the risk of erroneous *pars pro toto* thinking that overstresses this single factor at the expense of other significant facets of analytic technique. Indeed, my focus is on *mind use* as an analytic tool, function, and even technique, albeit certainly *not* as an omnipresent ideal or an all-encompassing aspect of psychoanalytic action. Thus, in privileging the analyst's relationship to his/her own mind, *four* important issues that are *not* highlighted in this chapter should be kept in mind: first, the analyst's mental experience is ubiquitous in guiding the analyst's understanding, yet its importance lies in its aim to help understand the patient's mind as the central focus; secondly, the nature of relating to one's mind is inevitably intermittent and thus, experienced analysts, akin to more developed individuals

generally, learn to trust the comings and goings as well as conscious and pre-conscious facets of such self-reflection so that when coming back to one's mind is necessary for analytic progress, they are better able to create the inner psychic space to do so; thirdly, the fact that mental events are fundamentally autonomous cannot be ignored nor can the mind's activities be dispassionately observed, but rather must be experienced and emotionally engaged with; and finally, detaching from or "letting go" of the effort to relate to one's mind or mentalizing experience is also vital for the analyst both in the analytic process and certainly for living life in general.

2. Mind and body are intimately related and mind is a function of the body. Nonetheless, reductive localization of mental states with brain regions, though popular within contemporary neuroscience (which actually carries forward that which Freud, 1895, ultimately abandoned with his "Scientific Project"), offers a different, though potentially useful level of understanding in contrast to what psychoanalysis imparts. In my view, the *mind* and *brain* are two ways of looking at the same thing, two differing levels of analysis: *mind* standing for a more experience-near, phenomenological, and metaphorical way of representing internal mental activities; whereas *brain* indicates the psychobiological, neuroscience level of discourse. Where there is mind, there is brain—yet the converse is *not* necessarily the case.

3. The basis of Freud's thinking about the mind emerged from Mill's (1843) philosophical perspective rooted in associationism and empiricism. Mill viewed the laws of the mind as pertaining to mental states that consist of thoughts, emotions, volitions, and sensations. Consequently, Mill's conclusive statement on the meaning of mind today seems clinically prescient.

4. The fact that analysts are impacted by their patients' unconscious and participate in their transference enactments is based on our biological sensitivity to a wide range of semiotic systems that are grasped by the senses, often without any conscious knowledge (e.g., Tuckett, 1983; Ahumada, 1994). Interestingly, recent findings from non-linear dynamics, chaos and complexity theory (see Galatzer-Levy, 2009) expand upon Freud's (1912b) original ideas about unconscious patient-analyst communication and are in line with Winnicott's (1949, 1971a) ideas about mutual influence, Kleinian views on systems of projective identification (Bion, 1962b), Racker's (1968) concept of "psychological symbiosis", Ogden's (1994) theorizing about intersubjectivity and the analytic third, Bolognini's (2004) commensal, co-operative "interpsychic" fusion that is part

of normal mental cohabiting, and Symington's (2006) notion of fundamental emotional linkages processed within a different channel of knowledge. In particular, the "linking of minds" (i.e., "mind-mind coupling") is posited to occur as the mind-brains of the two participants in a functioning psychoanalytic relationship form a unique system, which in the language of chaos theory creates a "new oscillator" making change possible (Galatzer-Levy, 2009).

5. This concept of self-reflexivity and the related notions of mentalization, theory of mind, insightfulness, and reflective function are more than just new terms for what was once called introspection, self-reflection, insight, and expanded awareness. Moreover, there is widespread convergence of interest in this area today that is chiefly based on Fonagy's (1993) notion of reflective self-function—for example, Fonagy and Target's (1996, 1998; Target & Fonagy, 1996) research on "reflective functioning" and "mentalization"; attachment-based work on "theory of mind" and "mentalized affectivity" (Mayes & Cohen, 1996; Fonagy & Target, 2007; Jurist, Slade & Bergner, 2008) as well as "insightfulness" (Sugarman, 2006); and trauma-based study of self-regulation, dissociation, and states of consciousness (Bromberg, 1998).

6. As noted in this volume's introductory chapter (Diamond & Christian), there is a consensus within the psychoanalytic literature that the mutative process involves both the *internalization of the relationship* with the analyst, described typically as relational or attachment factors, and the achievement of *insight through interpretation*, designated as insight- or understanding-based features (e.g., Loewald, 1960; Friedman, 1978; Cooper, 1992; Pulver, 1992; Baker, 1993; Gabbard, 1995). Here, I focus mainly on the former in terms of the patient's internalization of the analyst's mind use. It is beyond the scope of this chapter to discuss the interrelationship between these two factors, albeit neither factor occurs independently from the other (see also Bolgar, Chapter Thirteen in this volume).

7. Freud (1915a) discussed the latter in terms of a battle to be waged in the analyst's mind against "the forces which seek to drag him down from the analytic level" (p. 170) that are exacerbated by a cultural resistance to the unconscious; Ehrlich (2010) addresses this as analysts' ubiquitous ambivalence about practising analysis.

8. The phrase "evenly hovering attention" differs slightly from Freud's (1912b, 1922) notion of "evenly suspended attention". Though often treated as synonymous, "hovering" contrasts with the less elastic notion of "suspended" in implying a quality of being more easily shifted from the outside to the inside, or associating out and in from

what derives from the patient to what emerges from within the analyst.

9. Keats (1817) described "negative capability" as, "when man is capable of being in uncertainty, mysteries, and doubts, without any irritable reaching after fact and reason ... capable of remaining content with half knowledge" (pp. 477–478). Like Heidegger's (1959) concept of *Gelassenheit*, this refers to a form of thinking that permits us simply to let go of willing and subsequently let things be in their uncertainty and mystery.

10. In highlighting the significance of the analyst's active mental work, and in contrast to the overly used analytic term of *containment*, Symington (2006) employs the term *embrace* to emphasize more of the tactile-sensory realm of experience requiring subjective activity. In this respect, *embrace* suggests putting one's arms around an experience in contrast to the somewhat more distanced and less mentally active term of *contain*.

CHAPTER ELEVEN

From under long shadows: identification and disidentification in analysis

Thomas P. Helscher

An object-choice, an attachment of the libido to a particular person, had at one time existed; then, owing to a real slight or disappointment coming from this loved person, the object-relationship was shattered. The result was not the normal one of a withdrawal of the libido from this object and a displacement of it on to a new one, but something different, for whose coming-about various conditions seem to be necessary. The object cathexis proved to have little power of resistance and was brought to an end. But the free libido was not displaced on to another object; it was withdrawn into the ego. *There, however, it was not employed in any unspecified way, but served to establish an identification of the ego with the abandoned object. Thus the shadow of the object fell upon the ego, and the latter could henceforth be judged by a special agency, as if it were an object, the forsaken object.*

—Freud (1917, p. 249, italics added)

What was really wrong with his heart was, however, eloquently revealed in another dream—a dream in which he saw his heart lying on a plate and his mother lifting it with a spoon (i.e., in the act of eating it). Thus it was because he had internalized his mother as a bad object that he felt his heart to be affected by a fatal disease; and he had internalized her, bad object that she was for him, because as a child he needed her.

—Fairbairn (1943, p. 68)

Introduction

In this chapter I will describe the process by which a patient in analysis begins the complex and difficult process of disidentifying with powerful internal parental objects that have stunted the development of his unique potential, in much the same way as tall trees stunt the development of budding saplings in a forest. Using both Freud's theories of narcissism and the object relations theories of Melanie Klein and W. R. D. Fairbairn, I will first describe the dynamics of internalization and identification with the powerful internal parent. Then, I will describe the process in analysis in which the analyst uncovers the complex set of identifications through careful listening, exploration of countertransference, and a constant assessment of what Antonino Ferro (2009) calls the "analytic field", and then intervenes interpretively to help the patient unlock the crippling unconscious hold his internal objects have on him.

It is important to note that this process is more than simply the analysis of defence. Rather, by addressing the core of the patient's internal object world, and the ways in which this identification with internal objects limits and distorts his relationship to real objects in the here and now, this work is in fact a deconstruction of a core aspect of the patient's character as concretized in a few crucial repetitive relational dynamics—a much more difficult and risky proposition for both analyst and patient. As such, the analytic process of outlining and dismantling such internal object relationships involves much more than interpretation, since very often the links to these objects are not yet symbolized or even mentalized, but rather embodied—often quite literally as somatic symptoms, but also as destructive behavioural patterns, professional choices, or choices of partners. As a first stage, the links to the internal objects are hypothesized by the analyst, and then gradually brought into the analysis through careful interpretation and links to material or experiences in the sessions or in the transference/countertransference dynamic.

It is within the analytic field that the stultifying effects of such identifications can be experienced most intensely and immediately by both people in the room, and it is also here that what Michael Balint (1968) calls "a new beginning" can emerge (p. 131).

Role of identification in the formation of self

The concept of identification has become central to any psycho-analytic understanding of the formation of the self, particularly understandings that grow out of the object relations tradition. Freud himself returned repeatedly to the concept of identification, enlarging upon and elaborating its place within his thinking about the formation of a person's identity. As Laplanche and Pontalis (1967) note in *The Language of Psychoanalysis*, Freud's early interest in hysteria, for example, represents an extension of the interest of the time in imitation or "mental contagion". Thus, Freud (1900) stated, "… identification is not simple imitation but *assimilation* on the basis of a similar aetiological pretension; it expresses a resemblance and is derived from a common element which remains in the unconscious" (p. 150, original italics). It is in his first foray into what would become the foundations of object relations, however, in "Mourning and Melancholia", that Freud (1917) would begin to sketch out the central role identification plays in character formation.[1]

In this still clinically relevant work, Freud describes the psychological processes that form the foundations of contemporary psychoanalysis—the splitting of the ego in the face of a painful experience of loss, the internalization of an object, and the sado-masochistic relations within the self between the self-identified and other-identified parts. This would become the basis for the conception of the superego as the internalization of the parents, and the splitting of the ego described in detail here via identification would become the heart of the structural theory. The concept of the internalization of the object that Freud outlines here would also become the starting point for both Melanie Klein and W. R. D. Fairbairn's elaborations of this new field of internal object relations.

Despite decades of elaboration on the concept of melancholia and its relation to object loss, Freud's careful explication in both "Mourning and Melancholia" (1917) and "On Narcissism" (1914a) of the complicated dialectic of self and other remains unsurpassed.[2] Freud's nuanced distinction between normal mourning and pathological melancholia in this essay rests on something much more complex than the distinction between the internalized object of melancholia and the external object of mourning—namely, the kind of attachment the ego had to that object. To the extent that the relationship was predominantly anaclitic, the likely outcome would be mourning (i.e., following a loss, the person would eventually transfer his or her libido onto another object following a normal period of grief). To the extent that the object was bound by a narcissistic type object tie, however, the person was susceptible to the internalization of the object and the withdrawal of libido into the self. The pathological state of mourning introduced a complex set of object relations between the self and the internalized object. Freud's (1917) description of the unexpected reaction of the melancholic ego to the loss of the object is worth examining closely as its represents the foundational moment for object relations theory:

> The result [of the shattering of the object relationship] was not the normal one of a withdrawal of the libido from this object and a displacement of it on to a new one [the characteristic outcome of normal mourning], but something different, for whose coming-about various conditions seem to be necessary. The object-cathexis proved to have little power of resistance and was brought to an end. But the free libido was not displaced on to another object; it was withdrawn into the ego. There, however, it was not employed in any unspecified way, but served to establish an *identification* of the ego with the abandoned object [p. 249, original italics].

Rather than seeking out a new object for investment, the libido withdraws into the ego and is used to link the ego with the "abandoned" object. Note how the passive loss has been turned around into active abandonment (see also Ogden, 2002, p. 772). This identification splits the ego in two—what Freud (1917) describes as "a cleavage between the critical activity of the ego and the ego as altered by identification" (p. 249)—or, more precisely, between a sadistically critical part of the self and a part of the self that has become identified with and *as* the Other. Freud describes this other-identified part of the self as having fallen under "the shadow of the object", perhaps the most important and resonant phrase in this essay. As evocative as it is, the meaning of this phrase needs to be carefully interpreted.

In his recent rereading of this seminal Freudian text, Ogden (2002) focuses on what he calls the "thinness" of the experience of the Other implied in the figurative language of the shadow. Certainly there is implied a two-dimensionality that lacks colour, body, and warmth that seems consistent with the emotional register of narcissistic relations.[3] Yet within this passage, and taken together with Freud's (1917) subsequent description of suicide and being intensely in love as instances of the ego being "overwhelmed by the object" (p. 252), I would argue that Freud is pointing more urgently to the way the fragile ego is overshadowed by the object. What Freud brilliantly intuits as well, however, is that through the fluid vicissitudes of identification (what we will later come to see as projective identification) what seems at first glance as the small and vulnerable party—the ego—turns out to be the sadistic and critical agency, while the part of the ego identified with the other turns out to be weak and wretched, impoverished and diminished by these critical attacks. Thus, Freud describes as much in his figurative language as in his actual logic a pattern of reversal—the fragile ego is overshadowed or overwhelmed by the all-powerful object and, in revenge and as a defence, the ego turns the tables on the other through its identification. Now the ego as self or subject is powerful and overshadowing, and the Other is diminished and denigrated.

I will argue that this complex process of identification as a means of control, revenge, and intense ongoing connection with an all-powerful internal object is still the basis for understanding much of the most resistant dynamics within analytic treatment (see for example Fairbairn, 1943). To sum up, then, in Ogden's (2002) words, "[T]he painful experience of loss is short-circuited by the melancholic's identification with the object, thus denying the separateness of the object: the object is me and I am the object" (p. 773). This confusion between self and other internally creates enormous psychological difficulty for the melancholic in establishing and maintaining healthy relationships with external objects in the present, including the analyst. In what seems to me an admirably clear marriage of the phenomenology and libidinal dynamics of melancholia or depression, Ogden (2002) describes the melancholic's denial of object-loss and the price he pays for it:

"This avoidance [of the pain of loss] is achieved by means of an unconscious 'deal with the devil': in exchange for the evasion of the pain of object loss, the melancholic is doomed to experience the sense of lifelessness that comes as a consequence of discon- necting oneself from large portions of external reality" [p. 773].

This "deal with the devil" will come to represent, I will argue, an important juncture at which object relations will diverge with Melanie Klein and W. R. D. Fairbairn. For as we shall see, Freud's crucial distinction between the melancholic's withdrawal into an internal object world and the mourner's eventual return to external object relating will become lost in Melanie Klein's (1940) reformula- tion of this essay.

Melanie Klein and the internal object world

In the opening page of her seminal essay "Mourning and its rela- tion to manic depressive states", Melanie Klein (1940) takes Freud's thinking about the pathological process of melancholia and turns it into the foundation of the infant's normal psychological devel- opment, thereby collapsing the distinction between mourning and melancholia. In her words, "My contention is that the child goes through states of mind comparable to the mourning [really, melancholia] of the adult, *or rather*, that this early mourning is revived whenever grief is experienced in later life" (p. 344, italics added). With the phrase, "or rather", Klein reverses the sequence of child mourning mirroring adult melancholia and makes early mourning for the lost breast the normal course of development, as well as the basis for the later onset of melancholia.

It is important to underscore that Klein must essentially con- flate mourning and melancholia in her reformulation, and asserts that every child experiences a kind of early melancholia—which becomes her version of the infantile neurosis. What is missing from Freud's careful, if ultimately not fully satisfying, attempt to distin- guish normal mourning from pathological melancholia, however, is the distinction that Klein makes between internal object relating and relating to external objects. For Klein, the enduring legacy of the internalization of the object, first the mother's breast of course, is the creation of an internal object world, which we can think of as the proliferation of personified aspects of the child's mother and father, as experienced through the prism of the child's own needs and emotional capacities. From Klein's perspective, it follows then that psychological health depends upon the correspondence between a person's internal object world and the "real" world of external objects. For example, she (1940) declares that,

> It seems at this stage of development, the unification of external and internal, loved and hated, real and imaginary objects is carried out in such a way that each step in the unification leads again to a renewed splitting of the imagos. But as the adaptation to the external world increases, this splitting is carried out on planes which gradually become increasingly nearer and nearer to reality [p. 350].

Yet the internal object world with its foundations in early infancy remains the primary realm for emotional experience throughout life.

With her intuitive grasp of the heart of Freud's insight in "Mourning and Melancholia" concerning the internalization of a loved and hated all-powerful object by the narcissistically vulnerable early ego, Klein (1940) develops an object relations tradition nascent in Freud's work (1914a, 1917) yet overshadowed by the later ego psychological turn (see Cohen, 2007). For Klein and those who have elaborated on her original ideas, mental illness and psychological health have to do with managing the inescapable fact of our dependency upon others,[4] particularly in the earliest and most vulnerable stages of our development (see also Fairbairn, 1941; Meltzer, 2005; Ogden, 2010). Identification becomes in this way of thinking an essential method for establishing and maintaining these necessary object relations (see Padel, 1985).

Donald Meltzer (2005) describes this process from a contemporary Kleinian perspective whereby our psychological well-being depends upon our respectful relations with an internalized parental couple who come to represent the core of the self, and as he puts it, "[A]t the nucleus of this private core [of the personality] is the mysterious, sacred nuptial chamber of the internal objects, to which they must be allowed periodically to withdraw to repair and restore one another" (pp. xix). If Meltzer's conception of an internal object world founded upon respect for the necessary separateness of the Other-within represents a contemporary Kleinian perspective on mental health and emotional stability, its counterpart is the internal object relationship invaded by the anxious or envious projections of the immature or envious aspects of the ego. For Klein (1946), the dynamic counterpart to what she imagines to be a healthy and necessary introjection of the good object, a process modelled on the taking in of milk from the breast, is the violent splitting and projection of aspects of the self or object that are felt to be toxic or destructive.

This concept of projective identification, of course, is Klein's most significant contribution to the development of the concept of identification. Projective identification is a complex, dyadic process in which a part or aspect of the self is transferred via projection into the internalized object. As Klein (1946) observes, projective identification is a phantasy, yet one that has real psychological consequences, primarily for the ego, whose sense of the differentiation between self and other now becomes blurred (see also Grotstein, 1977).

Klein's notion of projective identification was conceived as the most primitive infantile defence against an overwhelming and potentially annihilating innate anxiety, which she linked to the death instinct. Following Freud's (1917) lead in "Mourning and Melancholia", Klein (1946) conceived of projective identification as necessarily the defence of the vulnerable and weak early ego against first an internal experience of unbearable anxiety and then following the deflection of the death instinct outwards, against an external environment that is felt to be all-powerful and persecutory. If splitting and projective identification are the first-line defences of the most vulnerable and imperilled aspects of the self, then *facilitating reintegration of the split-off aspects of the self—feelings and self-representations—becomes the goal of analysis and essential to maturation and to adequate reality-testing.* For example, in Freud's (1917) description of the reversal of crushed ego and abandoning object in the dynamics of the melancholic, we can see projective identification at work, with the resultant blurring of boundaries between ego and object. According to this understanding of projective identification, the analyst would help the patient reintegrate the split-off abandoned, unwanted, and often dangerous feelings that have been projected into the internal object.

The clinical implications of this theory have been profound and wide-reaching. Analysis creates the conditions in which the internal world, formed in infancy and then reconstituted continuously through a dynamic process of projection and reintrojection, could be re-created, and with the help of the analyst, distortions and confusions between internal and external reality, and between self and other, could be clarified. The equation of analyst/mother and patient/baby and the need for correspondence between the internal world, whose dynamics are established in infancy, and the external world of the here and now of the transference meant that projective identification clinically had to be conceived as passing from infant/ patient to mother/analyst. In short, this uni-directionality helped fuel the split between the Kleinians and the British Middle School analysts, who felt that Klein neglected the critical role played by real (and not merely phantasized) environmental failure in pathological development (e.g., Fairbairn, 1944a, b; Winnicott, 1954a, b; James, 1960; Khan, 1963; Kohon, 1986; Phillips, 1988). The assertion that Klein ignores the importance of the mother's caregiving role can be overstated, considering that it was Klein who in fact stressed how the mother's regular attuned feedings and care are responsible for breaking the cycle of projection and reintrojection of toxic feelings, and establishing in its place a benign cycle of love and trust.

Nonetheless, there is no doubt that the mother's or father's actual interactions with the child are subordinated to the role of internal phantasy in the development of psychopathology.

Projective identification, both in early life and in clinical practice, is pathological to the degree that the identifications are fixed rather than fluid (Grotstein, 1977). As Bion (1962c) noted, projective iden-tification can serve as a necessary early mode of communication of unsymbolized early affective states—infantile distress—that he calls "beta elements" (p. 119). Projective identification, however, need not move simply from infant/patient to mother/analyst. If we consider a complementary version of projective identification in early life, we can imagine that it would be just as likely to move from parents to children, particularly for parents whose internal object worlds are themselves subject to a confusion of self and other as well as a nar-cissistic use of objects. When used defensively by parents as a means of ridding themselves of unbearable aspects of their own person-alities and then internalized and established by their child as a core object relationship, these projective identifications form the basis of a pathological relational dynamic that is extremely resistant to change. They also serve as a model for understanding the transgen-erational transmission of trauma (see Faimberg, 2005).

Fairbairn's theory of identification as response to environmental failure

Starting, much as Klein did, from Freud's model of melancholia as introjection and identification with an all-powerful loved object, W. R. D. Fairbairn (1943) directs his attention to the caregivers rather than the infant's instinctual conflicts to locate the origins of psychopathology. As a result of her/his complete dependence upon necessarily limited and often pathologically flawed caregivers, the infant internalizes, identifies with, and then represses the parents' failures—their "badness"—as a means of attempting to manage a situation of utter helplessness. The infant has no choice over his or her parents, and no recourse to redress bad parenting. Fairbairn (1941) describes two kinds of identifications: initially, what he calls "primary identifications" that are characteristic of his phase of "early infantile dependency"; and later, "secondary identifications" that are transient phenomena modelled upon the first kind. As he describes it:

> I employ the term *"primary identification"* here to signify the cathexis of an object which has not yet been differentiated from the cathecting subject. The unqualified term "identification" is, of course, sometimes used in this sense; but it is more commonly used to signify the establishment of a relationship based on non-differentiation with an object which has already been differentiated in some measure at least. This latter process represents a revival of the type of relationship involved in primary identification, and should thus, strictly speaking, be described as *"secondary identification"*. The distinction is one which it is theoretically important to bear in mind; but, so long as it is not forgotten, the simple term identification may be used for convenience without any specific reference to the primary or secondary nature of the process in question [pp. 34–35].

Fairbairn (1943) argues that this unique situation—our primary identification with objects that may not be good for us—explains the fierce attachment to what in later life seem like really bad relationships, or addictions, or eating disorders. Something like food, for example, upon which we are utterly dependent, becomes for the binge eater "a bad object". Fairbairn stressed that for a child who is naturally dependent on the parents a bad object is better than no object at all, and given the situation of infantile helplessness, it feels as if that is the only choice—to the regressed personality, or perhaps more accurately, to the undeveloped and undifferentiated parts of the personality, there are no other objects available. The patient in the room with us may look for all intents and purposes like a mature 30-year-old man, but the object-relational stage in which he is trapped is infancy and its state of helpless dependency upon one's all-powerful internal objects.

Thus we have a situation of the infant's necessary tendency to absorb and to cling to aspects of his or her parents, "primary identi-fication" which, when combined with the parents' own narcissistic vulnerabilities, creates a fertile ground for projective identification from the parents to the infant of unwanted or unloved aspects of themselves. What Fairbairn stresses, particularly in his earlier work (1941), is the importance of helping patients differentiate between their states of infantile dependence upon internalized objects, their need to make it right with this particular object, and a more mature state of interdependence upon real external objects, relationships that are characterized by reciprocal giving and taking. Mature object-relating, as opposed to those relationships characteristic of the stage of infantile dependency, relies on one's ability to experi-ence an object as it is, rather than as one needs it to be. It requires a movement away from internality and towards experiences with real people—what Freud (1917) describes as the movement of normal mourning as opposed to melancholic fixation on internal-ized objects. As Ogden (2010) describes it, Fairbairn's conception of maturation depends upon an escape from imprisonment within the internal object world formed in early life:

> Psychological growth, for Fairbairn (as I read him), involves a form of acceptance of oneself that can be achieved only in the context of a real relationship with a relatively psychologically mature person. A relationship of this sort (including the analytic relationship) is the only possible exit from the solipsistic world of internal object relationships .... With psychological growth, one comes to know at a depth that one's early experiences with

one's unloving and unaccepting mother will never be other
than what they were .... In order to take part in experience in
a world populated by people whom one has not invented, and
from whom one may learn, the individual must first loosen the
unconscious bonds of resentment, addictive love, contempt,
and disillusionment that confine him to a life lived principally
in his mind [pp. 116–117].

Transgenerational transmission of parental narcissism

In *The Telescoping of Generations*, Haydee Faimberg (2005) describes
a process of transgenerational projective identification, in which
parents project unwanted aspects of themselves into their children, while appropriating for themselves what they feel is loveable
about their children. For Faimberg, what she calls the "alienating
identifications" with parental projections appear in the transference
as a secret, never-before-told history that exists latently in the person, a version of Christopher Bollas's (1987) "unthought known".
Through the act of listening to a dissonance between the voice of
the patient in the here and now and the anachronistic elements
in her material, the analyst arrives at a critical moment of grasping something that suddenly illuminates the transference and the
patient's history retrospectively—after the fact (i.e., *après-coup*).
While Faimberg sketches out with admirable lucidity the operation
of the parental narcissism as it establishes unconsciously its colonization of parts of the child's personality, her model depends upon
this moment of the analyst's dramatic recognition of *après-coup* that
seems unnecessary and clinically suspect, because it suggests that
dramatic revelations are at the heart of analytic change rather than
patient, painstaking, and ordinary analytic intercourse. If this work
of locating the parental narcissistic projections resembles a game of
hide-and-seek, it does so, I believe, like the case of the purloined letter in the short story by Edgar Allen Poe, in which the secreted letter
is hidden in plain sight on the mantelpiece as apparently a worthless
scrap of no import (Lacan, 1966). In other words, the secret history is
not so much a secret as it is lacking the proper significance provided
by an appropriate subjective context—in Bion's (1962c) terms, an
adequate "container". I think Winnicott's (1974) notion in "Fear of
Breakdown" is closer to the clinical situation here—the patient has

already had the experience he fears, but there was no one home—no capacity for appropriate subjective registration of it, so that it persists in the form of anxieties about the future, or anxious dreams, or well-worn and apparently amusing family anecdotes from childhood.

It is the persistent and typically undramatic work of disidentification over the course of the analysis on the part of both analyst and analysand that gradually allows for the past to become history rather than unconscious repetition. In Faimberg's (2005) words, "[W]ith this process of disidentification (with respect to an alienated identification), history can be re-established [*established for the first time I would argue*] with the quality of 'past.' Thus disidentification is the condition for the liberation of desire and the constitution of the future" (p. 11, my notation italicized). Disidentification in this sense does not mean the deletion or elimination of these early identifications from the unconscious; rather, by releasing them from repression as Fairbairn (1943) describes it, we loosen their hold upon us. There opens up a space within which what Winnicott (1954a, b) calls "the true self" can emerge.

Disidentification in the analytic field

If the necessary splitting of the early ego results from a combination of its fragility as well as its dependence upon the psychological support of the Other, whether conceived as propping, mirroring, holding, or containing, what Fairbairn (1941) calls its "infantile dependency", then psychological growth in analysis would depend upon the capacity to dismantle the relatively fixed identification with this Other, to undo the "primary identification". Such a process of disidentification, however, is fraught with peril, since the psychic survival of the self at its earliest stages depended upon this blurring of boundaries between the fragile and dependent self and its provider/protector.

Often the clinical picture that presents itself is what Hannah Segal (1955) describes as a "symbolic equation", in which the space between the self, the object, and the symbolized has either never reliably been established or has collapsed (p. 168). The experience of the analyst in this situation very often is feeling outside some sealed chamber, watching or hearing some drama re-enacted repeatedly, but unable to engage or influence the proceedings.[5]

The identification, which is by definition unconscious, presents itself indirectly. In a first session with a patient who describes the loss of a powerful and domineering father to cancer of the larynx, I am aware of an odd and persistent rattle in his throat when he speaks, that I come to understand as an unconscious link to this dead father. Another patient complains bitterly of her addiction to cigarettes, and how it seals her off from the rest of the world around as she drives around town in her car, smoking furiously. She is convinced that "they"—the other drivers she sees—are all healthy and hopeful. No one she knows smokes, none of her friends, clients, or boyfriend can know she smokes. Yet as soon as she is alone, especially in her car or at home late at night, she lights up. Months into the treatment she talks about her shameful feelings about her father who is dying young of emphysema from a life-long three pack a day habit. Over the course of the analysis, we return repeatedly to this secret and shameful identification with a dying father inside, and how the smoking soothes and deadens her.

In the analysis with her, I often feel deadened and hopeless myself, unable to break the hold of these powerful ties to her internal parents. This projective identification in the countertransference, this communication of a feeling of despair and hopelessness, represents a first step in the process of loosening the grip of the identification. Her devotion to this internal object relationship to a self-destructive father limits her capacity for a new experience with a man, either with me in the analysis, or with the numerous men she dates and discards. It is as if the present holds no interest for her; only the past embodied in this static relationship with an aspect of her father matters. In keeping with the confusion of the projective identifications going on internally, the patient is sometimes identified with the smoking and dying father, sometimes with the grieving and helpless child, sometimes with an angry and punishing child who turns the tables on the father who neglected her in childhood by her not returning his desperate phone calls in his final months. In the transference, I am experienced as the unavailable father whose phone calls—interpretations, interventions—are not returned. Regardless of which position she finds herself in, however, the result is unsatisfying for her, and ultimately inhibits her work establishing new relationships in the present, with new and different objects, including her work with me in the analysis.

So how does what I am calling a process of disidentification come about in the analysis? I believe we can point to a series of inter-related factors that allow for the possibility of psychic change and emotional development. First, we isolate and highlight a particu-lar area of fragility in the patient's personality that is connected to an early object relation breakdown. Most often, this breakdown can be traced to an environmental failure—a narcissistic vulnerability in a primary object that creates a corresponding narcissistic vulner-ability in the child or infant. It could also be the result of unavoid-able ruptures in the early relationship—an illness, sudden change in circumstances, arrival of a sibling that strains to the breaking point an already precarious libidinal economy between young child and parent. The typically preverbal period of these ruptures, along with the parents' lack of registration of them, makes them particularly difficult to work through in adulthood, not to mention childhood. In the early period of the analysis, they emerge first in the analyst's mind (or if the analyst is a candidate in training, perhaps in the mind of the supervisor) as a hypothesis, based on some experience with the patient—a story from childhood, a somatic symptom described, a dream recounted, a particular often recurrent relational pattern at work or with lovers, family, or friends.

This hypothesis then becomes a symbolic node in the intersub-jective field between patient and analyst. Tentatively, the analyst will begin to make links to this hypothesis in the patient's analytic material—the day-to-day conflicts and personal and professional challenges, their historical reflections on their relations with parents and siblings in their early life, and especially their dreams, which will most likely reveal these unconscious identifications most clearly. But it is within the field of the transference/countertransference dynam-ics that the analyst will find him or herself on more solid ground for understanding and unwinding this tangled bit of psychic history.

A woman who has not married and has struggled to sustain rela-tionships with men begins her analysis with me with an assumption that I am easily bored, and worries that my responsibilities in my institute and my work with other patients depletes me and leaves me unavailable to her. In my mind, I link this sense of me to her father, who came home from work exhausted and drained. Several months later, we return to this topic in a session in which she is wor-ried that because she has no pressing issue, she will wander vaguely and not get anything accomplished. She takes up several themes and discards them restlessly. I link this to her feeling that she is boring me and that she couldn't engage her father after work, and point out that in this case, she seems to be identified with a father inside who can't engage with her if she doesn't have an urgent need. She becomes aware of how often in her life she acts out this identification rather than allowing herself to try to engage new people in her life, and then reflects on how sad it is that so many potential relationships with men never had a chance because of this attachment to her internal unavailable father. My experience of being with her as an easily wounded child, resentful, unsoothable, gives way to a strong feeling of empathy with her grief—I feel with her in the session in a new way.

As a result then of this careful and gradual process of registration, notation, and interpretation, the identification becomes available to consciousness—it enters the symbolic field directly and is available to both analyst and patient as an explanation for conflicts, choices, behaviour. It might be useful to think of the primary identification process as similar to a magnetic field that orients the lines of force in the patient's life around the pole of his or her primary internal objects. The therapeutic process of disidentification which results from the gradual shared construction of a new symbolic field mapping the operation of this previously unconscious magnetic field works to reverse the polarity and to expand the potential for what we could think of from the perspective of non-linear dynamics and/or chaos theory (Galatzer-Levy, 2009) as "new attractors" to emerge, both from within the patient's own personality—new interests, habits, passions, feelings—and from without in the current environment of the patient—new love objects, new friends, new opportunities. At the centre of this altered field, however, is the relationship with the analyst who operates both like and unlike the primary object of identification (cf. Strachey, 1934).

If we conceive of the objective of analysis as helping patients escape from their imprisonment within their internal object relationships and be available to new experiences and new objects, then the analyst must offer her/himself up as both a representative of that primary object relationship, which is to say little more than s/he must offer herself as a transference figure, but more important, must also stand as a representative of the world outside the patient's internal object world—as irreducibly Other. We could say that the analyst functions in a way that resembles Winnicott's (1951) transitional object, in that while:

> … it is true that the piece of the blanket (or whatever it is) is symbolical of some part object, such as the breast[,] nevertheless, the point of it is not its symbolic value so much as its actuality. Its not being the breast (or mother), although real, is as important as the fact that it stands for the breast (or mother) [p. 233].

What is therapeutic, then, is the capacity of the analyst and the analytic situation to render the patient's experience of his or her relations to the primary object symbolic through the specific quality of the real Otherness of the analyst and the externality of the analytic setting.

The emergence of the true self

As a result of this clearing away of the dead-wood of powerful and suffocating identifications with powerful internalized parent figures, the unrealized or undeveloped aspects of the patient begin to emerge—often in the form of dreams of new babies, of new hopes for love or business, in new interests, or simply experiencing one's own desires and feelings for the first time. This represents the emergence of what Winnicott (1954a) has defined as the true self, whose development to this point has been arrested. Like so many of Winnicott's groundbreaking concepts, the true self is necessarily vague. The true self is separate from the analyst, neither identification with nor defiant rejection of her, but made possible by the work of both patient and analyst.

Conclusion

I believe that one powerful component of transformative analytic work is this *process of uncovering and dismantling an internal object relationship with an early parental figure whose maintenance has become the focus of a patient's emotional life, without conscious awareness.* The process of engaging with the analyst in bringing this early identification and this ongoing object relationship into the analytic field allows for new possibilities to emerge—which when engaged with represent moments of true self experiencing. As a result, the patient moves from the timelessness of a mythic and static past to the terrifying yet enlivening flux of the present opening to the future. I would argue that what I have described as true self-experiencing represents the creativity possible within developmental narratives—the particular and personal inflection of our generational, our cultural, and our personal historical narratives. I believe that this personal inflection of shared developmental stories is what makes for a richly experienced personal life. The process of disidentification I have described does not preclude the importance of other aspects of analytic work, including the more normative work of managing developmental challenges that necessarily involve healthy identification with parental figures. Nevertheless, I think the truly original contribution of psychoanalysis has been this conceptualization of the birth of the true self.

Notes

1. Thomas Ogden (2002) offers a rereading of "Mourning and Melancholia" to clarify its seminal role in the origins of objects relations in his article entitled, "A New Reading of the Origins of Object Relations Theory".

2. For a careful explication of how Freud's concept of narcissism is always already implicated with an object, see Laplanche's (1970) chapter "The Ego and Narcissism", in *Life and Death in Psychoanalysis*.

3. Jacques Lacan's (1949) description of the capture of the infant's subjectivity by his image in the mirror represents another version of this dynamic of the fragile early ego being captured by a powerful Other.

4. Some might argue against Klein's recognition of the importance of our dependency on others by pointing to her emphasis on the innateness of aggression linked to the death instinct, along with her retaining much of Freud's libido theory. As Stephen Mitchell (1995) notes, however, Klein reformulates the concept of the instinct and impulse in such a way as to include the object in our earliest impulses and instincts. Hunger, thus, is inseparable from an innate sense of an object that would satisfy it; hatred from an object that

warrants it. In particular, Klein's concept of the depressive position and the manic defences against dependency, which even Winnicott would retain, argue strongly for her inclusion in this tradition of an other-centered psychology.

5. Donald Meltzer (1992) in *The Claustrum* gives an excellent clinical description of patients who live sealed off from contact inside their internal objects.

CHAPTER TWELVE

Movement thinking and therapeutic action in psychoanalysis

Beth I. Kalish

In my analytic practice I work with a variety of patients, mostly adults (on the couch), some couples, and a few children. Thinking in movement terms has become second nature due to an extensive background in movement observation and assessment (Kalish, 1976); such thinking precedes and/or occurs simultaneously with listening. It has become my practice to utilize what I refer to as "muscle memory" in my own body as I observe and/or pick up aspects of my patients' body movement patterns as they talk. This method gives me an additional instrument for understanding what is occurring with the patient non-verbally. Repeatedly, it validates hypotheses for formulating interpretations. Later, I will illustrate the method with specific clinical examples. First, it is important to define and to elaborate what is meant by "movement thinking" and how I have come to make use of this concept as a psychoanalyst.

The term "movement thinking" originated with Rudolf Laban (1960), who began studying movement in Germany prior to World War II. He was involved with all dance forms as well as choreography. His first system of notation was developed in order to preserve dance for future performance. He named it "Labanotation". It continues, to this day, to be used by professional dancers for that purpose. In the late 1930s, Laban immigrated to England as a result of mounting dangers to artists in Germany. Already famous, he was hired by the British government to study factory workers' movements and to aid them in becoming more efficient while working. Thus, he developed a second method of notating movements. He and his English colleague, F. C. Lawrence, wrote a book about this investigation called *Effort* (Laban & Lawrence, 1947). The word "effort" was translated from the German word "*Antrieb*", which described the quality of the workers' exertion when moving in their tasks. It was *the moving body* in action that interested him. After the war, Laban became interested in the development of a system of notation representing all movement qualities observable in the body. To that end, he studied movements in various cultures: American Indians, African, Chinese as well as European individuals. Ritual and work movements were his focus. Finally, his extensive study of dance, of ritual, fighting, and work movements in varying societies, culminated in an enlarged comprehensive method of notation, developed with co-workers Warren Lamb and Irmgard Bartenieff, called "Effort-Shape Analysis" (Bartenieff & Davis, 1965; Lamb, 1965).

> With the same movement terms he could (now) describe functional, expressive and artistic movement. He found that just as the Effort-Shape variables describe how a worker moves in a task, they can describe how individuals act and react to each other in a discussion, or how dancers shape themselves through space and vary the intensity … in various dance styles [Bartenieff & Davis, 1965, p. 6].

Laban (1960) conceptualized a theory of movement behaviour and the universal qualities of its meaning. He stated that,

> [M]ovement thinking could be considered as a gathering of impressions of happenings [*in the body*] … *movement thinking* does not, as thinking in words does, serve orientation in the external world, but rather—orientation in man's inner world. in which impulses surge and seek an outlet in doing, acting and dancing [p. 17, italics added].

In earlier writings (Dratman & Kalish, 1967; Kalish, 1968, 1976), I suggested that Laban's concept of movement thinking allows for another dimension of understanding human behaviours, which is clearly far more expressive of more than movement activity or of motor skill. For example, *efforts* are those movement qualities that reveal a person's *attitudes* towards the use of space, weight, and time. Efforts manifest in the body as coping mechanisms in relation to the environment. This understanding of *efforts* could offer the analyst information regarding, for example, the patient's unconscious conflict towards or away from autonomy, given that autonomy is a highly important developmental achievement of the ego. All individuals gradually develop their own characteristic distribution of effort elements. According to Laban and other movement observers who have followed a similar line of thinking, a mature constellation of effort elements shows an individual's movement preferences in terms of attention, intention, and decision-making. These so-called bodily preferences originate from unconscious and/or conscious aspects of psyche and of soma (Bartenieff & Davis, 1965; Kestenberg, 1965, 1967, 1975; Kestenberg, Marcus, Robins, Berlow & Buelte, 1971; Laban, 1960; Loman & Brandt, 1992).

There are basic problems in any discussion such as this one, in which a non-verbal mode (i.e., movement) is described as an important variable of study. First, it is crucial to find a method that will make the data as reliable as possible. The method must allow for a way to make reliable the observations by means of a standard procedure of recording. Second, a theoretical rationale is needed on which to base interpretations. Third, one must deal with the problem of trying to discuss a non-verbal construct, like movement behaviours, by using only verbal terminology.

Dell (1970), an early movement researcher, was well versed in Laban's Effort-Shape Analysis.

> Someone moves. You want to describe the movement. What can you say? You could start by saying what the person did. You can choose from among the many intransitive verbs in your vocabulary—he ran, he stopped, he turned, he jumped.... Or the person might have done something involving an object, allowing you a larger choice of verbs—he threw it, he brushed it off, he laid it down. You might want to become more specific, describing which parts of his body moved in the action, or even which direction he moved in or how the direction of his movements related to various other people or objects

surrounding him. If you say this much and no more, you will
get something similar to the script of a play .... But when reading a play, you can never know the varying intonations, col-
orations, emphases, hesitations with which the actor delivered
the lines in the living theater. In the same way, a description of
movement, no matter how detailed, when limited to the action
itself, yields little information about how the mover really
moved. You know what he did but you do not know how he
did it [pp. 3–4].

She beautifully articulated that a language of movement terms with
universal meaning was needed. A language that could incorporate more than action; a language that could demonstrate qualitative differences among and between individuals. Laban's language
of movement terms does just that. Like music, it can be notated by
means of symbols and/or it can be translated into descriptive words
without losing the quality of meaning of the movements.

It was the language of Effort-Shape that I learned and then
applied while comparing the differing movements of autistic and
non-autistic children. This empirical research led to the development of a Body Movement Scale for Autistic and other Atypical
Children (Ruttenberg, Kalish, Wenar & Wolf, 1976; Kalish, 1976). The
Movement Scale assesses pure movement qualities as these qualities change chronologically during a child's early developmental
phases. Data was derived by trained raters from observations made
over a one year period of both typical and atypical (autistic) children
and how they move at specific chronological ages from 12 months to
five years. As part of descriptive terminology used in the Movement
Scale, I invented the word "echocorpia". Echocorpia refers to specific
repetitive movements observed that are without body integration or
expression of affect. These repetitive (habitual) movements appear
to be disassociated in the body-as-a-whole. That is, echocorpia is to
body movement as echolalia is to verbal language.

Observations of body movements and/or facial expression in
particular are not unique to psychology or to psychoanalysis. Charles
Darwin's (1896) classic *The Expressions of the Emotions of Man and Animals* represents the most fundamental scientific contribution to observational work. Later, there were a number of early psychoanalysts,
beginning with Freud, who subscribed to movement observation as

part of their daily analytic work. For example, Freud (1905a) gave a vivid description of his young patient, Dora, as he observed her playing with her pocketbook as she lay on his sofa and talked to him:

> ... opening it, putting a finger into it, shutting it again and so on. ... I give the name of symptomatic acts to those acts which people perform ... automatically, unconsciously, without attending to them .... They are actions to which people would like to deny any significance and which, if questioned about them they would explain as being indifferent and accidental. Closer observation, however will show that these actions, about which consciousness knows nothing or wishes to know nothing, in fact give expression to unconscious thoughts and impulses and are therefore most valuable and instructive as being manifestations of the unconscious thoughts and impulses ... [p. 75]. .

In Dora's case, Freud interpreted her actions as relating to early masturbation fantasies that she had previously denied.

Deutsch (1947), following Freud (1905a, 1923a), discussed that muscular movements of the body, face, fingers, hands, etc. are motor discharges of psychic tensions that have meaning. They relate to emotional processes and "may be a sensitive means of detecting conscious and unconscious psychic processes" (p. 195). He cites multiple clinical observations of "postural behaviors", which he termed "random observations which justify a more systematic investigation" (p. 198). Deutsch concluded that there are definite motivations for postural behaviour of every patient. He believed that postural attitudes reflect, substitute for, or accompany verbal expression of the unconscious and that each individual has his/her own characteristic posture to which s/he eventually returns when s/he has deviated from it. Postural changes can reflect a shift during an analysis. This can serve as vital information for the analyst, when and if s/he attends to the modality of movement behaviours that are ongoing as they change and evolve.

Rangell (1954a) wrote about the psychology of poise. He elaborated in great detail on the "psychic significance of the snout or perioral region" of the body (p. 313). He believed that the snout area plays a decisive role in revealing inner states in that the area around the mouth is closely related to affects and to the mimetic expressive system, "which is so much at the core of man's relation to man" (p. 320). Rangell as well as Hoffer (1949) each place special emphasis on the relation between mouth and hand movements and their intra-psychic implications throughout the life cycle.

In 1971, Greenacre, stated:

> I would be even more emphatic now about the need to pay attention to nonverbal communication than I have been in years past. The psychoanalytic situation stresses the impor- tance of speech in contrast to action. The analysand's position on the couch, by subtle suggestion, limits the extent of active movement and the suggestion is furthered by the direction to the analysand to speak whatever thoughts and feelings he becomes aware of during the hour. Yet the movements on the couch, postures, mannerism, changes in tone and intensity of voice, flushing, sweating and special states of body tensions are all part of the expression of feeling and may represent explicit communications [pp. 61–62].

Developmental aspects

In summarizing his relevant work, Mittelman (1954) discussed motility in infants, children, and adults. He presented a convincing argument that motility is a drive, dominant in the second year of life. As far as I can determine from the psychoanalytic literature, few psychoanalysts endorsed Mittelman's strongly held view of motility as a drive. However, in observing normal children from 12 months to five years of age during my doctoral research (Kalish, 1976), I found sufficient empirical evidence to support Mittelman's postulates about motility. Later, Siegel (1984), an early colleague in dance-movement therapy who also trained in psychoanalysis, wrote extensively about motility as a separate drive. She elaborated on motility as an important ego function in development. Although still a controversial concept, I believe that motility as a drive deserves attention and further exploration. One has only to observe children consistently during the first two years of life to see that "motor phenomena" are dominant. That is to say, that movement is pursued for movement's sake and not simply as a means to an end, such as getting somewhere. Drawing from Mittelman, I prefer to use "motility" rather than "motor", as the former is a more inclusive term.

Mittelman's (1954) theory and basic observations support motility dominance especially in the second year. He grouped these phenomena under the following age-specific headings:

> 1) So-called random movements of infants; 2) Affectomotor patterns that accompany emotional reactions such as joy, fear and so forth; 3) Well-organized, vigorous rhythmic patterns, referred to as "autoerotic"—for example, rocking or bouncing; 4) Skilled motor activity, including posture, locomotion and particularly, manipulation; and 5) Motor phenomena that are indispensable elements of the function of another organ or another striving—for example, motor patterns that subserve oral activities such as sucking or eating …. During the age period from about ten months to four or five years, there are motor manifestations that can be considered as evidence for the motor urge [drive], with individual variations in intensity [p. 145].

Intensity is revealed in shifting tension levels. Thus, shifting levels of tension are observable in the body at all times. I will discuss this later in the chapter. Motility appears as a dominant drive from the age of approximately 12 months to three years. The child can consistently be observed engaged in clear signs of drivenness in movements that serve no other visible purpose aside from the experience of movement itself; affective pleasure is present in actions such as crawling, running, bouncing, banging, and jumping. Rhythm and repetition are observable components of these activities during early childhood, when the precursors of a drive for mastery are developing. During the second and third years of life, motility is one of the most important expressions of early ego functions. These include mastery, integration, reality testing, and beginning control of impulses. Mittelman described this period as the motor level of ego and libidinal development.

Importantly, the need for motility and/or motor discharge and its various expression(s) in activity does not disappear with age. There are ongoing manifestations of motility throughout life in the same way that oral, anal, and genital urges remain, albeit in a more varied and modified form.

In a general sense, as one watches any individual moving, it is possible to observe that s/he either holds back, restricts, or binds the flow of movements in the body. Conversely, another person may go-with-the-flow; the body moves easily and even lyrically. The going-with-the-flow of movement is called "free" while the restriction of flow is termed "bound" when using Laban's terminology. Bound flow is what we think of as seen in a tense person; free flow would be seen as a relaxed (but not limp) overall quality of movements in the body. Both free and bound flow are aspects of muscle tensions discernable in the moving body. It is the relationship and degree of muscle tension that is important to observe. This can be seen in a moving body part, or in the body-as-a-whole. Another key parameter is that of shape-flow. This refers to the alternations of growing and shrinking in several dimensions of the body (e.g., width, length, and depth).

A key aspect of shape-flow can be observed in breathing styles. An individual grows as s/he inhales and shrinks with an exhale. For example, I recall a woman patient whose body-as-a-whole from the waist up was so tensely held that I could not discern her breathing cycle. After several sessions, I interpreted that she appeared to be "holding her breath", appearing not to be breathing in or out, even though, of course, I knew she was. Immediately, she sucked in air, began to laugh anxiously, saying she had been told that before, but "I do not know how to breathe deeply, if I stop to breathe in, I am afraid I will lose my thoughts." At that moment in the session, I began to mirror her breathing and then deepen mine. She picked up the cue and was able to imitate by deepening her own breathing (i.e., growing via shape-flow). She stated that my action made her feel I was taking her seriously, that the very intervention of breathing in/out together allowed her to "relax her mind" and concomitantly she felt more able to sort out her thoughts.

Another patient talked of a feeling experienced for years, that of "a heavy weight on my chest". This feeling was particularly strong for her when she would lie down to sleep at night, or when she was lying on my couch. She imagined this heavy weight as a rock that she wished she could lift off her body. She said she was "weighted down" by this rock and the feelings it evoked. Many years into her analytic work she associated the rock with her father and his "heavy hand on my chest" when he molested her at age four. Over time, she worked through this visualization and her feelings of helplessness that originated from the past experience. She imagined the rock as less and less heavy until it was no longer there for her. What was left was a "flabby spongy surface ... my inner self was so vulnerable, I had to hide all feelings from my parents, couldn't talk about the molestation. Now I have lifted that rock, there is less to hide ... there is hope. I can feel what I feel and think about my body—my inner centre. It helps to put the pieces together." I asked her to explain what she meant by her "inner centre". She said, "That is my strength that I did not know I had, now I can use it, then I couldn't. I do not feel like a victim any more."

It is part of my working hypothesis that the very act of moving together synchronously *is therapeutic*. Whether it takes the form of breathing (or a body motion), the motility mode can recapitulate a pre-language experience that functions as a soothing attunement with the other. This appears to be most intensely articulated in the patient's response when the analyst's intervention is directly tied to the patient's in-the-moment affective experience.

This hypothesis concurs with other contemporary movement writers who believe that variations in body shape express changes in one's affective relationship to the environment (Bloom, 2006; Kestenberg, 1975; La Barre, 2001; Loman & Brant, 1992; Sossin & Loman, 1992).

Free or bound flow and shape-flow represent only two of many parameters of observation derived from Laban's complex system. It should be noted that to learn all aspects of Effort-Shape Analysis, as well as how to notate it, requires intense study and practice. In addition, during the process of learning, it is imperative to "feel" those particular manifestations in one's *own* body in order to later empathize, identify, and understand another person's bodily experience. It is similar to that of learning to recognize (in order to utilize) one's countertransference experience, by first bringing the analyst's own feelings (somatic) to consciousness during a psychoanalysis. This kind of "knowing" takes years of concentration and daily practice. However, movement thinking can enhance an analyst's multi-dimensional assessment of psychic changes during treatment phases of the patient.

Kestenberg (1965, 1975) was uniquely astute at movement observation/notation in her psychoanalytic work. As a child psychoanalyst beginning to publish in the 1950s she became interested in, and studied with, several of the early disciples of Rudolf

Laban, most notably, Irmgard Bartenieff (Bartenieff & Davis, 1965; Bartenieff & Lewis, 1980) and Warren Lamb (1965). As stated earlier in this paper, Bartenieff and Lamb worked with Laban in Europe before bringing Laban's theory and methods to the United States. Lamb's (1965) contributions included the establishment of an assessed ratio between postural-gestural movements and their affective meanings (1965).

It was my good fortune to have studied and worked with Bartenieff, Lamb, and with Kestenberg during the years from 1965–1980. Lamb (1965) notated my movements as I worked with an autistic child. He commented that certain adults could excel in work with children because they have maintained a balanced posture/gesture ratio in their own bodies (Lamb, personal communication).

Kestenberg founded the Sands Point Movement Study Group for research as well as a Child Development Center. There she developed, to use her terminology, "movement re-training for mothers and their infants". After careful observation and notation of a mother's movement style while holding, touching, and interacting with her infant, Kestenberg could identify "mismatching" that was leading to difficulties in relating between the two. In her book, *Children and Parents* (1975), she devoted a detailed chapter to aspects of "attunement and clashing" in movement styles as well as their ramifications in mother/child dyads that she explained on both an interpersonal and intrapsychic level. After years of observational longitudinal research, she formulated the Kestenberg Movement Profile (KMP). Again, this represents a highly complex instrument for describing, assessing, and interpreting non-verbal behaviour based on stages of development and their manifestations in both children and in adults. The Profile can graph 120 movement factors and describes body attitude and qualifying numerical data partially derived from Laban's early work. (See Sossin & Loman, 1992 for clinical applications of the Kestenberg Movement Profile.)

For the most part, Kestenberg felt that she was not appreciated or well understood by her own psychoanalytic colleagues during her lifetime (Kestenberg, personal communication). Her work attempted to integrate movement behaviour, early development, and psychoanalytic theory. As my mentor, long before I became a psychoanalyst, she stands out in my mind as a beacon of inspiration for the creativity and foresight of her many unique contributions to research in both movement and in psychoanalysis. Kestenberg's interest in innate motor rhythms and the resulting tensions expressed in contractions of agonistic and antagonistic muscles led to her own theoretical formulations regarding drive(s) and the resulting observable "flow of tensions" throughout the body. Her early notation system (1965), which preceded the KMP, emphasized that certain types of tension flow in the body could be manifested as demonstrating a particular psychosexual stage of development. She collected specific observational data to illustrate the unique rhythms of orality, of anality, and of the phallic phases over the many years of her own research and that of her colleagues and students. The chart below shows her graph of the psychosexual stages and how she designated and taught us to notate specific bodily rhythms when observing an individual.

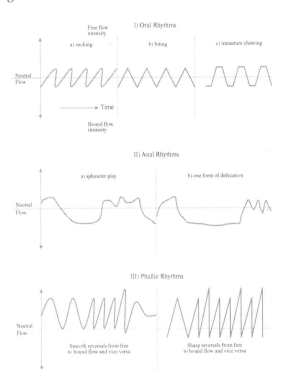

Figure 1. Diagrams of typical rhythms of tension flow that are appropriate for zonal discharge.

Kestenberg designed her graphic profiles to augment the narrative developmental assessments conducted by her longtime colleague Anna Freud (1965). Later, Kestenberg and Sossin (1979) emphasized that psychosexual rhythms are not "drives" per se. However, they were named for drive phases *because* they represent specific rhythms associated with those drives and, at the same time, such rhythms are observable in the muscular activity in the body.

I think of observable or "felt" muscular activity as "muscle memories" since they are often connected to early affective states and/or traumas repressed from childhood. For example, another young woman patient who had been sexually abused at a very early age described how certain positions in her yoga class caused her to be flooded with tears and she did not know why. Associations during her analysis revealed being held in a similar position when she was abused more than 30 years before. Such muscle memories (a body position, in this case) as well as bodily rhythms, while more subtly discernable in adults than they are in young children, clearly can provide important data during an analysis most especially when the analyst is attuned to this non-verbal mode.

Clinical vignette

The following vignette will illustrate further how I observed and then utilized the rhythm mode and concomitant tension flow with a patient in analysis after several years on the couch. On this particular Monday session, S entered the room without making eye contact (unusual for her) and went immediately to the couch, lying down more quickly than usual. She began to speak of her weekend in a flat, affectless tone. While talking, she absent-mindedly leaned down to the end of the couch and pulled the blanket (always there) up over herself, and, at the same time, she began to fiddle with the fringe while talking. After some minutes, she began to rub her cheek with the fringe on the blanket. While listening, observing, and waiting, I became aware that I was "picking up" her hand movements and rhythmically rubbing my own cheek as she was rubbing hers! Then, based on my knowledge of her and my countertransference reaction, I formulated an interpretation regarding the possibility that she may have experienced a sense of isolation from me over the weekend separation and now she seemed to be struggling to get "attuned" to me once more. She acknowledged that, indeed, this was true. She began to cry and expressed dismay at my interpretation, since she had said nothing about this verbally. She questioned how I "knew" about her loneliness and isolation over the break of the weekend. When I suggested that her hand movements were very compelling and that I found myself mirroring them in response, it seemed to me as if we were becoming "re-attuned". Quickly she retorted, "What hand movements? I wasn't doing anything with my hands, just playing around with the edge of the blanket." Even though the patient wanted to minimize this non-verbal movement play, I had become conscious of earlier movement "mis-matching" between us (similar to Kestenberg's descriptions of mother/infant misattunement). This alerted me to pick up and mirror her movement qualities in order to reconnect to her psychic state. In so doing, I experienced a sense of her (my?) isolation in the moment and thus formulated the interpretation. The interpretation revealed the deeper level of her unexpressed affect.

During the time I was listening to S, preceding the interpretation, my thoughts had drifted back to images of autistic children with whom I had worked long ago. Unlike them, one could reach this woman on a verbal level, albeit slowly. Gradually, she had begun to accept the meaning (and importance) of her actions as an expression of her inner reality. Many years after the described occurrence in her analysis, she referred to this session and its power for her, "a real break-through" she said. She began to acknowledge her own regressive neediness, which she had denied for so long. No longer could she defend against that which she unconsciously "knew" but could not previously express in words. It was her body movements that revealed the real affective response of her inner experience over the weekend. This marked a new stage for her in a long and fruitful analysis (Kalish-Weiss, 1997).

This clinical example is given to illustrate how conscious/ unconscious attunement to movement parameters, namely, movement thinking on the part of the analyst, can serve as an aspect for both deepening insight as well as for change in the patient. It has been my experience with both children and adults that affective movement attunement picked up and then interpreted by the analyst leads to *a sense of safety* within the psychoanalytic space. The analyst's thinking in this way on multiple levels can serve as a model of what

Bollas (1989) described as the bringing to consciousness "unthought known" aspects in the analysis (p. 10). Thus, over time, a patient can begin to value, and to clarify, first in his/her own mind and later to articulate vis-à-vis secondary process, the significant meaning(s) of his/her movement behaviours. It is as basic as a patient's growing interest in dream material along with personal recognition of the rich symbolic information such material can provide from the unconscious.

Kramer and Akhtar (1992) edited a volume focusing on the non-verbal aspects of communication in psychoanalysis. The book is titled, *When the Body Speaks*. Each chapter stemmed from a symposium held in honour of Margaret Mahler. Eight distinguished psychoanalysts grappled with the issue at hand: they pondered several questions including: does the talking cure consist of more than talking?, what can be learned from observing patients' gestures, posture, facial expressions, silences, tone of voice?, etc. Each analyst presented clinical case material from their own practices as well as pointing to the great value of using non-verbal phenomena in psychoanalysis. These clinicians approached their presentations as strong advocates for the role of non-verbal communication in their own practices while suggesting that other psychoanalysts and psychotherapists do so as well. They spoke to the need for in-depth knowledge and research in this area. Interestingly, only an occasional reference was made to the already extensive research of non-verbal dynamics that preceded their own contributions and subsequent publication. Not surprisingly, none referred to the work of Laban and his theories of observation in their references. Nor was a cross-disciplinary approach to this important topic evident.

More than 20 years before their publication, I reviewed much of the known literature on non-verbal communication (Kalish, 1976). At that time, a variety of writings under the following headings were available: body motion; kinesics; paralanguage, and proxemics. There was an avalanche of serious scientific work with no less than eight major books devoted to the theory and research in non-verbal communication in the social sciences (Birdwhistell, 1952, 1970; Condon, 1968, 1973; Dittman, 1972; Ekman, 1973; Ekman & Friesen, 1968; Ekman, Friesen & Ellsworth, 1972; Hinde, 1972; Mehrabian, 1972; Scheflen, 1972, 1974; Spiegel & Machotka, 1974).

However, none of these researchers were psychoanalysts nor did there seem to be any cross-referencing.

Of particular note were the outstanding contributions of an anthropologist, Ray Birdwhistell (1952, 1970) and his subsequent collaborative work with psychiatrist, Albert Scheflen (1972, 1974). Birdwhistell coined the term "kinesics". Drawing on his knowledge of descriptive linguistics, he argued that all movements of the body have meaning (i.e., are not accidental) and that non-verbal forms of language have a grammar that can be analysed in terms similar to spoken language. Thus, a "kineme" is "similar to a phoneme because it consists of a group of movements which are not identical, but which may be used interchangeably without affecting social meaning" (Knapp, 1972, pp. 94–95).

He, along with a group of psychiatrists working in kinesics research, emphasized the social impact and culture on the infant and later the adult in their body-motion behaviour and developing language. As Birdwhistell (1970) described it, body motion behaviour is just as much "learned behavior as is a language behavior; we simply have not, heretofore, known enough about it to teach it" (p. 8).

All kinesics research rested on the assumption that much that occurs between people, as they communicate, occurs through non-verbal action without awareness of the participants (Birdwhistell, 1963). This group of researchers used film extensively for study. By means of slow motion film analysis, body movements were revealed repeatedly that were not seen when viewing film at the usual 24 frames per second. Their groundbreaking research showed conflict and contradictions between verbal language of the subjects and their movement messages while they were engrossed during intense conversations (Birdwhistell, 1970).

The research of Condon (1968) and Condon and Bronsin (1973) involved the study of differences between normal and pathological subjects in movement behaviours. They emphasized, and I agree, that clusters of relationships between movements and speech could and should be studied as *units of behaviour*. This "self-synchrony", as they called it, was like an interactive dance between the listener and speaker. It clearly demonstrated rhythmic and directional coordination, as well as how the listener and speaker learned from each other. Condon and Bronsin (1973) examined diagnostic categories; they studied

30 films in detail, showing aphasia, Parkinsonism, Huntington's chorea, stuttering, childhood autism, and schizophrenia. They found that all pathological behaviours were self-synchronous at either the "micro or macro levels" (p. 38). The film of schizophrenic patients showed that "… one part of the body was often out of phase with the rest of the body. In several instances a micro strabismus was detected, in that one eye might move and the other remain still or one eye might track markedly faster than the other eye. In many other instances one part of the body would remain exceptionally still over long periods, which contrasted with the movement pattern of normal interaction …" (p. 38). Moreover, they found some tentative evidence that these patients appeared to become more self-synchronous as their pathological states improved.

Condon and Bronson's (1973) findings were similar to those I reported in the same journal. These findings were not based on the study of films. Instead, I simply observed and notated the movements of children using methods of Effort-Shape Analysis. This early study (Kalish, 1968), comparing severely disturbed and non-disturbed children, led to later research. Now, after many years of evidence in clinical practice, I am satisfied that it is possible to observe such phenomena *without* the need to use film slowed down to the micro-level (Kalish-Weiss, 1983, 1997, 2008a)! Clearly, it is a skill that can be developed and learned. Movement thinking for the analyst can become second nature over time.

How can it be explained that, in general, psychoanalysts have not incorporated the movement modality into their work to a greater degree? A psychoanalyst, McLaughlin (1992) addressed this same question, acknowledging that from the beginning of psychoanalysis to the present there has been a central importance placed on the spoken word. McLaughlin sees this as a misguided notion that to this day continues. As he put it (1992):

> Recognition of the full potentiality of gestural expressiveness for psychoanalytic work has been nearly as slow in coming as has been the acknowledgment of the unique powers of natural sign language for the congenitally deaf. For their field it would take many years of practical experience and research, documented by Oliver Sacks (1989) to override the prevailing bias that the deaf should learn oral speech, and to demonstrate the natural

signing of the deaf to be a complete and supple language in its own right, superior to mere words in its power of portrayal in a four-dimensional fashion [p. 154].

The importance placed on verbal communication in psychoanalysis stems from a psychoanalytic commitment to the overriding power of rational thinking and secondary processes to which the spoken language gives evidence. Most analysts consider that movement behaviour (with or without accompanying speech) tends to represent a regression to an infantile level of functioning. Unfortunately, this has resulted in a profound placement of body-ego in the realm of pre-language: that it is considered more psychically primitive in a developmental sense (Freud, 1923a).

Movement in the analyst's mind

Once the door is opened for a session, as the patient moves into the analytic space there is an opportunity for the analyst to observe more than verbal communications. If the analyst views the office environment as a laboratory (i.e., wherein the space does not change over time) s/he can consciously monitor each patient's use of that space in the few minutes it takes to enter, to approach the couch, to settle on the couch, and then to begin verbal discourse. Those few minutes create ample time for a potential observation of specific movement behaviours of any given patient. Initially, an analyst wishing to attune him- or herself to movement thinking might observe the following four dimensions:

> 1) *Element of use of Space*: Body-as-a-whole moves with a tendency towards filling up or shrinking within the available boundaries (of the room; or of the couch, etc.; 2) *Element of use of Time*: Body-as-a-whole moving with either a tendency towards "quickness" or "slowness" through the space; 3) *Element of use of Weight*: Body-as-a-whole moving with either a tendency towards "heaviness" or "lightness"; and 4) *Element of use of Tension Flow*: Body-as-a-whole or certain body parts are rigidly held; shallow breathing or deep breathing should be noted.

After observing each of these four dimensions, the analyst might then keep in mind whether or not any of these parameters are altered in the horizontal position on the couch and/or when the patient begins to speak. Later, at the end of the session, the analyst may note changes, as the patient exits the office space. Can the analyst account for these changes when reviewing the verbal content of the material(s) discussed?

A certain female patient of mine demonstrated extremes of "quickness" and "lightness" as well as high intensity (tension flow). She verbalized, "I am a troubled person" as she rushed into and through my office space on the initial visit. It felt to me like a tornado had overtaken the room. She described herself as living on a "treadmill of anxiety". She was talking non-stop even before sitting down in the chair opposite mine. Months later when she (reluctantly) began lying on the couch, I observed a startling shift in tension flow in her body attitude. She would rush to the couch, and then give into gravity (collapse) with heaviness in her body-as-a-whole. Often she curled into a foetal position while her speech remained pressured (quickness) and her breathing remained shallow. The differences in her vertical/horizontal movements were profound in as much as they revealed her conflict between her more regressed internal states and her verbally expressed, highly defended intellectualized verbal content. It was more than a year of repeating this pattern before she was able to take in the space around her, both visually and inhaling more air into her body. An important moment occurred for her when, lying on her back, she looked around and commented, "Oh, I never saw that picture on your wall, is it new?" Again, it was her movement behaviours more than her words that revealed her shifting anxiety states.

Although psychoanalysts such as Akhtar (1992), Balint (1968), Bromberg (1996), and Winnicott (1958b) have all emphasized the vital importance of the analyst's appreciating an attitude towards space and distancing (in the analysis as well as in the patient's individual development), none have put it in the context of an observational model of the patient's body-as-a whole that I am proposing as an important tool of observation.

During a psychoanalysis, in order to become conscious of one's feelings, there should also be a corresponding body awareness that can lead to changes in the patient's body image. As Schilder (1950) stated, "The image of the body means the picture of our own body which we form in our mind, that is to say the way in which the body appears to ourselves" (p. 11). Growing awareness of the kinesthetic process and one's changing body image during psychoanalysis can be integrating for the patient. Such integration leads to a more comprehensive understanding of mutative change in the analysis for both patient and analyst.

Today, psychoanalysts embrace the notion that mutative change is complex and rests on multiple factors during the course of any analytic process. Diamond (Chapter Ten in this volume) elaborates that a constant factor in the over-determined, multifaceted, and complex process of therapeutic action is invariably fashioned from the analyst's mental activities during the work. I underscore his view and suggest that the use of the non-verbal mode of the patient's motility *in the analyst's mind* adds to, and enriches, this complex process of therapeutic action.

In conclusion, it is evident in our literature that observations of motility as a modality have been greatly under-utilized by psychoanalysts, most especially in recent years. It is my thesis that an understanding of interdisciplinary integration of body-mind concepts along with the theoretical underpinnings of thinking in movement terms could reinstate an important dimension to the work of psychoanalysis.

SECTION V

REFLECTIONS: PSYCHOANALYTIC
DOGMA AND FLEXIBILITY

A centenarian's retrospective on psychoanalysis: an interview with Hedda Bolgar[1]

Interviewed by Michael J. Diamond

Biographical sketch[2]

Hedda Bolgar was born in Switzerland on August 19, 1909. She was the only child of two influential parents; her father was a social activist, history scholar, and diplomat representing Hungary, and her mother was the first female journalist on the staff of a German language newspaper in Budapest. Her family's political position was considered controversial, as her mother was a feminist and socialist, and her father was involved in aiding the start of the Hungarian Revolution in 1918.

Bolgar completed her PhD at the University of Vienna in 1934, taking psychology courses with Karl and Charlotte Bühler, studying infant observation and life cycle development, and gaining exposure to the group of Vienna psychoanalysts involved with Freud including Heinz Hartmann and Rene Spitz.

In the mid-1930s, Bolgar and Liselotte Fischer, who were close friends as well as psychoanalytically-oriented clinicians, collaborated to develop the "Little World Test" (also known as the "Bolgar-Fischer World Test", see Bolgar & Fischer, 1940). The test was developed as a nonverbal projective instrument through which a clinician could observe symbolic representations of human motivation, selection, and creative behaviour.

In 1938 at the age of 28 and already a strong public critic of the Nazi regime as well as being actively involved in anti-Nazi politics, Bolgar feared for her life and fled on the very day of Hitler's arrival. Upon arriving in the United States, she began a post-doctoral fellowship at Michael Reese Hospital in Chicago, in order to obtain her analytic training. At the time, she was the only woman in the Department of Psychology at the University of Chicago. While living in the Midwest, she gave training workshops in the use of the "Little World Test".

Leaving Chicago for a research position, Bolgar moved to New York for two years, where she arranged for her family and fiancé to immigrate to the United States. Unfortunately, she was unable to help her future in-laws, who perished in concentration camps at Auschwitz. After marrying in New York, Bolgar and her husband, Herbert Bekker, returned to Chicago in 1941.

Bolgar took a position on the faculty at the University of Chicago, and a few years later, she credits Franz Alexander for helping her gain entrance to the Chicago Psychoanalytic Institute. She subsequently became the first candidate with a non-medical degree to graduate from the Institute.

In 1954, Bolgar moved to Los Angeles and gained employment as a psychoanalyst/psychologist in the Department of Psychiatry and Behavioral Neuroscience, which was chaired by Franz Alexander, at Mt. Sinai Hospital (today Cedars-Sinai Medical Center). In 1970, she co-founded the Los Angeles Institute and Society for Psychoanalytic Studies (LAISPS) because she felt that Los Angeles offered insufficient training for non-medical analysts.

Her husband passed away in 1973 after 33 years of marriage. One year later, in 1974, Bolgar founded the Wright Institute in Los Angeles, a non-profit mental health training and service centre that today includes the Hedda Bolgar Psychotherapy Clinic, which treats people who cannot afford quality mental health services elsewhere.

Bolgar continues as one of our profession's most accomplished and creative members, having trained hundreds of psychoanalysts and psychoanalytically-oriented clinicians. She has been teaching and practising psychoanalysis for more than 70 years. Her current interests focus on aging, feminism, political activism, and psychoanalytic training and practice (e.g., Bolgar, 1999, 2002, 2009).

Today Hedda's comfortably elegant west Los Angeles home in Brentwood continues to serve as a welcoming centre for many of LAISPS's and the Wright Institute's functions. She currently hosts a salon on the first Wednesday of the month for colleagues to discuss a variety of topics ranging from clinical and theoretical psychoanalytic issues to the psychological implications of social problems (see Hollander, 2010). When recently asking Bolgar as to what accounts for her boundless energy, Hedda's answer is, as Hollander (2010) noted,

> ... always the same: "Diet, I've been a vegetarian for 85 years." And then she (Hedda) adds with a twinkle in her eye but quite seriously, "Oh, yes, and being engaged in the world, always fighting for the truth" [p. 2].

At the age of 101, Hedda balances a deep wisdom with an appreciation of the joy in life. She remains a practising psychoanalyst who sees patients several days a week, supervises, teaches, and lectures nationally. In concluding our interview for this chapter, Hedda noted that she still loves doing psychoanalysis but that she regrets that "really the only bad thing about being old is that I can't start anybody new except for very brief consultations." And then adding, in her own inimitable fashion, "You live with that .... It's not tragic, that's the difference, it isn't tragic, it just is!"

Interview

MD: *It's such a pleasure to be able to do this with you. We'll start with the historical influence on your work.*

HB: I was fortunate in coming to psychoanalysis at a time when psychoanalysis meant the theories and techniques of Freud. I read the four-volume "Collected Papers" and enjoyed both the richness of ideas that were all new to me and also Freud as a writer. That was long before I thought of becoming a psychoanalyst.

Academically, I came from psychology and anthropology and the only course in psychotherapy available at the University of Vienna in Freud's city (and mine) was taught in the department of urology. Why? Because it seemed there was somebody in the medical school who thought that male impotence might have something to do with the mind.

Eventually, the political events in Austria brought me to the United States and to clinical psychology, projective diagnostic techniques, and re-reading Freud. And finally as a faculty member of the Department of Psychology at the University of Chicago, I was accepted for psychoanalytic training at the Institute for Psychoanalysis in Chicago. I was a "special" student because I did not have a medical degree.

Franz Alexander was the director of the Institute and his views on analytic theory and technique were of considerable influence in my early years as an analyst. However, I had by that time attended seminars led by other analysts outside the Chicago Institute and I knew that there was considerable disagreement with Alexander's ideas.

Historical issues

MD: *I wanted to ask you about one of Alexander's main ideas and see how that might've influenced you. One of his ideas concerned the shortening of psychoanalysis.*

HB: Well, I think the really important issue was the battle about the corrective emotional experience. Which, I think, was largely misunderstood, but it really contained the essence of what he believed psychoanalysis was to become. I think the whole thing of flexibility, the non-orthodoxy, the idea that individual people and individual situations required individual treatment. Most importantly, he stressed that you should really understand the individuality of the patient.

As for shortening the analysis, I don't know if there is such a thing as a short analysis. There is short psychotherapy, psychoanalytic psychotherapy, but there is no short analysis. The difference, I think, is important to keep in mind. There are different things you can do. You can solve problems, specific problems anyway. In psychoanalytic psychotherapy, you can certainly make symptoms go away. You certainly can help with maladaptive defences as long as it's more or less limited to a certain type of pathology. But psychoanalysis requires time. I don't think it can be shortened.

MD: *Some would say that analyses have gotten longer over the years.*

HB: Yes, they have gotten longer because we know more and because we will analyse people who, when I started up, were considered not analysable. I haven't heard the discussion about people who are not analysable in a long, long time except for control cases of candidates. But, I think psychoanalysis takes time.

MD: *With a much wider spectrum of patients?*

HB: Wider spectrum of expectations. In psychoanalysis I think you're talking about a total makeover. It's not just solving one problem or two problems. People often come in with one problem, ... but as the exploration goes on the patient's whole life becomes involved. So it takes a while.

Influential figures

MD: *Who would you say is most influential on your work today?*

HB: I don't think any one theorist really. It's very hard to answer that. Everyone has been influential in a way. The so-called orientations (which I don't see as orientations), but I've always welcomed changes, just because, well, no matter how wonderful Freud's contributions were, there are holes in his system. And, I always feel that with every new person who has emphasized one particular aspect and added to it, and developed it, we have gained. It's not disagreement with the original standard Freudian psychoanalysis, but I think everybody should welcome creative expansion and value innovation. I know the excitement I felt every time I learned about a new emphasis in psychoanalysis or a new "orientation". It was a gain. It wasn't like having to give up something. It was not an either-or, it was and, and, and .... It just made one's work richer and more effective, perhaps, and helped one grow as a person and an analyst.

MD: *Well, as you've observed these trends then over the years, what makes you feel most hopeful about the future of psychoanalysis?*

HB: That psychoanalysis isn't static. It's not ... it's not a collection of what you cannot change out of veneration for the founder. I think the very flexibility of it, the openness to new ideas and to explorations. Psychoanalysis today is much richer. It is harder to imagine psychoanalysis without Klein, Hartmann, Kohut, Fairbairn, Winnicott, Bion, Lacan.

MD: *What gives you pause about the future?*

HB: Partly, the seeming forgetting of the original incredible discoveries of Freud. Partly the almost neglect, and even hostility to the whole idea of the unconscious. I think that was probably the greatest thing that ever came out of psychoanalysis. I also like the emphasis that not all of the unconscious is repression, but the unconscious that also happens to be there because you can contain just so much. A great many passing experiences may or may not become relevant at some point; [they] are not a matter of repressing.

MD: *It's not the dynamic of it …*

HB: It's not the dynamic, it's just somewhere; there is a limit to the human brain and that things do come up, but they're not necessarily conflict. I have a feeling that psychoanalysis will last forever because you will just discover new things all the time.

Kinds of analysts

MD: *You've sort of answered this, but I'm going to put it to you again. What kind of analyst do you consider yourself to be?*

HB: Well, I've always thought that ideally you should leave everything outside the door of the office; your own past, your own authority figures, your analyst, your supervisors, your institute and your referral sources. The "here and now" is a very valid and important concept. So is Bion's "without memory and desire" up to a point.

MD: *Do you believe though that you can leave that out of the room?*

HB: You can leave your own values out of the room at least as far as they are conscious. You can leave your own needs, to a large extent, out of the room. You can try and really listen and be what I used to call, "alone with the patient" and let the patients bring their past and their family and their important figures in. But yours should preferably be outside, so that you can really concentrate. You can really listen; you can really be there. And let your own reactions at the moment be available.

MD: *Would you encourage someone to go into psychoanalytic training today? Assuming you would, what kind of person would you encourage?*

HB: Well, I think that what you need to do to be a really effective analyst is to have a very rich life yourself. When I think of my classmates from the Institute who came out of medical school, it was pretty much the same social, economic background, with very little awareness of the variety of the world, and who may or may not have had some additional interests. But their life seemed very limited. And I don't think that helps because it's hard to understand the patient, if you haven't been somewhere there yourself. I have always liked [Robert] Stolorow's formulation of searching for the analogue when the patient talks. Search your own experience and connect with the patient's experience that way, so there is a readiness for identification. And it's hard to identify if you haven't had a lot of experiences of great variety yourself.

MD: *Which certainly argues for having experience in the world before you go into analytic training, not the coming right out of medical school or graduate school.*

HB: Not unless you've had a really varied life. Some people do. People who have had to, let's say, forcibly emigrate, leave their countries, leave their culture in their teens or later. Somebody did research on "normal people" and they turned out to be very boring and very dull. And, so I think a certain amount of abnormality in one's own life experience is a great help. Without that I think you get restless, you get bored, you get burned out. You're just not really fully there.

The other thing is language. Increasingly, I believe, we analyse patients whose "mother tongue" or original language is not ours or not the language in which the analysis is conducted. I think that a great deal of affect and unconscious communication is lost that way. When I analyse a patient with whom I do not share his or her first language I ask the patient to relate the significant events in their mother tongue. If I do not understand that language I ask the patient to translate later. That way the patient stays in the original experience.

I once listened to a colleague present his work with a patient whom he described as very difficult because she did not seem to connect with him. She would just talk without any feelings. In the history he mentioned that she spoke many languages and had lived in many different cultures. I asked my colleague which was her first language and he said he didn't know. I asked him if he knew what language she had spoken with her mother when she was very little. He became a bit irritated with me. He said, "I only speak English so why would I want to know all that?" I suggested that if he asked her to talk about some important memories in the language that she spoke at the time she might develop some emotional connection with him.

The psychoanalytic process

MD: *Let me turn then to another area we want to explore. That is, your thoughts about the psychoanalytic process and in particular what is it that makes for a psychoanalysis as opposed to a psychoanalytic psychotherapy?*

HB: As I said before about psychoanalytic psychotherapy, I think it is essentially problem solving, whereas psychoanalysis is the total exploration and remaking of one's self.

MD: *And can that be done in what some might consider more of a psychotherapeutic framework once or twice a week, for example?*

HB: Yes, it can be done once or twice a week with the right person. That depends really on the analyst of course, but also on the patient. There are patients who really do well with less than the standard four or five times per week. I've had those; I've had patients who've done a tremendous amount of work, psychoanalytic work on their own, in-between the hours. Once a week I don't think is enough, but twice a week can be enough. I've had one patient who said, "I couldn't do more … process the hour and I need an extra day or two to do that. If I came every day it would all pile up, it would be too much and I wouldn't be able to deal with it." So, I thought there was a lot of truth to that for some people. Some people would walk out of the analytic hour and it's gone until they're back; and other people process it, quite consciously. It depends.

MD: *Would you be able to describe a case that captures something of how you work?*

HB: There are a number of issues there. I would like to tell you about one patient about whom I have never stopped feeling guilty because I followed analytic technique instead of following my own feelings and wishes. It was a patient whose mother died when the patient was 18 months old. She had one child and then developed cancer. She was told not to get pregnant again because it would be very dangerous for her health. She decided she wanted a second child and she got pregnant and she had my patient. My patient never really had a mother. Mother was constantly in and out of hospitals, in and out of the country searching for cures. My patient had a vague memory of a big house. Everything was white and there was a long corridor and she was taken to her room and there was her mother in bed and she was told to say goodbye to her mother. So, she said goodbye and she was convinced, as she said, the hole in mother's breast was her doing. She felt terribly guilty. Father didn't know what to do with the two children after mother died and sent them to his family in Europe to a country in which the language was very different from English. The children didn't know the language. The older sister was taking mother's place in a way. The patient became mute. She didn't talk at all. She was totally devastated from the loss of even a mother who wasn't much of a mother. She felt she was among strangers. She was a stranger and the only person she could relate to really was this one sister. Gradually things became a little better. Father remarried and the two children returned to the United States, to a well-run, caring household.

My patient developed a career. She was very creative. She was an artist. She did very well. She was a high functioning person with a trend towards being an alcoholic, but it didn't interfere with her profession and her creativity.

She was chronically depressed. Not suicidal but really depressed. Life was just negative. People were negative. Everything was basically dangerous and bad. She was in analysis and after five years she said to me, "The first three years I didn't hear a word you said. I didn't know what you were talking about. I only listened to your voice. I came to hear your voice." I said, "How is it now?" "Now, I can listen to what you say," she replied. But she did something that I then called the waking dream. She would go into a dream-like state on the couch and she was almost always ending up in dark slippery dirty places and she was desperately looking for something which she couldn't find. And I figured she was looking for her dead mother.

One day, she was lying on the couch and she was very restless. She said there was something strange happening to her. I was inside her body. No, she was inside my body and she was being born and would I hold her. I sat down on the top of the couch and I put my arm around her shoulder and it was a long journey and a dangerous journey and eventually she was born and now she had a mother. She was very happy. She gave herself a new name, which in translation meant reborn. We didn't have anything about "born again" in those days. It didn't mean anything of that sort. She was a lesbian. I knew that all along but it had not entered into the analysis at that point. She left very happy. She came back the next day and she wanted me to hold her again and she wanted me to sit on the couch with her, lie on the couch with her, whatever. And here is where I committed probably the gravest mistake in my analytic practice. I wouldn't do it. I couldn't decide whether this was the beginning of a lesbian seduction or really she was the one-day-old infant that she said she was. She said, "You know I'm only a day old. I'll grow up, don't worry. I will grow up, but right now I'm an infant and you've got to treat me like an infant, you have to hold me." And I made the wrong decision. I said maybe we ought to continue with our analytic work. She stayed in analysis a long time. She continued. We resolved some problems, but she never lost the depression. It was better, it was less self-destructive, self-defeating. She found a life-long partner later on, but she never lost the depression but instead of being depressed, she started to develop a number of psychosomatic illnesses. And she never was as happy as she was on that first day after she was born. I think it was a mistake. It was too early in my life, in my career, and I fell into the frame.

MD: *How did she experience your holding the frame that tightly?*

HB: I talked to her later about it, one day. And I said I really have been wondering all along and I really felt I did not do the right thing. She had become a therapist actually and along the way, an analyst. And I reminded her when she had forgotten the whole episode and she looked at me and she said, "Well, I would've done what you did. I wouldn't hold the patient." So she had forgiven me in some way, or had identified with my mistake.

MD: *And you think if you had held her it would've made for a very different outcome?*

HB: I think so. (I think so.)

MD: *Um hm.*

HB: Today I think so. So that's it. I was thinking that that sort of situation never came up again. I don't know whether I am careful to not have it come up, or whether I can now be a "mother" to a patient without holding her, I don't know.

MD: *Well, and of course you're suggesting that it was earlier in your career.*

HB: It was earlier.

MD: *Your training, your supervisors, your psychoanalytic superego, they all played a part.*

HB: I was still using Alexander's couch, which I somehow inherited after he died. I still believed in one kind of frame, which actually was not Alexander's frame.

MD: *Interesting.*

The analytic frame

HB: In the meantime the frame has become a little more flexible. One day I asked myself, if that frame is a wonderful thing, what's it made of?

MD: *What was your answer?*

HB: Well, I said it isn't iron and it isn't very hard wood, it's something that is more like rubber, something that's flexible that will bend with the need.

MD: *And of course that always brings up that kind of touchy area, no pun intended, concerning how flexible you can be.*

HB: What is essential and what isn't, that's really the question. And I think that what is essential is part of the analysis; you have to know a patient well enough to know what's essential. And you have to be able to let the information come to you, from your own inside and from the patient. When the patient objects to something, it's not just resistance. I think resistance is an over-rated notion anyhow. I never use it—I say it's self-protection, so that it has to come from the patient. For one patient, it's all a terrible constraining thing, for another patient it's very welcome because they come from a chaotic, dysfunctional background and any order and any system and any regulation is welcome. And that's the corrective emotional experience. Patients need some things, they want some things, and they don't want some things. And you have to understand what that is and what it means.

MD: *And you're suggesting with the patient you described that you did know her well enough, but that you didn't trust yourself?*

HB: Absolutely. It was breaking the rules; it was violating, it was breaking the frame. I don't think it was threatening me particularly, but the patient was using an experience from yesterday to exploit it for her unresolved needs. It was always the patient, remember, it was never us.

Therapeutic action

MD: *The theme I'd like to pick up on now is the idea of therapeutic action. Why don't we start with your thoughts about the goals or aims of psychoanalysis?*

HB: Well, I don't think there are any concrete goals and I don't think there are any overall universal aims. I think it all depends on who the patient is, who the analyst is and what's needed, or what's possible. Um, I hardly ever think of psychopathology any more. I think of the total existence of a patient and I think that whatever they bring in makes sense somehow. It has a reason, [and] it helps to discover the reason. It helps to really understand what's going on. Why the patient is here. What he or she expects or needs. How much or what you can do as an analyst. So it's a total understanding, but not just a simple understanding of one feeling or one reaction or one trauma, but really to understand the total existence of the other. And that takes time, it takes a certain amount of knowledge and a certain kind of broad perspective on life, it takes a respect for the external reality of the patient.

I think it has been a problem in psychoanalysis until relatively recently and there are some notable exceptions. People who are really aware of the fact that people don't only live in the childhood family and they don't only live in their adult relationships or the lack of it, but there is a whole social and cultural life that people live in and that we somehow have to also understand and understand the patient's place in it. So it's a very complicated thing. Perhaps if there's one word that conveys what I hope patients will get out of the analysis, it is "liberation"—a sense of real freedom. A sense of self-determination, a sense of knowing oneself, of accepting oneself, of accepting other people. Empathy is sort of a word that's being thrown around an awful lot and it has become a technical term almost, but actually if you go to the origin of the word, it is really "suffering with". It takes some respect for the patient's suffering and a capacity to identify with it, even if it really is not part of your own life.

It raises the question of the similarity or difference between the patient and the analyst, which is a very interesting and very complicated question. How similar do you have to be, how different do you have to be? How able are you to really deal with and accept and respect and get to know the difference?

Differences between patients and analysts

MD: *Let's get back to the idea of difference, and how you're able to navigate the idea of difference, particularly if someone's difference is troubling for you?*

HB: OK. One day, a young man came in. I forget how he was referred to me. He came in. He was at a loss. Things were not going the way he wanted them to. He was fired from the police department because he was too violent. And that takes some violence, I guess. He was carrying a gun all the time and driving around the freeways, hoping he could catch "some nigger" doing something wrong and shoot him. He slept with a loaded rifle, hoping somebody would break in so he could shoot and kill him. And he looked at me and he said, "I don't like doctors and I don't pay my bills." And I remember saying to him very quietly, "You'll pay mine." And he said, "Wow, you think so but I know I won't." He told me that many times, that's all he was talking about, how angry he was and how the world wasn't treating him right. I was listening. I hardly ever said anything and one day I decided to make one intervention. And as he was raving about "the niggers" and everybody else who was doing wrong things and the police department guy who fired him because he was doing his job, I said as quietly as I could, "You must've had a terrible childhood." And he looked at me and he burst into tears and he said, "How did you know? I never talk about that." And I said, "Yes, I noticed that." And everything changed. Everything changed totally. One comment and everything changed. But the fact is, everything changed. He found a girlfriend who was really lovely, who made him pay his bills, who helped him with everything, who didn't criticize him no matter what he did.

MD: *What was it in you that allowed you to overcome whatever disturbance you were feeling when you were hearing about his violence, his racism?*

HB: He was my patient and really different from me. He'd had a terrible life and then he told me about his terrible life, it really was terrible. I mostly felt compassion for him. And I was lucky because I never knew such experiences.

How psychoanalysis works

MD: *I wanted to ask you about how psychoanalysis works, along with the theme of the book, of course. How do you think it works, and why doesn't it work for certain patients?*

HB: It works I think primarily because it's *not* a repetition in the reliving of the past only. Mostly it's different, because it happens in a relationship that is like no other. Because it's new, … because it's something that never happened to them before. I think you need to certainly go over the past and to look at the past together, but even in the looking at it together, it is different from the way it was when it happened. Because there is somebody who cares about you, there is somebody who wants to know, there is somebody who doesn't judge. There is somebody who really wants to be with that child that is abused or non-understood, or neglected, or over-controlled, or whatever it is, or intruded upon. You really have to go through it. But you go through it, [and] by going through it, it changes. The difference is [one] now becomes an adult. The ego psychologists are big on that. That was the Chicago phrase: "That was then, and now you are an adult and you can cope with it." Well, you're not much of an adult maybe, but you have somebody who looks at it with you [who] is sympathetic and understanding, and doesn't judge you. I think those things are still very important.

MD: *It's very much along the lines of what Strachey wrote about.*

HB: Yes, I think that's valid. I think that every single one of those things, the absence of traumatic experience, the presence of a caring attuned person matters. But it takes a long time for the patient to really trust that. And then we go back to Erikson and "basic trust". The analyst has to be really trustworthy. And you have to demonstrate that for a while for it to sink in, so that's why analysis is long.

MD: *And when it doesn't work?*

HB: When it doesn't work it's because one of those things is not there. Because with an analyst who is not *alone with the patient* and *with the patient* (*alone* is important just as *with* is important), can't be as helpful. An analyst I think who values his difference and who prefers his experience to the patient's experience and stays there … conveying, "You should be the way I am"—that doesn't work.

Interpretation versus relationship

MD: *We're getting back to how analysis helps a patient. Well, I have an idea of what you're going to say here, but I want to give you a chance to talk about the dichotomy that's often made in psychoanalytic thinking about the role of interpretation versus the importance of the relationship. What do you think?*

HB: I don't know why psychoanalysis loves these either-or statements. Of course both are important and there's no question in my mind. I don't like the word "interpretation" because it really means I know something you don't know. I usually call it "intervention" and sometimes it's a clarifying intervention and sometimes it's a reminder of something. We can describe whatever the intervention is, but of course it is in the relationship. And there's no question that you say things to a patient in a situation in an analytic hour that are different from what you say to your friends or what you say to an acquaintance or what you say to a child. So, it is very much part of the relationship as it exists between two specific people. And it's a very specific intervention each time you make it. But it's not often the "ah ha" experience because you now have said something totally fitting and real.

MD: *You are more dubious as to the so-called "magic" of interpretation?*

HB: The magic of interpretation and the fact that there are things that are endlessly repeated. The patient repeats it, relives it, retells it. You may say the same thing in different words and different aspects of whatever it is the patient talks about. Very often it's really a test of the degree of the analyst's understanding. Sometimes you're wrong. Maybe you're not wrong, but for the patient at that moment you are wrong. Is that helpful? You're lucky if it isn't hurtful. And that's the struggle that goes on between patient and analyst. Sometimes, you think you know something and the patient can't let you know it. Can't let himself or herself know it. It's too painful. It's too reminiscent of the real suffering. There are many reasons why interpretations really can be good or not so good. So, you have to be careful with it. And the relationship really governs the interpretation.

MD: *What do you think of the idea of the so-called "deep" interpretation?*

HB: Well, it better be deep or it doesn't make any sense. I mean what does deep mean? Deep means that so far it hasn't occurred to the patient. And so it's something really new and it may be challenging depending on the relationship— maybe something worth thinking about. It may come up again and again and again, in a memory, in a dream, in the transference, in the so-called enactment. It comes up in a variety of ways and so should the interpretation vary with whatever comes up. It should not always be the same. I think interpretation tends to be repetitious. Sometimes it has to be, but again, if we can adapt it to the content and the feeling and the quality of the memory as it comes up, it's more effective than if it's just the same interpretation over and over again.

MD: *Some analysts say that the deep interpretation, the deeper interpretation emerges from an experience that the analyst is having with a patient.*

HB: Yeah, absolutely.

MD: *As opposed to it's deriving from theory, or …*

HB: Absolutely, that's the way everything you say should come. I really think theory is something you refer to when you don't know what's going on. It's an aid. It's really an aid and there's nothing wrong with trying to understand theoretically what a patient's association might mean. You can think about it, but those are the times when your own insides aren't working. It's a lot better if you wait and see what comes up in you. I have always felt that there was, what people now talk about, unconscious communication; the patient's unconscious to the analyst's unconscious and vice versa. We are really motivated in our expression when this communication takes place.

MD: *I want to ask you about Freud's pessimism late in his life, in "Analysis Terminable and Interminable". And of course that essay was before countertransference was acceptable and understandable and an important source of data. So, I'm wondering, as you are in the latter stages of your life and your career, do you feel any pessimism about the future? And, how do you understand Freud's pessimism?*

HB: Well, Freud was still a medical man. He still somehow thought about cure. He still thought about fixing something. Analysis would somehow fix something rather definite, I think. Not just make life better, make the person liberated. End the analysis with a sense of self that's positive and gratifying. I think he still had a feeling that there was a goal to each analysis and that that had to be met. In a way, the pathology had to be removed. And that makes for pessimism. Because you know sometimes what we call, what we used to call pathology, is not terribly harmful, it's part of the character, part of the person's experience, and certain experiences make for certain development. I am referring to personality's character, the real person. And sometimes that can't be changed and doesn't have to be changed.

MD: *Well, I think what you're really saying is that in analysis we can develop a different relationship to our psychopathology.*

HB: Yes.

MD: *It doesn't necessarily get rid of …*

HB: No, no and it may not be psychopathology.

MD: *Yeah, right.*

HB: I mean what is "pathology" is a whole other thing. And I don't really think in terms of pathology any more.

Termination: can you ever really go back?

MD: *Well, that being said, then, what do you think of when you think about the notion of terminating an analysis?*

HB: I don't terminate, the patient does. And then we talk about why.

MD: *So you wait until it comes from the patient.*

HB: Yes. I remember one patient who I thought really was ready to go. Some things had changed and some hadn't. He was doing really well and he was lying on the couch and it was one office where the couch was parallel with the door and suddenly, I noticed that he was always looking at the door. Not always, but in certain parts of the hour he would sort of turn towards the door. And so I said at one point, "Are you thinking of leaving? You are looking at the door." Now I could've said, are you afraid someone's going to come in? But what I thought was my association to it—was he was looking to escape, while he was looking at the door. And he said, "Well, uh, I guess maybe I have been thinking what it would be like if I didn't come any more." So then we started talking about what brought that up. Why and how and what did he think it would be. Gradually you set a time and you allow plenty of time. That's another thing.

MD: *What criteria do you look for to make a decision that it's in the patient's best interest?*

HB: Well, I would sort of listen to my reaction to it. At some point I would think that it's an escape, at some point maybe I would even think that he was also looking at someone coming in, maybe someone to rescue him. Maybe somebody to attack him. Maybe going back over the entire experience, how more liberated does he feel now than he did when he came? Where does he feel like he can really act and do and say and be himself and accept himself and be accepted, feel accepted? So, termination is a very mutual review of something. It's not just saying goodbye.

MD: *It's an unfortunate word, "terminate".*

HB: In Chicago we didn't use it.

MD: *What did you use?*

HB: Interruption.

MD: *Oh.*

HB: We also assumed that people would come back.

MD: *I was going to ask you about that. What do you think of Freud's idea that every five years one returns to analysis?*

HB: Every five years [said simultaneously]. Well, as candidates we were told to re-read Freud every five years completely. Which I thought was a good idea.

MD: *It's a very different book every five years.*

HB: It's a very different book. It's a very different book after 40 years. But, analysing my own personal experiences, I knew I should've gone back. When I left my analysis, I said we only scratched the surface—it was a pretty good ego psychology, psychoanalysis. It was. My analyst had a very interesting idea that I've sort of agreed with more or less. She said that the transference can only be resolved in the friendship with the analyst, a post-analytic friendship. I said that seems to be working for candidates who grow up in the Institute and stay in the Institute and eventually we sit in committees, and disagree, and in the meantime, we have season tickets together. And [laugh], we never talk about the analysis any more. No matter what we think. And sometimes we go back and sometimes we don't and I was very clear that I could not get myself to go back and live through another transference.

It was too hard and too painful. I just didn't feel I wanted to do it again.

MD: *It seems that many analysts, experienced analysts, still carry some sense of shame though about the idea of going back.*

HB: That's because they were raised when pathology was "bad" and it was supposedly resolved—whereas going back means that I'm still "pathological". That never bothered me.

MD: *As if it were a failure.*

HB: No, that never bothered me. But I would really have loved to go back to a very contemporary analysis—an inter-subjective one.

MD: *What would be different about that?*

HB: Oh, everything would be different. I would say all the things I didn't say in my original analysis.

MD: *Why wouldn't you have said it in your original?*

HB: Because I was in an institute. It was a non-reporting institute theoretically. But I was a special student. I had to be really on my best behaviour.

MD: *So you are really bringing up one of the problems with training analysis per se.*

HB: Absolutely. There is an education committee, there is a pro-gression committee …

MD: *Sure …*

HB: Your analyst walks out of it, but …

MD: *And you're going to have to live in the same world [with your ana-lyst]… so part of what you're saying is that it's a lot harder to bring out the negative transference in the training analysis.*

HB: Absolutely, and things that you are ashamed of about yourself.

The real person of the analyst

MD: *Sure …. I want now to bring it to the heart of what you originally suggested that your interview-based chapter might be about, which is the "real person" of the analyst and the patient-analyst match. So, first of all could you say a little more about what you mean by the real person of the analyst?*

HB: The short form of that is: everything other than analytic theo-ry and analytic technique. That's the short form. And the long form is everything that the analyst has experienced early and late and is experiencing in relationships, interests, participation in society, appreciation of the real life of both the patient and the analyst. And the space, the social space they live in, the allowing of social issues to enter into the analysis. I always say that when a patient comes in limping for six weeks and doesn't mention it, eventually, you will say, "I noticed you are limping and you haven't talked about it. What's that all about?" That's a legitimate question. But I say, what do you think of Bush? It's not a legitimate question. In my waiting room there are a bunch of magazines and I remember one young patient who walked in here one day and he looked at them and said, "If my dad knew what you are reading, he wouldn't pay for my analysis." That's the real analyst.

MD: *That's quite a change from the old blank screen idea.*

HB: Absolutely, the blank screen was really I think the undoing of analysis for so many years. You can't be a blank screen. You are not a blank screen. You sit here for 50 minutes or now 45 and things happen in you all the time: you have thoughts, you have feelings, you have bodily reactions. So that's the you. And you have them for good reasons. But also, I was thinking of [Christopher] Bollas the other day. I was reading one of his case histories where he made a wonderful interpretation on the basis of King Lear and Hamlet, the fact that he knows Shakespeare as well as he does is part of the real person of Christopher Bollas. When you read Grotstein's book about who is the dreamer, it's full of classical education. It's full of knowledge of a lot of things in the world. When you think of Kohut and his self psychology and all the rest of it, he also was really consumed with music. Music was an important part of his real life. And I'm sure it entered into how he worked. And what he associated to. I think what we associate to during an analytic hour when the patient talks about whatever they do, is part of our personality—it has nothing to do with theory. Sometimes it has to do with theory. Sometimes we will think, "Oh yeah, Klein said such and such. And do I want to use or don't I want to use it?" But, and sometimes, you remember what you were taught about boundaries and do you want to use it or don't you? And whether or not you want to use it has to do with who you are. So, it's there all the time, it's basic. When a patient tells me, "You are so contained. You sit still. You look at me. Your face hardly ever shows any expression. [You are] so contained." Well, is that good or bad, [laugh] and is it true? And am I really that contained? Well, maybe with that particular patient during a number of hours I am because it's necessary and that's my judgment that it's necessary and also comes from the fact [of] who I am.

MD: *You're talking about the analyst's subjectivity now.*

HB: Yes.

MD: *As an instrument of the therapy.*

HB: Absolutely. It is an instrument if it's used with a certain amount of permissiveness (within ourselves). When it isn't, "I mustn't think about that, I've got to listen to the patient." Well, I listen to the patient really carefully and this is what comes up in me. And is this me, [who has] learned the theory? Or [who has] been trained in a certain technique? Or is it me, [who has] lived in a lot of different cultures and a lot of different languages, and social changes? Is it the me that has political opinion? Is it the me that has been interested in Buddhism? Which me is it? Is it the me that prefers the stage to movies?

MD: *You're saying something that I think is a very important notion, the whole idea of what we go through in analytic training and then in a sense what has to be unlearned so we can be free to decide to be spontaneous with ourselves, to be permissive.*

HB: And, be able to see what's going on with the patient other than in a given [theoretical] framework.

MD: *Yes.*

What is a good match?

MD: *I wanted to ask you about a kind of a match, the whole idea of the matching between patient and analyst and what makes for a good match, or at least a "good enough" match?*

HB: I had one patient with whom I really failed and I think it was a bad match because he was a minimalist. He walked in here and he said, "My god, this is terrible." "What's terrible?" "All that stuff you have around." So I asked him what particularly bothered him. He said, "Everything." I said, "What would be a good place for you to be in?" He said, "I would want a whitewashed office, with a couch and one chair, maybe two." So then he told me that he had a fairly high position in a big business. He lived in a totally substandard apartment. He told me he owned one fork and one plate. And he never turned on more than one light at a time. He never went on vacation. And after four years, well, he changed considerably. He bought himself a Porsche. And he built a house for himself in Malibu of all places.

I usually took a month of vacation. I don't know what happened in the first three years, whether those years I didn't take quite so long a vacation in the summer. I told every patient before we started that I take one month in the summer and I take two weeks at Christmas and two weeks during the spring so I don't know what happened. What happened in the fourth year, I took my usual vacation and when I came back he left me. He would not even come back for the traditional one hour to talk about it.

I thought he felt that I used the money he paid me to go to Europe and leave him. And I didn't care what happened to him during those four weeks. And he said he had had it with me. And that was it.

MD: *But you said you'd failed with him? I'm curious about why you think that.*

HB: Because I did not see that my leaving him at that particular point in the analysis was different from the earlier times. I did not see that I was becoming important to him.

MD: *You feel you missed that somehow?*

HB: Yes. I somehow missed that. It was the timing more than anything else. I'm sure I took long vacations even in previous years, but he wasn't involved as he was then. I just somehow did not see that.

MD: *What would you have done differently if you had seen that?*

HB: I would have talked about it; I would've made him talk about it. I would've taken him back to the point where he thought he didn't deserve anything but one fork. More so than I did. I did, but I didn't do it in relationship to me. And I was delighted when he got that car, and I was delighted when he started building that house. And I thought we are really getting somewhere. He was still living in the substandard apartment.

MD: *Let me ask you about when you make a referral to another psychoanalyst. How do you decide who to refer to, what goes through you?*

HB: Well, in reality, I would like to give you a theoretical answer, but in reality, what I do is I never refer to anybody I have not analysed or supervised. I really want to know how they work. You know, people write beautifully, and they may not be such good analysts. So that's one thing.

MD: *You want to really know them.*

HB: I want to know what they do and I want to have heard it from them. And I don't want to see it in beautifully edited theoretical papers. I mean some people write beautifully, and some people are good analysts, and some people do both.

Analytic curricula

MD: *Let me ask you then, staying with the idea of the real person. What do you think is most useful for analysts who are going to read and listen to you talk about this? What is most useful for them to know that they can do in order to develop that "subjective" person inside?*

HB: Well, they might want to expand their lives. They might want to do things that might be interesting to them. They might read a novel occasionally. They might, um, well, what, go to a concert; they might even go to an opera maybe. They might decide to go to Europe on their vacation, or to Asia. Or to Africa. They might want to read different things than they have been reading. They might look at paintings. They might really read Shakespeare and forget that they had to read it in high school. I don't know.

MD: *Do you think of anything in a psychoanalytic curriculum that might be changed to foster more of that?*

HB: Well, certainly there should be at this point, a course on growing old. I don't use aging, because we age from the day we are born. So, aging is a euphemism, it covers old. And when I talk about it, I talk about growing old. That I think is just from a practical point of view, the population that we're going to see is going to be older. The other thing is, when I was a candidate at the Chicago Institute we had an elective course in Greek tragedy.

MD: *You are stressing the value of life experience and liberal arts education.*

HB: … and humanities and history. And sociology and anthropology. It's tremendously important. It's really much more important than the medical background. And some of us knew that early.

MD: *Well, Freud wrote about that, didn't he?*

HB: Right, right. And I would add to it to have a richer life and a variety of relationships.

MD: *And you certainly model that as you continue to live life so fully.*

HB: So far, yeah.

MD: *Hedda, we're going to stop here. Thank you very much.*

HB: Thank you!

Notes

1. This two-hour face-to-face interview took place at Hedda Bolgar's home on August 11, 2010. This chapter is an edited transcript of the interview. Edits were made to facilitate reading and understanding—such as making complete sentences, omitting disfluencies, and adding references that were mutually understood. We have minimized our inclusion of laughter, pauses, and overlapping commentary that characterized this lively interchange. Recorded interview transcribed by Trudy Milburn, PhD.

2. Portions of this biographical sketch were used with permission from the website: http://www.feministvoices.com (see Sohi & Rutherford, 2010).

REFERENCES

Abend, S. (1979). Unconscious fantasy and theories of cure. *Journal of the American Psychoanalytic Association, 27*: 579–596.

Abend, S. (1990). The psychoanalytic process: Motives and obstacles in the search for clarification. *Psychoanalytic Quarterly, 59*: 532–549.

Abend, S. (1996). The problem of therapeutic alliance. *Journal of Clinical Psychoanalysis, 5*: 213–226.

Abend, S. (2002). Factors influencing change in patients in psychoanalytic treatment. *Journal of Clinical Psychoanalysis, 11*: 209–223.

Abend, S. (2007). Therapeutic action in modern conflict theory. *Psychoanalytic Quarterly, 76 (Suppl.)*: 1417–1442.

Abend, S. (2009). Freud, transference and therapeutic action. *Psychoanalytic Quarterly, 78*: 871–892.

Adler, E. & Bachant, J. (1998). Intrapsychic and interactive dimensions of resistance: a contemporary perspective. *Psychoanalytic Psychology, 15*: 451–479.

Ahumada, J. L. (1994). Interpretation and creationism. *International Journal of Psychoanalysis, 75*: 695–707.

Ainsworth, M. D. S. & Bell, S. M. (1970). Attachment, exploration and separation: illustrated by the behavior of one-year-olds in a strange situation. *Child Development, 41*: 49–67.

Akhtar, S. (1992). Tethers, orbits and invisible fences: Clinical, developmental, sociocultural and technical aspects of optimal distance. In: S. Kramer & S. Akhtar (Eds.), *When the Body Speaks* (pp. 21–59). Northvale, NJ: Jason Aronson.

Alexander, F. (1950). Analysis of the therapeutic factors in psychoanalytic treatment. *Psychoanalytic Quarterly, 19*: 482–500.

Alexander, F. (1954). Some quantitative aspects of psychoanalytic technique. *Journal of the American Psychoanalytic Association, 2*: 685–701.

Alexander, F. (1956). Two forms of regression and their therapeutic implications. *Psychoanalytic Quarterly, 25*: 178–196.

Alexander, F. & French, T. (1946). *Psychoanalytic Therapy: Principles and Application.* New York: The Ronald Press Company.

Althusser, L. (1971). Ideology and ideological state apparatuses (Notes toward an investigation). In: L. Althusser (Ed.), *Lenin and Philosophy and Other Essays* (pp. 127–186). New York: Monthly Review Press.

Apfelbaum, B. (1962). Some problems in contemporary ego. *Journal of the American Psychoanalytic Association, 10*: 526–537.

Apfelbaum, B. (1966). Ego psychology: A critique of the structural approach to psychoanalytic theory. *International Journal of Psychoanalysis, 41*: 451–475.

Arlow, J. A. (1969). Fantasy, memory, and reality testing. *Psychoanalytic Quarterly, 38*: 28–51.

Arlow, J. A. (1972). Some dilemmas in psychoanalytic education. *Journal of the American Psychoanalytic Association, 20*: 556–566.

Arlow, J. A. (1979). The genesis of interpretation. *Journal of the American Psychoanalytic Association, 27 (Suppl.)*: 193–206.

Arlow, J. A. (1990). Psychoanalysis and character development. *Psychoanalytic Review, 77*: 1–10.

Arlow, J. A. (1993a). Training for psychoanalysis and psychotherapy. *Psychoanalytic Review, 80*: 183–197.

Arlow, J. A. (1993b). Two discussions of "The Mind of the Analyst" and a response from Madeleine Baranger. *International Journal of Psychoanalysis, 74*: 1147–1155.

Arlow, J. A. (1996). The concept of psychic reality—How useful? *International Journal of Psychoanalysis, 77*: 659–666.

Arlow, J. A. & Brenner, C. (1990). The psychoanalytic process. *Psychoanalytic Quarterly, 59*: 678–692.

Aron, L. (1991). The patient's experience of the analyst's subjectivity. *Psychoanalytic Dialogues, 1*: 29–51.

Aron, L. (2000). Self-reflexivity and the therapeutic action of psychoanalysis. *Psychoanalytic Psychology, 17*: 667–689.

Bacal, H. (1985). Optimal responsiveness and the therapeutic process. In: A. Goldberg (Ed.), *Progress in Self Psychology, Volume 1* (pp. 202–227). Hillsdale, NJ: The Analytic Press.

Bach, S. (1994). *The Language of Perversion and the Language of Love.* New York: Jason Aronson.

Bach, S. (2006). *Getting from Here to There: Analytic Love, Analytic Process.* New York: Analytic Press.

Baker, R. (1993). The patient's discovery of the psychoanalyst as a new object. *International Journal of Psychoanalysis, 74*: 1223–1233.

Baldwin, S. A., Wampold, B. E. & Imel, Z. E. (2007). Untangling the alliance-outcome correlation: Exploring the relative importance of therapist and patient variability in the alliance. *Journal of Consulting and Clinical Psychology, 75*: 842–852.

Balint, M. (1949). Early developmental states of the ego. Primary object love. *International Journal of Psychoanalysis, 30*: 265–273.

Balint, M. (1968). *The Basic Fault.* London: Tavistock.

Balter, L., Lothane, Z. & Spencer, J. H. (1980). On the analyzing instrument. *Psychoanalytic Quarterly, 49*: 474–504.

Barber, J., Luborsky, L., Gallop, R., Crits-Christoph, P., Frank, A., Weiss, R., et al. (2001). Therapeutic alliance as a predictor of outcome and retention in the National Institute on Drug Abuse Collaborative cocaine treatment study. *Journal of Consulting and Clinical Psychology, 69*: 119–124.

Barranger, M. & Barranger, W. (2008). The analytic situation as a dynamic field. *International Journal of Psychoanalysis, 89*: 795–826.

Bartenieff, I. & Davis, M. (1965). *Effort-Shape Analysis of Movement.* New York: Dance Notation Bureau.

Bartenieff, I. & Lewis, D. (1980). *Body Movement: Coping with the Environment.* New York: Gordon and Breach.

Beebe, B. & Lachmann, F. (1994). Representations and internalization in infancy: Three principles of salience. *Psychoanalytic Psychology, 11*: 127–165.

Benjamin, J. (1990). An outline of intersubjectivity: The development of recognition. *Psychoanalytic Psychology, 7 (Suppl.)*: 33–46.

Benjamin, J. (1999). Recognition and destruction: An outline of inter-subjectivity (and Afterword). In: S. Mitchell & L. A. Aron (Eds.), *Relational Psychoanalysis: The Emergence of a Tradition* (pp. 181–210). Hillsdale, NJ: Analytic Press.

Bergmann, M. S. (1997). The historical roots of psychoanalytic orthodoxy. *Journal of the International Psychoanalytical Association, 78*: 69–86.

Berman, L. (1949). Countertransferences and attitudes of the analyst in the therapeutic process. *Psychiatry, 12*: 159–166.

Bernardi, R. (1992). On pluralism in psychoanalysis. *Psychoanalytic Inquiry, 12*: 506–525.

Bettelheim, B. (1983). *Freud and Man's Soul*. New York: Knopf.

Bibring, E. (1937). Symposium on the theory of the therapeutic results of psycho-analysis. *International Journal of Psychoanalysis, 18*: 165–184.

Bibring, E. (1954). Psychoanalysis and the dynamic psychotherapies. *Journal of the American Psychoanalytic Association, 2*: 745–770.

Bick, I. J. (1990). Outatime: Recreationism and the adolescent experience in Back to the Future. *Psychoanalytic Review, 77*: 587–608.

Billig, M. (1982). *Ideology and Social Psychology*. Oxford: Basil Blackwell.

Bion, W. R. (1954). Notes on the theory of schizophrenia. *International Journal of Psychoanalysis, 35*: 113–118.

Bion, W. R. (1956). Development of schizophrenic thought. *International Journal of Psychoanalysis, 37*: 344–346.

Bion, W. R. (1957). Differentiation of the psychotic from the non-psychotic personalities. *International Journal of Psychoanalysis, 38*: 266–275.

Bion, W. R. (1959). Attacks on linking. *International Journal of Psychoanalysis, 40*: 308–315.

Bion, W. R. (1962a). *Learning from Experience*. London: Tavistock.

Bion, W. R. (1962b). The psycho-analytic study of thinking: II. A theory of thinking. *International Journal of Psychoanalysis, 43*: 306–310.

Bion, W. R. (1962c). A theory of thinking. In: *Second Thoughts: Selected Papers in Psychoanalysis* (pp. 110–119). Northvale, NJ: Aronson, 1977.

Bion, W. R. (1963). *Elements of Psychoanalysis*. London: William Heinemann.

Bion, W. R. (1967). Notes on memory and desire. In: E. Spillius (Ed.), *Melanie Klein Today, Volume 2* (pp. 178–186). London: Routledge, 1988.

Bion, W. R. (1970). *Attention and Interpretation*. New York: Basic.

Bion, W. R. (1976). Evidence. In: F. Bion (Ed.), *Clinical Seminars and Four Papers* (pp. 239–246). Abingdon, UK: Fleetwood Press, 1987.

Bion, W. R. (1977). *Seven Servants*. New York: Jason Aronson.

Bird, B. (1972). Notes on transference: Universal phenomenon and hardest part of analysis. *Journal of the American Psychoanalytic Association, 20*: 267–301.

Birdwhistell, R. (1963). The kinesic level in the investigation of the emotions. In: P. H. Knapp (Ed.), *Expression of the Emotions in Man*. New York: International Universities Press.

Birdwhistell, R. (1970). Kinesic analysis of filmed behavior of children. In: *Kinesics and Context* (pp. 47–50). Philadelphia: University of Pennsylvania Press.

Blass, R. B. (2010). An introduction to "Distinguishing psychoanalysis from psychotherapy". *International Journal of Psychoanalysis, 91*: 15–21.

Blatt, S. J. & Behrends, R. S. (1987). Internalization, separation-individuation, and the nature of therapeutic action. *International Journal of Psychoanalysis, 68*: 279–297.

Bloom, K. (2006). *The Embodied Self: Movement and Psychoanalysis.* London: Karnac.

Boesky, D. (1990). The psychoanalytic process and its components. *Psychoanalytic Quarterly, 59*: 550–584.

Boesky, D. (1994). Dialogue on the Brenner paper between Charles Brenner, M.D. and Dale Boesky, M.D. *Journal of Clinical Psychoanalysis, 3*: 509–522.

Bolgar, H. (1999). Regression, re-living and repair of very early traumatization. *Psychotherapy in Private Practice, 17*: 39–51.

Bolgar, H. (2002). When the glass is full. *Psychoanalytic Inquiry, 22*: 640–651.

Bolgar, H. (2009). A century of essential feminism. *Studies in Gender and Sexuality, 10*: 195–199.

Bolgar, H. & Fischer, L. K. (1940). The toy test: A psychodiagnostic method. *Psychological Bulletin, 37*: 517–518.

Bollas, C. (1979). The transformational object. *International Journal of Psychoanalysis, 60*: 97–107.

Bollas, C. (1983). Expressive uses of the countertransference: Notes to the patient from oneself. *Contemporary Psychoanalysis, 19*: 1–34.

Bollas, C. (1987). *The Shadow of the Object: Psychoanalysis of the Unthought Known.* New York: Columbia University Press.

Bollas, C. (1989). *Forces of Destiny: Psychoanalysis and Human Idiom.* London: Free Association.

Bolognini, S. (1997). Empathy and "empathism". *International Journal of Psychoanalysis, 78*: 279–293.

Bolognini, S. (2001). Empathy and the unconscious. *Psychoanalytic Quarterly, 70*: 447–471.

Bolognini, S. (2004). Intrapsychic-Interpsychic. *International Journal of Psychoanalysis, 85*: 337–358.

Bolognini, S. (2011). *Secret Passages: The Theory and Technique of Interpsychic Relations.* New York: Routledge.

Bonanno, G., Keltner, D., Holen, A. & Horowitz, M. (1995). When avoiding unpleasant emotions might not be such a bad thing: Verbal-autonomic response dissociation and midlife conjugal bereavement. *Journal of Personality and Social Psychology, 69*: 975–989.

Bornstein, R. F. (2001). The impending death of psychoanalysis. *Psychoanalytic Psychology, 18*: 3–20.

Bornstein, R. F. (2002). The impending death of psychoanalysis: From destructive obfuscation to constructive dialogue. *Psychoanalytic Psychology, 19*: 580–590.

Bowlby, J. (1940). The influence of early environment in the development of neurosis and neurotic character. *International Journal of Psychoanalysis, 21*: 154–178.

Bowlby, J. (1958). The nature of the child's tie to his mother. *International Journal of Psychoanalysis, 39*: 350–373.

Bowlby, J. (1963). Pathological mourning and childhood mourning. *Journal of the American Psychoanalytic Association, 11*: 500–541.

Bowlby, J. (1969). *Attachment and Loss, Volume 1. Attachment*. New York: Basic.

Bowlby, J. (1973). *Attachment and Loss, Volume 2. Separation*. New York: Basic.

Bowlby, J. (1980). *Attachment and Loss, Volume 3. Loss, Sadness, and Depression*. New York: Basic.

Bowlby, J. (1988). *A Secure Base: Parent-child Attachment and Healthy Human Development*. New York: Basic.

Brenner, C. (1953a). An addendum to Freud's theory of anxiety. *International Journal of Psychoanalysis, 34*: 18–24.

Brenner, C. (1953b). *An Elementary Textbook of Psychoanalysis*. Madison, CT: International Universities Press.

Brenner, C. (1959). The masochistic character: Genesis and treatment. *Journal of the American Psychoanalytic Association, 7*: 197–226.

Brenner, C. (1969). Discussion. *Journal of the American Psychoanalytic Association, 17*: 41–53.

Brenner, C. (1975). Affects and psychic conflict. *Psychoanalytic Quarterly, 44*: 5–28.

Brenner, C. (1976). *Psychoanalytic Technique and Psychic Conflict*. Madison, CT: International Universities Press.

Brenner, C. (1979a). The components of psychic conflict and its consequences in mental life. *Psychoanalytic Quarterly, 48*: 547–567.

Brenner, C. (1979b). Working alliance, therapeutic alliance, and transference. *Journal of the American Psychoanalytic Association, 27 (Suppl.)*: 137–157.

Brenner, C. (1982). *The Mind in Conflict*. Madison, CT: International Universities Press.

Brenner, C. (1985). Countertransference as compromise formation, *The Psychoanalytic Quarterly, 54*: 155–163.

Brenner, C. (1987). A structural theory perspective. *Psychoanalytic Inquiry, 7*: 167–171.

Brenner, C. (1992). The structural theory and clinical practice. *Journal of Clinical Psychoanalysis, 1*: 369–380.

Brenner, C. (1993). Contribution to discussion of pre-published papers at the 38th congress of the IPA. *Journal of the International Psychoanalytical Association, 74*: 1191–1192.

Brenner, C. (1994). The mind as conflict and compromise formation. *Journal of Clinical Psychoanalysis, 3*: 473–488.

Brenner, C. (1995). Some remarks on psychoanalytic technique. *Journal of Clinical Psychoanalysis, 4*: 413–428.

Brenner, C. (1996). The nature of knowledge and the limits of authority in psychoanalysis. *Psychoanalytic Quarterly, 65*: 21–31.

Brenner, C. (1998). Beyond the ego and the id revisited. *Journal of Clinical Psychoanalysis, 7*: 165–180.

Brenner, C. (2000). Observations on some aspects of current psychoanalytic theories. *Psychoanalytic Quarterly, 69*: 597–632.

Brenner, C. (2002). Conflict, compromise formation, and structural theory. *Psychoanalytic Quarterly, 71*: 397–417.

Brenner, C. (2008). Aspects of psychoanalytic theory: Drives, defense, and the pleasure-unpleasure principle. *Psychoanalytic Quarterly, 77*: 707–717.

Brenner, C. (2009). Memoir. *Psychoanalytic Quarterly, 78*: 637–673.

Breuer, J. & Freud, S. (1893). On the psychical mechanism of hysterical phenomena. *S. E., 2*: 3–17. London: Hogarth.

Britton, R. (1989). The missing link: Parental sexuality in the Oedipus complex. In: R. Britton, M. Feldman & E. O'Shaughnessy (Eds.), *The Oedipus Complex Today: Clinical Implications* (pp. 83–101). London: Karnac.

Bromberg, P. M. (1995). Resistance, object-usage, and human relatedness. *Contemporary Psychoanalysis, 31*: 173–191.

Bromberg, P. M. (1996). Standing in the spaces. The multiplicity of self in the psychoanalytic relationship. *Contemporary Psychoanalysis, 32*: 509–535.

Bromberg, P. M. (1998). *Standing in the Spaces: Essays on Clinical Process.* Hillsdale, NJ: Analytic Press.

Brown, L. J. (2010). Klein, Bion, and intersubjectivity: Becoming, transforming, and dreaming. *Psychoanalytic Dialogues, 20*: 669–682.

Brown, L. J. (2011). *Intersubjective Processes and the Unconscious: An Integration of Freudian, Kleinian, and Bionian Perspectives.* London: Routledge.

Busch, F. (1993). "In the neighborhood": Aspects of a good interpretation and a "developmental lag" in ego psychology. *Journal of the American Psychoanalytic Association, 41*: 151–177.

Busch, F. (1994). Some ambiguities in the method of free association and their implications for technique. *Journal of the American Psychoanalytic Association, 42*: 363–384.

Busch, F. (1995). Do actions speak louder than words? A query into an enigma in analytic theory and technique. *Journal of the American Psychoanalytic Association, 43*: 61–82.

Busch, F. (2000). What is a deep interpretation? *Journal of the American Psychoanalytic Association, 48*: 237–254.

Busch, F. (2009). "Can you push a camel through the eye of a needle?" Reflections on how the unconscious speaks to us and its clinical implications. *International Journal of Psychoanalysis, 90*: 53–68.

Busch, F. (2010). Distinguishing psychoanalysis from psychotherapy. *International Journal of Psychoanalysis, 91*: 23–34.

Canestri, J. (2007). Comments on therapeutic action. *Psychoanalytic Quarterly, 76 (Suppl.)*: 1601–1634.

Canestri, J. (2009). Comments on Sandor M. Abend's "Freud, transference and therapeutic action". *Psychoanalytic Quarterly, 78*: 903–911.

Caper, R. (1992). Does psychoanalysis heal? A contribution to the theory of psychoanalytic technique. *International Journal of Psychoanalysis, 73*: 283–292.

Caper, R. (1997). A mind of one's own. *International Journal of Psychoanalysis, 78*: 265–278.

Caper, R. (2009). *Building Out into the Dark: Theory and Observation in Science and Psychoanalysis.* New York: Routledge.

Carpy, D. (1989). Tolerating the countertransference: A mutative process. *International Journal of Psychoanalysis, 70*: 287–294.

Chodorow, N. J. (2004). The American independent tradition: Loewald, Erikson, and the (possible) rise of intersubjective ego psychology. *Psychoanalytic Dialogues, 14*: 207–232.

Chodorow, N. J. (2010). Beyond the dyad: Individual psychology, social world. *Journal of the American Psychoanalytic Association, 58*: 207–230.

Christian, C. (2007). Sibling loss, guilt, and reparation: A case study. *International Journal of Psychoanalysis, 88*: 41–54.

Cohen, D. W. (2007). Freud's baby: Beyond autoerotism and narcissism. *International Journal of Psychoanalysis, 88*: 883–893.

Condon, W. S. (1968). Linguistic-kinesic research and dance therapy. *Proceedings of Third Annual Conference of American Dance Therapy Association* (pp. 21–42), Columbia, MD.

Condon, W. S. & Bronsin, H. W. (1973). Microlinguistic-kinesic events in schizophrenic behavior. Paper presented at Conference on Schizophrenia: Current concepts and research, New York.

Cooper, A. M. (1986). Some limitations on therapeutic effectiveness: The "burnout syndrome" in psychoanalysts. *Psychoanalytic Quarterly, 55*: 576–598.

Cooper, A. M. (1992). Psychic change: Development in the theory of psychoanalytic technique. *International Journal of Psychoanalysis, 73*: 245–250.

Couch, A. S. (2002). Extra-transference interpretation: A defense of classical technique. *Psychoanalytic Study of the Child, 57*: 63–92.

Darwin, C. (1896). *The Expression of the Emotions in Man and Animals.* New York: Appleton, Crofts.

Davies, J. (1996). Linking the "pre-analytic" with the postclassical: integration, dissociation, and the multiplicity of unconscious process. *Contemporary Psychoanalysis, 32*: 553–576.

Davison, W. T., Pray, M. & Bristol, C. (1990). Mutative interpretation and close process monitoring in a study of psychoanalytic process. *Psychoanalytic Quarterly, 59*: 599–628.

Davison, W. T., Pray, M., Bristol, C. & Welker, R. (1996). Defense analysis and mutative interpretation. In: M. Goldberger (Ed.), *Danger and Defense: The Technique of Close Process Attention* (pp. 1–51). Northvale, NJ: Jason Aronson.

de Leon de Bernardi, B. (2000). The countertransference: A Latin American view. *International Journal of Psychoanalysis, 81*: 331–351.

De M'Uzan, M. (1994). *La bouche de l'inconscient.* Paris: Gallimard.

Dell, C. (1970). *A Primer for Movement Description: Using Effort-Shape and Supplementary Concepts.* New York: Dance Notations Bureau.

Derrida, J. (1998). *Resistances of Psychoanalysis.* Stanford, CA: Stanford University Press.

Deutsch, F. (1947). Analysis of postural behavior. *Psychoanalytic Quarterly, 16*: 195–213.

Diamond, M. J. (1989). Stagnation, chaos, and severe character neuroses. *Psychoanalytic Psychology, 6*: 455–473.

Diamond, M. J. (1997). The unbearable agony of being: Interpreting tormented states of mind in the psychoanalysis of sexually traumatized patients. *Bulletin of the Menninger Clinic, 61*: 495–519.

Dimen, M. (2010). Reflections on cure, or "I/Thought/It." *Psychoanalytic Dialogues, 20*: 254–268.

Dittman, A. T. (1972). *Interpersonal Messages of Emotion.* New York: Springer.

Dratman, M. & Kalish, B. I. (1967). Reorganization of psychic structures in autism: A study using body movement therapy. In: *Proceedings of the 2nd Annual Conference of the American Dance Therapy Association.* Reprinted in: *American Dance Therapy Association Monograph, 1,* 1971.

Eagle, M. N. (1993). Enactment, transference, and symptomatic cure: A case history. *Psychoanalytic Dialogues, 3*: 93–110.

Eagle, M. N. (2003). The postmodern turn in psychoanalysis: A critique. *Psychoanalytic Psychology, 20*: 411–424.

Eagle, M. N. (2011). *From Classical to Contemporary Psychoanalysis: A Critique and Integration.* New York: Routledge.

Eagle, M. N., Wakefield, J. & Wolitzky, D. L. (2003). Interpreting Mitchell's constructivism: Reply to Altman and Davies. *Journal of the American Psychoanalytic Association, 51 (Suppl.)*: 163–178.

Eagle, M. N., Wolitzky, D. L. & Wakefield, J. (2001). The analyst's knowledge and authority: A critique of the "New View" in psychoanalysis. *Journal of the American Psychoanalytic Association, 49*: 457–488.

Eagleton, T. (1991). *Ideology.* London: Verso.

Ehrlich, L. T. (2010). The analyst's ambivalence about continuing and deepening an analysis. *Journal of the American Psychoanalytic Association, 58*: 515–532.

Eissler, K. (1950). The "Chicago Institute of Psychoanalysis" and the sixth period of the development of psychoanalytic technique. *The Journal of General Psychology, 19*: 103–157.

Eissler, K. (1953). The effect of the structure of the ego on psychoanalytic technique. *Journal of the American Psychoanalytic Association, 1*: 104–143.

Eizirik, C. L. (2010). Panel report—Analytic practice: Convergences and divergences. *International Journal of Psychoanalysis, 91*: 371–375.

Ekman, P. (Ed.) (1973). *Darwin and Facial Expression: A Century of Research in Review.* New York: Academic Press.

Ekman, P. & Friesen, W. V. (1968). Nonverbal behavior in psychotherapy research. In: J. M. Schlein (Ed.), *Research in Psychotherapy Volume 3* (pp. 179–216). Washington, DC: American Psychological Association.

Ekman, P., Friesen, W. V. & Ellsworth, P. (1972). *Emotion in the human face: Guidelines for research and an integration of findings.* New York: Pergamon Press.

Ellenberger, H. (1970). *The Discovery of the Unconscious.* New York: Basic.

Elliott, A. & Spezzano, C. (1996). Psychoanalysis at its limits: Navigating the postmodern turn. *Psychoanalytic Quarterly, 65*: 52–83.

Ellman, S. J. (2005). Rothstein as a self and object Freudian. *Psychoanalytic Dialogues, 15*: 459–471.

Ellman, S. J. (2010). *When Theories Touch: A Historical and Theoretical Integration of Psychoanalytic Thought.* London: Karnac.

Erikson, E. H. (1950). *Childhood and Society.* New York: W. W. Norton.

Erikson, E. H. (1956). The problem of ego identity. *Journal of the American Psychoanalytic Association, 4*: 56–121.

Etchegoyen, R. H. (1983). Fifty years after the mutative interpretation. *International Journal of Psychoanalysis, 64*: 445–460.

Etchegoyen, R. H., Lopez, B. M. & Rabih, M. (1987). On envy and how to interpret it. *International Journal of Psychoanalysis, 68*: 49–60.

Faimberg, H. (1992). The countertransference position and the counter-transference. *International Journal of Psychoanalysis, 73*: 541–547.

Faimberg, H. (1996). Listening to listening. *International Journal of Psychoanalysis, 77*: 667–677.

Faimberg, H. (2005). *The Telescoping of Generations: Listening to the Narcissistic Links Between Generations.* London: Routledge.

Fairbairn, W. R. D. (1941). A revised psychopathology of the psychoses and psychoneuroses. *International Journal of Psychoanalysis, 22*: 250–279. Also in: *Psychoanalytic Studies of the Personality* (pp. 28–58). London: Tavistock, 1952.

Fairbairn, W. R. D. (1943). The repression and the return of bad objects. In: *Psychoanalytic Studies of the Personality* (pp. 59–81). London: Tavistock, 1952.

Fairbairn, W. R. D. (1944). Endopsychic structure considered in terms of object-relationships. In: *Psychoanalytic Studies of the Personality* (pp. 82–136). London: Tavistock, 1952.

Fairbairn, W. R. D. (1952a). *An Object-Relations Theory of the Personality.* New York: Basic.

Fairbairn, W. R. D. (1952b). *Psychoanalytic Studies of The Personality.* London: Tavistock.

Fairbairn, W. R. D. (1955). Observations in defence of the object-relations theory of the personality. *British Journal of Medical Psychology, 28*: 144–156.

Fairbairn, W. R. D. (1958). On the nature and aims of psycho-analytical treatment. *International Journal of Psychoanalysis, 39*: 374–385.

Fairbairn, W. R. D. (1963). Synopsis of an object-relations theory of the personality. *International Journal of Psychoanalysis, 44*: 224–226.

Feldman, M. (1993). The dynamics of reassurance. *International Journal of Psychoanalysis, 74*: 275–285.

Fenichel, O. (1941a). The ego and the affects. *Psychoanalytic Review, 28*: 47–60.

Fenichel, O. (1941b). *Problems of Psychoanalytic Technique.* Albany, NY: The Psychoanalytic Quarterly.

Fenichel, O. (1945a). Nature and classification of the so-called psychosomatic phenomena. *Psychoanalytic Quarterly, 14*: 287–312.

Fenichel, O. (1945b). *The Psychoanalytic Theory of Neurosis.* New York: W. W. Norton.

Fenichel, O. (1954). The study of defense mechanisms and its importance to psychoanalysis. In: *The Collected Papers of Otto Fenichel: Second Series* (pp. 183–197). New York: W. W. Norton.

Ferenczi, S. (1919). On the technique of psychoanalysis. In: *Further Contributions to the Theory and Technique of Psycho-Analysis*, 2nd edition (pp. 177–189). London: Hogarth, 1950.

Ferenczi, S. (1920). The further development of an active therapy in psychoanalysis. In: *Further Contributions to the Theory and Technique of Psycho-Analysis*, 3rd edition (pp. 198–217). London: Hogarth, 1950.

Ferenczi, S. (1932). *The Clinical Diary of Sandor Ferenczi* (J. Dupont, Trans.). Cambridge, MA: Harvard University Press, 1988.

Ferenczi, S. & Rank, O. (1924). *The Development of Psychoanalysis*. New York: Dover, 1956.

Ferraro, F. & Garella, A. (2009). *Endings: On Termination in Psychoanalysis*. New York: Rodopi.

Ferro, A. (2008). *Mind Works: Technique and Creativity in Psychoanalysis* (P. Slotkin, Trans.). London: Routledge.

Ferro, A. (2009). Transformations in dreaming and characters in the psychoanalytic field. *International Journal of Psychoanalysis, 90*: 209–230.

Ferro, A. & Basile, R. (2009). *The Analytic Field: A Clinical Concept*. London: Karnac.

Firman, G. J. & Kaplan (Porter) M. P. (1978). Staff "splitting" on medical-surgical wards. *Psychiatry, 41*: 289–295.

Fliess, R. (1942). The metapsychology of the analyst. *Psychoanalytic Quarterly, 11*: 211–227.

Fonagy, P. (1982). The integration of psychoanalysis and experimental science: A review. *International Review of Psychoanalysis, 9*: 125–145.

Fonagy, P. (1993). Psychoanalytic and empirical approaches to developmental psychopathology: An object-relations perspective. *Journal of the American Psychoanalytic Association, 41*: 245–260.

Fonagy, P. (1999). Points of contact and divergence between psychoanalytic and attachment theories: Is psychoanalytic theory truly different? *Psychoanalytic Inquiry, 19*: 448–480.

Fonagy, P. (2001). *Attachment Theory and Psychoanalysis*. New York: Other Press.

Fonagy, P. & Target, M. (1996). Playing with reality: I. Theory of mind and the normal development of psychic reality. *International Journal of Psychoanalysis, 77*: 217–233.

Fonagy, P. & Target, M. (1998). Mentalization and the changing aims of child psychoanalysis. *Psychoanalytic Dialogues, 8*: 87–114.

Fonagy, P. & Target, M. (2007). The rooting of the mind in the body: New links between attachment theory and psychoanalytic thought. *Journal of the American Psychoanalytic Association, 55*: 411–456.

Fonagy, P., Target, M. & Gergely, G. (2000). Attachment and borderline personality disorder: A theory and some evidence. *Psychiatric Clinics of North America, 23*: 103–122.

Freeden, M. (1996). *Ideologies and Political Theory.* Oxford: Clarendon Press.

Freud, A. (1936). *The Ego and the Mechanisms of Defense.* New York: International Universities Press, 1946.

Freud, A. (1954). The widening scope of indications for psychoanalysis. *Journal of the American Psychoanalytic Association, 2*: 607–620.

Freud, A. (1965). *Normality and Pathology in Childhood: Assessments in Development.* New York: International Universities Press.

Freud, A. (1966). *The Ego And The Mechanism Of Defense* (Rev. Ed.). New York: International Universities Press.

Freud, A. (1966–1980). *The Writings of Anna Freud: 8 Volumes.* New York: International Universities Press.

Freud, A. (1976). Changes in psychoanalytic practice and experience. *International Journal of Psychoanalysis, 57*: 257–260.

Freud, S. (1894). The neuro-psychoses of defence. *S. E., 3*: 41–61. London: Hogarth.

Freud, S. (1895). *A Project for a Scientific Psychology. S. E., 1*: 283–397. London: Hogarth.

Freud, S. (1896). *The Aetiology of Hysteria. S. E., 3*: 187–221. London: Hogarth.

Freud, S. (1900). *The Interpretation of Dreams. S. E., 4*: 1–338. London: Hogarth.

Freud, S. (1901). Letter from Freud to Fliess, January 25, 1901. In: J. M. Masson (Ed.), *The Complete Letters of Sigmund Freud to Wilhelm Fliess, 1887–1904* (pp. 432–433). Cambridge, MA: Harvard University Press, 1985.

Freud, S. (1905a). *Fragment of an Analysis of a Case of Hysteria. S. E., 7*: 15–122. London: Hogarth.

Freud, S. (1905b). Three essays on the theory of sexuality. *S. E., 7*: 123–245. London: Hogarth.

Freud, S. (1905c). Psychical (or mental) treatment. *S. E., 7*: 281–302. London: Hogarth.

Freud, S. (1909). Family romances. *S. E., 9*: 235–241. London: Hogarth.

Freud, S. (1910a). Five Lectures on Psycho-analysis. *S. E., 11*: 1–56. London: Hogarth.

Freud, S. (1910b). Future prospects of psycho-analysis. *S. E., 11*: 141–151. London: Hogarth.

Freud, S. (1912a). The dynamics of transference. *S. E., 12*: 97–108. London: Hogarth.

Freud, S. (1912b). Recommendations to physicians practicing psychoanalysis. *S. E., 12*: 109–120. London: Hogarth.

Freud, S. (1913). On beginning the treatment (Further recommendations on the technique of psycho-analysis, I). *S. E., 12*: 121–144. London: Hogarth.

Freud, S. (1914a). On narcissism: An introduction. *S. E., 14*: 67–104. London: Hogarth.

Freud, S. (1914b). Papers on technique: Remembering, repeating, and working-through: (Further recommendations on the technique of psychoanalysis, II). *S. E., 12*: 147–156. London: Hogarth.

Freud, S. (1915a). Observations on transference love. *S. E., 12*: 157–171. London: Hogarth.

Freud, S. (1915b). Repression. *S. E., 14*: 141–158. London: Hogarth.

Freud, S. (1916–1917). *Introductory Lectures on Psycho-analysis, Part 3. S. E., 16*: 243–496. London: Hogarth.

Freud, S. (1917). Mourning and melancholia. *S. E., 14*: 239–258. London: Hogarth.

Freud, S. (1919). Lines of advance in psycho-analytic therapy. *S. E., 17*: 157–168. London: Hogarth.

Freud, S. (1920). *Beyond the Pleasure Principle. S. E., 18*: 1–64. London: Hogarth.

Freud, S. (1922). Two encyclopaedia articles. *S. E., 18*: 235–259. London: Hogarth.

Freud, S. (1923a). *The Ego and the Id. S. E., 19*: 1–66. London: Hogarth.

Freud, S. (1923b). The infantile genital organization: an interpolation into the theory of sexuality. *S. E., 19*: 141–145. London: Hogarth.

Freud, S. (1924). The economic problem of masochism. *S. E., 19*: 167–189. London: Hogarth.

Freud, S. (1926a). Inhibitions, symptoms and anxiety. *S. E., 20*: 75–175. London: Hogarth, 1978.

Freud, S. (1926b). The question of lay analysis. *S. E., 20*: 179–258. London: Hogarth.

Freud, S. (1933). New introductory lectures on psycho-analysis. *S. E., 20*: 1–182. London: Hogarth.

Freud, S. (1937). *Analysis Terminable and Interminable. S. E., 23*: 209–254. London: Hogarth.

Freud, S. (1938a). *An Outline of Psycho-analysis. S. E., 23*: 139–208. London: Hogarth.

Freud, S. (1938b). Some elementary lessons in psycho-analysis. *S. E.*, 23: 209–253. London: Hogarth.

Friedman, L. (1978). Trends in the psychoanalytic theory of treatment. *Psychoanalytic Quarterly, 47*: 524–567.

Friedman, L. (1991). A reading of Freud's papers on technique. *Psychoanalytic Quarterly, 60*: 564–595.

Friedman, L. (2007). Who needs theory of therapeutic action? *Psychoanalytic Quarterly, 76 (Suppl.)*: 1635–1662.

Friedman, R. & Natterson, J. (1999). Enactment: An intersubjective perspective. *Psychoanalytic Quarterly, 68*: 220–247.

Frosch, J. (1959). Transference derivatives of the family romance. *Journal of the American Psychoanalytic Association, 7*: 503–522.

Gabbard, G. O. (1995). Countertransference: The emerging common ground. *International Journal of Psychoanalysis, 76*: 475–485.

Gabbard, G. O. (2009). What is a "good enough" termination? *Journal of the American Psychoanalytic Association, 57*: 575–594.

Gabbard, G. O. & Westen, D. (2003). Rethinking therapeutic action. *International Journal of Psychoanalysis, 84*: 823–841.

Galatzer-Levy, R. M. (2009). Good vibrations: Analytic process as coupled oscillations. *International Journal of Psychoanalysis, 90*: 983–1007.

Gerson, S. (2004). The relational unconscious: a core element of intersubjectivity, thirdness and clinical process. *Psychoanalytic Quarterly, 73*: 63–98.

Gill, M. M. (1954). Psychoanalysis and exploratory psychotherapy. *Journal of the American Psychoanalytic Association, 2*: 771–797.

Gill, M. M. (1983). The interpersonal paradigm and the degree of the therapist's involvement. *Contemporary Psychoanalysis, 19*: 200–237.

Gitelson, M. (1962). The curative factors in psycho-analysis. *International Journal of Psychoanalysis, 43*: 194–205.

Glover, E. (1931). The therapeutic effect of the inexact interpretation: A contribution to the theory of suggestion. *International Journal of Psychoanalysis, 12*: 397–411.

Godbout, C. (2004). Reflections on Bion's 'elements of psychoanalysis': Experience, thought and growth. *International Journal of Psychoanalysis, 85*: 1123–1136.

Godbout, C. (2005). The "economic problem" of interpretation, 1. *Canadian Journal of Psychoanalysis, 13*: 77–93.

Gray, J. (2005). Althusser, ideology, and theoretical foundations: Theory and communication. *The Journal of New Media and Culture, 3*(1). Retrieved from http://www.ibiblio.org/nmediac/winter2004/gray.html (June 1, 2010).

Gray, P. (1973). Psychoanalytic technique and the ego's capacity for viewing intrapsychic activity. *Journal of the American Psychoanalytic Association, 21*: 474–494.

Gray, P. (1982). "Developmental lag" in the evolution of technique for psychoanalysis of neurotic conflict. *Journal of the American Psychoanalytic Association, 30*: 621–655.

Gray, P. (1987). On the technique of analysis of the superego: An introduction. *Psychoanalytic Quarterly, 56*: 130–154.

Gray, P. (1990). The nature of therapeutic action in psychoanalysis. *Journal of the American Psychoanalytic Association, 38*: 1083–1096.

Gray, P. (1991). On transferred permissive or approving superego functions: The analysis of the ego's superego activities, Part II. *Psychoanalytic Quarterly, 60*: 1–21.

Gray, P. (1993). A brief didactic guide to analysis of the ego in conflict. *Journal of Clinical Psychoanalysis, 2*: 325–340.

Gray, P. (1994a). *The Ego and Analysis of Defense*. Northvale, NJ: Jason Aronson.

Gray, P. (1994b). On helping analysands observe intrapsychic activity. In: *The Ego and Analysis of Defense* (pp. 63–86). Northvale, NJ: Jason Aronson.

Gray, P. (1996). Undoing the lag in the technique of conflict and defense analysis. *Psychoanalytic Study of the Child, 51*: 87–101.

Gray, P. (2000). On the receiving end: facilitating the analysis of conflicted drive derivatives of aggression. *Journal of the American Psychoanalytic Association, 48*: 219–236.

Greenacre, P. (1971). Discussion of Eleanor Galenson's paper, "A consideration of the nature of thought in childhood play". In: J. B. McDevitt & C. F. Settlage (Eds.), *Separation-Individuation: Essays in Honor of Margaret S. Mahler* (pp. 61–62). New York: International Universities Press.

Greenberg, J. R. (1986). Theoretical models and the analyst's neutrality. *Contemporary Psychoanalysis, 22*: 87–106.

Greenberg, J. R. (2007). Therapeutic action: Convergence without consensus. *Psychoanalytic Quarterly, 76 (Suppl.)*: 1675–1688.

Greenberg, J. R. (2009). Comments on Sandor M. Abend's "Freud, transference and therapeutic action". *Psychoanalytic Quarterly, 78*: 925–935.

Greenberg, J. R. & Mitchell, S. (1983). *Object Relations in Psychoanalytic Theory*. Cambridge, MA: Harvard University Press.

Greenson, R. (1965). The working alliance and the transference neurosis. *Psychoanalytic Quarterly, 34*: 155–181.

Greenwald, A. (1980). The totalitarian ego: Fabrication and revision of personal history. *American Psychologist, 35*: 603–618.

Grinberg, L. (1990). *The Goals of Psychoanalysis*. London: Karnac.

Grotjahn, M. (1967). Sigmund Freud and the art of letter writing. In: H. M. Ruitenbeck, (Ed.), *Freud As We Knew Him* (pp. 433–447). Detroit, MI: Wayne State University Press, 1973.

Grotstein, J. S. (1977). *Splitting and Projective Identification.* Northvale, NJ: Jason Aronson.

Grotstein, J. S. (2005). Projective transidentification: An extension of the concept of projective identification. *International Journal of Psychoanalysis, 86*: 1051–1069.

Grunbaum, A. (1984). *The Foundations of Psychoanalysis: A Philosophical Critique*. Berkeley, CA: University of California Press.

Guntrip, H. J. S. (1961). *Personality Structure and Human Interaction: The Developing Synthesis of Psychodynamic Theory*. New York: International Universities Press.

Guntrip, H. J. S. (1969). *Schizoid Phenomena, Object-Relations, and the Self.* New York: International Universities Press.

Haartman, K. (2008). *Treating Attachment Pathology.* New York: Jason Aronson.

Hale, N. (1995). *The Rise and Crisis of Psychoanalysis in the United States: Freud and the Americans, 1917–1985*. New York: Oxford University Press.

Harris, A. (2005). *Gender as Soft Assembly.* Hillsdale, NJ: The Analytic Press.

Hartmann, H. (1939a). *Ego Psychology and the Problem of Adaptation.* New York: International Universities Press.

Hartmann, H. (1939b). Psychoanalysis and the concept of health. *International Journal of Psychoanalysis, 20*: 308–321.

Hartmann, H., Kris, E. & Loewenstein, R. M. (1946). Comments on the formation of psychic structure. *Psychoanalytic Study of the Child*, 2: 11–38.

Heidegger, M. (1959). *Discourse on Thinking: A Translation of Gelassenheit* (J. M. Anderson & E. H. Freund, Trans.). New York: Harper and Row, 1969.

Heimann, P. (1950). On counter-transference. *International Journal of Psychoanalysis, 31*: 81–84.

Hinde, R. A. (Ed.) (1972). *Nonverbal Communication.* Cambridge: Cambridge University Press.

Hinshelwood, R. (1989). *A Dictionary of Kleinian Thought.* Northvale, NJ: Jason Aronson.

Hoffer, W. (1949). Mouth, hand and ego integration. *Psychoanalytic Study of the Child, 3*: 49–56.

Hoffman, I. Z. (1983). The patient as interpreter of the analyst's experience. *Contemporary Psychoanalysis, 19*: 389–422.

Hoffman, I. Z. (1992). Some practical implications of a social constructivist view of the psychoanalytic situation. *Psychoanalytic Dialogues, 2*: 287–304.

Hoffman, I. Z. (1996). The intimate and ironic authority of the psycho-analyst's presence. *Psychoanalytic Quarterly, 65*: 102–136.

Hoffman, I. Z. (1998). *Ritual and Spontaneity in the Psychoanalytic Process: A Dialectical Constructivist Point of View.* Hillsdale, NJ: The Analytic Press.

Hoffman, I. Z. (2007). "Doublethinking" our way to scientific legiti-macy: The desiccation of human experience. Plenary address at the American Psychoanalytic Association, Winter Meeting, New York.

Hoffman, I. Z. (2009). Doublethinking our way to "scientific" legitimacy. The desiccation of human experience. *Journal of the American Psycho-analytic Association, 57*: 1043–1069.

Hoffman, L. (2010). One hundred years after Sigmund Freud lectures in America: Towards an integration of psychoanalytic theories and techniques within psychiatry. *History of Psychiatry, 21*: 1–16.

Hollander, N. C. (2009a). Ideology, psyche and the historical significance of 9/11. *Psychoanalysis, Culture & Society, 14*: 171–182.

Hollander, N. C. (2009b). When not knowing allies with destructiveness: Global warning and psychoanalytic ethical non-neutrality. *Interna-tional Journal of Applied Psychoanalytic Studies, 6*: 1–11.

Hollander, N. C. (2010). *Uprooted Minds: Surviving the Politics of Terror in the Americas.* New York: Routledge.

Hollander, N. C. & Gutwill, S. (2006). Despair and hope in a culture of denial. In: L. Layton, N. C. Hollander & S. Gutwill (Eds.), *Psychoa-nalysis, Class, and Politics: Encounters in the Clinical Setting* (pp. 81–91). New York: Routledge.

Holt, R. R. (1976). Drive or wish: A reconsideration of the psychoana-lytic theory of motivations. In: M. M. Gill & P. S. Holzman (Eds.), *Psy-chology Versus Metapsychology* (pp. 158–197). New York: International Universities Press.

Holt, R. R. (1989). *Freud Reappraised: A Fresh Look at Psychoanalytic Theory.* New York: Guilford Press.

Horney, K. (1937). *The Neurotic Personality of Our Time.* New York: W. W. Norton.

Horvath, A. O. & Symonds, B. D. (1991). Relations between working alliance and outcome in psychotherapy: A metanalysis. *Journal of Counseling Psychology, 38*: 139–149.

Hutchinson, J. (1996). Use of the close process attention technique in patients with impulse disorders. In: M. Goldberger (Ed.), *Danger and Defense: The Technique of Close Process Attention* (pp. 131–178). Northvale, NJ: Jason Aronson.

Isakower, O. (1963). In: Unpublished Minutes of the Faculty Meeting of the New York Psychoanalytic Institute, October 14 & November 20.

Isakower, O. (1992). Chapter Two: Preliminary thoughts on the analyzing instrument. *Journal of Clinical Psychoanalysis, 1*: 184–194.

James, M. (1960). Premature ego development. *International Journal of Psychoanalysis, 41*: 288–294.

Jiménez, J. P. (2009). Grasping psychoanalysts' practice in its own merits. *International Journal of Psychoanalysis, 90*: 231–248.

Johansson, H. & Eklund, M. (2006). Helping alliance and early drop-out rate from outpatient psychiatric care: The influence of patient factors. *Social Psychiatry and Psychiatric Epidemiology, 41*: 140–147.

Jones, E. (1920). The pathology of morbid anxiety. In: *Papers on Psychoanalysis* (pp. 474–499). London: Bailliere, Tindall & Cox.

Jones, E. (1972). *Sigmund Freud: Life and Work, Volume One: The Young Freud 1856–1900*. London: Hogarth.

Joseph, B. (1975). The patient who is difficult to reach. In: M. Feldman & E. B. Spillius (Eds.), *Psychic Equilibrium and Psychic Change: Selected Papers of Betty Joseph* (pp. 75–87). London: Routledge, 1989.

Joseph, B. (1989). *Psychic Equilibrium and Psychic Change*. London: Routledge.

Jurist, E. L., Slade, A. & Bergner, S. (2008). *Mind to Mind: Infant Research, Neuroscience, and Psychoanalysis*. New York: Other Press.

Kalish, B. I. (1968). Body movement therapy for autistic children. *Journal of American Dance Therapy Association, 1*: 7–9.

Kalish, B. I. (1976). Body Movement Scale for Autistic and Other Atypical Children: An exploratory study using a normal group and an atypical group. (Doctoral dissertation, Bryn Mawr College, 1976.) *Dissertation Abstracts International*, 1977, *36*: 10.

Kalish-Weiss, B. I. (1997). Through dance/movement therapy to psychoanalysis. *American Journal of Dance Therapy, 19*: 5–14.

Kalish-Weiss, B. I. (2008). The case of Richard: Assessment and analytic treatment of a two year old twin with autistic-like states. *Journal of Infant, Child and Adolescent Psychotherapy, 7*: 37–57.

Kalish-Weiss, B. I. (with Ruttenberg, B. A., Fiese, B. A. & D'Orazio, A.) (1983). Early infant assessment using the behavior-rating instrument for autistic and atypical children (BRIAAC). In: J. Call, E. Galenson & R. L. Tyson (Eds.), *Frontiers of Infant Psychiatry* (pp. 413–424). New York: Basic.

Kazdin, A. (2007). Mediators and mechanisms of change in psychotherapy research. *Annual Review of Clinical Psychology, 3*: 1–27.

Kazdin, A. (2008). Evidence-based treatment and practice: New opportunities to bridge clinical research and practice, enhance the knowledge base, and improve patient care. *American Psychologist, 63*: 146–159.

Kazdin, A. (2010). Mending the split, the Kazdin way. *Monitor on Psychology (American Psychological Association)*, 41: 45.

Keats, J. (1817). From a letter to George and Thomas Keats, December 21, 1817. In: J. P. Hunter (Ed.), *The Norton Introduction to Literature: The Poetry* (pp. 477–478). New York: W. W. Norton, 1973.

Kernberg, O. F. (1979). Some implications of object relations theory for psychoanalytic technique. *Journal of the American Psychoanalytic Association, 27 (Suppl.)*: 207–240.

Kernberg, O. F. (2001). Object relations, affects, and drives: Toward a new synthesis. *Psychoanalytic Inquiry, 21*: 604–619.

Kestenberg, J. S. (1965). The role of movement patterns in development: I. Rhythms of movement, II. Flow of tension and effort. *Psychoanalytic Quarterly, 34*: 1–36 & 517–563.

Kestenberg, J. S. (1967). The role of movement patterns in development: III. The control of shape. *Psychoanalytic Quarterly, 36*: 356–409.

Kestenberg, J. S. (1975). *Children and Parents: Psychoanalytic Studies in Development*. New York: Jason Aronson.

Kestenberg, J. S. & Sossin, M. K. (1979). *The Role of Movement Patterns in Development II*. New York: Dance Notation Bureau.

Kestenberg, J. S. Marcus, H. Robins, E. Berlowe, J. & Buelte, A. (1971). Development of a young child as expressed through bodily movement. *Journal of the American Psychoanalytic Association, 10*: 746–763.

Khan, M. (1963). The concept of cumulative trauma. In: *The British School of Psychoanalysis* (pp. 117–135). New Haven, CT: Yale University Press, 1986.

King, P. & Steiner, R. (Eds.) (1991). *The Controversial Discussions, 1941–1945*. London and New York: Tavistock/Routledge.

Kirsner, D. (2000). *Unfree Associations Inside Psychoanalytic Institutes*. London: Process Press.

Klein, G. S. (1969). Freud's two theories of sexuality. In: M. M. Gill & P. S. Holzman (Eds.), *Psychology Versus Metapsychology* (pp. 14–70). New York: International Universities Press.

Klein, M. (1932). *The Psycho-Analysis of Children*. London: Hogarth.

Klein, M. (1935). A contribution to the psychogenesis of manic-depressive states. *International Journal of Psychoanalysis, 16*: 145–174.

Klein, M. (1940). Mourning and its relation to manic-depressive states. In: *The Writings of Melanie Klein, Volume 1* (pp. 344–369). London: Free Press, 1975.

Klein, M. (1946). Notes on some schizoid mechanisms. *International Journal of Psychoanalysis, 27*: 99–110.

Klein, M. (1948). A contribution to the theory of anxiety and guilt. *International Journal of Psychoanalysis, 29*: 114–123.

Klein, M. (1957). *Envy and Gratitude and Other Works: 1946–1963*. New York: Free Press.

Klein, M. (1975a). *The Writings of Melanie Klein (1921–1945), Volume 1*. London: Hogarth.

Klein, M. (1975b). *The Writings of Melanie Klein (1946–1963), Volume 2*. London: Hogarth.

Knapp, P. (1972). *Nonverbal Communication in Human Interaction*. New York: Holt, Reinhart and Winston.

Kohon, G. (1986). Notes on the history of the psychoanalytic movement in Great Britain. In: *The British School of Psychoanalysis: The Independent Tradition* (pp. 24–50). New Haven, CT: Yale University Press.

Kohut, H. (1971). *The Analysis of the Self: A Systematic Approach to the Psychoanalytic Treatment of Narcissistic Personality Disorders*. New York: International Universities Press.

Kohut, H. (1977). *The Restoration of the Self*. New York: International Universities Press.

Kohut, H. (1984). *How Does Analysis Cure?* (A. Goldberg & P. Stepansky, Eds.). Chicago: University of Chicago Press.

Kramer, S. & Akhtar, S. (Eds.) (1992). *When the Body Speaks. Psychological Meanings in Kinetic Clues*. Northvale, NJ: Jason Aronson.

Kris, A. O. (1990). The Analyst's Stance and the Method of Free Association. *Psychoanalytic Study of the Child, 45*: 25–41.

Kris, E. (1950). The significance of Freud's earliest discoveries. *International Journal of Psychoanalysis, 31*: 108–116.

Kwawer, J. S. (1998). Fundamentalism reconsidered: reflections on psychoanalytic technique. *Contemporary Psychoanalysis, 34*: 565–576.

La Barre, F. (2001). *On Moving and Being Moved*. Hillside, NJ: The Analytic Press.

Laban, R. (1960). *The Mastery of Movement*. London: Macdonald & Evans.

Laban, R. & Lawrence, F. C. (1947). *Effort*. London: Macdonald & Evans.

Lacan, J. (1949). The mirror stage as formative of the *i* function as revealed in psychoanalytic experience (B. Fink, Trans.). In: *Ecrits: The First Complete Edition in English* (pp. 75–82). New York: W. W. Norton, 2006.

Lacan, J. (1966). Seminar on the Purloined Letter (B. Fink, Trans.). In: *Ecrits: The First Complete Edition in English* (pp. 6–50). New York: W. W. Norton, 2006.

Lamb, W. (1965). *Posture and Gesture: An Introduction to the Study of Physical Behavior*. London: Gerald Duckworth.

Lambert, M. & Barley, D. (2001). Research summary on the therapeutic relationship and psychotherapy outcome. *Psychotherapy, 38*: 357–361.

LaMothe, R. (2001). Vitalizing objects and psychoanalytic psychotherapy. *Psychoanalytic Psychology, 18*: 320–339.

Langs, R. J. (1975). The therapeutic relationship and deviations in technique. *International Journal of Psychoanalytic Psychotherapy,* 4: 106–141.

Langs, R. J. (1981). The therapeutic interaction. In: *Classics in Psychoanalytic Technique* (pp. 359–360). New York: Jason Aronson.

Langs, R. J. (1985). The communicative approach and the future of psychoanalysis. *Contemporary Psychoanalysis, 21*: 403–424.

Laplanche, J. (1970). The ego and narcissism. In: *Life and Death in Psychoanalysis* (pp. 66–84). Baltimore, MD: Johns Hopkins University Press, 1976.

Laplanche, J. & Pontalis, J.-B. (1967). Identification (D. Nicholson-Smith, Trans.). In: *The Language of Psychoanalysis* (pp. 205–208). New York: W. W. Norton, 1973.

Lear, J. (1990). *Love and Its Place in Nature: A Philosophical Interpretation of Freudian Psychoanalysis.* New York: Farrar, Straus and Giroux.

Lear, J. (2003). *Therapeutic Action: An Earnest Plea for Irony.* New York: Other Press.

Levenson, E. A. (1983). *The Ambiguity of Change.* New York: Basic.

Levenson, E. A. (1987a). An interpersonal perspective. *Psychoanalytic Inquiry, 7*: 207–214.

Levenson, E. A. (1987b). The purloined self. *Journal of the American Academy of Psychoanalysis, 15*: 481–490.

Levin, C. (2010). The mind as a complex internal object: Inner estrangement. *Psychoanalytic Quarterly, 79*: 95–127.

Little, M. (1951). Counter-transference and the patient's response to it. *International Journal of Psychoanalysis, 32*: 32–40.

Loewald, H. W. (1960). On the therapeutic action of psycho-analysis. *International Journal of Psychoanalysis, 41*: 16–33.

Loewald, H. W. (1975). Psychoanalysis as an art and the fantasy character of the psychoanalytic situation. *Journal of the American Psychoanalytic Association, 23*: 277–299.

Loewald, H. W. (1986). Transference-countertransference. *Journal of the American Psychoanalytic Association, 34*: 275–287.

Loewenstein, R. M. (1951). The problem of interpretation. *Psychoanalytic Quarterly, 20*: 1–14.

Loman, S. & Brandt, R. (Eds.) (1992). *The Body-Mind Connection in Human Movement Analysis.* Keene, NH: Antioch New England Graduate School.

Lopez, D. (2004). Some critical observations on Gabbard and Westen's paper, 'Rethinking therapeutic action.' *Gli Argonauti: Psicoanalisi e Societa, 26*: 291–308.

Lyons-Ruth, K., Bruschweiler-Stern, N., Harrison, A., Morgan, A., Nahum, J., Sander, L., et al. (1998). Implicit relational knowing: Its role in development and psychoanalytic treatment. *Infant Mental Health Journal, 19*: 282–289.

Mahler, M. S., Pine, F. & Bergman, A. (1975). *The Psychological Birth of the Human Infant: Symbiosis and Individuation.* New York: Basic.

Main, M. (1993). Discourse, prediction and recent studies in attachment: Implication for psychoanalysis. *Journal of the American Psychoanalytic Association, 41(Suppl.)*: 209–244.

Makari, G. (1998). The seductions of history: Sexual trauma in Freud's theory and historiography. *International Journal of Psychoanalysis, 79*: 857–869.

Makari, G. (2008). *Revolution in Mind: The Creation of Psychoanalysis.* New York: Harper Collins.

Malcolm, J. (1982). *Psychoanalysis: The Impossible Profession.* New York: Vintage.

Malin, A. (1993). A self-psychological approach to the analysis of resistance: A case report. *International Journal of Psychoanalysis, 74*: 505–518.

Malin, A. & Grotstein, J. S. (1966). Projective identification in the therapeutic process. *International Journal of Psychoanalysis, 47*: 26–31.

Marcus, E. R. (1999). Modern ego psychology. *Journal of the American Psychoanalytic Association, 47*: 843–871.

Martin, A. R. (1952). The dynamics of insight. *American Journal of Psychoanalysis, 12*: 24–28.

Martin, D., Graske, J. & Davis, M. (2000). Relation of the therapeutic alliance with outcome and other variables: A meta-analytic review. *Journal of Consulting and Clinical Psychology, 68*: 438–450.

Masson, J. M. (1985). *The Complete Letters of Sigmund Freud to Wilhelm Fliess, 1887–1904.* Cambridge, MA: Harvard University Press.

Mayes, L. (1994). Understanding adaptive processes in a developmental context: A reappraisal of Hartmann's problem of adaptation. *Psychoanalytic Study of the Child, 49*: 12–35.

Mayes, L. C. & Cohen, D. J. (1996). Children's developing theory of mind. *Journal of the American Psychoanalytic Association, 44*: 117–142.

McGuire, W. (1974). *The Freud/Jung Letters: The Correspondence Between Sigmund Freud and C. G. Jung* (R. Mannheim & R. F. C. Hull, Trans.). Princeton, NJ: Princeton University Press.

McLaughlin, J. T. (1981). Transference, psychic reality, and countertransference. *Psychoanalytic Quarterly, 50*: 639–664.

McLaughlin, J. T. (1992). Nonverbal behaviors in the analytic situation: The search for meaning in nonverbal cues. In: S. Kramer & S. Akhtar (Eds.), *When the Body Speaks* (pp. 131–161). New York: Jason Aronson.

Mehrabian, A. (1972). *Nonverbal Communication*. Chicago: Aldine-Atherton.

Meltzer, D. (1992). *The Claustrum: An Investigation of Claustrophic Phenomena*. London: Clunie Press.

Meltzer, D. (2005). Introduction. In: M. Harris Williams (Ed.), *The Vale of Soulmaking: The Post-Kleinian Model of the Mind* (pp. xi–xix). London: Karnac.

Merleau-Ponty, M. (1962). *Phenomenology of Perception* (C. Smith, Trans.). London: Routledge & Kegan Paul.

Michels, R. (2007). The theory of therapeutic action. *Psychoanalytic Quarterly, 76 (Suppl.)*: 1725–1733.

Mill, J. S. (1843). Of the laws of the mind. In: J. M. Robson (Ed.), *Collected Works of John Stuart Mill—A System of Logic: Book VI: On the Logic of the Moral Sciences* (pp. 24–36). Toronto: University of Toronto Press, 1963.

Mitchell, S. A. (1988). *Relational Concepts in Psychoanalysis: An Integration*. Cambridge, MA: Harvard University Press.

Mitchell, S. A. (1990). Discussion: A relational view. *Psychoanalytic Inquiry, 10*: 523–540.

Mitchell, S. A. (1993). *Hope and Dread in Psychoanalysis*. New York: Basic.

Mitchell, S. A. (1995). *Freud and Beyond: A History of Modern Psychoanalytic Thought*. New York: Basic.

Mitchell, S. A. (1998). The analyst's knowledge and authority. *Psychoanalytic Quarterly, 67*: 1–31.

Mitchell, S. A. (2000a). *Relationality: From Attachment to Intersubjectivity*. Hillsdale, NJ: The Analytic Press.

Mitchell, S. A. (2000b). Reply to Silverman. *Psychoanalytic Psychology, 17*: 153–159.

Mitchell, S. A. & Aron, L. (1999). *Relational Psychoanalysis: The Emergence of a Tradition*. Hillsdale, NJ: The Analytic Press.

Mitrani, J. L. (2001). "Taking the transference": Some technical implications in three papers by Bion. *International Journal of Psychoanalysis, 82*: 1085–1104.

Mittelman, B. (1954). Motility in infants, children and adults: patterning and psychodynamics. *The Psychoanalytic Study of the Child, 9*: 142–177.

Modell, A. H. (1976). The "holding environment" and the therapeutic action of psychoanalysis. *Journal of the American Psychoanalytic Association, 24*: 285–307.

Modell, A. H. (1991). The therapeutic relationship as a paradoxical experience. *Psychoanalytic Dialogues, 1*: 13–28.

Money-Kyrle, R. E. (1956). Normal countertransference and some of its deviations. *International Journal of Psychoanalysis, 37*: 360–366.

Money-Kyrle, R. E. (1958). On the process of psycho-analytical inference. *International Journal of Psychoanalysis, 39*: 129–133.

Moran, R. (2001). *Authority and Estrangement: An Essay on Self-Knowledge.* Princeton, NJ: Princeton University Press.

Nacht, S. (1963). The non-verbal relationship in psycho-analytic treatment. *International Journal of Psychoanalysis, 44*: 334–339.

Natterson J. (2003). Love in psychotherapy. *Psychoanalytic Psychology, 20*: 509–521.

Natterson, J. & Friedman, R. (1995). *A Primer of Clinical Intersubjectivity.* Northvale, NJ: Jason Aronson.

Newbury, M. (1967). *Just Dropped In.* [Recorded by Kenny Rogers & The First Edition.] On *The First Edition* [CD]. Los Angeles: Reprise Records (released in 1968).

Newman, K. (1988). Countertransference: Its role in facilitating the use of the object. *Annual of Psychoanalysis, 16*: 251–276.

Newman, K. (1999). The usable analyst: The role of the affective engagement of the analyst in reaching usability. *Annual of Psychoanalysis, 26*: 175–194.

Newman, K. (2007). Therapeutic action in self psychology. *Psychoanalytic Quarterly, 76*: 1513–1546.

Nunberg, H. (1937). Symposium on the theory of the therapeutic results of psychoanalysis. *International Journal of Psychoanalysis, 18*: 157–165.

Ogden, T. H. (1985a). The mother, the infant and the matrix: Interpretations of aspects of the work of Donald Winnicott. *Contemporary Psychoanalysis, 21*: 346–371.

Ogden, T. H. (1985b). On potential space. *International Journal of Psychoanalysis, 66*: 129–142.

Ogden, T. H. (1986). *The Matrix of the Mind.* Northvale, NJ: Jason Aronson.

Ogden, T. H. (1994). The analytic third: Working with intersubjective clinical facts. *International Journal of Psychoanalysis, 75*: 3–19.

Ogden, T. H. (1997). *Reverie and Interpretation: Sensing Something Human.* Northvale, NJ: Jason Aronson.

Ogden, T. H. (2002). A new reading of the origins of object relations theory. *International Journal of Psychoanalysis, 83*: 767–782.

Ogden, T. H. (2005). This art of psychoanalysis: Dreaming undreamt dreams and interrupted cries. In: *This Art of Psychoanalysis* (pp. 1–18). London: Routledge.

Ogden, T. H. (2010). Why read Fairbairn? *International Journal of Psychoanalysis, 91*: 101–118.

Ornstein, A. (1995). The fate of the curative fantasy in the psychoanalytic treatment process. *Contemporary Psychoanalysis, 31*: 113–123.

Ornstein, A. & Ornstein, P. H. (2005). Conflict in contemporary clinical work: A self psychological perspective. *Psychoanalytic Quarterly, 74*: 219–251.

Ornstein, P. H. & Ornstein, A. (1977). On the continuing evolution of psychoanalytic psychotherapy: Reflections and predictions. *Annual of Psychoanalysis, 5*: 329- 370.

Osman, M. P. & Tabachnick, N. D. (1988). Introduction and survey of some previous views. *Psychoanalytic Review, 75*: 195–215.

Padel, J. (1985). Ego in current thinking. *International Journal of Psychoanalysis, 12*: 273–283.

Panel (1967). On acting-out and its role in the psychoanalytic process. International Psychoanalytic Association, Copenhagen, July 28.

Panel (1995). Therapist-patient enactments: Recognizing, understanding and working with them. 45th Anniversary of the Southern California Psychoanalytic Society and Institute, Los Angeles, November 18.

Panel (1999). Enactment: An open panel discussion, IPTAR, October 18, 1997. *Journal of Clinical Psychoanalysis, 8*: 7–92.

Paniagua, C. (1991). Patient's surface, clinical surface, and workable surface. *Journal of the American Psychoanalytic Association, 39*: 669–685.

Paniagua, C. (2001). The attraction of topographical technique. *International Journal of Psychoanalysis, 82*: 671–684.

Parsons, M. (2006). The analyst's countertransference to the psychoanalytic process. *International Journal of* Psychoanalysis, *87*: 1183–1198.

Parsons, M. (2009). An independent theory of clinical technique. *Psychoanalytic Dialogues, 19*: 221–236.

Phillips, A. (1988). *Winnicott* (pp. 62–126). Cambridge, MA: Harvard University Press.

Pick, I. B. (1985). Working through in the countertransference. *International Journal of Psychoanalysis, 66*: 157–166.

Pine, F. (1988). The four psychologies of psychoanalysis and their place in clinical work. *Journal of the American Psychoanalytic Association, 86*: 571–596.

Poland, W. S. (2000). The analyst's witnessing and otherness. *Journal of the American Psychoanalytic Association, 48*: 17–34.

Polanyi, M. (1967). *The Tacit Dimension*. Chicago: University of Chicago Press.

Porter, P. & Kalish-Weiss, B. (2008). Whatever possessed me? Discussion group working with the "split off" psyche. Presentation at the Division of Psychoanalysis (39) 28th Annual Spring Meeting, New York, April.

Portuges, S. (2004). On Emanuel Berman's "Fear of Relating"—Freudian conflict theory perspective. Paper presented at the International Association of Relational Psychoanalysis, Santa Monica, CA, April.

Portuges, S. (2005). Technical problems in the analysis of transference and counter-transference. Paper presented at Hominis '05: Convención Intercontinental de Psicología y Ciencias Sociales y Humanas ante los Problemas Contemporaneos, Havana, Cuba, November.

Portuges, S. (2009). The politics of psychoanalytic neutrality. *International Journal of Applied Psychoanalytic Studies, 6*: 61–73.

Psychoanalytic Quarterly (2007). Supplemental issue on "Comparing theories of therapeutic action". *76 (Suppl.)*: 1413–1761.

Pulver, S. E. (1992). Psychic change: Insight or relationship? *International Journal of Psychoanalysis, 73*: 199–206.

Pulver, S. E. (1993). The eclectic analyst, or the many roads to insight and change. *Journal of the American Psychoanalytic Association, 41*: 339–357.

Racker, H. (1953). The meanings and uses of countertransference. In: *Transference and Countertransference* (pp. 127–173). New York: International Universities Press, 1968.

Racker, H. (1968). *Transference and Countertransference*. New York: International Universities Press.

Rangell, L. (1952a). The analysis of a doll phobia. *International Journal of Psychoanalysis, 33*: 43–53.

Rangell, L. (1952b). Panel report: The theory of affects. *Bulletin of the American Psychoanalytic Association, 8*: 300–315.

Rangell, L. (1954a). The psychology of poise—with a special elaboration on the psychic significance of the snout or perioral region. *International Journal of Psychoanalysis, 35*: 313–332.

Rangell, L. (1954b). Panel report: "Psychoanalysis and dynamic psychotherapy—similarities and differences". *Journal of the American Psychoanalytic Association, 2*: 152–166.

Rangell, L. (1954c). Similarities and differences between psychoanalysis and dynamic psychotherapy. *Journal of the American Psychoanalytic Association, 2*: 734–744.

Rangell, L. (1968). A point of view on acting out. *International Journal of Psychoanalysis, 49*: 195–201.

Rangell, L. (1969). The intrapsychic process and its analysis: A recent line of thought and its current implications. *International Journal of Psychoanalysis, 50*: 65–77.

Rangell, L. (1972). Aggression, Oedipus, and historical perspective. *International Journal of Psychoanalysis, 53*: 3–11.

Rangell, L. (1981a). From insight to change. *Journal of the American Psychoanalytic Association, 29*: 119–141.

Rangell, L. (1981b). Psychoanalysis and dynamic psychotherapy: Similarities and differences twenty-five years later. *Psychoanalytic Quarterly, 50*: 665–693.

Rangell, L. (1985). Frontiers in psychoanalysis. Between the dream and psychic pain. *Journal of the American Psychoanalytic Association, 33 (Suppl.)*: 153–158.

Rangell, L. (1989). Action theory within the structural view. *Journal of the International Psychoanalytical Association, 70*: 189–203.

Rangell, L. (1999). My view on enactment and related revisions. Discussion. *Journal of Clinical Psychoanalysis, 8*: 77–92.

Rangell, L. (2004). *My Life in Theory.* New York: Other Press.

Rangell, L. (2007). *The Road to Unity in Psychoanalytic Theory.* New York: Jason Aronson.

Rapaport, D. (1959). The structure of psychoanalytic theory: A systematizing attempt. In: S. Koch (Ed.), *Psychology: A study of science, Study I: Conceptual Systematic, Volume 3: Formulations of the Person and the Social Context* (pp. 55–183). New York: McGraw-Hill.

Rapaport, D. (1967). *The Collected Papers of David Rapaport* (M. M. Gill, Ed.). New York: Basic.

Rapaport, D. & Gill, M. M. (1959). The points of view and assumptions of metapsychology. In: M. M. Gill (Ed.), *The Collected Papers of David Rapaport* (pp. 795–811). New York: Basic, 1967.

Rayner, E. (1991). *The Independent Mind in British Psychoanalysis.* London: Free Association.

Reich, W. (1926). The sources of neurotic anxiety: A contribution to the theory of psycho-analysis. *International Journal of Psychoanalysis, 7*: 381–391.

Reich, W. (1933). *Character Analysis* (V. R. Carfagno, Trans.). New York: Farrar, Straus and Giroux, 1972.

Reik, T. (1948). *Listening with the Third Ear: The Inner Experience of a Psychoanalyst.* New York: Jove Publications/Harcourt Brace Jovanovich.

Renik, O. (1993a). Analytic interaction: Conceptualizing technique in light of the analyst's irreducible subjectivity. *Psychoanalytic Quarterly*, 62: 553–571.

Renik, O. (1993b). Countertransference enactment and the psychoanalytic process. In: M. Horowitz, O. Kernberg & E. Weinshel (Eds.), *Psychic Structure and Psychic Change* (pp. 137–160). Madison, CT: International Universities Press.

Renik, O. (1996). The perils of neutrality. *Psychoanalytic Quarterly*, 65: 495–517.

Richards, A. D. (1999). A. A. Brill and the politics of exclusion. *Journal of the American Psychoanalytic Association*, 47: 9–28.

Richfield, J. (1954). An analysis of the concept of insight. *Psychoanalytic Quarterly*, 23: 390–408.

Rogers, C. (1951). *Client-centered Therapy: Its Current Practice, Implications and Theory*. London: Constable.

Rorty, R. (1991). *Objectivity, Relativism, and Truth: Philosophical Papers, Volume 1*. New York: Cambridge University Press.

Rosenfeld, H. (1971). A clinical approach to the psycho-analytical theory of the life and death instincts: An investigation into the aggressive aspects of narcissism. *International Journal of Psychoanalysis*, 52: 169–178.

Rosenfeld, H. (1983). Primitive object relations and mechanisms. *International Journal of Psychoanalysis*, 64: 261–267.

Rosenfeld, H. (1987). *Impasse and Interpretation*. London: Tavistock.

Rosenzweig, S. (1934). An experimental study of memory in relation to the theory of repression. *British Journal of Psychoanalysis*, 24: 247–265.

Roughton, R. (1995). Action and acting out. In: B. Moore & B. Fine (Eds.), *Psychoanalysis: The Major Concepts* (pp. 130–148). New Haven, CT: Yale University Press.

Ruttenberg, B. A., Kalish, B. I., Wenar, C. & Wolf, E. (1976). *The Behavior Rating Instrument for Autistic and Other Atypical Children (BRIAAC)*. Chicago: Stoelting. Amsterdam: Svets and Zeitlinger (publ. in Dutch).

Sacks, O. (1989). *Seeing Voices: A Journey into the World of the Deaf*. Berkeley, CA: University of California Press.

Samberg, E. (2004). Resistance. *Journal of the American Psychoanalytic Association*, 52: 243–253.

Samstag, L., Batchelder, S., Muran, J., Safran, J. & Winston, A. (1998). Early identification of treatment failures in short-term psychotherapy: An assessment of therapeutic alliance and interpersonal behavior. *Journal of Psychotherapy Practice and Research*, 7: 126–143.

Sander, L. W. (1992). Countertransference. *International Journal of Psychoanalysis, 73*: 582–584.

Sandler, A. (1984). On interpretation and holding. *Scandinavian Psychoanalytic Review, 7*: 161–176.

Sandler, J. (1976). Countertransference and role-responsiveness. *International Review of Psychoanalysis, 3*: 43–47.

Sandler, J. (1981). Character traits and object relationships. *Psychoanalytic Quarterly, 50*: 694–708.

Sandler, J. (1992). Reflections on developments in the theory of psychoanalytic technique. *International Journal of Psychoanalysis, 73*: 189–198.

Sanville, J. (1991). *The Playground of Psychoanalytic Therapy*. Hillsdale, NJ: The Analytic Press.

Sarnoff, C. (1976). *Latency*. New York: Jason Aronson.

Schafer, R. (1959). Generative empathy in the treatment situation. *Psychoanalytic Quarterly, 28*: 342–373.

Schafer, R. (1970). An overview of Heinz Hartmann's contributions to psychoanalysis. *International Journal of Psychoanalysis, 51*: 425–446.

Schafer, R. (1983). *The Analytic Attitude*. New York: Basic.

Schafer, R. (1994). *Retelling a Life: Narration and Dialogue in Psychoanalysis*. New York: Basic.

Schafer, R. (1997). *The contemporary Kleinians of London*. New York: International Universities Press.

Scheflen, A. (1972). *Body Language and the Social Order*. Englewood Cliffs, NJ: Prentice-Hall.

Scheflen, A. (1974). *How Behavior Means*. New York: Jason Aronson.

Schilder, P. (1950). *The Image & Appearance of the Human Body*. New York: John Wiley.

Schlesinger, H. J. (1995). The process of interpretation and the moment of change. *Journal of the American Psychoanalytic Association, 43*: 663–688.

Schlessinger, H. J. (2005). *Endings and Beginnings: On Terminating Psychotherapy and Psychoanalysis*. Hillsdale, NJ: The Analytic Press.

Schore, A. N. (1994). *Affect Regulation and the Origin of the Self: The Neurobiology of Emotional Development*. Mahwah, NJ: Lawrence Erlbaum.

Schore, A. N. (2001). Effects of a secure attachment relationship on right brain development, affect regulation, and infant mental health. *Infant Mental Health Journal, 22*: 7–66.

Schore, A. N. (2002). Advances in neuropsychoanalysis, attachment theory, and trauma research: implications for self psychology. *Psychoanalytic Inquiry, 22*: 433–484.

Schore, A. N. (2003). *Affect Regulation and the Repair of the Self*. New York: W. W. Norton.

Searle, J. (1998). *Mind, Language, and Society: Philosophy in the Real World.* New York: Basic.

Searles, H. F. (1973). Concerning therapeutic symbiosis. *Annual of Psychoanalysis, 1*: 247–262.

Searles, H. F. (1975). The patient as therapist to his analyst. In: P. L. Giovacchini (Ed.), *Tactics and Techniques in Psychoanalytic Therapy, Volume 2* (pp. 95–151). New York: Jason Aronson.

Segal, H. (1950). Some aspects of the analysis of a schizophrenic. *International Journal of Psychoanalysis, 31*: 268–278.

Segal, H. (1955). Notes on symbol formation. In: *Melanie Klein Today: Developments in Theory and Practice, Volume 1* (pp. 160–177). London: Routledge, 1988.

Segal, H. (1956). Depression in the schizophrenic. *International Journal of Psychoanalysis, 37*: 339–343.

Segal, H. (1964). *Introduction to the Work of Melanie Klein.* New York: Basic.

Shedler, J. (2010). The efficacy of psychodynamic psychotherapy. *American Psychologist, 65*: 98–109.

Shevrin, H. (2003). The consequences of abandoning a comprehensive psychoanalytic theory: "Revisiting Rapaport's systematizing attempt". *Journal of the American Psychoanalytic Association, 51*: 1005–1020.

Shulman, D. G. (1990). Psychoanalysis and the quantitative research tradition. *Psychoanalytic Review, 77*: 245–261.

Siegel, D. (1999). *The Developing Mind: How Relationships and the Brain Interact and Shape Who We Are.* New York: Guilford Press.

Siegel, E. V. (1984). *Dance-Movement Therapy: Mirror of Our Selves, the Psychoanalytic Approach.* New York: Human Sciences Press.

Siqueland, L., Crits-Christoph, P., Gallop, R., Barber, J. P., Griffin, M. L., Thase, M. E., et al. (2002). Retention in psychosocial treatment of cocaine dependence: predictors and impact on outcome. *American Journal on Addictions, 11*: 24–40.

Smith, H. F. (2007). In search of a theory of therapeutic action. *Psychoanalytic Quarterly, 76 (Suppl.)*: 1735–1761.

Smith, H. F. (2008). Charles Brenner (1913–2008). *Psychoanalytic Quarterly, 77*: 705.

Sohi, S. & Rutherford, A. (2010). Hedda Bolgar. Reprinted from *Psychology's feminist voices* (http://www.feministvoices.com/hedda-bolgar/) (retrieved January 1, 2011).

Sossin, M. & Loman, S. (1992). Clinical applications of the Kestenberg Movement Profile. In: S. Loman & R. Brandt (Eds.), *The Body Mind Connection in Human Movement Analysis* (pp. 21–54). Keene, NH: Antioch New England Graduate School.

Spence, D. (1982). *Narrative Truth and Historical Truth: Meaning and Interpretation in Psychoanalysis.* London: W. W. Norton.

Spezzano, C. (2007). A home for the mind. *Psychoanalytic Quarterly,* 76: 1563–1583.

Spiegel, J. P. & Machotka, P. (1974). *Messages of the Body.* New York: Free Press.

Spillius, E. (2007). *Encounters With Melanie Klein: Selected Papers of Elizabeth Spillius.* Hove, UK: Routledge.

Steele, H. & Steele, M. (1998). Attachment and psychoanalysis: Time for a reunion. *Social Development,* 7: 92–119.

Steingart, I. (1995). *A Thing Apart: Love and Reality in the Therapeutic Partnership (Critical Issues in Psychoanalysis: 2).* Northvale, NJ: Jason Aronson.

Stepansky, P. (2010). *Psychoanalysis at the Margins.* New York: Other Press Professional.

Sterba, R. (1934). The fate of the ego in analytic therapy. *International Journal of Psychoanalysis,* 15: 117–126.

Stern, D. B. (1989). The analyst's unformulated experience of the patient. *Contemporary Psychoanalysis,* 25: 1–33.

Stern, D. B. (2003). *Unformulated Experience: From Dissociation to Imagination in Psychoanalysis.* New York: Routledge.

Stern, D. N. (1985). *The Interpersonal World of the Infant.* New York: Basic.

Stern, D. N. (2004). *The Present Moment in Psychotherapy and Everyday Life.* New York: W. W. Norton.

Stolorow, R. (1990). Converting psychotherapy to psychoanalysis: a critique of the underlying assumptions. *Psychoanalytic Inquiry,* 1: 119–130.

Stolorow, R., Atwood, G. & Brandschaft, B. (1994). *The Intersubjective Perspective.* Northvale, NJ: Jason Aronson.

Stolorow, R., Brandchaft, B. & Atwood, G. (1987). *Psychoanalytic Treatment: An Intersubjective Approach.* Hillsdale, NJ: The Analytic Press.

Stone, A. (1997). Where will psychoanalysis survive? *Harvard Magazine,* 99: 35–39.

Stone, L. (1954). The widening scope of indications for psychoanalysis. *Journal of the American Psychoanalytic Association,* 2: 567–594.

Stone, L. (1961). *The Psychoanalytic Situation: An Examination of Its Development and Essential Nature.* New York: International Universities Press.

Strachey, J. (1934). The nature of the therapeutic action of psychoanalysis. *International Journal of Psychoanalysis,* 15: 127–159.

Strachey, J. (1969). The nature of the therapeutic action of psychoanalysis. *International Journal of Psychoanalysis,* 50: 275–292.

Strupp, H. H. & Binder, J. L. (1984). *Psychotherapy in a New Key: A Guide to Time-Limited Psychotherapy*. New York: Basic.

Sugarman, A. (2006). Mentalization, insightfulness, and therapeutic action: The importance of mental organization. *International Journal of Psychoanalysis, 87*: 965–987.

Sullivan, H. S. (1953). *The Interpersonal Theory of Psychiatry* (H. S. Perry & M. L. Gawel, Eds.). New York: W. W. Norton.

Sulloway, F. J. (1979). *Freud: Biologist of the Mind*. New York: Basic.

Symington, N. (2006). *A Healing Conversation*. London: Karnac.

Target, M. & Fonagy, P. (1996). Playing with reality: II. The development of psychic reality from a theoretical perspective. *International Journal of Psychoanalysis, 77*: 459–479.

Taylor, S. & Brown, J. (1994). Positive illusions and well-being revisited: Separating fact from fiction. *Psychological Bulletin, 116*: 21–27.

Taylor, S., Kemeny, M., Reed, G., Bower, J. & Gruenewald, T. (2000). Psychological resources, positive illusions, and health. *American Psychologist, 55*: 99–109.

Thompson, C. (1943). The therapeutic technique of Sandor Ferenczi: A comment. *International Journal of Psychoanalysis, 24*: 64–66.

Tuckett, D. (1983). Words and the psychoanalytical interaction. *International Review of Psychoanalysis, 10*: 407–413.

Valenstein, A. F. (1981). Insight as an embedded concept in the early historical phase of psychoanalysis. *Psychoanalytic Study of the Child, 36*: 307–315.

Varga, M. (2005). Analysis of transference as transformation of enactment. *The Psychoanalytic Review, 92*: 509–523.

Wachtel, P. (1977). *Psychoanalysis, Behavior Therapy, and the Relational World*. Washington, DC: American Psychological Association.

Waelder, R. (1936). The principle of multiple function: Observations on over-determination. *Psychoanalytic Quarterly, 5*: 45–62.

Wallerstein, R. S. (1983). Self psychology and "classical" psychoanalytic psychology. *Psychoanalysis and Contemporary Thought, 6*: 553–595.

Wallerstein, R. S. (1984). Anna Freud: Radical innovator and staunch conservative. *Psychoanalytic Study of the Child, 39*: 65–80.

Wallerstein, R. S. (1988). One psychoanalysis or many? *International Journal of Psychoanalysis, 69*: 5–21.

Weinshel, E. M. (1984). Some observations on the psychoanalytic process. *Psychoanalytic Quarterly, 53*: 63–92.

Weiss, J. Sampson, H. & The Mount Zion Psychotherapy Research Group (1986). *The Psychoanalytic Process: Theory, Clinical Observation, And Empirical Research*. New York: Guilford Press.

White, R. (2006). The legacy of Paul Gray. *Journal of the American Psychoanalytic Association* Psychoanalytic Netcast (November). Retrieved from http://www.apsa.org/Publications/JAPA/Netcast. aspx (June 15, 2010).

Wille, R. S. G. (2008). Psychoanalytic identity: Psychoanalysis as an internal object. *Psychoanalytic Quarterly, 77*: 1193–1229.

Winnicott, D. W. (1935). The manic defence. In: *Through Pediatrics to Psycho-Analysis* (pp. 129–144). New York: Basic, 1975.

Winnicott, D. W. (1941). The observation of infants in a set situation. *International Journal of Psychoanalysis, 22*: 229–249.

Winnicott, D. W. (1945). Primitive emotional development. *International Journal of Psychoanalysis, 26*: 137–143.

Winnicott, D. W. (1949). Hate in the countertransference. *International Journal of Psychoanalysis, 30*: 69–74.

Winnicott, D. W. (1951). Transitional objects and transitional phenomena. In: *Through Paediatrics to Psycho-Analysis* (pp. 229–242). New York: Basic, 1975.

Winnicott, D. W. (1953). Transitional objects and transitional phenomena—A study of the first not-me possession. *International Journal of Psychoanalysis, 34*: 89–97.

Winnicott, D. W. (1954a). Letter to W. Clifford M. Scott. In: F. Robert Rodman (Ed.), *The Spontaneous Gesture: Selected Letters of D. W. Winnicott* (pp. 61–62). Cambridge, MA: Harvard University Press, 1987.

Winnicott, D. W. (1954b). Metapsychological and clinical aspects of regression within the psycho-analytical set-up. In: *Through Paediatrics to Psycho-Analysis* (pp. 279–294). New York: Basic, 1975.

Winnicott, D. W. (1956). On transference. *International Journal of Psychoanalysis, 37*: 386–388.

Winnicott, D. W. (1958a). The capacity to be alone. *International Journal of Psychoanalysis, 39*: 416–420.

Winnicott, D. W. (1958b). *Through Paediatrics to Psychoanalysis*. London: Tavistock.

Winnicott, D. W. (1960). The theory of the parent-infant relationship. *International Journal of Psychoanalysis, 41*: 585–595.

Winnicott, D. W. (1965). *The Maturational Process and the Facilitating Environment*. New York: International Universities Press.

Winnicott, D. W. (1968a). *Holding and Interpretation*. London: Hogarth and the Institute of Psycho-Analysis.

Winnicott, D. W. (1968b). Playing: its theoretical status in the clinical situation. *International Journal of Psychoanalysis, 49*: 591–599.

Winnicott, D. W. (1969). The use of an object. *International Journal of Psychoanalysis, 50*: 711–716.

Winnicott, D. W. (1971a). Interrelating apart from instinctual drive and in terms of cross-identifications. In: *Playing and Reality* (pp. 119–137). London: Tavistock.

Winnicott, D. W. (1971b). *Playing and Reality*. London: Tavistock.

Winnicott, D. W. (1971c). *Therapeutic Consultations in Child Psychiatry*. London: Hogarth and the Institute of Psycho-Analysis.

Winnicott, D. W. (1974). Fear of breakdown. *International Review of Psychoanalysis, 1*: 103–107.

Winnicott, D. W. (1975). *Through Paediatrics to Psycho-Analysis*. London: Hogarth.

Wolf, E. (1988). *Treating the Self*. New York: Guilford Press.

Wolson, P. (2005). The existential dimension of psychoanalysis (EDP): Psychic survival and the fear of psychic death (nonbeing). *Psychoanalytic Review, 92*: 675–699.

Wolson, P. (2006). The relational Unconscious: An integration of intrapsychic and relational analysis. Scientific Meeting Presentation, Los Angeles Institute and Society for Psychoanalytic Studies, Los Angeles, CA, March.

Wordsworth, W. (1807). Character of the Happy Warrior. In: S. Gill (Ed.), *William Wordsworth—The Major Works* (pp. 320–321). New York: Oxford University Press, 1984.

Young-Bruehl, E. (2002). Review of "Anna Freud: A view of development, disturbance and therapeutic techniques" by Rose Edgcumbe. *Psychoanalytic Review, 89*: 757–760.

Zeligs, M. A. (1957). Acting in—A contribution to the meaning of some postural attitudes observed during analysis. *Journal of the American Psychoanalytic Association, 5*: 685–706.

Zetzel, E. R. (1956). Current concepts of transference. *International Journal of Psychoanalysis, 37*: 369–375.

Zetzel, E. R. (1965). The theory of therapy in relation to a developmental model of the psychic apparatus. *International Journal of Psychoanalysis, 46*: 39–52.

Žižek, S. (1989). *The Sublime Object of Ideology*. London: Verso.

INDEX

interpersonal psychoanalysts 17,
181
interpretation xxv–xxx, 10–14,
43–46, 55–57, 59–60, 62, 78–79,
109, 121–122, 126–127, 129–132,
134–141, 143–144, 293–295,
334–335
analysand's 131
analyst's 25, 43, 56–57, 111, 131,
167, 172, 181
classical analyst's
understanding 171
content 132, 138
correct 223
deep 81–82, 88, 295, 312
effective 123, 177
experience-distant 172
experience-near 172, 180
explicit 59–64
extra-transference 124, 130, 313
inexact 10, 319
insight-inducing 169, 181, 185
making 81–82, 139, 176, 220
mutative 8, 10, 130, 313, 315
non-transference 43
objective xxvi
primacy of 12, 45
silent 61–62, 64
interpsychic xxvi, xxx, 208–209,
212–214, 221, 223–224, 232–233,
309
communication xxx, 224
intersubjective 35, 71, 76, 137–138,
181–182, 185, 207, 212–213, 230,
251, 311–312, 319, 329, 336
interventions 17, 55–56, 58, 75,
78–79, 82–85, 95, 155, 177, 184,
208, 223, 250, 292, 294
analyst's 81, 90, 265
intrapsychic ix, xxiv, xxvi, xxviii,
7, 10, 16–18, 22, 24, 90–92, 106,
135, 212–213, 223, 320

change ix, xxvi, 18, 135, 205
process, patient's 88, 91–92
introspection 113, 184, 200, 234
Isakower, O. 223–224, 323
isolation 98, 215, 268–269

James, M. 191, 245, 323
Jiménez, J. P. xxiii, 35, 323
Johansson, H. 58, 323
Jones, E. 4, 24, 323
Joseph, B. 35, 175, 177, 208, 323
Jurist, E. L. 234, 323

Kalish, B. I. ix, xviii, xxx, 196, 200,
214, 257–258, 260, 262, 269–270,
272, 313, 323, 331, 333
Kalish-Weiss, B. I. 196, 269, 272,
323, 331
Kazdin, A. xxvii, 19, 58–59,
323–324
Keats, J. 228, 235, 324
Keltner, D. 309
Kemeny, M. 337
Kernberg, O. F. 19, 324, 333
Kestenberg, J. S. 259, 265–269, 324,
335
Kestenberg Movement Profile
(KMP) 266–267, 335
Khan, M. 245, 324
kinesthetic 275
King, P. 105, 299, 324
King Lear 299
Kirsner, D. 33, 324
Klein, G. S. 100, 324
Klein, M. xxx, 15–17, 27, 33, 75,
95, 105, 126, 175–176, 182, 192,
238–239, 242–246, 324–325,
335–336
Kleinians and Kleinian theory 12,
15, 19, 28, 30, 32–33, 35, 113,
132, 139, 175–177, 185, 192–194,
214, 233